AF322919

Clean C++

Sustainable Software Development Patterns and Best Practices with C++ 17

Stephan Roth

apress®

Clean C++: Sustainable Software Development Patterns and Best Practices with C++ 17

Stephan Roth
Bad Schwartau, Schleswig-Holstein, Germany

ISBN-13 (pbk): 978-1-4842-2792-3   ISBN-13 (electronic): 978-1-4842-2793-0
DOI 10.1007/978-1-4842-2793-0

Library of Congress Control Number: 2017955209

Copyright © 2017 by Stephan Roth

This work is subject to copyright. All rights are reserved by the Publisher, whether the whole or part of the material is concerned, specifically the rights of translation, reprinting, reuse of illustrations, recitation, broadcasting, reproduction on microfilms or in any other physical way, and transmission or information storage and retrieval, electronic adaptation, computer software, or by similar or dissimilar methodology now known or hereafter developed.

Trademarked names, logos, and images may appear in this book. Rather than use a trademark symbol with every occurrence of a trademarked name, logo, or image we use the names, logos, and images only in an editorial fashion and to the benefit of the trademark owner, with no intention of infringement of the trademark.

The use in this publication of trade names, trademarks, service marks, and similar terms, even if they are not identified as such, is not to be taken as an expression of opinion as to whether or not they are subject to proprietary rights.

While the advice and information in this book are believed to be true and accurate at the date of publication, neither the authors nor the editors nor the publisher can accept any legal responsibility for any errors or omissions that may be made. The publisher makes no warranty, express or implied, with respect to the material contained herein.

Cover image by Freepik (`www.freepik.com`)

Managing Director: Welmoed Spahr
Editorial Director: Todd Green
Acquisitions Editor: Steve Anglin
Development Editor: Matthew Moodie
Technical Reviewer: Marc Gregoire
Coordinating Editor: Mark Powers
Copy Editor: Karen Jameson

Distributed to the book trade worldwide by Springer Science+Business Media New York, 233 Spring Street, 6th Floor, New York, NY 10013. Phone 1-800-SPRINGER, fax (201) 348-4505, e-mail `orders-ny@springer-sbm.com`, or visit `www.springeronline.com`. Apress Media, LLC is a California LLC and the sole member (owner) is Springer Science + Business Media Finance Inc (SSBM Finance Inc). SSBM Finance Inc is a **Delaware** corporation.

For information on translations, please e-mail `rights@apress.com`, or visit `http://www.apress.com/rights-permissions`.

Apress titles may be purchased in bulk for academic, corporate, or promotional use. eBook versions and licenses are also available for most titles. For more information, reference our Print and eBook Bulk Sales web page at `http://www.apress.com/bulk-sales`.

Any source code or other supplementary material referenced by the author in this book is available to readers on GitHub via the book's product page, located at `www.apress.com/9781484227923`. For more detailed information, please visit `http://www.apress.com/source-code`.

Printed on acid-free paper

To Caroline and Maximilian: my beloved and marvelous family.

Contents at a Glance

Contents

Comments 48

Functions 56

About Old C-style in C++ Projects 72

Chapter 5: Advanced Concepts of Modern C++ 85

Managing Resources 85

We Like to Move It 94

About the Author

Stephan Roth, born on May 15, 1968, is a passionate coach, consultant, and trainer for Systems and Software Engineering with German consultancy company *oose Innovative Informatik eG* located in Hamburg. Before he joined oose, Stephan worked for many years as a software developer, software architect, and systems engineer in the field of radio reconnaissance and communication intelligence systems. He has developed sophisticated applications, especially for distributed systems with ambitious performance requirements, and graphical user interfaces using C++ and other programming languages. Stephan is also a speaker at professional conferences and author of several publications. As a member of the *Gesellschaft für Systems Engineering e.V.*, the German chapter of the international Systems Engineering organization INCOSE, he is also engaged in the Systems Engineering community. Furthermore, he is an active supporter of the Software Craftsmanship movement and concerned with principles and practices of Clean Code Development (CCD).

Stephan Roth lives with his wife Caroline and their son Maximilian in Bad Schwartau, a spa in the German federal state of Schleswig-Holstein near the Baltic Sea.

You can visit Stephan's website and blog about Systems Engineering, Software Engineering, and Software Craftsmanship via the URL `roth-soft.de`. Please note that the articles there are mainly written in German.

On top of that, you can contact him via e-mail or follow him at the networks listed below.

E-Mail: `stephan@clean-cpp.com`

Twitter: @_StephanRoth (`https://twitter.com/_StephanRoth`)

Google+ Profile Page: `http://gplus.to/sro`

LinkedIn: `http://www.linkedin.com/pub/stephan-roth/79/3a1/514`

About the Technical Reviewer

Marc Gregoire is a software engineer from Belgium. He graduated from the University of Leuven, Belgium, with a degree in "Burgerlijk ingenieur in de computer wetenschappen" (equivalent to Master of Science in engineering in computer science). The year after, he received a master's degree, cum laude, in artificial intelligence at the same university. After his studies were completed, Marc started working for a software consultancy company called Ordina Belgium. As a consultant, he worked for Siemens and Nokia Siemens Networks on critical 2G and 3G software running on Solaris for telecom operators. This required working in international teams stretching from South America and the United States to EMEA and Asia. Marc is now working for Nikon Metrology on industrial 3D laser scanning software.

His main expertise is C/C++, and specifically Microsoft VC++ and the MFC framework. He has experience in developing C++ programs running 24x7 on Windows and Linux platforms: for example, KNX/EIB home automation software. Next to C/C++, Marc also likes C# and uses PHP for creating web pages.

Since April 2007, he has received the yearly Microsoft MVP (Most Valuable Professional) award for his Visual C++ expertise.

Marc is the founder of the Belgian C++ Users Group (`www.becpp.org`), author of *Professional C++* and a member of the CodeGuru forum (as Marc G). He maintains a blog on `www.nuonsoft.com/blog/`.

Acknowledgments

Writing a book like this one is never just the work of an individual person, the author. There are always numerous, fabulous people who contribute significantly to such a great project.

First of all, I would like to thank Steve Anglin of Apress. Steve contacted me in March 2016 and has persuaded me to continue my book project with Apress Media LLC, which has been self-published at Leanpub until then. That was such great luck, and I thank you, dear Steve. In July 2016 the contracts were signed. Nevertheless, I would also like to thank the superb Leanpub self-publishing platform that served some years as a kind of "incubator" for this book.

Next, I would like to thank Mark Powers, Editorial Operations Manager at Apress, for his great support during the writing of the manuscript. Mark was not only always available to answer questions: his incessant follow-up on the progress of the manuscript was a positive incentive for me. I am very grateful to you, dear Mark. In addition, many thanks also to Matthew Moodie, Lead Development Editor at Apress, who has provided proper help throughout the whole book development process.

A special thank you goes out to my technical reviewer Marc Gregoire. Marc, thank you for critically examining every single chapter. You've found many issues that I probably would have never found. You pushed me hard to improve several sections, and that was really valuable to me.

Of course, I would also like to say a big thank you to the whole production team at Apress. They've done an excellent job regarding the finalization (copy editing, indexing, composition/layout, etc.) of the whole book until the distribution of the final print (and eBook) files.

Of course, I also thank all my colleagues at oose. Thank you for the many inspiring discussions.

Last but not least, I would like to thank my beloved and unique family, especially for their understanding that a book project takes a great deal of time. Maximilian and Caroline, you're just wonderful.

CHAPTER 1

Introduction

How it is done is as important as having it done.

—Eduardo Namur

It is still a sad reality that many software development projects are in bad conditions, and some might even be in a serious crisis. The reasons for this are manifold. Some projects, for example, are afflicted because of lousy project management. In other projects, the conditions and requirements are constantly changed, but the process does not support this high-dynamic environment.

In some projects there are pure technical reasons: their code is of poor quality. That does not necessarily mean that the code is not working correctly. Its **external quality**, measured by the quality assurance department using blackbox, user, or acceptance tests, can be pretty high. It can pass the QA without complaints, and the test report says that they find nothing wrong. Also users of the software may be satisfied and happy, and its development has been completed on time and budget (... which is rare, I know). Everything seems to be fine ... really everything?

Nevertheless, the **internal quality** of this code, which might work correctly, can be very poor. Often the code is difficult to understand and horrible to maintain and extend. Countless software units, like classes, or functions, are very large, some of them with thousands of lines of code. Too many dependencies between software units lead to unwanted side effects if something is changed. The software has no perceivable architecture. Its structure seems to be randomly originated and some developers speak about "historically grown software" or "architecture by accident." Classes, functions, variables, and constants have bad and mysterious names, and the code is littered with lots of comments: some of them are outdated, just describe obvious things, or are plain wrong. Developers are afraid to change something or to extend the software because they know that it is rotten and fragile, and they know that unit test coverage is poor, if there are any unit tests at all. "Never touch a running system" is a statement that is frequently heard in such kinds of projects. The implementation of a new feature doesn't need a few days until it is ready for deployment; it takes several weeks or even months.

Such a kind of bad software is often referred to as a *Big Ball Of Mud*. This term was first used in 1997 by Brian Foote and Joseph W. Yoder in a paper for the Fourth Conference on Patterns Languages of Programs (PLoP '97/EuroPLoP '97). Foote and Yoder describe the Big Ball Of Mud as "... a haphazardly structured, sprawling, sloppy, duct-tape-and-baling-wire, spaghetti-code jungle." Such software systems are costly and time-wasting maintenance nightmares, and they can bring a development organization to its knees!

The pathological phenomena just described can be found in software projects in all industrial sectors and domains. The programming language used doesn't matter. You'll find Big Ball Of Muds written in Java, PHP, C, C#, C++, or any other more or less popular language. But why is that so?

© Stephan Roth 2017

S. Roth, *Clean C++*, DOI 10.1007/978-1-4842-2793-0_1

Software Entropy

First of all, there is something that seems to be like a natural law. Just like any other closed and complex system, software tends to get messy over time. This phenomenon is called *software entropy*. The term is based on the second law of thermodynamics. It states that a closed system's disorder cannot be reduced; it can only remain unchanged or increase. Software seems to behave this way. Every time a new function is added or something is changed, the code is getting a little bit more disordered. There are also numerous influencing factors that could forward software entropy, for instance, the following:

- Unrealistic project schedules that will raise the pressure, and hence will compel developers to botch things and to do their work in a bad and unprofessional way.

- Immense complexity of software systems nowadays.

- Developers have different skill levels and experience.

- Globally distributed, cross-cultural teams, enforcing communication problems.

- The development mainly pays attention to the functional aspects (functional requirements and the system's use cases) of the software, whereby the quality requirements (a.k.a. nonfunctional requirements), such as performance efficiency, maintainability, usability, portability, security, etc., are neglected or at worst are being fully forgotten.

- Inappropriate development environment and bad tools.

- Management is focused on earning quick money and doesn't understand the value of sustainable software development.

- Quick and dirty hacks and non-design-conformable implementations (a.k.a. *Broken Windows*).

THE BROKEN WINDOW THEORY

The Broken Window Theory was developed in U.S.-American crime research. The theory states that a single destroyed window at an abandoned building can be the trigger for the dilapidation of an entire neighborhood. The broken window sends a fatal signal to the environment: "Look, nobody cares about this building!" This attracts further decay, vandalism, and other antisocial behavior. The Broken Window Theory has been used as the foundation for several reforms in criminal policy, especially for the development of Zero-Tolerance strategies.

In software development, this theory was taken up and applied to the quality of code. Hacks and bad implementations, which are not compliant with the software design, are called "broken windows." If these bad implementations are not repaired, more hacks to deal with them may appear in their neighborhood. And thus, the dilapidation of code is set into motion.

Don't tolerate "broken windows" in your code – **fix them!**

However, it seems to be that particular C and C++ projects are prone for mess and tend more than others to slip off into a bad state. Even the World Wide Web is full of bad, but apparently very fast and highly optimized C++ code examples, with a cruel syntax and completely ignoring elementary principles for good design and well-written code.

One reason for this might be that C++ is a multi-paradigm programming language on an intermediate level, that is, it comprises both high-level and low-level language features. With C++ you are able to write large and distributed business software systems with sophisticated user interfaces, as well as software for small embedded systems with real-time behavior, tied very closely to the underlying hardware. Multi-paradigm language means that you are able to write procedural, functional, or object-oriented programs, or even a mixture of all three paradigms. In addition, C++ allows *Template Metaprogramming* (TMP), a technique in which so-called templates are used by a compiler to generate temporary source code, which is merged by the compiler with the rest of the source code and then compiled. And ever since the release of ISO standard C++11, even more ways have been added, for example, functional programming with anonymous functions are now supported in a very elegant manner by lambda expressions. As a consequence of these diverse capabilities, C++ has the reputation to be very complex, complicated, and cumbersome.

Another cause for bad software could be that many developers didn't have an IT background. Anyone can begin to develop software nowadays, no matter if she has a university degree or any other apprenticeship in computer science. A vast majority of C++ developers are (or were) non-experts. Especially in the technological domains automotive, railway transportation, aerospace, electrical/electronics, or mechanical engineering, many engineers slipped into programming during the last decades without having an education in computer science. As the complexity grew and technical systems contained more and more software, there was an urgent need for programmers. This demand was covered by the existing workforce. Electrical engineers, mathematicians, physicists, and also lots of people from strictly nontechnical disciplines started to develop software and learn it mainly by self-education and hands-on by simply doing it. And they have done it to their best knowledge and belief.

Basically, there is absolutely nothing wrong with it. But sometimes just knowing the tools and the programming language is not enough! Software development is not the same as programming. The world is full of software that was tinkered together by improperly trained software developers. There are many things on abstract levels a developer must consider to create a sustainable system, for example, architecture and design. How should a system be structured to achieve certain quality goals? What is this object-oriented thing good for and how do I use it efficiently? What are the advantages and drawbacks of a certain framework or library? What are the differences between various algorithms, and why doesn't one algorithm fit all similar problems? And what the heck is a deterministic finite automaton, and why does it help to cope with complexity?!

But there is no reason to lose heart! What really matters for a software's ongoing health is that someone cares about it, and clean code is the key!

Clean Code

A major misunderstanding is to confuse clean code with something that can be called "beautiful code." Clean code has no beauty reasons. Professional programmers are not paid for writing beautiful or pretty code. They are hired by development companies as experts to create customer value.

Code is clean if it can be understood and maintained easily by any team member.

Clean code is the basis for being fast. If your code is clean and test coverage is good, a change or a new function just take a few hours or a couple of days – and not weeks or months – until it is implemented, tested, and deployed.

Clean code is the foundation for sustainable software and keeps a software development project running over a long time without accumulating a large amount of technical debt. Developers must actively tend the software and ensure it stays in shape because the code is crucial for survival of a software development organization.

Clean code is also a key to make you a happier developer. It leads to a stress-free life. If your code is clean and you're feeling comfortable with it, you can keep calm in every situation, even in front of a tight project deadline.

All of the points mentioned above are true, but the key point is this: **Clean code saves money!** In essence, it's about economic efficiency. Each year, development organizations lose a lot of money because their code is in bad shape.

Why C++?

C makes it easy to shoot yourself in the foot. C++ makes it harder, but when you do, you blow away your whole leg!

—Bjarne Stroustrup, *Bjarne Stroustrup's FAQ: Did you really say that?*

Each programming language is a tool, and each one has its strengths and weaknesses. An important part of the job of a software architect is to choose the programming language — or nowadays the set of programming languages — that suits the project perfectly. It is an important architectural decision that should never be made on the basis of a gut feeling or personal preferences. Similarly, a principle like "In our company we do everything with *<replace this with the language of your choice>*" might not be a good guide.

As a multi-paradigm programming language, C++ is a melting pot that blends different ideas and concepts together. The language has always been an excellent choice when it comes to the development of operating systems, device drivers, embedded systems, database management systems, ambitious computer games, 3D animations and computer aided design, real time audio and video processing, big data management, and many other performance-critical applications. There are certain domains in which C++ is the lingua franca. Large C++ code bases with billions of lines of code are still out there and in use.

A few years ago a widely spread opinion was that C++ is hard to learn and use. The language can be complex and daunting to programmers who are often shouldered with the task of writing large, complex programs. Due to this, mainly interpreted and managed languages, such as Java or C#, were getting popular. An excessive marketing by the manufacturer of these languages did the rest. In consequence, managed languages have come to dominate in certain domains, but natively compiled languages still dominate in others. A programming language is not a religion. If you don't need the performance of C++, but Java, for instance, makes your work easier, then by all means use it.

C++11 – The Beginning of a New Era

Some people say that C++ is currently undergoing a renaissance. Some even speak of a revolution. They say that the modern C++ of today is no longer comparable with the "historical C++" of the early 1990s. The catalyst for this trend was mainly the appearance of the C++ Standard ISO/IEC 14882:2011 [ISO11], better known as *C++11*, in September 2011.

No doubt, C++11 has brought some great innovations. It looked as if the publication of this standard has set some stuff in motion. And while this book is in production, the C++ standardization committee has completed their work on the new C++17 standard, which is now in its final ISO balloting process. Furthermore, C++20 is already getting off the starting blocks.

Currently there are a lot of things happening in the native development space, especially in companies of the manufacturing industry, because software has become the most important value-adding factor for technical systems. Development tools for C++ are much more powerful nowadays and a multitude of useful libraries and frameworks are available. But I would not necessarily call this whole development a revolution. I think it is usual evolution. Also programming languages must be continually improved and adapted to meet new requirements, and C++98 respectively C++03 (which was primarily just a bug fix release on C++98) was a bit long in the tooth.

Who This Book Is For

As a trainer and consultant I have the opportunity to take a look into many companies that are developing software. Furthermore, I observe very closely what is happening in the developer scene. And I've recognized a gap.

My impression is that C++ programmers have been ignored by those promoting Software Craftsmanship and Clean Code development. Many principles and practices, which are relatively well-known in the Java environment, and in the hip world of web or game development, seems to be largely unknown in the C++ world. Pioneering books, such as Andrew Hunt and David Thomas's *The Pragmatic Programmer* [Hunt99], or Robert C. Martin's *Clean Code* [Martin09], are often not even known.

This book tries to close that gap a little, because even with C++, code can be written clean! If you want to teach yourself about writing clean C++, this book is for you.

This book is not a C++ primer! You should already be familiar with the basic concepts of the language to use the knowledge from this book efficiently. If you just want to start with C++ development and still have no basic knowledge of the language, you should first learn them, which can be done with other books or a good C++ introduction training.

Furthermore, this book doesn't contain any esoteric hack or kludge. I know that a lot of nutty and mind-blowing things are possible with C++, but these are usually not in the spirit of clean code and should only seldom be used for a clean and modern C++ program. If you are really crazy about mysterious C++ pointer calisthenics, this book is not for you.

For some code examples in this book, various language features of the standards C++11 (ISO/IEC 14882:2011), C++14 (ISO/IEC 14882:2014), and also a few from the latest C++17 are used. If you are not familiar with these features, don't worry. I will briefly provide introductions about some of them with the help of sidebars. Please note that actually not every C++ compiler supports all new language features completely.

Apart from that, this book is written to help C++ developers of all skill levels and shows by example how to write understandable, flexible, maintainable and efficient C++ code. Even if you are a seasoned C++ developer, there are some nuggets and data points in this book that I think you will find useful in your work. The presented principles and practices can be applied to both new software systems, sometimes called *greenfield projects*; as well as legacy systems with a long history, which are often called *brownfield projects* pejoratively.

Conventions Used in This Book

The following typographical conventions are used in this book:

> *Italic font* is used to introduce new terms and names.

> **Bold font** is used within paragraphs to emphasize terms or important statements.

> `Monospaced font` is used within paragraphs to refer to program elements such as class, variable or function names, statements, and C++ keywords. This font is also used to show command line inputs, an address of a website (URL), a keystroke sequence, or the output produced by a program.

Sidebars

Sometimes I'm passing on small bits of information to you that are tangentially related to the content around it, which could be considered separate from that content. Such sections are known as sidebars. Sometimes I use a sidebar to present an additional or contrasting discussion about the topic around it. Example:

THIS HEADER CONTAINS THE TITLE OF A SIDEBAR

This is the text in a sidebar.

Notes, Tips, and Warnings

Another kind of sidebar for special purposes is used for notes, tips, and warnings. They are used to give some special information to you, to provide a useful piece of advice, or to warn you about things that can be dangerous and should be avoided. Example:

■ **Note**   This is the text of the note.

Code Samples

Code examples and code snippets will appear separately from the text, syntax-highlighted (keywords of the C++ language are bold) and in a monospaced font. Longer code sections usually have titles. To reference to specific lines of the code example in the text, code samples are sometimes decorated with line numbers.

Listing 1-1. A line-numbered code sample

```
01  class Clazz {
02  public:
03    Clazz();
04    virtual ~Clazz();
05    void doSomething();
06
07  private:
08    int _attribute;
09
10    void function();
11  };
```

To better focus on specific aspects of the code, irrelevant parts are sometimes obscured and represented by a comment with ellipsis (…), like in this example:

```
void Clazz::function() {
  // ...
}
```

Coding Style

Just a few words about the coding style I've used in this book.

You may get the impression that my programming style has a strong likeness to typical Java code, mixed up with the Kernighan and Ritchie (K&R) style. In my nearly 20 years as a software developer, and even later in my career, I still have learned other programming languages than C++, for instance ANSI-C, Java, Delphi, Scala, and several scripting languages. Hence I've adopted my own programming style, which is a melting pot of different influences.

Maybe you do not like my style, and you prefer Linus Torvald's Kernel style, the Allman style, or any other popular C++ coding standard. This is of course perfectly OK. I like my style, and you like yours.

Companion Website and Source Code Repository

This book is accompanied by a companion website: `www.clean-cpp.com`.

The website includes:

- A discussion forum where readers can discuss specific topics with other readers and, of course, with the author.

- The discussion of additional topics that may not yet have been covered in this book.

- High-resolution version of all the figures in this book.

Most of the source code examples in this book, and other useful additions, are available on GitHub at:

`https://github.com/clean-cpp`

You can check out the code using Git with the following command:

`$> git clone https://github.com/clean-cpp/book-samples.git`

You can get a .zip archive of the code by going to `https://github.com/clean-cpp/book-samples` and clicking on the "Download ZIP" button.

UML Diagrams

Some illustrations in this book are UML diagrams. The *Unified Modeling Language* (UML) is a standardized graphical language to create models of software and other systems. In its current version 2.5, UML offers 14 diagram types to describe a system entirely.

Don't worry if you are not familiar with all diagram types; I use in this book only a few of them. I present UML diagrams from time to time to provide a quick overview of certain issues that possibly cannot be detected fast enough by just reading the code. In Appendix A you find a brief overview of the used notations.

CHAPTER 2

Build a Safety Net

Testing is a skill. While this may come as a surprise to some people it is a simple fact.

—Mark Fewster and Dorothy Graham, *Software Test Automation,* 1999

That I start the main part of this book with a chapter about testing may be surprising to some readers, but this is for several good reasons. During the past few years, testing on certain levels has become an essential cornerstone of modern software development. The potential benefits of a good test strategy are enormous. All kinds of tests, if well engineered, can be helpful and useful. In this chapter I will describe why I think that Unit Tests, especially, are indispensable to ensure a fundamental level of excellent quality in software.

Please note that this chapter is about what is sometimes called POUT ("Plain Old Unit Testing") and not the design-supporting tool Test-Driven Development (TDD), which I will discuss later in this book.

The Need for Testing

1962: NASA MARINER 1

The Mariner 1 spacecraft was launched on July 22, 1962, as a Venus flyby mission for planetary exploration. Due to a problem with its directional antenna, the Atlas-Agena B launching rocket worked unreliably and lost its control signal from ground control shortly after launch.

This exceptional case had been considered during design and construction of the rocket. The Atlas-Agena launching vehicle switched to automatic control by the on-board guidance computer. Unfortunately, an error in the software of this computer led to incorrect control commands that caused a critical course deviation and made steering impossible. The rocket was directed toward earth and pointed to a critical area.

At T+293 seconds the Range Safety Officer sent the destruct command to blow the rocket. A NASA examination report[1] mentions a typo in the computer's source code, the lack of a hyphen ('-'), as the cause of the error. The total loss was $18.5 million, which was a huge amount of money in those days.

---

[1] NASA National Space Science Data Center (NSSDC): Mariner 1, `http://nssdc.gsfc.nasa.gov/nmc/spacecraft-Display.do?id=MARIN1`, retrieved 2014-04-28.

© Stephan Roth 2017
S. Roth, *Clean C++*, DOI 10.1007/978-1-4842-2793-0_2

If software developers are asked why tests are good and essential, I suppose that the most common answer will be the reduction of bugs, errors, or flaws. No doubt, this is basically correct: testing is an elementary part of the quality assurance.

Software bugs are usually perceived as an unpleasant nuisance. Users are annoyed about the wrong behavior of the program, which produces invalid output, or they are seriously ticked off about regular crashes. Sometimes even odds and ends, such as a truncated text in a dialogue box of a user interface, are enough to significantly bother users of software in their daily work. The consequence may be an increasing dissatisfaction about the software, and at worst its replacement by another product. In addition to a financial loss, the image of the software's manufacturer suffers from bugs. At worst, the company gets into serious trouble and many jobs get lost.

But the previously described scenario does not apply to every piece of software. The implications of a bug can be much more dramatic.

1986: THERAC-25 MEDICAL ACCELERATOR DISASTER

This case is probably the most consequential failure in the history of software development. The Therac-25 was a radiation therapy device. It was developed and produced from 1982 until 1985 by the state-owned enterprise Atomic Energy of Canada Limited (AECL). Eleven devices were produced and installed in clinics in the USA and Canada.

Due to bugs in the control software, an insufficient quality assurance process, and other deficiencies, three patients lost their life caused by a radiation overdose. Three other patients were irradiated and carried away permanent, heavy health damages.

An analysis of this case has the result that, among other things, the software was written by only one person who was also responsible for the tests.

When people think of computers, they usually have a Desktop PC, laptop, tablet, or smartphone in their mind. And if they think about software, they usually think about web shops, office suites, or business IT systems.

But these kinds of software and computers make up only a very small percentage of all systems with which we have contact every day. Most of the software that surrounds us controls machines that physically interact with the world. Our whole life is managed by software. In a nutshell: **There is no life today without software!** Software is everywhere and an essential part of our infrastructure.

If we board an elevator, we give our lives are in the hands of software. Aircrafts are controlled by software, and the entire, worldwide air traffic control system depends on software. Our modern cars contain a significant amount of small computer systems with software that communicate over a network, responsible for many safety-critical functions of the vehicle. Air conditioning, automatic doors, medical devices, trains, automated production lines in factories ... No matter what we're doing nowadays, we permanently come into touch with software. And with the *Digital Revolution* and the *Internet of Things* (IoT), the relevance of software for our life will again increase significantly. Hardly any other topic is this more evident than with the autonomous (driverless) car.

I think it is unnecessary to emphasize that any bug in these software-intense systems can have catastrophic consequences. A fault or malfunction of these important systems can be a threat to life or physical condition. At worst, hundreds of people can lose their life during a plane crash, possibly caused by a wrong `if`-statement in a subroutine of the Fly-by-Wire subsystem. Quality is under no circumstances negotiable in these kinds of systems. **Never!**

But even in systems without functional safety requirements, bugs can have serious implications, especially if they are subtler in their destructiveness. It is easy to imagine that bugs in financial software could be a trigger for a worldwide bank crisis nowadays. Just assume that the financial software of an arbitrary big bank carries out every posting twice due to a bug, and this issue will not be noticed for a couple of days.

1990: THE AT&T CRASH

On January 15th, 1990, the AT&T long distance telephone network crashed and 75 million phone calls failed during 9 hours. The blackout was caused by a single line of code (a wrong `break` statement) in a software upgrade that AT&T deployed to all 114 of its computer-operated electronic switches (4ESS) in December 1989. The problem began the afternoon of January 15 when a malfunction in AT&T's Manhattan control center led to a chain reaction and disabled switches throughout half the network.

The estimated loss for AT&T was $60 million, and probably a huge amount of losses for businesses that relied on the telephone network.

Introduction into Testing

There are different levels of quality assurance measures in software development projects. These levels are often visualized in the form of a pyramid – the so-called Test Pyramid. The fundamental concept was developed by the American software developer Mike Cohn, one of the founders of the Scrum Alliance. He described the Test Automation Pyramid in his book *Succeeding with Agile* [Cohn09]. With the aid of the pyramid, Cohn describes the degree of automation required for efficient software testing. In the following years, the Test Pyramid has been developed further by different people. The one depicted in Figure 2-1 is my version of it.

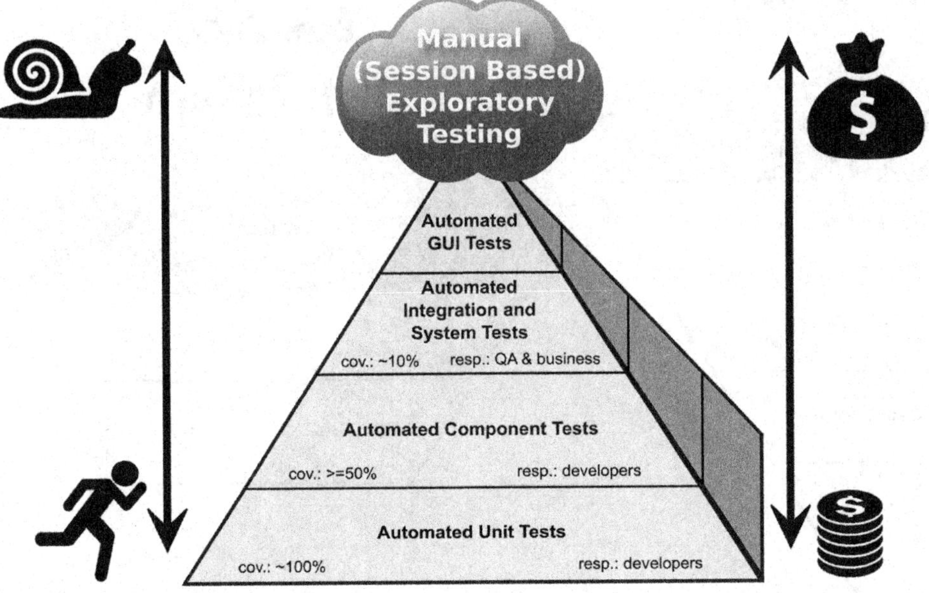

Figure 2-1. *The Test Pyramid*

The pyramid shape, of course, is no coincidence. The message behind it is that you should have many more low-level unit tests (approximately 100% code coverage) than other kind of tests. But why is that?

Experience has shown that the total costs regarding implementation and maintenance of tests are increasing toward the top of the pyramid. Large system tests and manual user acceptance tests are usually complex, often require extensive organization, and cannot be automated easily. For instance, an automated UI test is hard to write, often fragile, and relatively slow. Therefore, these tests are often performed manually, which is suitable for customer approval (acceptance tests) and regular exploratory tests by QA, but far too time consuming and expensive for everyday use during development.

Furthermore, large system tests, or UI-driven tests, are totally improper to check all possible paths of execution through the whole system. There's lots of code in a software system that deals with alternative paths, exceptions and error-handling, cross-cutting concerns (security, transaction handling, logging ...) and other auxiliary functions that are required, but often cannot be reached through the normal user interface.

Above all, if a test on a system level fails, the exact cause of the error can be difficult to locate. System tests typically are based upon the system's use cases. During the execution of a use case, many components are involved. This means that many hundreds, or even thousands, of lines of code are executed. Which one of these lines was responsible for the failed test? This question often cannot be answered easily and requires a time-consuming and costly analysis.

Unfortunately, in several software development projects you'll find degenerated Test Pyramids as shown in Figure 2-2. In such projects an enormous effort is put into the tests on the higher level, whereas the elementary unit tests are neglected (*Ice Cream Cone Anti-Pattern*). In the extreme case they are completely missing (*Cup Cake Anti-Pattern*).

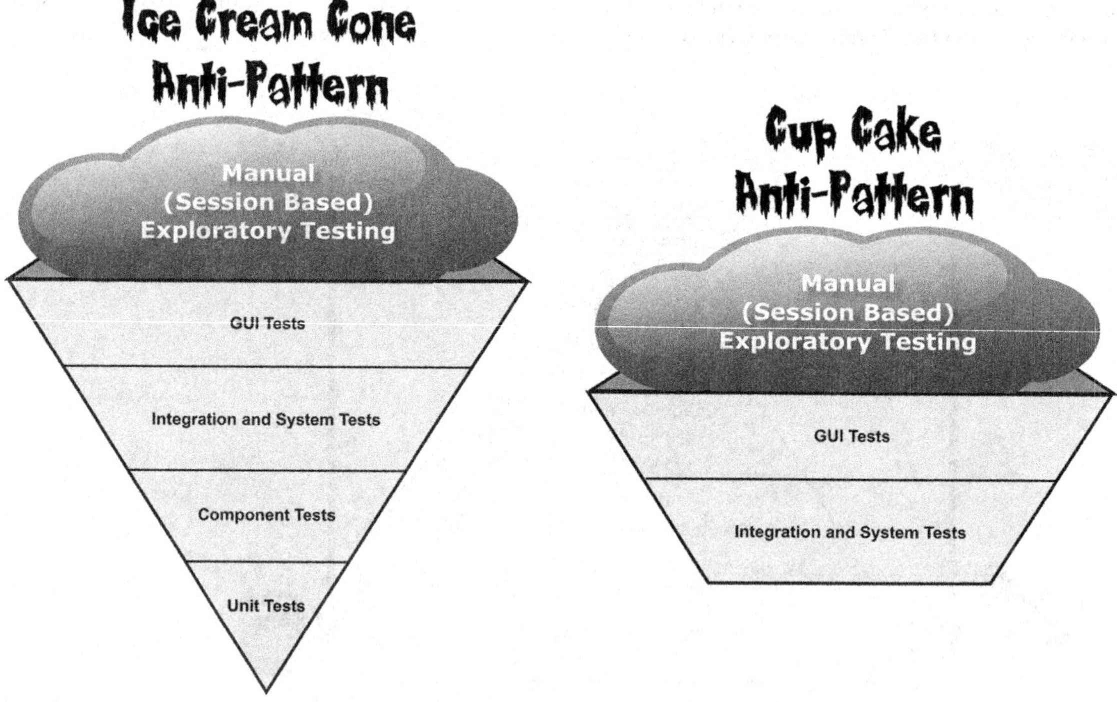

Figure 2-2. *Degenerated Test Pyramids (Anti-Patterns)*

Therefore, a broad base of inexpensive, well-crafted, very fast, regularly maintained, and fully automated unit tests, supported by a selection of useful component tests, can be a solid foundation to ensure a pretty high quality of a software system.

Unit Tests

"refactoring" without tests isn't refactoring, it is just moving shit around.

—Corey Haines (@coreyhaines), December 20, 2013, on Twitter

A unit test is a piece of code that executes a small part of your production code base in a particular context. The test will show you in a split second that your code works as you expect it to work. If unit test coverage is pretty high, and you can check in less than a minute that all parts of your system under development are working correctly, it will have numerous advantages:

- Numerous investigations and studies have proven that fixing bugs after software is shipped has been proven to be much more expensive than having unit tests in place.

- Unit tests give an immediate feedback about your entire code base. Provided that test coverage is sufficiently high (approx. 100%), developers know in just a few seconds if the code works correctly.

- Unit tests give developers the confidence to refactor their code without fear of doing something wrong that breaks the code. In fact, a structural change in a code base without a safety net of unit tests is dangerous and should not be called Refactoring.

- A high coverage with unit tests can prevent time-consuming and frustrating debugging sessions. The often hours-long searches for the causation of a bug using a Debugger can be reduced dramatically. Of course, you will never be able to completely eliminate the use of a Debugger. This tool can still be used to analyze subtle problems, or to find the cause of a failed unit test. But it will no longer be the pivotal developer tool to ensure the quality of the code.

- Unit tests are a kind of executable documentation because they show exactly how the code is designed to be used. They are, so to speak, something of a usage example.

- Unit tests can easily detect regressions, that is, they can immediately show things that used to work, but have unexpectedly stopped working after a change in the code was made.

- Unit testing fosters the creation of clean and well-formed interfaces. It can help to avoid unwanted dependencies between units. A Design for Testability is also a good Design for Usability, that is, if a piece of code can be mounted against a test fixture easily, then it can usually also be integrated with less effort into the system's production code.

- Unit testing makes the development faster.

Especially the last item in this list appears to be paradoxical and needs a little bit of explanation. Unit testing helps the development to go ahead faster – how can that be? That doesn't seem logic.

No doubt about it: writing unit tests means effort. First and foremost, managers just see that effort and do not understand why developers should invest time for tests. And especially in the initial phase of a project, the positive effect of unit testing on development speed may not be visible. In these early stages of a project, when the complexity of the system is relatively low and most everything works fine, writing unit tests seems at first just to take effort. But times are changing ...

When the system becomes bigger and bigger (+ 100,000 LOC) and the complexity increases, it becomes more difficult to understand and verify the system (remember software entropy I've described in Chapter 1). Frequently when many developers in different teams are working on a huge system, they are confronted with code written by other developers every day. Without unit tests in place, this can become a very frustrating job. I'm sure everyone knows those stupid, endless debugging sessions, walking through the code in single-step mode while analyzing the values of variables again and again and again. ... This is a huge waste of time! And it will slow down development speed significantly.

Particularly in the mid-to-late stages of development, and in the maintenance phase after delivery of the product, good unit tests unfold their positive effects. The greatest time savings from unit testing comes a few months or years after a test was written, when a unit or its API needs to be changed or extended.

If test coverage is high it's nearly irrelevant, whether a piece of code that is edited by a developer was written by himself or by another developer. Good unit tests help developers to understand a piece of code written by another person quickly, even if it was written three years ago. If a test fails, it exactly shows where some behavior is broken. Developers can trust that everything still works correctly if all tests pass. Lengthy and annoying debugging sessions become a rarity, and the Debugger serves mainly to find the cause of a failed test quickly if this cause is not obvious. And that's great because it's fun to work that way. It's motivating, and it leads to faster and better results. Developers will have greater confidence in the code base and will feel comfortable with it. Changing requirements or new feature requests? No problem, because they are able to ship the new product quick and often, and with excellent quality.

UNIT TEST FRAMEWORKS

There are several different unit test frameworks available for C++ development, for example, CppUnit, Boost.Test, CUTE, Google Test, and a couple more.

In principle, all these frameworks follow the basic design of so-called *xUnit*, which is a collective name for several unit test frameworks that derive their structure and functionality from Smalltalk's *SUnit*. Apart from the fact that the content of this chapter is not fixated on a specific unit test framework, and because its content is applicable to unit testing in general, a full and detailed comparison of all available frameworks would be beyond the scope of this book. Furthermore, choosing a suitable framework is dependent on many factors. For instance, if it is very important to you that you can add new tests with a minimal amount of work quickly, so this might be a knock-out criterion for certain frameworks.

What about QA?

A developer could have the following attitude: "Why should I test my software? We have testers and a QA department, it's their job."

The essential question is this: Is software quality a sole concern of the quality assurance department? The simple and clear answer: **No!**

I've said this before, and I'll say it again. Despite the fact that your company may have a separate QA group to test the software, it should be the goal of the development group that QA find nothing wrong.

—Robert C. Martin, *The Clean Coder* [Martin11]

It would be extremely unprofessional to hand over a piece of software to QA from which is known that it contains bugs. Professional developers never foist off the responsibility for a system's quality on other departments. On the contrary, professional software craftspeople build productive partnerships with the people from QA. They should work closely together and complement each other.

Of course it is a very ambitious goal to deliver 100% defect-free software. From time to time, QA will find something wrong. And that's good. QA is our second safety net. They check whether the previous quality assurance measures were sufficient and effective.

From our mistakes we can learn and get better. Professional developers remedy those quality deficits immediately by fixing the bugs that were found by QA, and by writing automated unit tests to catch them in the future. Then they should carefully think about this: "How in God's name could it happen that we've overlooked this issue?" The result of this retrospective should serve as an input to improve the development process.

Rules for Good Unit Tests

I've seen many unit tests that are pretty unhelpful. Unit tests should add value to your project. To achieve this goal, some essential rules should be followed, which I will describe in this section.

Test Code Quality

The same high-quality requirements for the production code have to be valid for the unit test code. I'll go even further: Ideally, there should be no judgmental distinction between production and test code – both are equal. If we say that there is production code on the one hand, and test code on the other hand, we separate things that belong together inseparably. Don't do that! Thinking about production and test code in two categories lays the foundation to be able to neglect tests later in the project.

Unit Test Naming

If a unit test fails, the developer wants to know immediately:

- What is the name of the unit; whose test was failed?

- What was tested, and what was the environment of the test (the test scenario)?

- What was the expected test result, and what is the actual test result of the failed test?

Hence an expressive and descriptive naming of unit tests is very important. My advice is to establish naming standards for all tests.

First of all, it's good practice to name the unit test module (depending on the unit test framework, they are called *Test Harnesses* or *Test Fixtures*) in such a way so that the tested unit can be easily derived from it. They should have a name like `<Unit_under_Test>Test`, whereby the placeholder `<Unit_under_Test>` must be substituted by the name of the test subject, obviously. For instance, if your system under test (SUT) is the unit `Money`, the corresponding test fixture that attaches to that unit and contains all unit test cases, should be named `MoneyTest` (see Figure 2-3).

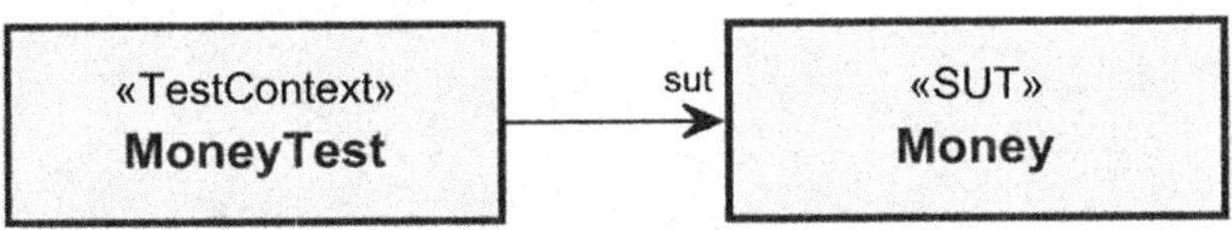

Figure 2-3. *The system under test (SUT) and its Test Context*

Beyond that, unit tests must have expressive and descriptive names. It is not helpful if unit tests have more or less meaningless names like `testConstructor()`, `test4391()`, or `sumTest()`. Here are two suggestions to find a good name for them.

For general, multipurpose classes that can be used in different contexts, an expressive name could contain the following parts:

- The precondition of the test scenario, that is, the state of the SUT before the test was executed.

- The tested part of the unit under test, typically the name of the tested procedure, function, or method (API).

- The expected test result.

That leads to a name template for unit test procedures/methods, like this one:

```
<PreconditionAndStateOfUnitUnderTest>_<TestedPartOfAPI>_<ExpectedBehavior>
```

Here are a few examples:

Listing 2-1. Some examples for good and expressive unit test names

```
void CustomerCacheTest::cacheIsEmpty_addElement_sizeIsOne();
void CustomerCacheTest::cacheContainsOneElement_removeElement_sizeIsZero();
void ComplexNumberCalculatorTest::givenTwoComplexNumbers_add_Works();
void MoneyTest:: givenTwoMoneyObjectsWithDifferentBalance_theInequalityComparison_Works();
void MoneyTest::createMoneyObjectWithParameter_getBalanceAsString_returnsCorrectString();
void InvoiceTest::invoiceIsReadyForAccounting_getInvoiceDate_returnsToday();
```

Another possible approach to build expressive unit test names is to manifest a specific requirement in the name. These names typically reflect requirements of the application's domain. For instance, they are derived from stakeholder requirements.

Listing 2-2. Some more examples of unit test names that verify domain-specific requirements

```
void UserAccountTest::creatingNewAccountWithExistingEmailAddressThrowsException();
void ChessEngineTest::aPawnCanNotMoveBackwards();
void ChessEngineTest::aCastlingIsNotAllowedIfInvolvedKingHasBeenMovedBefore();
void ChessEngineTest::aCastlingIsNotAllowedIfInvolvedRookHasBeenMovedBefore();
void HeaterControlTest::ifWaterTemperatureIsGreaterThan92DegTurnHeaterOff();
void BookInventoryTest::aBookThatIsInTheInventoryCanBeBorrowedByAuthorizedPeople();
void BookInventoryTest::aBookThatIsAlreadyBorrowedCanNotBeBorrowedTwice();
```

As you read these test method names, it becomes clear that even if the implementation of the tests and the test methods are not shown here, a lot of useful information can be derived easily from it. And this is also a great advantage if such a test will fail. Nearly all unit test frameworks write the name of the failed test on standard output (stdout). Thus, error location is greatly facilitated.

Unit Test Independence

Each unit test must be independent to all the others. It would be fatal if tests must be executed in a specific order because one test is based on the result of the previous one. Never write a unit test whose result is the prerequisite for a subsequent test. Never leave the unit under test in an altered state, which is a precondition for the following tests.

Major problems can be caused by global states, for example, the usage of Singletons or static members in your unit under test. Not only is it that Singletons increase the coupling between software units. They also often hold a global state that circumvents unit test independence. For instance, if a certain global state is the precondition for a successful test, but the previous test has mutated that global state, it can cause serious trouble.

Especially in legacy systems, which are often littered with Singletons, this begs the question: how can I get rid of all those nasty dependencies to those Singletons and make my code better testable? Well, that's an important question I discuss in section Dependency Injection in Chapter 6.

DEALING WITH LEGACY SYSTEMS

If you are confronted with so-called Legacy Systems and you are facing many difficulties while trying to add unit tests, I recommend the book *Working Effectively with Legacy Code* [Feathers07] by Michael C. Feathers. Feathers's book contains many strategies for working with large, untested legacy code bases. It also includes a catalogue of 24 dependency-breaking techniques. These strategies and techniques are beyond the scope of this book.

One Assertion per Test

I know that this is a controversial topic, but I will try to explain why I think this is important. My advice is to limit a unit test to use one assertion only, like this:

Listing 2-3. A unit test that checks the not-equal-operator of a Money class

```
void MoneyTest::givenTwoMoneyObjectsWithDifferentBalance_theInequalityComparison_Works() {
  const Money m1(-4000.0);
  const Money m2(2000.0);
  ASSERT_TRUE(m1 != m2);
}
```

One could now argue that we could also check whether other comparison operators (e.g., Money::operator==()) are working correctly in this unit test. It would be easy to do that by simply adding more assertions, like this:

Listing 2-4. Question: Is it really a good idea to check all comparison operators in one unit test?

```
void MoneyTest::givenTwoMoneyObjectsWithDifferentBalance_testAllComparisonOperators() {
  const Money m1(-4000.0);
  const Money m2(2000.0);
  ASSERT_TRUE(m1 != m2);
  ASSERT_FALSE(m1 == m2);
  ASSERT_TRUE(m1 < m2);
  ASSERT_FALSE(m1 > m2);
  // ...more assertions here...
}
```

I think the problems with this approach are obvious:

- If a test can fail for several reasons, it can be difficult for developers to find the cause of the error quickly. Above all, an early assertion that fails obscures additional errors, that is, it hides subsequent assertions, because the execution of the test is stopped.

- As already explained in section Unit Test Naming, we should name a test in a precise and expressive way. With multiple assertions, a unit test really tests many things (which is, by the way, a violation of the Single Responsibility Principle; see Chapter 6), and it would be difficult to find a good name for it. The above ... `testAllComparisonOperators()` is not precise enough.

Independent Initialization of Unit Test Environments

This rule is somewhat akin to Unit Test Independence. When a clean implemented test completes, all states related to that test must disappear. In more specific terms: when running all unit tests, each test must be an isolated partial instantiation of an application. Each test has to set up and initialize its required environment completely on its own. The same applies to cleaning up after the execution of the test.

Exclude Getters and Setters

Don't write unit tests for usual getters and setters of a class, like this:

Listing 2-5. A simple setter and getter

```
void Customer::setForename(const std::string& forename) {
  this->forename = forename;
}


std::string Customer::getForename() const {
  return forename;
}
```

Do you really expect that something could go wrong with such straightforward methods? These member functions are typically so simple that it would be foolish to write unit tests for them. Furthermore, usual getters and setters are implicitly tested by other and more important unit tests.

Attention, I just wrote that it is not necessary to test **usual and simple** getters and setters. Sometimes, getters and setters are not that simple. According to the Information Hiding Principle (see section, Information Hiding in Chapter 3) that we will discuss later, it should be hidden for the client if a getter is simple and stupid, or if it has to make complex things to determine its return value. Therefore, it can sometimes be useful to write an explicit test for a getter or setter.

Exclude Third-Party Code

Don't write tests for third-party code! We don't have to verify that libraries or frameworks do work as expected. For example, we can assume with a clear conscience that the countless times used member function `std::vector::push_back()` from the C++ Standard Library works correctly. On the contrary, we can expect that third-party code comes with its own unit tests. It can be a wise architectural decision to not use libraries or frameworks in your project that don't have own unit tests and whose quality are doubtful.

Exclude External Systems

The same as for third-party code is true for external systems. Don't write tests for systems that are in the context of your system to be developed, and thus not in your responsibility. For instance, if your financial software uses an existing, external currency conversion system that is connected via Internet, you should not test this. Besides the fact that such a system cannot provide a defined answer (the conversion factor between currencies varies minute by minute), and that such a system might be impossible to reach due to network issues, we are not responsible for the external system.

My advice is to mock (see section Test doubles (Fake objects) later in this chapter) these things out and to test your code, **not** theirs.

And What Do We Do with the Database?

Many IT systems contain (relational) databases nowadays. They are required to persist huge amounts of objects or data into longer-term storage, so that these objects or data can be queried in a comfortable way and survive a shutdown of the system.

An important question is this: what shall we do with the database during unit testing?

> *My first and overriding piece of advice on this subject is: When there is **any** way to test without a database, test **without** the database!*

> —Gerard Meszaros, *xUnit Patterns*

Databases can cause diverse and sometimes subtle problems during unit testing. For instance, if many unit tests use the same database, the database tends to become a large central storage that those tests must share for different purposes. This sharing may adversely affect the independence of the unit tests I've discussed earlier in this chapter. It could be difficult to guarantee the required precondition for each unit test. The execution of one unit test can cause unwanted side effects for other tests via the commonly used database.

Another problem is that databases are basically slow. They are much slower than access to local computer memory. Unit tests that interact with the database tend to run magnitudes slower than tests that can run entirely in memory. Imagine you have a few hundred unit tests, and each test needs an extra time span of 500 ms on average, caused by the database queries. In sum all tests take several minutes longer than without a database.

My advice is to mock out the database (see section about Test Doubles/Mock Objects later in this chapter), and execute all unit tests solely in memory. Don't worry: the database, if it exists, will be involved on the integration and system testing level.

Don't Mix Test Code with Production Code

Sometimes developers come up with the idea to equip their production code with test code. For example, a class might contain code to handle a dependency to a collaborating class during a test in the following manner:

Listing 2-6. One possible solution to deal with a dependency during test

```cpp
#include <memory>
#include "DataAccessObject.h"
#include "CustomerDAO.h"
#include "FakeDAOForTest.h"

using DataAccessObjectPtr = std::unique_ptr<DataAccessObject>;
```

```cpp
class Customer {
public:
  Customer() {}
  explicit Customer(bool testMode) : inTestMode(testMode) {}

  void save() {
    DataAccessObjectPtr dataAccessObject = getDataAccessObject();
    // ...use dataAccessObject to save this customer...
  };

  // ...

private:
  DataAccessObjectPtr getDataAccessObject() const {
    if (inTestMode) {
      return std::make_unique<FakeDAOForTest>();
    } else {
      return std::make_unique<CustomerDAO>();
    }
  }
  // ...more operations here...

  bool inTestMode{ false };
  // ...more attributes here...
};
```

DataAccessObject is the abstract base class of specific DAO's, in this case, CustomerDAO and FakeDAOForTest. The last one is a so-called fake object, which is nothing else than a test double (see section about Test doubles (Fake objects) later in this chapter). It is intended to replace the real DAO, since we do not want to test it, and we don't want to save the customer during test (remember my advice about databases). Which one of both DAO's is used is controlled by the Boolean data member inTestMode.

Well, this code would work, but the solution has several disadvantages.

First of all, our production code is cluttered with test code. Although it does not appear dramatically at first sight, it can increase complexity and reduce readability. We need an additional member to distinguish between test mode and production usage of our system. This Boolean member has nothing to do with a customer, not to mention with our system's domain. And it's easy to imagine that such kind of member is required in many classes in our system.

Moreover, our class Customer has dependencies to CustomerDAO and FakeDAOForTest. You can see it in the list of includes at the top of the source code. This means that the test dummy FakeDAOForTest is also part of the system in the production environment. It is to be hoped that the code of the test double is never called in production, but it is compiled, linked, and deployed.

Of course there are more elegant ways to deal with these dependencies and to keep the production code free from test code. For instance, we can inject the specific DAO as a reference parameter in Customer::save().

Listing 2-7. Avoiding dependencies to test code (1)

```cpp
class DataAccessObject;

class Customer {
public:
  void save(DataAccessObject& dataAccessObject) {
    // ...use dataAccessObject to save this customer...
  }
```

```
  // ...
};
```

Alternatively, this can be done during construction of instances of type `Customer`. In this case we must hold a reference to the DAO as an attribute of the class. Furthermore, we have to suppress the automatic generation of the default constructor through the compiler because we don' t want that any user of the `Customer` can create an improperly initialized instance of it.

Listing 2-8. Avoiding dependencies to test code (2)

```cpp
class DataAccessObject;

class Customer {
public:
  Customer() = delete;
  Customer(DataAccessObject& dataAccessObject) : dataAccessObject(dataAccessObject) {}
  void save() {
    // ...use member dataAccessObject to save this customer...
  }

  // ...
private:
  DataAccessObject& dataAccessObject;
  // ...
};
```

DELETED FUNCTIONS [C++11]

In C++, the compiler automatically generates the so-called *special member functions* (default constructor, copy constructor, copy-assignment operator, and destructor) for a type if it does not declare its own. Since C++11, this list of special member functions is extended by the move constructor and move-assignment operator. C++11 (and higher) provides an easy and declarative way to suppress the automatic creation of any special member function, as well as normal member functions and non-member functions: you can delete them. For instance, you can prevent the creation of a default constructor this way:

```cpp
class Clazz {
public:
  Clazz() = delete;
};
```

And another example: you can delete operator new to prevent classes from being dynamically allocated on the heap:

```cpp
class Clazz {
public:
  void* operator new(std::size_t) = delete;
};
```

A third alternative could be that the specific DAO is created by a Factory (see section Factory in Chapter 9 about Design Patterns) the Customer knows. This Factory can be configured from the outside to create the kind of DAO that is required if the system runs in a test environment. No matter which one of these possible solutions you choose, the Customer is free of test code. There are no dependencies to specific DAO's in Customer.

Tests Must Run Fast

In large projects, one day you will reach the point where you have thousands of unit tests. This is great in terms of software quality. But an awkward side effect might be that people will stop running these tests before they're doing a check-in into the source code repository, because it takes too long.

It is easy to imagine that there is a strong correlation between the time it takes to run tests and a team's productivity. If running all unit tests takes 15 minutes, 1/2 hour, or more, developers are impeded in doing their work and waste their time with waiting for the test results. Even if the execution of each unit test takes "only" half a second on average, it takes more than 8 minutes to carry out 1,000 tests. That means that the execution of the whole test suite 10 times per day will result in almost 1.5 hours of waiting time in total. As a result, developers will run the tests less often.

My advice is: **Tests must run fast!** Unit tests should establish a rapid feedback loop for developers. The execution of all unit tests for a large project should not last longer than about 3 minutes, and rather less time than that. For a faster, local test execution (<= a few seconds) during development, the test framework should provide an easy way to turn off irrelevant groups of tests temporarily.

Needless to say, that on the automated build system all tests must be executed without exception continuously every time before the final product will be built. The development team should get an immediate notification if one or more tests fail on the build system. For instance, this can be done via e-mail or with the help of an optical visualization (e.g., due to a flat screen on the wall, or a "traffic light" controlled by the build system) at a prominent place. If even just one test fails, under no circumstances should you release and ship the product!

Test Doubles (Fake Objects)

Unit tests should only be called "unit tests" if the units to be tested are completely independent from collaborators during test execution, that is, the unit under test does not use other units or external systems. For instance, while the involvement of a database during an integration test is uncritical and required, because that's the purpose of an integration test, an access (e.g., a query) to this database during a real unit test is proscribed (see section And What Do We Do with the Database? earlier in this chapter). Thus, dependencies of the unit to be tested to other modules or external systems should be replaced by so-called *Test Doubles*, also known as *Fake Objects*, or *Mock-Ups*.

In order to work in an elegant way with such Test Doubles, loose coupling of the unit under test is to be striven for (see section Loose coupling in the chapter Be Principled). For instance, an abstraction (e.g., an interface in the form of a pure abstract class) can be introduced at the point where an access is made to a collaborator that is unwanted for the test, as shown in Figure 2-4.

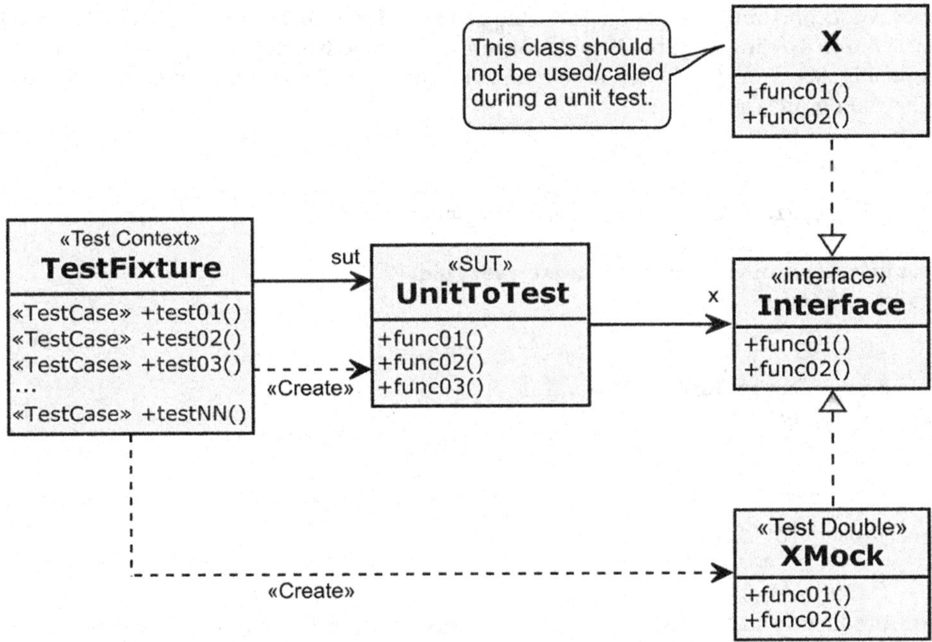

Figure 2-4. *An interface makes it easy to replace X with a Test Double XMock*

Let's assume that you want to develop an application that uses an external web service for current currency conversions. During a unit test you cannot use this external service naturally, because it delivers different conversion factors every second. Furthermore, the service is queried via Internet, which is basically slow and can fail. And it is impossible to simulate borderline cases. Hence you have to replace the real currency conversion by a test double during the unit test.

At first, we have to introduce a variation point in our code, where we can replace the module that communicates with the currency conversion service by a test double. This can be done with the help of an interface, which is in C++ an abstract class with solely pure virtual member functions.

Listing 2-9. An abstract interface for currency converters

```cpp
class CurrencyConverter {
public:
  virtual ~CurrencyConverter() { }
  virtual long double getConversionFactor() const = 0;
};
```

The access to the currency conversion service via Internet is encapsulated in a class that implements the CurrencyConverter interface.

Listing 2-10. The class that accesses the realtime currency conversion service

```cpp
class RealtimeCurrencyConversionService : public CurrencyConverter {
public:
  virtual long double getConversionFactor() const override;
  // ...more members here that are required to access the service...
};
```

For testing purposes a second implementation exists: the Test Double `CurrencyConversionServiceMock`. Objects of this class will return a defined and predictable conversion factor as it is required for unit testing. Furthermore, objects of this class provide additionally the capability to set the conversion factor from outside, for example, to simulate borderline cases.

Listing 2-11. The Test Double

```cpp
class CurrencyConversionServiceMock : public CurrencyConverter {
public:
  virtual long double getConversionFactor() const override {
    return conversionFactor;
  }

  void setConversionFactor(const long double value) {
    conversionFactor = value;
  }

private:
  long double conversionFactor{0.5};
};
```

At the place in the production code where the currency converter is used, the interface is now used to access the service. Due to this abstraction it is totally transparent for the client's code which kind of implementation is used during runtime – either the real currency converter or its Test Double.

Listing 2-12. The header of the class that uses the service

```cpp
#include <memory>

class CurrencyConverter;

class UserOfConversionService {
public:
  UserOfConversionService() = delete;
  UserOfConversionService(const std::shared_ptr<CurrencyConverter>& conversionService);
  void doSomething();
  // More of the public class interface follows here...

private:
  std::shared_ptr<CurrencyConverter> conversionService;
  //...internal implementation...
};
```

Listing 2-13. An excerpt from the implementation file

```cpp
UserOfConversionService::UserOfConversionService    (const std::shared_
ptr<CurrencyConverter>& conversionService) :
  conversionService(conversionService) { }

void UserOfConversionService::doSomething() {
  long double conversionFactor = conversionService->getConversionFactor();
  // ...
}
```

In a unit test for class `UserOfConversionService`, the test case is now able to pass in the mock object through the initialization constructor. On the other hand, at normal operation of the software, the real service can be passed through the constructor. This technique is known as a design pattern named Dependency Injection, which is discussed in detail in the eponymous section of the chapter Design Pattern.

Listing 2-14. An example how UserOfConversionService gets its required CurrencyConverter object

```
std::shared_ptr<CurrencyConverter> serviceToUse = std::make_shared<name of the desired class
here */>();
UserOfConversionService user(serviceToUse);
// The instance of UserOfConversionService is ready for use...
user.doSomething();
```

CHAPTER 3

Be Principled

I would advise students to pay more attention to the fundamental ideas rather than the latest technology. The technology will be out-of-date before they graduate. Fundamental ideas never get out of date.

—David L. Parnas

In this chapter, I introduce the most important and fundamental principles of well-designed and well-crafted software. What is special about these principles is that they are not tied to certain programming paradigms or programming languages. Some of them are not even specific to software development. For instance, the discussed KISS principle can be relevant to many areas of life: generally speaking, it is not a bad idea to make everything as simple in life as possible – not only software development.

That is, you should not learn of the following principles once and then forget them. These advices are given for you to internalize. These principles are so important that they should, ideally, become second nature to every developer. And many of the more concrete principles that I discuss later in this book have their roots in the following basic principles.

What Is a Principle?

In this book you will find various principles for better C++ code and well-designed software. But what is a principle in general?

Many people have principles that guide them through their life. For example, if you're against eating meat for several reasons, that would be a principle. If you want to protect your child, you give him principles along the way, guiding him to make the right decisions on their own, for example "Be careful and don't talk to strangers!" With this principle in mind, the child can deduce the correct behavior in certain specific situations.

A principle is a kind of rule, belief, or idea that guides you. Principles are often directly coupled to values or a value system. For instance, we don't need to be told that cannibalism is wrong because humans have an innate value regarding human life. And as a further example, the Agile Manifesto [Beck01] contains twelve principles that are guiding project teams in implementing Agile projects.

Principles are not irrevocable laws. They are not carved in stone. Willful violations of principles are sometimes necessary in programming. If you have very good reasons to violate principles, do it, but do it very carefully! It should be an exception.

Some of the following basic principles are, at various points later in the book, revisited and deepened.

© Stephan Roth 2017
S. Roth, *Clean C++*, DOI 10.1007/978-1-4842-2793-0_3

KISS

Everything should be made as simple as possible, but not simpler.

—Albert Einstein, theoretical physicist, 1879 - 1955

KISS is an acronym for "Keep it simple, stupid" or "Keep it simple and stupid" (OK, I know, there are other meanings for this acronym, but these two are the most common ones). In eXtreme Programming (XP), this principle is represented by a practice named "Do the simplest thing that could possibly work" (DTSTTCPW). The KISS principle states that simplicity should be a major goal in software development, and that unnecessary complexity should be avoided.

I think that KISS is one of those principles that developers usually forget when they are developing software. Software developers tend to write code in some elaborate way and make things more complicated than they should be. I know, we are all excellently skilled and highly motivated developers, and we know everything about design and architecture patterns, frameworks, technologies, tools, and other cool and fancy stuff. Crafting cool software is not our 9-to-5-job - it is our mission and we achieve fulfillment through our work.

But you have to keep in mind that any software system has an intrinsic complexity that is already challenging in itself. No doubt, complex problems often require complex code. The intrinsic complexity cannot be reduced. This kind of complexity is just there, due to the requirements to be fulfilled by the system. But it would be fatal to add unnecessary, homemade complexity to this intrinsic complexity. Therefore, it is advisable not to use every fancy feature of your language or cool design patterns just because you can. On the other hand, do not overplay simplicity. If ten decisions are necessary in a switch-case, that's just how it is.

Keep your code as simple as you can! Of course, if there are high prioritized quality requirements about flexibility and extensibility, you have to add complexity to fulfill these requirements. For instance, you can use the well-known Strategy Pattern (see Chapter 9 about Design Patterns) to introduce a flexible variation point into your code when requirements demand it. But be careful and add only that amount of complexity that makes things easier.

Focusing on simplicity is probably one of the most difficult things to do for a programmer. And it is a life long learning experience.

—Adrian Bolboaca (@adibolb), April 3, 2014, on Twitter

YAGNI

Always implement things when you actually need them, never when you just foresee that you need them.

—Ron Jeffries, *You're NOT gonna need it!* [Jeffries98]

This principle is tightly coupled to the previously discussed KISS principle. YAGNI is an acronym for "You Aren't Gonna Need It!" Sometimes it is translated to "You Ain't Gonna Need It!" YAGNI is the declaration of war against speculative generalization and over-engineering. It states that you should not write code that is not necessary at the moment, but might be in the future.

Probably every developer knows these kinds of tempting impulses in his daily work: "Maybe we could use it later...", or "We're going to need..." **No, you aren't gonna need it!** At any case you should resist to produce something for a possible later use. You might not need it after all. But if you have implemented that unnecessary thing, you've wasted your time and the code has been getting more complicated than it should be! And of course, you also violate the KISS principle. Even worse consequences could be that these code pieces for the future are buggy and cause serious problems!

My advice is this: Trust in the power of refactoring and build things not before you know that they are actually necessary.

DRY

Copy and paste is a design error.

—David L. Parnas

Although this principle is one of the most important, I'm quite sure that it is often violated, unintentionally or intentionally. DRY is an acronym for "Don't repeat yourself!" and states that we should avoid duplication, because duplication is evil. Sometimes this principle is also referred to as "Once And Only Once" (OAOO).

The reason why duplication is very dangerous is obvious: when one piece is changed, its copies must be changed accordingly. And don't have high hopes. It is a safe bet that change will occur. I think it's unnecessary to mention that any copied piece will be forgotten sooner or later and we can say hello to bugs.

OK, that's it – nothing more to say? Wait, there is still something and we need to go deeper.

In their brilliant book, *The Pragmatic Programmer* [Hunt99], Dave Thomas and Andy Hunt state that applying the DRY principle means that we have to ensure that "every piece of knowledge must have a single, unambiguous, authoritative representation within a system." It is noticeable that Dave and Andy did not explicitly mention the code, but they talk about the knowledge. And a system's knowledge is far broader than just its code. For instance, the DRY principle is also valid for the documentation, project, and test plans, or the system's configuration data. DRY affects everything! Perhaps you can imagine that strict compliance with this principle is not as easy as it seems to be at first sight.

Information Hiding

Information hiding is a long-known and fundamental principle in software development. It was first documented in the seminal paper "On the Criteria to Be Used in Decomposing Systems Into Modules" [Parnas72] written by noted David L. Parnas in 1972.

The principle states that one piece of code that calls another piece of code should not know internals about that other piece of code. This makes it possible to change internal parts of the called piece of code without being forced to change the calling piece of code accordingly.

David L. Parnas describes information hiding as the basic principle for decomposing systems into modules. Parnas argued that system modularization should concern the hiding of difficult design decisions or design decisions that are likely to change. The fewer internals a software unit (e.g., a class or component) exposes to its environment, the lesser is the coupling between the implementation of the unit and its clients. As a result, changes in the internal implementation of a software unit will not be propagated to its environment.

There are numerous advantages of information hiding:

- Limitation of the consequences of changes in modules

- Minimal influence on other modules if a bug fix is necessary

- Significantly increasing the reusability of modules

- Better testability of modules

Information hiding is often confused with encapsulation, but it's not the same. I know that both terms have been used in many noted books synonymously, but I don't agree. Information hiding is a design principle for aiding developers in finding good modules. The principle works at multiple levels of abstraction and unfolds its positive effect, especially in large systems.

Encapsulation is often a programming-language dependent, technique for restricting access to the innards of a module. For instance, in C++ you can precede a list of class members with the `private` keyword to ensure that they cannot be accessed from outside the class. But just because we use such kind of guards for access control, we are still far away from getting information hiding automatically. Encapsulation facilitates, but does not guarantee, information hiding.

The following code example shows an encapsulated class with poor information hiding:

Listing 3-1. A class for automatic door steering (excerpt)

```cpp
class AutomaticDoor {
public:
  enum class State {
    closed = 1,
    opening,
    open,
    closing
  };

private:
  State state;
  // ...more attributes here...

public:
  State getState() const;
  // ...more member functions here...
};
```

This is not information hiding, because parts of the internal implementation of the class are exposed to the environment, even if the class looks well encapsulated. Note the type of the return value of getState. The enumeration class State is required by clients using this class, as the following example demonstrates:

Listing 3-2. An example how AutomaticDoor must be used to query the door's current state

```cpp
#include "AutomaticDoor.h"

int main() {
  AutomaticDoor automaticDoor;
  AutomaticDoor::State doorsState = automaticDoor.getState();
  if (doorsState == AutomaticDoor::State::closed) {
    // do something...
  }
  return 0;
}
```

ENUMERATION CLASS (STRUCT) [C++11]

With C++11 there has also been an innovation on enumerations types. For downwards compatibility to earlier C++ standards, there is still the well-known enumeration with its keyword enum. Since C++11, there are also the enumeration classes respectively enumeration structs.

One problem with those old C++ enumerations is that they export their enumeration literals to the surrounding namespace, causing name clashes, like in the following example:

```
const std::string bear;
// ...and elsewhere in the same namespace...
enum Animal { dog, deer, cat, bird, bear }; // error: 'bear' redeclared as different
kind of symbol
```

Furthermore, old C++ enums implicitly convert to int, causing subtle errors when such a conversion is not expected or wanted:

```
enum Animal { dog, deer, cat, bird, bear };
Animal animal = dog;
int aNumber = animal; // Implicit conversion: works
```

These problems no longer exist when using enumeration classes, also called "new enums," or "strong enums." Their enumeration literals are local to the enumeration, and their values do not implicitly convert to other types (like to another enumeration or an int).

```
const std::string bear;
// ...and elsewhere in the same namespace...
enum class Animal { dog, deer, cat, bird, bear }; // No conflict with the string named
'bear'
Animal animal = Animal::dog;
int aNumber = animal; // Compiler error!
```

It is strongly recommended to use enumeration classes instead of plain old enums for a modern C++ program, because it makes the code safer. And because enumeration classes are also classes, they can be forward declared.

What will happen if the internal implementation of AutomaticDoor must be changed and the enumeration class State is removed from the class? It is easy to see that it will have a significant impact on the client's code. It will result in changes everywhere where member function AutomaticDoor::getState() is used.

The following is an encapsulated AutomaticDoor with good information hiding:

Listing 3-3. A better designed class for automatic door steering

```
class AutomaticDoor {
public:
  bool isClosed() const;
  bool isOpening() const;
```

```cpp
  bool isOpen() const;
  bool isClosing() const;
  // ...more operations here...

private:
  enum class State {
    closed = 1,
    opening,
    open,
    closing
  };

  State state;
  // ...more attributes here...
};
```

Listing 3-4. An example how elegant class AutomaticDoor can be used after it was changed

```cpp
#include "AutomaticDoor.h"

int main() {
  AutomaticDoor automaticDoor;
  if (automaticDoor.isClosed()) {
    // do something...
  }
  return 0;
}
```

Now it's much easier to change the innards of AutomaticDoor. The client code does not depend on internal parts of the class anymore. You are now able to remove the enumeration State and replace it by another kind of implementation without any user of the class noticing this.

Strong Cohesion

A general piece of advice in software development is that any software entity (synonyms: module, component, unit, class, function …) should have a strong (or high) cohesion. In very general terms, cohesion is strong when the module does a well-defined job.

To dive deeper into this principle, let's take a look at two examples where cohesion is weak, starting with Figure 3-1.

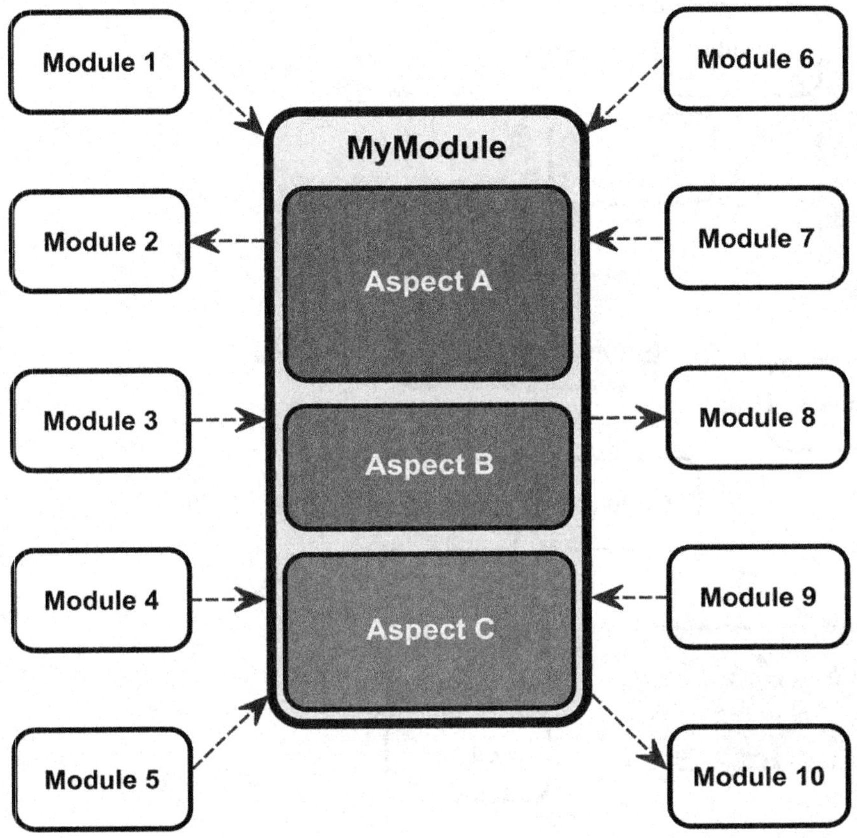

Figure 3-1. `MyModule` *has too many responsibilities, and this leads to many dependencies from and to other modules*

In this illustration of the modularization of an arbitrary system, three different aspects of the business domain are placed inside one single module. Aspects A, B, and C have nothing, or nearly nothing, in common, but all three are placed inside `MyModule`. A look into the module's code could reveal that the functions of A, B, and C are operating on different, and completely independent, pieces of data.

Now take a look at all the dashed arrows in that picture. Each of them is a dependency. The element at the tail of such an arrow requires the element at the head of the arrow for its implementation. In this case, any other module of the system that wants to use services offered by A, or B, or C, will make itself dependent from the whole module `MyModule`. The major drawback of such a design is obvious: it will result in too many dependencies and the maintainability goes down the drain.

To increase cohesion, the aspects of A, B, and C should be separated from each other, and moved into their own modules (Figure 3-2).

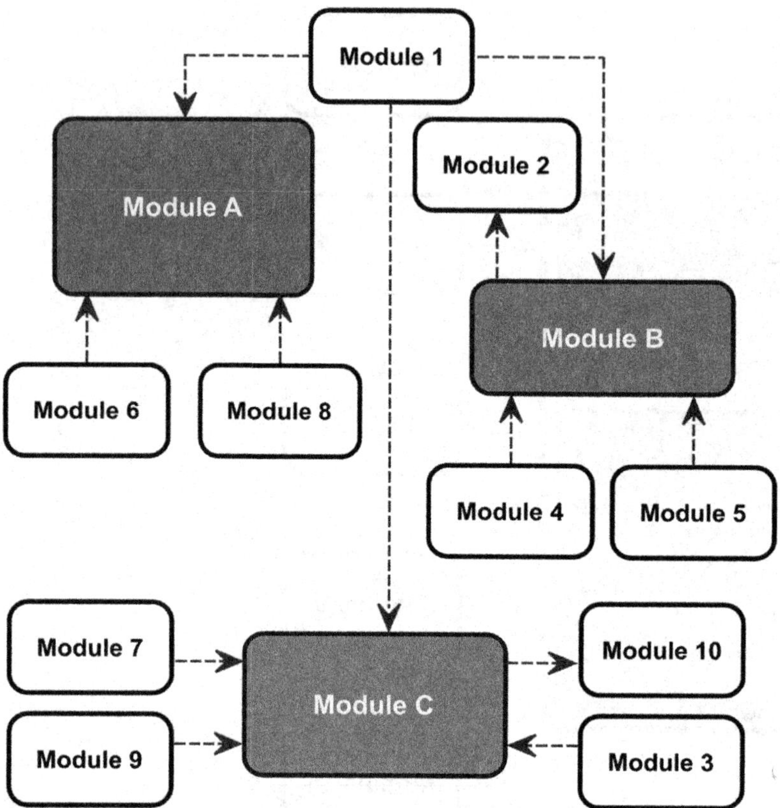

Figure 3-2. *High cohesion: The previously mixed aspects A, B, and C have been separated into discrete modules*

Now it is easy to see that each of these modules has far fewer dependencies than our old `MyModule`. It is clear that A, B, and C have nothing to do with each other directly. The only module, that depends on all three modules A, B, and C, is the one that is named `Module 1`.

Another form of weak cohesion is called the ***Shot Gun Anti-Pattern***. I think it is generally known, that a shot gun is a firearm that shoots a huge amount of small spherical pellets. The weapon has typically a large scatter. In software development, this metaphor is used to express that a certain domain aspect, or single logical idea, is highly fragmented and distributed across many modules. Figure 3-3 depicts such a situation.

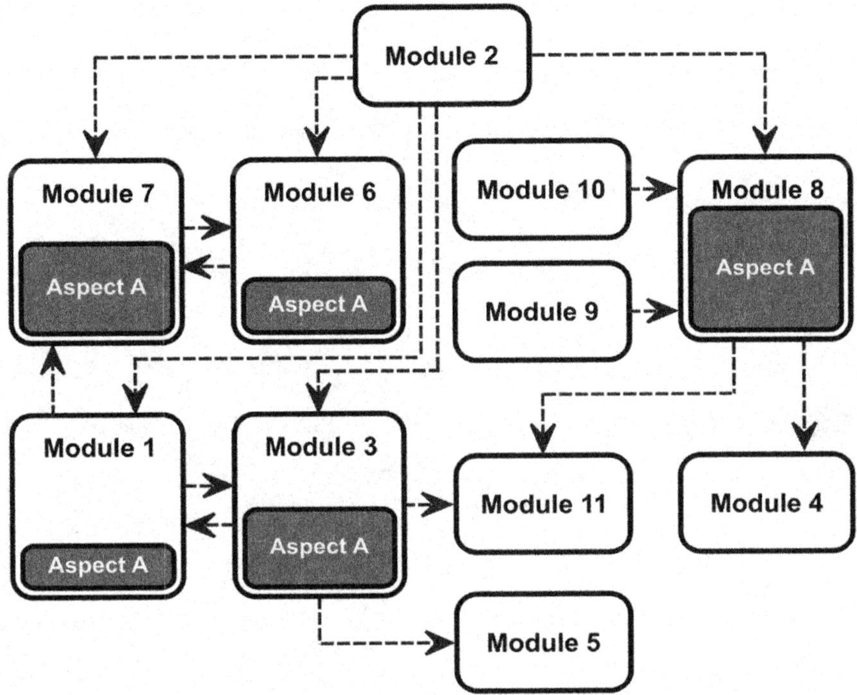

Figure 3-3. *The Aspect A was scattered over five modules*

Even with this form of weak cohesion, many unfavorable dependencies arose. The distributed fragments of Aspect A must work closely together. That means that every module that implements a subset of Aspect A must interact at least with one other module containing another subset of Aspect A. This leads to a large number of dependencies crosswise through the design. At worst, it can lead to cyclic dependencies, like between module 1 and 3, or between module 6 and 7. This has, once again, a negative impact on the maintainability and extendibility. And of course the testability of this design is extremely bad.

Such kind of design will lead to something that is called *Shotgun Surgery*. A certain type of change regarding Aspect A leads to making lots of small changes to many modules. That's really bad and should be avoided. We have to fix this by pulling all the parts of the code that are fragments of the same logical aspect together into a single cohesive module.

There are certain other principles – for instance, the Single Responsibility Principle (SRP) of object-oriented design (see Chapter 6) –, that fosters high cohesion. High cohesion often correlates with loose coupling, and vice versa.

Loose Coupling

Consider the following small example:

Listing 3-5. A switch that can power on and off a lamp

```cpp
class Lamp {
public:
  void on() {
```

```cpp
    //...
  }

  void off() {
    //...
  }
};

class Switch {
private:
  Lamp& lamp;
  bool state {false};

public:
  Switch(Lamp& lamp) : lamp(lamp) { }

  void toggle() {
    if (state) {
      state = false;
      lamp.off();
    } else {
      state = true;
      lamp.on();
    }
  }
};
```

Basically, this piece of code will work. You can first create an instance of class Lamp. Then this is passed by reference when instantiating class Switch. Visualized with UML, this small example would look like that in Figure 3-4.

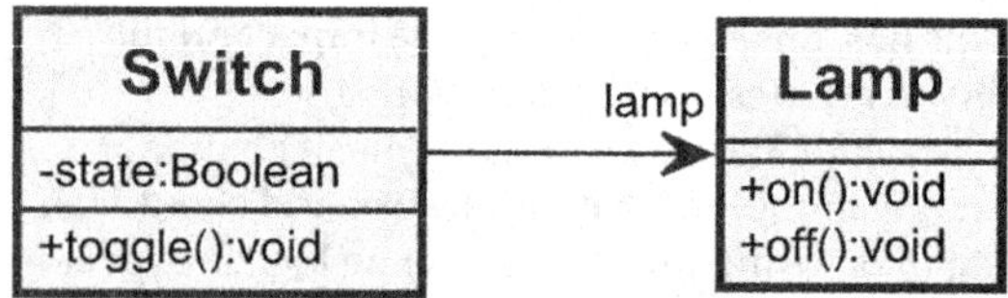

Figure 3-4. *A class diagram of Switch and Lamp*

What's the problem with this design?

The problem is that our Switch contains a reference directly to the concrete class Lamp. In other words: the switch knows that there is a lamp.

Maybe you will argue: "Well, but that's the purpose of the switch. It has to power on and off lamps." I would say: Yes, if that is the one and only thing the switch should do, then this design might be adequate. But please go to a DIY store then and have a look at the switches that you can buy there. Do they know that lamps exist?

And what do you think about the testability of this design? Can the switch be tested independently as it is required for unit testing? No, this is not possible. And what shall we do when the switch has to power on not only a lamp, but a fan, or an electric roller blind?

In our example above, the switch and the lamp are **tightly coupled**.

In software development, a loose coupling (also known as low or weak coupling) between modules should be sought. That means that you should build a system in which each of its modules has, or makes use of, little or no knowledge of the definitions of other separate modules.

The key to loose coupling in software development is interfaces. An interface declares publicly accessible behavioral features of a class without committing to a particular implementation of that class. An interface is like a contract. Classes that implement an interface are committed to fulfill the contract, that is, these classes must provide implementations for the method signatures of the interface.

In C++, interfaces are implemented using abstract classes, like this:

Listing 3-6. The Switchable interface

```cpp
class Switchable {
public:
  virtual void on() = 0;
  virtual void off() = 0;
};
```

The class Switch doesn't contain a reference to the Lamp any more. Instead it holds a reference to our new interface class Switchable.

Listing 3-7. The modified Switch class, where Lamp is gone

```cpp
class Switch {
private:
  Switchable& switchable;
  bool state {false};

public:
  Switch(Switchable& switchable) : switchable(switchable) {}

  void toggle() {
    if (state) {
      state = false;
      switchable.off();
    } else {
      state = true;
      switchable.on();
    }
  }
};
```

The Lamp class implements our new interface.

Listing 3-8. Class 'Lamp' implements the 'Switchable' interface

```cpp
class Lamp : public Switchable {
public:
  void on() override {
    // ...
  }

  void off() override {
    // ...
  }
};
```

Expressed in UML, our new design looks like the one in Figure 3-5.

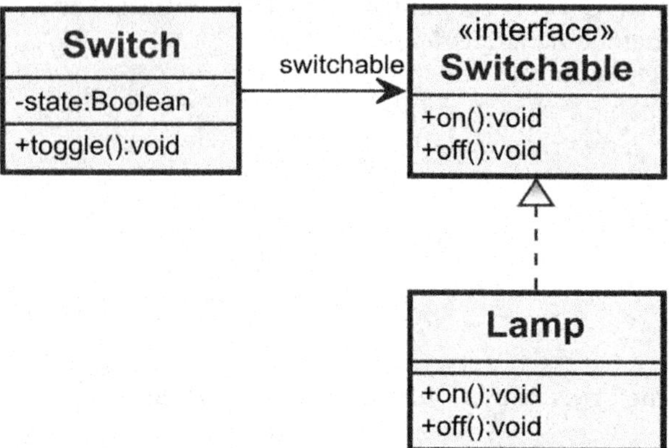

Figure 3-5. *Loosely coupled Switch and Lamp via an interface*

The advantages of such a design are obvious. Switch is completely independent from concrete classes that shall be controlled by it. Furthermore, Switch can be tested independently by providing a test double implementing the Switchable interface. You want to control a fan instead of a lamp? No problem: this design is open for extension. Just create a class Fan or other classes representing electrical devices that implements the interface Switchable, as shown in Figure 3-6.

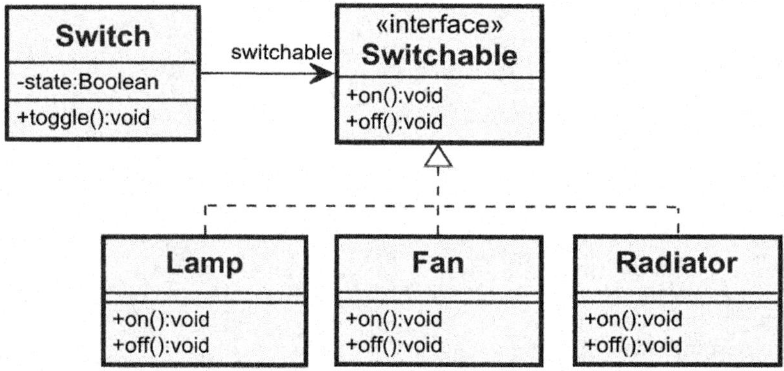

Figure 3-6. *Via an interface, a Switch is able to control different classes for electrical devices*

Attention on loose coupling can provide a high degree of autonomy for individual modules of a system. The principle can be effective on different levels: both at the smallest modules, as well as on the system's architecture level for large components. High cohesion fosters loose coupling, because a module with a clearly defined responsibility usually depends on less collaborators.

Be Careful with Optimizations

Premature optimization is the root of all evil (or at least most of it) in programming.

—Donald E. Knuth, American computer scientist [Knuth74]

I've seen developers starting time-wasting optimizations just with vague ideas of overhead, but not really knowing where the performance is lost. They often fiddled on individual instructions; or tried to optimize small, local loops, to squeeze out even the last drop of performance. Just as a footnote, one of these programmers I'm talking about was me.

The success of these activities was generally marginal. The expected performance advantages usually did not arise. In the end it was just a waste of precious time. On the contrary, often the understandability and maintainability of the allegedly optimized code suffers drastically. Particularly bad: sometimes it even happens that subtly bugs are slipped into the code during such optimization measures. My advice is this: **As long as there are no explicit performance requirements to satisfy, keep your hands off optimizations.**

The comprehensibility and maintainability of our code should be our first goal. And as I explain in the section "But the Call Time Overhead!" in Chapter 4, compilers are nowadays very good at optimizing code. Whenever you feel just a desire to optimize something, think about YAGNI.

Only when explicit performance requirements, which are expressly requested by a stakeholder, are not satisfied, should you spring into action. But then you should carefully analyze first where the performance gets lost. Don't make any optimizations just on the basis of a gut feeling. For instance, you can use a Profiler to find out where the bottlenecks are. After the use of such a tool, developers are usually surprised that the performance gets lost at a completely different location than where it was originally assumed to be.

■ **Note**   A Profiler is a tool for dynamic program analysis. It measures, among other metrics, the frequency and duration of function calls. The gathered profiling information can be used to aid program optimization.

Principle of Least Astonishment (PLA)

The Principle of Least Astonishment (POLA/PLA), also known as Principle of Least Surprise (POLS), is well known in user interface design and ergonomics. The principle states that the user should not be surprised by unexpected responses of the user interface. The user should not be puzzled by appearing or disappearing controls, confusing error messages, unusual reactions on established keystroke sequences (remember: Ctrl + C is the de facto standard for copying applications on Windows operating systems, and not to exit a program), or other unexpected behavior.

This principle can also be well transferred to API design in software development. Calling a function should not surprise the caller with unexpected behavior or mysterious side effects. A function should exactly do what its function name implies (see section about "Function Naming" in Chapter 4). For instance, calling a getter on an instance of a class should not modify the internal state of that object.

The Boy Scout Rule

This principle is about you and your behavior. It reads as follows: **Always leave the campground cleaner than you found it.**

Boy scouts are very principled. One of their principles states that they should clean up a mess or pollution in the environment immediately, once they've found such bad things. As responsible software craftspeople we should apply this principle to our daily work. Whenever we find something in a piece of code that needs to be improved, or which is a bad code smell, we should fix it immediately. And it does not matter who the original author of this piece of code was.

The advantage of this behavior is that we continuously prevent the dilapidation of our code. If we all behave this way, the code simply could not rot. The tendency of growing software entropy has little chance to take dominance of our system. And the improvement doesn't have to be a big deal. It may be a very small clean-up, for example:

- Renaming a poorly named class, variable, function, or method (see section "Good Names and Function Naming" in Chapter 4).

- Decomposing the innards of a large function into smaller pieces (see section "Let Them Be Small" in Chapter 4).

- Deleting a comment by making the commented piece of code self-explanatory (see section "Avoid Comments" in Chapter 4).

- Cleaning up a complex and puzzling if-else-compound.

- Removing a small bit of duplicated code (see section about the DRY principle in this chapter).

Since most of these improvements are code refactorings, a solid safety net consisting of good unit tests, as described in Chapter 2, is essential. Without unit tests in place, you cannot be sure that you do not break something.

Beside good unit test coverage, we still need a special culture in our team: *Collective Code Ownership*.

Collective Code Ownership means that we should truly work as a community. Every team member, at any time, is allowed to make a change or extension on any piece of code. There should be no attitude like "This is Peter's code, and that's Fred's module. I don't touch them!" It should be considered to be a high value that other people can take over the code we wrote. Nobody in a real team should be afraid, or have to obtain permission, to clean up the code, or to add new features. With a culture of collective code ownership, the Boy Scout Rule will work fine.

CHAPTER 4

Basics of Clean C++

As I have already explained in this book's Introduction (see Chapter 1), lots of C++ code out there is not clean. In many projects, software entropy has gotten the upper hand. Even if you are dealing with an ongoing development project, for example, with a piece of software under maintenance, large parts of the code base are often very old. The code looks as it was written in the last century. This is not surprising, because most of that code *was* written in the last century! There are many projects with a long life cycle, which have their roots in the 1990s or even the 1980s. Furthermore, many programmers just copy code snippets out of legacy projects and modify them to get things done.

Some programmers treat the language just like one of many tools. They see no reason to improve something, because what they cobble together works somehow. It should not be that way because it will quickly lead to increased software entropy, and the project will turn into a big mess quicker than you think.

In this chapter I describe the general basics of clean C++. These are sometimes universal things that are often programming language independent. For example, giving a good name is essential in all programming languages. Several other aspects, like const correctness, the usage of smart pointers, or the great advantages of move semantics, are specific for C++.

But before I discuss specific topics, I want to point out a general piece of advice:

If you are not already doing so, start using C++11 (or higher) now!

With the new standard that came up in 2011, C++ has been improved in many ways, and some features of C++11, but also of the following standards C++14, and C++17, are too useful to ignore. And it's not just about performance. The language has definitely become much easier to use and it has even become more powerful. C++11 cannot only make your code shorter, clearer, and easier to read: it can increase your productivity. Moreover, the features of this language standard and its successors enable you to write more correct and exception safe code.

But now let's explore the key elements of clean and modern C++ step by step...

Good Names

Programs must be written for people to read, and only incidentally for machines to execute.

—Hal Abelson and Gerald Jay Sussman, 1984

© Stephan Roth 2017
S. Roth, *Clean C++*, DOI 10.1007/978-1-4842-2793-0_4

The following piece of source code is taken from the well-known *Apache OpenOffice* version 3.4.1, an open source office software suite. Apache OpenOffice has a long history, which dates back to the year 1984. It descends from Oracles *OpenOffice.org* (OOo), which was an open sourced version of the earlier *StarOffice*. In 2011, Oracle stopped the development of OpenOffice.org, fired all developers, and contributed the code and trademarks to the *Apache Software Foundation*. Therefore, please be tolerant and keep in mind that the Apache Software Foundation has inherited a nearly 30-year-old ancient beast and a vast technical debt.

Listing 4-1. An excerpt from Apache's OpenOffice 3.4.1 source code

```cpp
// Building the info struct for single elements
SbxInfo* ProcessWrapper::GetInfo( short nIdx )
{
    Methods* p = &pMethods[ nIdx ];
    // Wenn mal eine Hilfedatei zur Verfuegung steht:
    // SbxInfo* pResultInfo = new SbxInfo( Hilfedateiname, p->nHelpId );
    SbxInfo* pResultInfo = new SbxInfo;
    short nPar = p->nArgs & _ARGSMASK;
    for( short i = 0; i < nPar; i++ )
    {
        p++;
        String aMethodName( p->pName, RTL_TEXTENCODING_ASCII_US );
        sal_uInt16 nInfoFlags = ( p->nArgs >> 8 ) & 0x03;
        if( p->nArgs & _OPT )
            nInfoFlags |= SBX_OPTIONAL;
        pResultInfo->AddParam( aMethodName, p->eType, nInfoFlags );
    }
    return pResultInfo;
}
```

I have a simple question for you: **What does this function do?**

It seems easy to give an answer at first sight, because the code snippet is small (less than 20 LOC) and the indentation is OK. But in fact, it is not possible to say at a glance what this function really does, and the reason for this lies not only in the domain that might be unknown to you.

This short code snippet has many bad smells (e.g., commented-out code, comments in German, magic literals like 0x03, etc.) but a major problem is the poor naming. The function's name GetInfo() is very abstract and gives us at most a vague idea of what this function actually does. Also the namespace name ProcessWrapper is not very helpful. Perhaps you can use this function to retrieve information about a running process? Well, wouldn't RetrieveProcessInformation() be a much better name for it?

After an analysis of the function's implementation you will also notice that the name is misleading, because GetInfo() is not just a simple getter as you might suspect. There is also something created with the new operator. Maybe you also noticed the comment above the function that speaks about building, and not just getting something. In other words, the call site will receive a resource that was allocated on the heap and must take care of it. To emphasize this fact, wouldn't a name like CreateProcessInformation() be much better?

Next take a look at the argument and the return value of the function. What is SbxInfo? What is nIdx? Maybe the argument nIdx holds a value that is used to access an element in a data structure (that is, an index), but that would just be a guess. In fact, we don't know it exactly.

Source code is read much more often by developers than translated by a compiler. Therefore, source code should be readable, and good names are a key factor to increase its readability. If you are working on a project with multiple people, good naming is essential so that you and your teammates can understand your code quickly. And even if you have to edit or read a piece of code written by yourself after a few weeks, or a few months, good class-, method-, and variable names will help you to recall what you had intended.

So, here is my basic advice:

Source code files, namespaces, classes, templates, functions, arguments, variables, and constants should have meaningful and expressive names.

When I'm designing software or write code, I spend a lot of time thinking about names. I believe that it is well-invested time to think about good names, even if it's sometimes not easy and takes 5 minutes or longer. I seldom find the perfect fitting name for a thing immediately. Therefore, I rename often, which is easy with a good editor or an Integrated Development Environment (IDE) with refactoring capabilities.

If finding a proper name for a variable, function, or class seems to be difficult or nearly impossible, it potentially indicates that something else might be wrong. Perhaps a design issue exists and you should find and solve the root cause for your naming problem.

Here are a few bits of advice for finding good names.

Names Should Be Self-Explanatory

I've committed myself to the concept of self-documenting code. Self-documenting code is code where no comments are required to explain its purpose (see also the following section on comments and how to avoid them). And self-documenting code requires self-explanatory names for its namespaces, classes, variables, constants, and functions.

Use simple but descriptive and self-explaining names.

Listing 4-2. Some examples of bad names

```
unsigned int num;
bool flag;
std::vector<Customer> list;
Product data;
```

Variable naming conventions can often turn into a religious war, but I am very sure that there is broad agreement that num, flag, list, and data are really bad names. What is data? Everything is data. This name has absolutely no semantics. It is like you would wrap up your goods and chattels in moving boxes and instead of writing on them what they really contain, for example, "Cookware," you would write the word "Things" on every single carton. In the new house when the cartons arrive, this information is completely useless.

Here is an example of how we could better name the four variables from the previous code example:

Listing 4-3. Some examples of good names

```cpp
unsigned int numberOfArticles;
bool isChanged;
std::vector<Customer> customers;
Product orderedProduct;
```

One can now argue that names are better the longer they are. Consider the following example:

Listing 4-4. A very exhaustive variable name

```cpp
unsigned int totalNumberOfCustomerEntriesWithMangledAddressInformation;
```

No doubt, this name is extremely expressive. Even without knowing where this code comes from, the reader knows quite well what this variable is used for. However, there are problems with names like this. For example, you can not easily remember such long names. And they are difficult to type. If such extremely verbose names are used in expressions, the readability of the code may even suffer:

Listing 4-5. A naming chaos, caused by too verbose names

```cpp
totalNumberOfCustomerEntriesWithMangledAddressInformation =
    amountOfCustomerEntriesWithIncompleteOrMissingZipCode +
    amountOfCustomerEntriesWithoutCityInformation +
    amountOfCustomerEntriesWithoutStreetInformation;
```

Too long and verbose names are not appropriate or desirable when trying to make our code clean. If the context is clear in which a variable is used, shorter and less descriptive names are possible. If the variable is a member (attribute) of a class, for instance, the class's name usually provides sufficient context for the variable:

Listing 4-6. The class's name provides enough context information for the attribute

```cpp
class CustomerRepository {
private:
  unsigned int numberOfMangledEntries;
  // ...
};
```

Use Names from the Domain

You may have already heard of Domain-Driven Design (DDD) before now. The term "Domain-Driven Design" was coined by Eric Evans in his eponymous book from 2004 [Evans04]. DDD is an approach in the complex object-oriented software development that primarily focuses on the core domain and domain logic. In other words, DDD is about trying to make your software a model of a real-life system by mapping business domain things and concepts into the code. For instance, if the software to be developed shall support the business processes in a car rental, then the things and concepts of car rental (e.g., rental car, car pool, rentee, rental period, rental confirmation, accounting, etc.) should be discoverable in the design of this software. If, on the other hand, software is developed in the aerospace industry, the aerospace domain should be reflected in it.

The advantages of such an approach are obvious: the use of terms from the domain facilitates, above all, the communication between the developers and other stakeholders. DDD helps the software development team to create a common model between the business and IT stakeholders in the company that the team can use to communicate about the business requirements, data entities, and process models.

A detailed introduction to Domain-Driven Design is beyond the scope of this book. However, it is basically always a very good idea to name components, classes, and functions in a way that elements and concepts from the application's domain can be rediscovered. This enables us to communicate software designs as naturally as possible. It will make code more understandable to anyone involved in solving a problem, for example, a tester or a business expert.

Take, for example, the abovementioned car rental. The class that is responsible for the use case of the reservation of a car for a certain customer could be as follows:

Listing 4-7. The interface of a use case controller class to reserve a car

```cpp
class ReserveCarUseCaseController {
public:
  Customer identifyCustomer(const UniqueIdentifier& customerId);
  CarList getListOfAvailableCars(const Station& atStation, const RentalPeriod&
  desiredRentalPeriod) const;
  ConfirmationOfReservation reserveCar(const UniqueIdentifier& carId, const RentalPeriod&
  rentalPeriod) const;

private:
  Customer& inquiringCustomer;
};
```

Now take a look at all those names used for the class, the methods, and the arguments and return types. They represent things that are typical for the car rental domain. If you read the methods from top to bottom, these are the individual steps that are required for renting a car. This is C++ code, but there is a great chance that also nontechnical stakeholders with domain knowledge can understand it.

Choose Names at an Appropriate Level of Abstraction

To keep the complexity of today's software systems under control, these systems are usually hierarchically decomposed. Hierarchical decomposition of a software system means that the entire problem is partitioned into smaller parts, respectively, as subtasks until developers get the confidence that they are able to manage these smaller parts. There are different methods and criteria to make this kind of decomposition. The Domain-Driven Design that was mentioned in the previous section, and also the Object-Oriented Analysis and Design (OOAD) are two methods for such decomposition, whereby the basic criteria for the creation of components and classes in both methods is the business domain.

With such decomposition, software modules are created at different levels of abstraction: starting from large components or subsystems down to very small building blocks like classes. The task, which a building block at a higher abstraction level fulfills, should be fulfilled by interaction of the building blocks on the next, lower abstraction level.

The abstraction levels introduced by this approach also have an impact on naming. Every time we go one step deeper down the hierarchy, the names of the elements are getting more concrete.

Imagine a Webshop. On the top level there might exist a large component whose single responsibility is to create invoices. This component could have a short and descriptive name like `Billing`. Usually, this component consists of further smaller components or classes. For instance, one of these smaller modules could be responsible for the calculation of a discount. Another module could be responsible for the creation of invoice line items. Thus, good names for these modules could be `DiscountCalculator` and `LineItemFactory`. If we now dive deeper into the decomposition hierarchy, the identifiers for components, classes, and also functions or methods become more and more concrete, verbose, and thus also longer. For example, a small method in a class at the deepest level could have a very detailed and elongated name, like `calculateReducedValueAddedTax()`.

Avoid Redundancy When Choosing a Name

It is redundant to pick up a class name or other names that provide a clear context, and use them as a part to build the name of a member variable, for example, like this:

Listing 4-8. Don't repeat the class's name in its attributes

```cpp
#include <string>

class Movie {
private:
  std::string movieTitle;
  // ...
};
```

Don't do that! It is an, albeit, only very tiny violation of the DRY principle. Instead, name it `Title`. The member variable is in the namespace of class `Movie`, so it's clear without ambiguity whose title is meant: the movie's title!

Here is another example of redundancy:

Listing 4-9. Don't include the attribute's type in its name

```cpp
#include <string>

class Movie {
  // ...
private:
  std::string stringTitle;
};
```

It is the title of a movie, so obviously it is a string and not an integer! Do not include the type of a variable or constant in its name.

Avoid Cryptic Abbreviations

When choosing a name for your variables or constants, use full words instead of cryptic abbreviations. The reason is obvious: cryptic abbreviations reduce the readability of your code significantly. Furthermore, when developers talk about their code, variable names should be easy to pronounce.

Remember the variable named `nPar` on line 8 from our Open Office code snippet. Neither is its meaning clear, nor it can be pronounced in a good manner.

Here are a few more examples for Do's and Dont's:

Listing 4-10. Some examples for good and bad names

```cpp
std::size_t idx;           // Bad!
std::size_t index;         // Good; might be sufficient in some cases
std::size_t customerIndex; // To be preferred, especially in situations where
                           // several objects are indexed
```

```
Car ctw;        // Bad!
Car carToWash;  // Good

Polygon ply1;         // Bad!
Polygon firstPolygon; // Good

unsigned int nBottles;        // Bad!
unsigned int bottleAmount;    // Better
unsigned int bottlesPerHour;  // Ah, the variable holds a work value,
                              // and not an absolute number. Excellent!

const double GOE = 9.80665; // Bad!
const double gravityOfEarth = 9.80665; // More expressive, but misleading. The constant is
                                       // not a gravitation, which would be a force in physics.
const double gravitationalAccelerationOnEarth = 9.80665; // Good.
constexpr Acceleration gravitationalAccelerationOnEarth = 9.80665_ms2; // Wow!
```

Look at the last line, which I have commented with "Wow!" That looks pretty convenient, because it is a familiar notation for scientists. It looks almost like teaching physics at school. And yes, that's really possible in C++, as you will learn in one of the following sections about Type-rich programming in Chapter 5.

Avoid Hungarian Notation and Prefixes

Do you know Charles Simonyi? Charles Simonyi is a Hungarian-American computer software expert who worked as a Chief Architect at Microsoft in the 1980s. Maybe you remember his name in a different context. Charles Simonyi is a space tourist and has made two trips into space, one of them to the International Space Station (ISS).

But he also developed a notation convention for naming variables in computer software, named the Hungarian notation, which has been widely used inside Microsoft and later, also, by other software manufacturers.

When using Hungarian Notation, the type, and sometimes also the scope, of a variable are used as a naming prefix for that variable. Here are a few examples:

Listing 4-11. Some examples for Hungarian notation with explanations

```
bool fEnabled;        // f = a boolean flag
int nCounter;         // n = number type (int, short, unsigned, ...)
char* pszName;        // psz = a pointer to a zero-terminated string
std::string strName; // str = a C++ stdlib string
int m_nCounter;       // The prefix 'm_' marks that it is a member variable,
                      // i.e. it has class scope.
char* g_pszNotice;    // That's a global(!) variable. Believe me, I've seen
                      // such a thing.
int dRange;           // d = double-precision floating point. In this case it's
                      // a stone-cold lie!
```

My advice in the 21th century is this:

Do not use Hungarian notation, or any other prefix-based notation, encoding the type of a variable in its name!

Hungarian notation was potentially helpful in a weakly typed language like C. It may have been useful at a time when developers have used simple editors for programming, and not IDEs that have a feature like "IntelliSense."

Modern and sophisticated development tools today support the developer very well and show the type and scope of a variable. There are no more good reasons to encode the type of a variable in its name. Far from it, such prefixes can impede the train of readability of the code.

At worst, it may even happen that during development the type of a variable gets changed without adapting the prefix of its name. In other words: the prefixes tend to turn into lies, as you can see from the last variable in the example above. That's really bad!

And another problem is that in object-oriented languages that support polymorphism, the prefix cannot be specified easily, or a prefix can even be puzzling. Which Hungarian prefix is suitable for a polymorphic variable that can be an integer or a double? `idX`? `diX`? How to determine a suitable and unmistakable prefix for an instantiated C++ template?

By the way, even Microsoft's so-called General Naming Conventions emphasize that you should not use Hungarian notation.

Avoid Using the Same Name for Different Purposes

Once you've introduced a meaningful and expressive name for any kind of software entity (e.g., a class or component), a function, or a variable, you should take care about that its name is never used for any other purpose.

I think it is pretty obvious that using the same name for different purposes can be puzzling and can mislead readers of the code. Don't do that. That's all I have to say about that topic.

Comments

Truth can only be found in one place: the code.

—Robert C. Martin, *Clean Code* [Martin09]

Do you remember your beginnings as a professional software developer? Do you still remember the coding standards in your company during those days? Maybe you're still young and not long in business, but the older ones will confirm that most of those standards contained a rule that proper professional code must always be properly commented. The absolutely comprehensible reasoning for this rule was that any other developer, or a new team member, could easily understand the intent of the code.

On first sight, this rule seems like a good idea. In many companies, the code was therefore commented extensively. In some projects, the ratio between productive lines of code and comments were almost 50:50. Unfortunately, it was **not** a good idea. On the contrary: **This rule was an absolutely bad idea!** It was, and it is completely wrong in several respects, because in the predominantly number of cases comments are a code smell. Comments are necessary when there is need for explanation and clarification. And that often means that the developer was not able to write simple and self-explanatory code.

Please do not misunderstand: there are some reasonable use cases for comments. In some situations a comment might actually be helpful. I will present a few of these rather rare cases at the end of this section. But for any other case this rule should apply, and that's also the heading of the next section: "Let the Code Tell a Story!"

Let the Code Tell a Story

Just imagine a movie at the cinema, which would only be understandable if individual scenes are explained using a textual description below the picture. This film would certainly not be a success. On the contrary, it would be picked to pieces by the critics. No one would watch such a bad movie. Good films are therefore very successful, because they can mainly tell a gripping story, only through the pictures and the dialogues of the actors.

Storytelling is basically a successful concept in many domains, not only in film production. When you think about building a great software product, then you should think about it in a way as you would tell the world a great and enthralling story. It's not surprising that Agile project management frameworks like Scrum use things called "user stories" as a way to capture requirements from the perspective of the user. As I've already explained in a section about preferring domain-specific names, you should talk to stakeholders in their own language.

So, here is my advice:

Code should tell a story and be self-explanatory. Comments must be avoided whenever possible.

Comments are not subtitles. Whenever you feel the desire to must write a comment in your code because you want to explain something, you should think about how you can write the code better so that it is self-explanatory and the comment gets superfluous. Modern programming languages like C++ have everything that's necessary to write clear and expressive code. Good programmers take advantage of that expressiveness to tell stories.

> *Any fool can write code that a computer can understand. Good programmers write code that humans can understand.*

> —Martin Fowler, 1999

Do Not Comment Obvious Things

Once again, we take a look at a small and typical piece of source code that was commented extensively.

Listing 4-12. Are these comments useful?

```
customerIndex++;                                        // Increment index
Customer* customer = getCustomerByIndex(customerIndex); // Retrieve the customer at the
                                                        // given index
CustomerAccount* account = customer->getAccount();      // Retrieve the customer's account
account->setLoyaltyDiscountInPercent(discount);         // Grant a 10% discount
```

Please, don't insult the reader's intelligence! It is obvious that these comments are **totally useless**. The code itself is largely self-explanatory. And they do not only add absolutely no new or relevant information. Much worse is that these useless comments are a kind of duplication of the code. They violate the DRY principle we've discussed in Chapter 3.

Maybe you've noticed another detail. Take a look at the last line. The comment speaks literally of a 10% discount, but in the code there is a variable or constant named discount that is passed into the function or method setLoyaltyDiscountInPercent(). What has happened here? A reasonable suspicion is that this comment has turned into a lie because the code was changed, but the comment was not adapted. That's really bad and misleading.

Don't Disable Code with Comments

Sometimes comments are used to disable a bunch of code that shall not be translated by the compiler. An often delivered reasoning by some developers for this practice is that one could possibly use this piece of code again later. They think, "Maybe one day … we'll need it again."

Listing 4-13. An example for commented-out code

```cpp
// This function is no longer used (John Doe, 2013-10-25):
/*
double calcDisplacement(double t) {
  const double goe = 9.81; // gravity of earth
  double d = 0.5 * goe * pow(t, 2); // calculation of distance
  return d;
}
*/
```

A major problem with commented-out code is that it adds confusion with no real benefit. Just imagine that the disabled function in the example above is not the only one, but one of a lot of places where code has been commented-out. The code will soon turn into a big mess and the commented-out code snippets will add a lot of noise that impedes the readability. Furthermore, commented-out code snippets are not quality assured, that is, they are not translated by the compiler, not tested, and not maintained. My advice is this:

Except for the purpose to try out something quickly, don't use comments to disable code. There is a version control system!

If code is no longer used, simply delete it. Let it go. You have a "time machine" to get it back, if necessary: your version control system. However, it often turns out that this case is very rare. Just take a look at the timestamp the developer has added in the above example. This piece of code is age old. What is the likelihood that it will ever be needed again?

To try out something quickly during development, for example, while searching for the causation for a bug, it is of course helpful to comment-out a code section temporarily. But it must be ensured that such modified code is not checked-in in the version control system.

Don't Write Block Comments

Comments like the follwing ones can be found in many projects.

Listing 4-14. An example of block comments

```cpp
#ifndef _STUFF_H_
#define _STUFF_H_

// -------------------------------------
// stuff.h: the interface of class Stuff
// John Doe, created: 2007-09-21
// -------------------------------------
```

```
class Stuff {
public:
  // ----------------
  // Public interface
  // ----------------

  // ...

protected:
  // -------------
  // Overrideables
  // -------------

  // ...

private:
  // -----------------------
  // Private member functions
  // -----------------------

  // ...

  // -----------------
  // Private attributes
  // -----------------

  // ...

};

#endif
```

These kinds of comments (and I do not mean the ones I used to obscure irrelevant parts) are called "Block Comments," or "Banners." They are often used to put a summary about the content at the top of a source code file. Or they are used to mark a special position in the code. For instance, they're introducing a code section where all private member functions of a class can be found.

These kinds of comments are mostly pure clutter and should be deleted immediately.

There are very few exceptions where such comments could have a benefit. In some rare cases, a bunch of functions of a special category can be gathered together underneath such a comment. But then you should not use noisy character trains consisting of hyphens (-), slashes (/), number signs (#), or asterisks (*) to envelop it. A comment like the following one is absolutely sufficient to introduce such a region:

Listing 4-15. Sometimes useful: a comment to introduce a category of functions

```
private:
  // Event handlers:
  void onUndoButtonClick();
  void onRedoButtonClick();
  void onCopyButtonClick();
  // ...
```

In some projects the coding standards say that big headers with copyright and license text at the top of any source code file are mandatory. They can look like this:

Listing 4-16. The license header in any source code file of Apache OpenOffice 3.4.1

```
/**************************************************************
 *
 * Licensed to the Apache Software Foundation (ASF) under one
 * or more contributor license agreements.  See the NOTICE file
 * distributed with this work for additional information
 * regarding copyright ownership.  The ASF licenses this file
 * to you under the Apache License, Version 2.0 (the
 * "License"); you may not use this file except in compliance
 * with the License.  You may obtain a copy of the License at
 *
 *   http://www.apache.org/licenses/LICENSE-2.0
 *
 * Unless required by applicable law or agreed to in writing,
 * software distributed under the License is distributed on an
 * "AS IS" BASIS, WITHOUT WARRANTIES OR CONDITIONS OF ANY
 * KIND, either express or implied.  See the License for the
 * specific language governing permissions and limitations
 * under the License.
 *
 **************************************************************/
```

First I want to say something fundamental about copyrights. You don't need to add comments about the copyright, or do anything else, to have copyright over your works. According to the *Berne Convention for the Protection of Literary and Artistic Works* [Wipo1886] (or *Berne Convention* in short), such comments have no legal meaning.

There were times where such comments were required. Before the United States had signed the Berne Convention in 1989, such copyright notices were mandatory if you wanted to enforce your copyright in the United States. But that is a thing of the past. Nowadays these comments are no longer needed.

My advice is to simply omit them. They are just cumbersome and useless baggage. However, if you want to, or even need to offer copyright and license information in your project, then you better write them in separate files, like `license.txt` and `copyright.txt`. If a software license requires under all circumstances that license information has to be included in the head area of every source code file, then you can hide these comments if your IDE has a so-called folding editor.

Don't Use Comments to Substitute Version Control

Sometimes – and this is extremely bad – banner comments are used for a change log, like in the following example.

Listing 4-17. Managing the change history in the source code file

```
// ################################################################
// Change log:
// 2016-06-14 (John Smith) Change method rebuildProductList to fix bug #275
// 2015-11-07 (Bob Jones) Extracted four methods to new class ProductListSorter
// 2015-09-23 (Ninja Dev) Fixed the most stupid bug ever in a very smart way
// ################################################################
```

Don't do this! To track the change history of every file in your project is one of the main tasks of your version control system. If you are using Git for example, you can use `git log -- [filename]` to get the history of changes of a file. The programmers who have written the comments above are more than likely those who always leave the Check-In Comments box empty on their commits.

The Rare Cases Where Comments Are Useful

Of course, not all source code comments are basically useless, false, or bad. There are some cases where comments are important or even indispensable.

In a few and very specific cases it may happen that, even if you had used perfect names for all variables and functions, some sections of your code need some further explanations to support the reader. For example, a comment is justified if a section of code has a high degree of inherent complexity so that it cannot be understood easily by everyone who did not have deep expert knowledge. This can be the case, for example, with a sophisticated mathematical algorithm or formula. Or the software system deals with a not everyday (business) domain, i.e. an area or field of application that is not comprehensible easily for everyone, for instance, experimental physics, complex simulations of natural phenomenons, or ambitious ciphering methods. In such cases, some well-written comments explaining things can be very valueable.

Another good reason to write a comment for once is a situation in which you must deliberately deviate from a good design principle. For example, the DRY principle (see Chapter 3) is, of course, valid under most circumstances, but there may be some very rare cases where you must willful duplicate a piece of code, for example, to fulfill ambitious quality requirements regarding performance. This justifies a comment explaining why you have violated the principle; otherwise your teammates may not be able to comprehend your decision.

The challenge is this: Good and meaningful comments are hard to write. It can be more difficult than writing the code. Just as not every member of a development team is good at designing a user interface, so not everyone is good at writing. Technical writing is a skill for which usually there are specialists.

So, here are a few bits of advice for writing comments that are inevitable because of the abovementioned reasons:

- **Make sure that your comments add value to the code.** Value in this context means that comments adds important pieces of information for other human beings (usually other developers) that are not evident from the code itself.

- **Explain always the Why, not the How.** How a piece of code works should be pretty clear from the code itself, and meaningful naming for variables and functions are the keys to achieving this goal. Use comments solely to explain why a certain piece of code exists. For example, you can provide a rationale for why you chose a particular algorithm or method.

- **Try to be as short and expressive as possible.** Prefer short and concise comments, ideally one-liners, and avoid long and garrulous texts. Always keep in mind that comments also need to be maintained. It is actually much easier to keep short comments than extensive and wordy explanations.

■ **Tip** In Integrated Development Environments (IDE) with syntax coloring, the color for comments is usually preconfigured to green or teal. You should change this color to red! A comment in the source code should be something special, which should attract the attention of the developer.

Documentation Generation from Source Code

A special form of comments is annotations that can be extracted by a documentation generator. An example of such a tool is Doxygen (`http://doxygen.org`) that is widespread in the C++ world and published under a GNU General Public License (GPLv2). Such a tool parses the annotated C++ source code and can create a documentation in the form of a readable and printable document (e.g., PDF), or a set of interlinked web documents (HTML) that can be viewed with a browser. And in combination with a visualization tool, Doxygen can even generate class diagrams, include dependency graphs, and call graphs. Thus, Doxygen can also be used for code analysis.

So that a meaningful documentation comes out of such a tool, the source code must be annotated intensely with specific comments. Here is a not-so-good example with annotations in Doxygen style:

Listing 4-18. A class annotated with documentation comments for Doxygen

```cpp
//! Objects of this class represent a customer account in our system.
class CustomerAccount {
  // ...

  //! Grant a loyalty discount.
  //! @param discount is the discount value in percent.
  void grantLoyaltyDiscount(unsigned short discount);

  // ...
};
```

What? Objects of class `CustomerAccount` represent customer accounts? Oh, really?! And `grantLoyaltyDiscount` grants a loyalty discount? Duh!

But seriously folks! For me, this form of documentation cuts both ways.

On the one hand, it may be very useful to annotate, especially the public interface (API) of a library or a framework with such kind of comments, and to generate documentation from it. Particularly if the clients of the software are unknown (the typical case with public available libraries and frameworks), such documentation can be very helpful if they want to use the software in their projects.

On the other hand, such comments add a huge amount of noise to your code. The ratio of code to comment lines can quite quickly reach 50:50. And as it can be seen from the example above, such comments also tend to explain obvious things (remember the section in this chapter, "Do Not Comment Obvious Things"). Finally, the best documentation ever – an "executable documentation" – is a set of well-crafted Unit Tests (see section about Unit Tests in Chapter 2 and Chapter 8 section about Test-Driven Development), which exactly can show how the library's API has to be used.

Anyway, I have no final opinion about this topic. If you want to, or have to, annotate the public API of your software components with Doxygen-style comments at all costs, then, for God's sake, do it. If it is well done, it can be pretty helpful. I strongly advise you to pay sole attention to your public API headers! For all other parts of your software, for instance, internally used modules, or private functions, I recommend that you not equip them with Doxygen annotations.

The above example can be significantly improved if terms and explanations from the applications domain are used.

Listing 4-19. A class annotated with comments from a business perspective for Doxygen

```cpp
//! Each customer must have an account, so bookings can be made. The account
//! is also necessary for the creation of monthly invoices.
//! @ingroup entities
//! @ingroup accounting
class CustomerAccount {
  // ...

  //! Regular customers occasionally receive a regular discount on their
  //! purchases.
  void grantDiscount(const PercentageValue& discount);

  // ...
};
```

Maybe you've noticed that I have not commented on the method's parameter with Dogygen's `@param` tag anymore. Instead, I have changed its type from a meaningless `unsigned short` to a const reference of a custom type named `PercentageValue`. Due to this, the parameter has become self-explanatory. Why this is a much better approach than any comment, you can read in a section about Type-Rich Programming in Chapter 5.

Here are a few final tipps for Doxygen-style annotations in source code:

- Don't use Doxygen's `@file [<name>]` tag to write the name of the file somewhere into the file itself. On the one hand, this is useless, because Dogygen reads the name of the file anyway and automatically. On the other hand, it violates the DRY principle (see Chapter 3). It is redundant information, and if you have to rename the file, you must remember to rename the `@file` tag as well.

- Do not edit the `@version`, `@author`, and `@date` tags manually, because your version control system can manage and keep track of this information a lot better than any developer that should edit them manually. If such management information should appear in the source code file under all circumstances, these tags should be filled automatically by the version control system. In all other cases I would do without them entirely.

- Do not use the `@bug` or `@todo` tags. Instead, either you should fix the bug immediately, or use an issue-tracking software to file bugs for later troubleshooting respectively manage open points.

- It is strongly recommended to provide a descriptive project home page using the `@mainpage` tag (ideally in a separate header file just for this purpose), since such a home page serves as a getting started guide and orientation aid for developers who are currently not familiar with the project at hand.

- I would not use the `@example` tag to provide a comment block containing a source code example about how to use an API. As already mentioned, such comments add a lot of noise to the code. Instead, I would offer a suite of well-crafted unit tests (see Chapter 2 about Unit Tests and Chapter 8 about Test-Driven Development), as these are the best examples of use at all – executable examples! In addition, unit tests are always correct and up to date, as they must be adjusted when the API changes (otherwise the tests will fail). A comment with a usage example, on the other hand, can become wrong without anyone noticing it.

- Once a project has been grown to a particular size, it is advisable to pool certain categories of software units with the help of Dogygen's grouping mechanism (Tags: @defgroup <name>, @addtogroup <name>, and @ingroup <name>). This is, for example, very useful when you want to express the fact that certain software units belong to a cohesive module on a higher level of abstraction (e.g., a component or subsystem). This mechanism also allows certain categories of classes to be grouped together, for example all entities, all adapters (see Adapter Pattern in Chapter 9), or all object factories (see Factory Pattern in Chapter 9). The class CustomerAccount from the previous code example is, for instance, in the group of entities (a group that contains all business objects), but it is also part of the accounting component.

Functions

Functions (synonyms: methods, procedures, services, operations) are the heart of any software system. They represent the first organizational unit above the lines of code. Well-written functions foster the readability and maintainability of a program considerably. For this reason, they should be crafted well and in a careful manner. In this section I give several important clues for writing good functions.

However, before I explain the things that I consider to be important for well-crafted functions, let's examine a deterrent example again, taken from Apache's OpenOffice 3.4.1.

Listing 4-20. Another excerpt from Apache's OpenOffice 3.4.1 source code

```
1780  sal_Bool BasicFrame::QueryFileName(String& rName, FileType nFileType, sal_Bool bSave )
1781  {
1782      NewFileDialog aDlg( this, bSave ? WinBits( WB_SAVEAS ) :
1783                          WinBits( WB_OPEN ) );
1784      aDlg.SetText( String( SttResId( bSave ? IDS_SAVEDLG : IDS_LOADDLG ) ) );
1785
1786      if ( nFileType & FT_RESULT_FILE )
1787      {
1788        aDlg.SetDefaultExt( String( SttResId( IDS_RESFILE ) ) );
1789        aDlg.AddFilter( String( SttResId( IDS_RESFILTER ) ),
1790             String( SttResId( IDS_RESFILE ) ) );
1791         aDlg.AddFilter( String( SttResId( IDS_TXTFILTER ) ),
1792             String( SttResId( IDS_TXTFILE ) ) );
1793         aDlg.SetCurFilter( SttResId( IDS_RESFILTER ) );
1794      }
1795
1796      if ( nFileType & FT_BASIC_SOURCE )
1797      {
1798          aDlg.SetDefaultExt( String( SttResId( IDS_NONAMEFILE ) ) );
1799          aDlg.AddFilter( String( SttResId( IDS_BASFILTER ) ),
1800             String( SttResId( IDS_NONAMEFILE ) ) );
1801          aDlg.AddFilter( String( SttResId( IDS_INCFILTER ) ),
1802             String( SttResId( IDS_INCFILE ) ) );
1803          aDlg.SetCurFilter( SttResId( IDS_BASFILTER ) );
1804      }
1805
1806      if ( nFileType & FT_BASIC_LIBRARY )
1807      {
1808          aDlg.SetDefaultExt( String( SttResId( IDS_LIBFILE ) ) );
```

```
1809          aDlg.AddFilter( String( SttResId( IDS_LIBFILTER ) ),
1810               String( SttResId( IDS_LIBFILE ) ) );
1811          aDlg.SetCurFilter( SttResId( IDS_LIBFILTER ) );
1812      }
1813
1814      Config aConf(Config::GetConfigName( Config::GetDefDirectory(),
1815          CUniString("testtool") ));
1816      aConf.SetGroup( "Misc" );
1817      ByteString aCurrentProfile = aConf.ReadKey( "CurrentProfile", "Path" );
1818      aConf.SetGroup( aCurrentProfile );
1819      ByteString aFilter( aConf.ReadKey( "LastFilterName") );
1820      if ( aFilter.Len() )
1821          aDlg.SetCurFilter( String( aFilter, RTL_TEXTENCODING_UTF8 ) );
1822      else
1823          aDlg.SetCurFilter( String( SttResId( IDS_BASFILTER ) ) );
1824
1825      aDlg.FilterSelect(); // Selects the last used path
1826 //   if ( bSave )
1827      if ( rName.Len() > 0 )
1828          aDlg.SetPath( rName );
1829
1830      if( aDlg.Execute() )
1831      {
1832          rName = aDlg.GetPath();
1833 /*       rExtension = aDlg.GetCurrentFilter();
1834          var i:integer;
1835          for ( i = 0 ; i < aDlg.GetFilterCount() ; i++ )
1836              if ( rExtension == aDlg.GetFilterName( i ) )
1837                  rExtension = aDlg.GetFilterType( i );
1838 */
1839          return sal_True;
1840      } else return sal_False;
1841  }
```

Question: What did you expect when you see a member function named `QueryFileName()` for the first time?

Would you expect that a file selection dialog box is opened (remember the Principle of Least Astonishment discussed in Chapter 3)? Probably not, but that is exactly what is done here. The user is obviously asked to do some interaction with the application, so a better name for this member function would be `AskUserForFilename()`.

But that's not enough. If you look at the first lines in detail, you will see that there is a Boolean parameter bSave used to distinguish between a file dialogue box for opening, and a file dialog box for saving files. Did you expect that? And how does the term Query... in the function name match to that fact? So, a better name for this member function may be `AskUserForFilenameToOpenOrSave()`.

The following lines deal with the function's argument nFileType. Apparently, three different file types are distinguished. The parameter nFileType is masked out with something named `FT_RESULT_FILE`, `FT_BASIC_SOURCE`, and `FT_BASIC_LIBRARY`. Depending on the result of this bitwise AND operation, the file dialogue box is configured differently, for example, filters are set. As already the Boolean parameter bSave has done before, the three `if`-statements introduce alternative paths. That increases what is known as the cyclomatic complexity of the function.

CYCLOMATIC COMPLEXITY

The quantitative software metric cyclomatic complexity was developed by Thomas J. McCabe, a U.S.-American mathematician, in 1976.

The metric is a directly count of the number of linearly independent paths through a section of source code, for example, a function. If a function contains no `if`- or `switch`-statement, and no `for`- or `while`-loop, there is just one single path through the function and its cyclomatic complexity is 1. If the function contains one `if`-statement representing a single decision point, there are two paths through the function and the cyclomatic complexity is 2.

If cyclomatic complexity is high, the affected piece of code is typically more difficult to understand, test, and modify, and thus prone to bugs.

The three `if`'s raise another question: Is this function the right place to do such kind of configuration? Definitely not! This does not belong over here.

The following lines (starting from 1814) are taking access to additional configuration data. It cannot be determined exactly, but it looks as if the last used file filter ("LastFilterName") is loaded from a source that contains configuration data, either a configuration file or the Windows registry. Especially confusing is that the already defined filter, which was set in the previous three `if`-blocks (`aDlg.SetCurFilter(...)`), will be **always** overwritten at this place (see lines 1820-1823). So, what is the sense of setting this filter in the three `if`-blocks before?

Shortly before the end, the reference parameter `rName` comes into play. Hold it ... name of what, please?! It is probably the file name, yes, but why is it not named `filename` to exclude all possibilities of doubt? And why is the file name not the return value of this function? (The reason why you should avoid so-called output arguments is a topic that is discussed later in this chapter.)

As if this were not bad enough, the function also contains commented-out code.

Well, this function consists of about 50 lines only, but it has many bad code smells. The function is too long, has a high cyclomatic complexity, mixes different concerns, has many arguments, and contains dead code. The function name `QueryFileName()` is unspecific and can be misleading. Who is queried? A database? `AskUserForFilename()` would be much better, because it emphasizes the interaction with the user. Most of the code is hard to read and difficult to understand. What does `nFileType & FT_BASIC_LIBRARY` mean?

But the essential point is, that the task to be performed by this function (file name selection) justifies an own class, because the class `BasicFrame`, which is part of the application's UI, is definitely not responsible for such things.

Enough of that. Let's take a look what has to be considered by a software crafter while designing good functions.

One Thing, No More!

A function has to have a very precise defined task that should be represented by its significant name. In his brilliant book *Clean Code*, the U.S.-American Software Developer Robert C. Martin formulates it as follows:

> *Functions should do one thing. They should do it well. They should do it only.*
>
> —Robert C. Martin, *Clean Code [Martin09]*

You may ask now: But how do I know when a function does too many things? Here are some possible indications:

1. The function is large, that is, it contains many lines of code (see following section about small functions).

2. You try to find a meaningful and expressive name for the function that exactly describes its purpose, but you cannot avoid using conjunctions, such as "and" or "or," to build the name. (See also one of the following sections on names.)

3. The body of a function is vertically separated using empty lines into groups that represent subsequent steps. Often these groups are also introduced with comments that are like headlines.

4. The cyclomatic complexity is high. The function contains many 'if', 'else', or 'switch-case' statements.

5. The function has many arguments (see section about Arguments and Return Values later in this chapter), especially one or more flag arguments of type bool.

Let Them Be Small

A central question regarding functions is this: What should be the maximum length of a function?

There are many rules of thumb and heuristics for the length of a function. For example, some say that a function should fit on the screen vertically. OK, at first glance that seems to be a not-so-bad rule. If a function fits on the screen, there is no need for the developer to scroll. On the other hand, should the height of my screen really determine the maximum size of a function? Screen heights are not all the same. So, I personally don't think that it is a good rule. Here is my advice on this topic:

Functions should be pretty small. Ideally 4–5 lines, maximum 12–15 lines, but not more.

Panic! I can already hear the outcry: "Lots of tiny functions? ARE YOU SERIOUS?!"

Yes, I am serious. As Robert C. Martin already wrote in his book *Clean Code* [Martin09]: Functions should be small, and they should be smaller than that.

Large functions usually have a high complexity. Developers are often not able to tell at a glance what such a function does. If a function is too large, it typically has too many responsibilities (see previous section), and does not do exactly one thing. The larger a function is, the harder it is to understand and maintain. Such functions often contain many, mostly nested decisions (if, else, switch) and loops. This is also known as high cyclomatic complexity.

Of course, as with any rule, there can be few justified exceptions. For instance, a function that contains a single large switch statement might be acceptable if it is extremely clean and straightforward to read. You can have a 400-line switch statement in a function (sometimes required to handle different kinds of incoming data in telecommunication systems), and it is perfectly OK.

"But the Call Time Overhead!"

People now might raise the objection that many small functions reduce the execution speed of a program. They might argue that any function call is costly.

Let me explain why I think that these fears are unfounded in most cases.

Yes, there were times when C++ compilers were not very good at optimizing, and CPU's were comparatively slow. It was at a time when the myth was spread, that C++ is generally slower than C. Such myths are propagated by individuals that did not know the language very well. And the times have changed.

Nowadays, modern C++ compilers are very good at optimizing. For instance, they can perform manifold local and global speed-up optimizations. They can reduce many C++ constructs, like loops or conditional statements, to functionally similar sequences of very efficient machine code. And they are now smart enough to inline functions automatically, if those functions can be basically inlined (... of course, sometimes it is not possible to do that).

And even the Linker is able to perform optimizations. For example, Microsofts Visual-Studio Compiler/ Linker provides a feature called *Whole Program Optimization* that allows the compiler and linker to perform global optimizations with information on all modules in the program. And with another Visual-Studio feature called *Profile-Guided Optimizations,* the compiler optimizes a program using gathered data from profiling test runs of the .exe or .dll file.

Even if we do not want to use the optimization options of the compiler, what are we talking about when we consider a function call?

An Intel Core i7 2600K CPU is able to perform 128,300 million instructions per second (MIPS) at a clock speed of 3.4 GHz. Ladies and gentleman, when we are talking about function calls, we are talking about a few nanoseconds! Light travels approximately 30 cm in one nanosecond (0.000000001 sec). Compared to other operations on a computer, like memory access outside of the cache, or hard disk access, a function call is magnitudes faster.

Developers should rather spend their precious time on real performance issues, which usually have their roots in bad architecture and design. Only under very special circumstances do you have to worry about function call overhead.

Function Naming

In general it can be said that the same naming rules as those for variables and constants are as far as possible applicable, also, for functions respectively methods. Function names should be clear, expressive, and self-explanatory. You should not have to read the body of a function to know what it does. Because functions define the behavior of a program, they typically have a verb in their name. Some special kind of functions is used to provide informations about a state. Their names often start with "is ...," or "has...."

The name of a function should start with a verb. Predicates, that is, statements about an object that can be true or false, should start with "is" or "has."

Here are some examples for expressive method names:

Listing 4-21. Just a few examples of expressive and self-explanatory names for member functions

```cpp
void CustomerAccount::grantDiscount(DiscountValue discount);
void Subject::attachObserver(const Observer& observer);
void Subject::notifyAllObservers() const;
int Bottling::getTotalAmountOfFilledBottles() const;
bool AutomaticDoor::isOpen() const;
bool CardReader::isEnabled() const;
bool DoubleLinkedList::hasMoreElements() const;
```

Use Intention-Revealing Names

Take a look at the following line of code, which is, of course, just a small excerpt from a larger program:

```
std::string head = html.substr(startOfHeader, lengthOfHeader);
```

This line of code looks good in principle. There is a C++ string (header `<string>`) named `html`, containing a piece of HTML (Hypertext Mark-Up Language) obviously. When this line is executed a copy of a substring of `html` is retrieved and assigned to a new string named `head`. The substring is defined by two parameters: one that sets the starting index of the substring, and another that defines the number of characters to include in the substring.

OK, I've just explained in detail **how** the header from a piece of HTML is extracted. Let me show you another version of the same code:

Listing 4-22. After introducing an intention-revealing name the code is better understandable.

```
std::string ReportRenderer::extractHtmlHeader(const std::string& html) {
  return html.substr(startOfHeader, lengthOfHeader);
}

// ...

std::string head = extractHtmlHeader(html);
```

Can you see how much clarity a small change like this could bring to your code? We have introduced a small member function that explains its intention by its semantic name. And at the place where the string operation originally could be found, we've replaced the direct invocation of `std::string::substr()` by a call of our new function.

The name of a function should express its intention/purpose, and not explain how it works.

How the job is done, that's what you should see from the code in the function's body. Don't explain the How in a functions name. Instead, express the purpose of the function from a business perspective.

In addition, we have another advantage. The partial functionality of how the header is extracted from the HTML page has been quasi-isolated and is now more easily replaceable without fumbling around at those places where the function is called.

Arguments and Return Values

After we have discussed function names in detail, there is another aspect that is important for good and clean functions: the function's arguments and return values. These both also contribute significantly to the fact that a function or method can be well understood and is easy usable for clients.

Number of Arguments

How many arguments (aka parameters) should a function (synonyms: method, operation) have at most? In Clean Code we find the following recommendation:

> *The ideal number of arguments for a function is zero (niladic). Next comes one (monadic), followed closely by two (dyadic). Three arguments (triadic) should be avoided where possible. More than three (polyadic) requires very special justification — and then shouldn't be used anyway.*

> — Robert C. Martin, *Clean Code* [Martin09]

This advice is therefore very interesting since Martin recommends that an ideal function should have no arguments. This is a bit weird because a function in the pure mathematical sense ($y = f(x)$) always has at least one argument (see also chapter about Functional Programming). This means that a "function without arguments" usually must have some kind of side effect.

Note that Martin uses code examples written in Java in his book, so he actually means the methods of a class when he talks about functions. We have to consider that there is an additional implicit "argument" available to methods of an object: this! The this pointer represents the context of execution. With the help of this, a member function can access the attributes of its class, read, or manipulate them. In other words: from the perspective of a member function, attributes of a class are nothing else as global variables. So, Martin's rule seems to be a proper guideline, but I think it's mainly appropriate for object-oriented designs.

But why are too many arguments bad?

First, every argument in a function's argument list can lead to a dependency, with the exception of arguments of standard built-in types like int or double. If you use a complex type (e.g., a class) in a function's argument list, your code depends on that type. The header file containing the used type must be included.

Furthermore, every argument must be processed somewhere inside of a function (if not, the argument is unnecessary and should be deleted immediately). Three arguments can lead to a relatively complex function, as we have seen by example of member function BasicFrame::QueryFileName() from Apache's OpenOffice.

In procedural programming it may sometimes be very difficult not to exceed three arguments. In C, for instance, you will often see functions with more arguments. A deterrent example is the hopeless antiquated Windows Win32-API.

Listing 4-23. The Win32 CreateWindowEx function to create windows

```cpp
HWND CreateWindowEx
(
  DWORD dwExStyle,
  LPCTSTR lpClassName,
  LPCTSTR lpWindowName,
  DWORD dwStyle,
  int x,
  int y,
  int nWidth,
  int nHeight,
  HWND hWndParent,
  HMENU hMenu,
  HINSTANCE hInstance,
  LPVOID lpParam
);
```

Well, this ugly code comes from ancient times, obviously. I'm pretty sure that if it would be designed nowadays, the Windows API would not look like that any more. Not without reason, there are numerous frameworks, such as *Microsoft Foundation Classes* (MFC), *Qt* (https://www.qt.io), or *wxWidgets* (https://www.wxwidgets.org), which wraps this creepy interface and offers simpler and more object-oriented ways to create a graphical user interface (UI).

And there are few possibilities to reduce the number of arguments. You could combine x, y, nWidth, and nHeight to a new structure named Rectangle, but then there are still nine arguments. An aggravating factor is that some of the arguments of this function are pointers to other complex structures, which for their part are composed of many attributes.

In good object-oriented designs, such long argument lists are usually not required. But C++ is not a pure object-oriented language, such as Java or C#. In Java, everything must be embedded in a class, which sometimes leads to much boiler-plate code. In C++ this is not required. You are allowed to implement free-standing functions in C++, that is, functions that are not members of a class. And that's quite OK.

So here is my advice on this topic:

Real functions should have as few arguments as possible. One argument is the ideal number. Member functions (methods) of a class often have no arguments. Usually those functions are manipulating the internal state of the object, or they are used to query something from the object.

Avoid Flag Arguments

A flag argument is a kind of argument that tells a function to perform a different operation depending on its value. Flag arguments are mostly of type bool, and sometimes even an enumeration.

Listing 4-24. A flag argument to control the level of detail of an invoice

```cpp
Invoice Billing::createInvoice(const BookingItems& items, const bool withDetails) {
  if (withDetails) {
    //...
  } else {
    //...
  }
}
```

The basic problem with flag arguments is that you introduce two (or sometimes even more) paths through your function. Such an argument is typically evaluated somewhere inside the function in an if- or switch/case-statement. It is used to determine whether or not to take a certain action. It means that the function is not doing one thing exactly right, as it should be (see section "One Thing, No More," earlier in this chapter). It's a case of weak cohesion (see Chapter 3) and violates the Single Responsibility Principle (see Chapter 6 about Object Orientation).

And if you see the function call somewhere in the code, you do not know exactly what a true or false means without analyzing the function Billing::createInvoice() in detail:

Listing 4-25. Baffling: What does the 'true' in the argument list mean?

```cpp
Billing billing;
Invoice invoice = billing.createInvoice(bookingItems, true);
```

My advice is that you should simply avoid flag arguments. Such kinds of arguments are always necessary if the concern of performing an action is not separated from its configuration.

One solution could be to provide separate, well-named functions instead:

Listing 4-26. Easier to comprehend: two member functions with intention-revealing names

```cpp
Invoice Billing::createSimpleInvoice(const BookingItems& items) {
  //...
}

Invoice Billing::createInvoiceWithDetails(const BookingItems& items) {
  Invoice invoice = createSimpleInvoice(items);
  //...add details to the invoice...
}
```

Another solution would be a specialization hierarchy of billings:

Listing 4-27. Different levels of details for invoices, realized the object-oriented way

```cpp
class Billing {
public:
  virtual Invoice createInvoice(const BookingItems& items) = 0;
  // ...
};

class SimpleBilling : public Billing {
public:
  virtual Invoice createInvoice(const BookingItems& items) override;
  // ...
};

class DetailedBilling : public Billing {
public:
  virtual Invoice createInvoice(const BookingItems& items) override;
  // ...
private:
  SimpleBilling simpleBilling;
};
```

The private member variable of type `SimpleBilling` is required in class `DetailedBilling` to be able to first perform a simple invoice creation without code duplication, and to add the details to the invoice afterwards.

OVERRIDE SPECIFIER [C++11]

Since C++11, it can explicitly be specified that a virtual function shall override a base class virtual function. For this purpose, the `override` identifier has been introduced.

If `override` appears immediately after the declaration of a member function, the compiler will check that the function is virtual and is overriding a virtual function from a base class. Thus, developers are protected from subtle errors that can arise when they merely think that they have overridden a virtual function, but in fact they have altered/added a new function, for example, due to a typo.

Avoid Output Arguments

An output parameter, sometimes also called a *result parameter,* is a function argument that is used for the function's return value.

One of the frequently mentioned benefits of using output arguments is that functions that use them can pass back more than one value at a time. Here is a typical example:

```cpp
bool ScriptInterpreter::executeCommand(const std::string& name,
                        const std::vector<std::string>& arguments,
                        Result& result);
```

This member function of class `ScriptInterpreter` returns not only a `bool`. The third argument is a non-const reference to an object of type `Result`, which represents the real result of the function. The Boolean return value is for determining whether the execution of the command was successful by the interpreter. A typical call of this member function might look like this:

```cpp
ScriptInterpreter interpreter;
// Many other preparations...
Result result;

if (interpreter.executeCommand(commandName, argumentList, result)) {
  // Continue normally...
} else {
  // Handle failed execution of command...
}
```

My simple advice is this:

Avoid output arguments at all costs.

Output arguments are unintuitive and can lead to confusion. The caller can sometimes not easily find out whether a passed object is treated as an output parameter and will possibly be mutated by the function.

Furthermore, output parameters complicate the easy composition of expressions. If functions have only one return value, they can be interconnected quite easily to chained function calls. In contrast, if functions have multiple output parameters, developers are forced to prepare and handle all the variables that will hold the result values. Therefore, the code that is calling these functions can turn into a mess quickly.

Especially if immutability should be fostered and side effects must be reduced, then output parameters are an absolutely terrible idea. Unsurprisingly, it is still impossible to pass an immutable object (see Chapter 9) as an output parameter.

If a method should return something to its callers, let the method return it as the methods return value. If the method must return multiple values, redesign it to return a single instance of an object that holds the values. Alternatively, a `std::tuple` (see Side Bar) or a `std::pair` can be used.

---

std::tuple AND std::make_tuple [C++11]

A sometimes useful class template is available since C++11 that can hold a fixed-size collection of heterogeneous values resp. objects: `std::tuple`. It is defined in header `<tuple>` as follows:

```cpp
template< class... Types >
class tuple;
```

It is a so-called *variadic template*, that is, it is a template that can take a variable number of template arguments. For instance, if you must hold several different values of different types as one single object, you can write the following:

```cpp
using Customer = std::tuple<std::string, std::string, std::string, Money, unsigned int>;
// ...
Customer aCustomer = std::make_tuple("Stephan", "Roth", "Bad Schwartau",
  outstandingBalance, timeForPaymentInDays);
```

`std::make_tuple` creates the tuple object, deducing the target type from the types of arguments. With the `auto` keyword you can let the compiler deduce the type of `aCustomer` from its initializer:

```cpp
auto aCustomer = std::make_tuple("Stephan", "Roth", "Bad Schwartau",
  outstandingBalance, timeForPaymentInDays);
```

Access to individual elements of an instance of `std::tuple` is unfortunately only possible via its index. For example, to retrieve the city from aCustomer, you have to write the following code:

```cpp
auto city = std::get<2>(aCustomer);
```

This is counterintuitive and can reduce the readability of the code.

My advice is to use the `std::tuple` class template only in exceptional cases. It should only be used to combine things temporarily, which do not belong together anyway. Once data (attributes, objects) must be kept together, because their cohesion is high, it usually justifies the introduction of an explicit type for this bunch of data: a class!

If you must also still basically distinguish between success and failure, then you can use the so-called Special Case Object Pattern (see Chapter 9 about Design Patterns) to return an object representing an invalid result.

Don't Pass or Return 0 (NULL, nullptr)

THE BILLION DOLLAR MISTAKE

Sir Charles Antony Richard Hoare, commonly known as Tony Hoare or C. A. R. Hoare, is a famous British computer scientist. He is primarily known for the Quick Sort algorithm. In 1965, Tony Hoare worked together with the Swiss computer scientist Niklaus E. Wirth on the further development of the programming language ALGOL. He introduced Null references in programming language ALGOL W, which was the predecessor of PASCAL.

More than 40 years later, Tony Hoare regrets this decision. In a talk at the QCon 2009 Conference in London, he said that the introduction of Null references had probably been a historically Billion Dollar Mistake. He argued that Null references had already caused so many problems during the past centuries, that the cost for it could probably be approximately $USD1 billion.

In C++, pointers can point to NULL or 0. Concretely, this means that the pointer points to the memory address 0. NULL is just a macro definition:

```
#define NULL    0
```

Since C++11, the language provides the new keyword `nullptr`, which is of type `std::nullptr_t`. Sometimes I see functions like this one:

```cpp
Customer* findCustomerByName(const std::string& name) const {
  // Code that searches the customer by name...
  // ...and if the customer could not be found:
  return nullptr; // ...or NULL;
}
```

Receiving NULL or nullptr (Starting from here, I will only use `nullptr` in the following text for the sake of simplicity) as a return value from a function can be confusing. What should the caller do with it? What does it mean? In the above example, it might be that a customer with the given name does not exist. But it can also mean that there might have been a critical error. A `nullptr` can mean failure, can mean success, and can mean almost anything.

My advice is this:

If it is inevitable to return a regular pointer as the result from a function or method, do not return `nullptr`!

In other words: If you're forced to return a regular pointer as the result from a function (we will see later on that there may be better alternatives), ensure that the pointer you're returning always points to a valid address. Here are my reasons why I think this is important.

The main rationale why you should not return `nullptr` from a function is that you shift the responsibility to decide what to do onto your callers. They have to check it. They have to deal with it. If functions can potentially return `nullptr`, this leads to many null checks, like this:

```cpp
Customer* customer = findCustomerByName("Stephan");

if (customer != nullptr) {
  OrderedProducts* orderedProducts = customer->getAllOrderedProducts();
  if (orderedProducts != nullptr) {
    // Do something with orderedProducts...
  } else {
    // And what should we do here?
  }
} else {
  // And what should we do here?
}
```

Many null checks reduce the readability of the code and increase its complexity. And there is another problem visible that leads us directly to the next point.

If a function can return a valid pointer or `nullptr`, it introduces an alternative flow path that needs to be continued by the caller. And it should lead to a reasonable and senseful reaction. This is sometimes quite problematic. What would be the correct, intuitive response in our program when our pointer to `Customer` is not pointing to a valid instance, but `nullptr`? Should the program abort the running operation with a message? Are there any requirements that a certain type of program continuation is mandatory in such cases? These questions sometimes cannot be answered well. Experience has shown that it is often relatively easy for stakeholders to describe all the so-called Happy Day Cases of their software, which are the positive cases during normal operation. It is much more difficult to describe the desired behavior of the software for the exceptions, errors, and special cases.

The worst consequence may be this: If any null check is forgotten, this can lead to critical runtime errors. Dereferencing a null pointer will lead to a segmentation fault and your application crashes.

In C++ there is still another problem to consider: **object ownership**.

For the caller of the function it is vague what to do with the resource pointed to by the pointer after its usage. Who is its owner? Is it required to delete the object? If yes: How is the resource to be disposed? Must the object be deleted with `delete`, because it was allocated with the new operator somewhere inside the function? Or is the ownership of the resource object managed differently, so that a `delete` is forbidden and will result in undefined behavior (see section "Don't allow undefined behaviour" in Chapter 5)? Is it perhaps even an operating system resource that has to be handled in a very special manner?

According to the Information Hiding Principle (see Chapter 3) this should have no relevance for the caller, but in fact we've imposed the responsibility for the resource to him. And if the caller does not handle the pointer correctly, it can lead to serious bugs, for example, memory leaks, double deletion, undefined behaviour, and sometimes security vulnerabilities.

Strategies to Avoid Regular Pointers

Prefer simple object construction on the stack instead of on the heap

The simplest way to create a new object is simply by creating it on the stack, like this way:

```cpp
#include "Customer.h"
// ...
Customer customer;
```

In the above example, an instance of class `Customer` (defined in header `Customer.h`) is created on the stack. The line of code that creates the instance can usually be found somewhere inside a function's or method's body. That means that the instance is destroyed automatically if the function or method runs out of scope, which happens when we will return from the function respectively method.

So far, so good. But what shall we do if an object that was created in a function or method must be returned to the caller?

In old-style C++, this challenge was often coped with in such a way that the object was created on the heap (using operator `new`) and then returned from the function as a pointer to this allocated resource.

```cpp
Customer* createDefaultCustomer() {
  Customer* customer = new Customer();
  // Do something more with customer, e.g. configuring it, and at the end...
  return customer;
}
```

The comprehensible reason for this approach is that, if we are dealing with a large object, an expensive copy construction can be avoided this way. But we have already discussed the drawbacks of this solution in the section above. For instance, what shall the caller do if the returned pointer is `nullptr`? Furthermore, the caller of the function is forced to be in charge of the resource management (e.g., deleting the returned pointer in the correct manner).

Good news: Since C++11, we can simply return large objects as values without being worried about a costly copy construction.

```cpp
Customer createDefaultCustomer() {
  Customer customer;
  // Do something with customer, and at the end...
  return customer;
}
```

The reason why we no longer have to worry about resource management in this case are the so-called **move semantics**, which are supported since C++11. Simply speaking, the concept of move semantics allows that resources are "moved" from one object to another instead of copying them. The term "move" means in this context, that the internal data of an object is removed from the old source object and placed into a new object. It is a transfer of ownership of the data from one object to another object, and this can be performed extremely fast (C++11 move semantics are discussed in detail in the following Chapter 5).

With C++11, all Standard Library container classes have been extended to support move semantics. This not only has made them very efficient, but also much easier to handle. For instance, to return a large vector containing strings from a function in a very efficient manner, you can do it like what is shown in the following example:

Listing 4-28. Since C++11, a locally instantiated and large object can be easily returned by value

```cpp
#include <vector>
#include <string>

using StringVector = std::vector<std::string>;
const StringVector::size_type AMOUNT_OF_STRINGS = 10000;

StringVector createLargeVectorOfStrings() {
  StringVector theVector(AMOUNT_OF_STRINGS, "Test");
  return theVector; // Guaranteed no copy construction here!
}
```

The exploitation of move semantics is one very good way to get rid of lots of regular pointers. But we can do much more...

In a function's argument list, use (const) references instead of pointers

Instead of writing...

```
void function(Type* argument);
```

...you should use C++ references, like this:

```
void function(Type& argument);
```

The main advantage of using references instead of pointers for arguments is that there's no need to check that the reference is not a `nullptr`. The simple reason for this is that references are never "NULL." (OK, I know that there are some subtle possibilities where you can still end up with a null reference, but these presuppose a very foolish or amateurish programming style.)

And another advantage is, that you don't need to dereference anything inside the function with the help of the dereference operator (*). That will lead to cleaner code. The reference can be used inside the function as it has been created locally on the stack. Of course, if you don't want to have any side effects, you should make it a const reference (see upcoming section about Const Correctness).

If it is inevitable to deal with a pointer to a resource, use a smart one

If it is unavoidable to use a pointer because the resource must be created on the heap mandatorily, you should wrap it immediately and take advantage of the so-called RAII idiom (Resource Acquisition is Initialization). That means that you should use a smart pointer for it. Since smart pointers and the RAII idiom play an important role in modern C++, there is a dedicated section about this topic in Chapter 5.

If an API returns a raw pointer...

..., well, then we have an "it-depends-problem."

Pointers are often returned from API's that are more or less out of our hands. Typical examples are third-party libraries.

In the lucky case that we are confronted with a well-designed API that provides factory methods to create resources, and also provides methods to hand them back to the library for safe and proper disposal, we have won. In this case we can once again take advantage of the RAII idiom (Resource Acquisition Is Initialization; see Chapter 5). We can create a custom smart pointer to wrap the regular pointer, whose allocator resp. deallocator could handle the managed resource as expected by the third- party library.

The Power of const correctness

Const correctness is a powerful approach for better and safer code in C++. The use of `const` can save a lot of trouble and debugging time, because violations of `const` cause compile-time errors. And as a kind of side effect, the use of `const` can also support the compiler in applying some of its optimization algorithms. That means that the proper usage of this qualifier is also an easy way to raise the execution performance of the program a little bit.

Unfortunately, the benefits of an intense use of const are undervalued by many developers. My advice is this:

Pay attention to const correctness. Use const as much as possible, and choose always a proper declaration of variables or objects as mutable or immutable.

In general, the keyword const in C++ prevents that objects can be mutated by the program. But const can be used in different contexts. The keyword has many faces.

Its simplest use is to define a variable as a constant:

```cpp
const long double PI = 3.141592653589794;
```

Another use is to prevent parameters that are passed into a function from being mutated. Since there are several variations, it often leads to confusion. Here are some examples:

```cpp
unsigned int determineWeightOfCar(Car const* car); // 1
void lacquerCar(Car* const car); // 2
unsigned int determineWeightOfCar(Car const* const car); // 3
void printMessage(const std::string& message); // 4
void printMessage(std::string const& message); // 5
```

1. The pointer car points to a **constant object** of type Car, that is, the Car object (the "pointee") cannot be modified.

2. The pointer car is a **constant pointer** of type Car, that is, you can modify the Car object, but you cannot modify the pointer (e.g., assigning a new instance of Car to it).

3. In this case, both the pointer and the pointee (the Car object) cannot be modified.

4. The argument message is passed by const reference to the function, that is, the string variable being referenced is not allowed to be changed inside the function.

5. This is just an alternative notation for a const reference argument. It is functionally equivalent to line 4 (...which I prefer, by the way).

Tip   There is a simple rule of thumb to read const qualifiers in the right manner. If you read them from right to left, then any appearing const qualifier modifies the thing to the left of it. **Exception:** If there is nothing on the left, for example, at the beginning of a declaration, then const modifies the thing to its right hand.

Another use of the const keyword is to declare a (non-static) member-function of a class as const, like in this example on line 5:

```cpp
#include <string>

class Car {
public:
  std::string getRegistrationCode() const;
  void setRegistrationCode(const std::string& registrationCode);
  // ...

private:
  std::string _registrationCode;
  // ...
};
```

As opposed to the setter on line 6, the member function getRegistrationCode on line 5 cannot modify member variables of class Car. The following implementation of getRegistrationCode will cause a compiler error, because the function tries to assign a new string to _registrationCode:

```cpp
std::string Car::getRegistrationCode() {
  std::string toBeReturned = registrationCode;
  registrationCode = "foo"; // Compile-time error!
  return toBeReturned;
}
```

About Old C-style in C++ Projects

If you take a look into relatively new C++ programs (for example, on GitHub or Sourceforge), you will be surprised at how many of these allegedly "new" programs still contain countless lines of old C code. Well, C is still a subset of the C++ language. This means that the language elements of C are still available. Unfortunately, many of these old C constructs have significant drawbacks when it comes to writing clean, safe, and modern code. And there are clearly better alternatives.

Therefore, a basic piece of advice is to quit using those old and error-prone C constructs wherever better C++ alternatives exist. And there are many of these possibilities. Nowadays you can nearly completely do without C programming in modern C++.

Prefer C++ Strings and Streams over Old C-Style char*

A so-called C++ string is part of the C++ Standard Library and is of type std::string or std::wstring (both defined in header <string>). In fact, both are type definitions on class template std::basic_string<T> and are defined this way:

```cpp
typedef basic_string<char> string;
typedef basic_string<wchar_t> wstring;
```

To create such a string, an object of one of these two templates must be instantiated, for example, with their initialization constructor:

```
std::string name("Stephan");
```

Compared to this, a so-called C-style string is simply an array of characters (type `char` or `wchar_t`) that ends with a so-called zero terminator (Sometimes also called null terminator). A zero terminator is a special character (`'\0'`, ASCII code 0) used to indicate the end of the string. A C-style string can be defined this way:

```
char name[] = "Stephan";
```

In this case, the zero terminator is automatically added at the end of the string, that is, the length of the string is 8 characters. An important point is that we have to keep in mind that we're still dealing with an array of characters. This means, for instance, that it has a fixed size. You can change the content of the array using the index operator, but no further characters can be added to the end of the array. And if the zero terminator at the end is accidentally overwritten, this can cause various issues.

The character array is often used with the help of a pointer pointing to the first element, for example, when it is passed as a function argument:

```
char* pointerToName = name;

void function(char* pointerToCharacterArray) {
  //...
}
```

However, in many C++ programs, as well as in textbooks, C-strings are still frequently used. Are there any good reasons to use C-style strings in C++ nowadays?

Yes, there are some situations where you can still use C-style strings. I will present a few of these exceptions. But for the overwhelming number of strings in a modern C++ program applies, they should be implemented using C++ strings. Objects of type `std::string` respectively `std::wstring` provide numerous advantages compared to old C-style strings:

- C++ string objects manage their memory by themselves, so that you can copy, create, and destroy them easily. That means that they free you from managing the lifetime of the string's data, which can be a tricky and daunting task using C-style character arrays.

- They are mutable. The string can be manipulated easily in various ways: adding strings or single characters, concatenate strings, replacements of parts of the string, etc.

- C++ strings provide a convenient iterator interface. As with all other Standard Library container types, `std::string` respectively `std::wstring` allows you to iterate over their elements (i.e., over their characters). This also means that all suitable algorithms that are defined in header `<algorithm>` can be applied to the string.

- C++ strings work perfectly together with C++ I/O streams (e.g., `ostream`, `stringstream`, `fstream`, etc.) so that you can take advantage of all those useful stream facilities easily.

- Since C++11, the Standard Library uses move semantics extensively. Many algorithms and containers are now move-optimized. This also applies to C++ strings. For example, an instance of a `std::string` can often simply be returned as the return value from a function. The formerly still necessary approaches with pointers or references to efficiently return large string objects from a function, that is, without costly copying of the string's data, are now no longer required.

In summary, the following advice can be given:

Apart from a few exceptions, strings in a modern C++ program should be represented by C++ strings taken from the Standard Library.

Well, but what are the few exceptions that justify the use of old C-style strings?

On the one hand, there are string constants, that is, immutable strings. If you just need a fixed array of fixed characters, then `std::string` provides little advantage. For instance, you can define such a string constant this way:

```cpp
const char* const PUBLISHER = "Apress Media LLC";
```

In this case, neither the value being pointed to can be changed, nor the pointer itself can be modified (see also the section about Const Correctness).

Another reason to work with C strings is compatibility with C-style API's respectively libraries. Many third-party libraries often have low-level interfaces to ensure backward compatibility and to keep their area of use as broad as possible. Strings are often expected as C-style strings on such an API. However, even in this case the use of the C-style strings should be locally limited to the handling of this interface. Away from the data exchange with such an API, the much more comfortable C++ strings should be used whereever possible.

Avoid Using printf(), sprintf(), gets(), etc.

`printf()`, which is part of the C library to perform Input/Output operations (defined in header `<cstdio>`), prints formatted data to standard output (stdout). Some developers are still using a lot of `printf`s for tracing/logging purposes in their C++ code. They often argue that `printf` is ... no ... it must be much faster than C++ I/O-Streams, since the whole C++ overhead is missing.

First, I/O is a bottleneck anyway, no matter if you're using `printf()` or `std::cout`. To write anything on standard output is generally slow, with magnitudes slower than most of the other operations in a program. Under certain circumstances, `std::cout` can be slightly slower than `printf()`, but in relation to the general cost of an I/O operation those few microseconds are usually negligible. At this point I would also like to remind everyone to be careful with (premature) optimizations (remember the section "Be Careful with Optimizations" in Chapter 3).

Second, `printf()` is fundamentally type-unsafe and thus prone to error. The function expects a sequence of non-typed arguments that are related to a C-string filled with format specifiers, which is the first argument. Functions that cannot be used safely should never be used, because this can lead to subtle bugs, undefined behavior (see section about Undefined Behavior in Chapter 5), and security vulnerabilities.

std::to_String() [C++11]

Don't use the C-function `sprintf()` (header `<cstdio>`) for conversion purposes in a modern C++ program. Since C++11, all variables of a numerical type can be easily converted to a C++ string using the safe and convenient `std::to_string()` respectively `std::to_wstring()` function, defined in header `<string>`. For example, a signed integer can be converted to a `std::string` containing a textual representation of the value in the following way:

```cpp
int value { 42 };
std::string valueAsString = std::to_string(value);
```

`std::to_string()` respectively `std::to_wstring()` is available for all integral or floating-point types, like `int`, `long`, `long long`, `unsigned int`, `float`, `double`, etc. But one of the major drawbacks of this simple conversion helper is its inaccuracy in certain cases.

```cpp
double d { 1e-9 };
std::cout << std::to_string(d) << "\n"; // Caution! Output: 0.000000
```

Furthermore, there are no configuration capabilities to control how `to_string()` formats the output string, for example, the amount of decimal places. That means that this function can de facto only be used to a minor extent in a real program. If you need a more precise and customized conversion, you have to provide it yourself. Instead of using `sprintf()` you can take advantage of string-streams (header `<sstream>`) and the configuration capabilities of the I/O Manipulators defined in header `<iomanip>`, like in the following example:

```cpp
#include <iomanip>
#include <sstream>
#include <string>

std::string convertDoubleToString(const long double valueToConvert, const int
precision) {
  std::stringstream stream { };
  stream << std::fixed << std::setprecision(precision) << valueToConvert;
  return stream.str();
}
```

Third, unlike `printf`, C++ I/O streams allow that complex objects can be easily streamed by providing a custom insertion operator (`operator<<`). Suppose we have a class `Invoice` (defined in a header file named `Invoice.h`) that looks like this:

Listing 4-29. An excerpt from file Invoice.h with line numbers

```cpp
01  #ifndef INVOICE_H_
02  #define INVOICE_H_
03
04  #include <chrono>
05  #include <memory>
06  #include <ostream>
```

```cpp
07  #include <string>
08  #include <vector>
09
10  #include "Customer.h"
11  #include "InvoiceLineItem.h"
12  #include "Money.h"
13  #include "UniqueIdentifier.h"
14
15  using InvoiceLineItemPtr = std::shared_ptr<InvoiceLineItem>;
16  using InvoiceLineItems = std::vector<InvoiceLineItemPtr>;
17
18  using InvoiceRecipient = Customer;
19  using InvoiceRecipientPtr = std::shared_ptr<InvoiceRecipient>;
20
21  using DateTime = std::chrono::system_clock::time_point;
22
23  class Invoice {
24  public:
25    explicit Invoice(const UniqueIdentifier& invoiceNumber);
26    Invoice() = delete;
27    void setRecipient(const InvoiceRecipientPtr& recipient);
28    void setDateTimeOfInvoicing(const DateTime& dateTimeOfInvoicing);
29    Money getSum() const;
30    Money getSumWithoutTax() const;
31    void addLineItem(const InvoiceLineItemPtr& lineItem);
32    // ...possibly more member functions here...
33
34  private:
35    friend std::ostream& operator<<(std::ostream& outstream, const Invoice& invoice);
36    std::string getDateTimeOfInvoicingAsString() const;
37
38    UniqueIdentifier invoiceNumber;
39    DateTime dateTimeOfInvoicing;
40    InvoiceRecipientPtr recipient;
41    InvoiceLineItems invoiceLineItems;
42  };
43  // ...
```

The class has dependencies to an invoice recipient (which in this case is an alias for the `Customer` defined in header `Customer.h`; see line no. 18), and uses an identifier (type `UniqueIdentifier`) representing an invoice number that is guaranteed to be unique among all invoice numbers. Furthermore, the Invoice uses a data type that can represent money amounts (see also section "Money Class" in Chapter 9 about design patterns), as well as a dependency to another data type that represents a single invoice line item. The latter is used to manage a list of invoice items inside the invoice using a `std::vector` (see line no. 16 respectively 41). And to represent the time of invoicing, we use the data type `time_point` from the Chrono library (defined in header `<chrono>`), which has been available since C++11.

Now let's imagine further that we want to stream the entire invoice with all its data to standard output. Wouldn't it be pretty simple and convenient if we could write something like...

```cpp
std::cout << instanceOfInvoice;
```

Well, that's possible with C++. The insertion operator (<<) for output streams can be overloaded for any class. We just have to add an operator<< function to our class declaration in the header. It is important to make this function a friend of the class (see line no. 35) because it would be called without creating an object.

Listing 4-30. The insertion operator for class Invoice

```cpp
43  // ...
44  std::ostream& operator<<(std::ostream& outstream, const Invoice& invoice) {
45    outstream << "Invoice No.: " << invoice.invoiceNumber << "\n";
46    outstream << "Recipient: " << *(invoice.recipient) << "\n";
47    outstream << "Date/time: " << invoice.getDateTimeOfInvoicingAsString() << "\n";
48    outstream << "Items:" << "\n";
49    for (const auto& item : invoice.invoiceLineItems) {
50      outstream << "      " << *item << "\n";
51    }
52    outstream << "Amount invoiced: " << invoice.getSum() << std::endl;
53    return outstream;
54  }
55  // ...
```

All structural components of the class Invoice are written into an output stream inside the function. This is possible, because also class UniqueIdentifier, InvoiceRecipient, and InvoiceLineItem, have their own insertion operator functions (not shown here) for output streams. To print all line items in the vector, a C++11 range-based for-loop is used. And to get a textual representation of the date of invoicing, we use an internal helper method named getDateTimeOfInvoicingAsString() that returns a well-formatted date/time string.

So, my advice for a modern C++ program is this:

Avoid using printf(), and also other unsafe C-functions, such as sprintf(), puts(), etc.

Prefer Standard Library Containers over Simple C-style Arrays

Instead of using C-style arrays, you should use the std::array<TYPE, N> template that is available since C++11 (header <array>). Instances of std::array<TYPE, N> are fixed-size sequence containers and are as efficient as ordinary C-style arrays.

The problems with C-style arrays are more or less the same as with C-style strings (see section above). C-arrays are bad, because they are passed around as a raw pointer to their first element. This could be potentially dangerous, because there are no bound checks that protect users of that array to access nonexistent elements. Arrays built with std::array are safer, because they don't decay to pointers (see also section "Strategies to Avoid Regular Pointers," earlier in this chapter).

An advantage of using std::array is that it knows its size (number of elements). When working with arrays, the size of that array is important information that is often required. Ordinary C-style arrays don't know their own size. Thus, the size of the array must often be handled as an additional piece of information, for example, in an additional variable. For example, the size must be passed as an additional argument to function calls like in the following example.

```cpp
const std::size_t arraySize = 10;
MyArrayType array[arraySize];

void function(MyArrayType const* array, const std::size_t arraySize) {
  // ...
}
```

Strictly speaking, in this case the array and its size doesn't form a cohesive unit (see section about Strong Cohesion in Chapter 3). Furthermore, we already know from a previous section about Arguments and Return Values that the number of function arguments should be as small as possible.

In contrast, instances of std::array carry their size and any instance can be queried about it. Thus, the argument lists of functions, or methods, don't require additional parameters about the array's size:

```cpp
#include <array>

using MyTypeArray = std::array<MyType, 10>;

void function(const MyTypeArray& array) {
  const std::size_t arraySize = array.size();
  //...
}
```

Another noteworthy advantage of std::array is that it has an STL-compatible interface. The class template provides public member functions so it looks like every other container in the Standard Library. For example, users of an array can get an iterator pointing to the begin and the end of the sequence using std::array::begin() respectively std::array::end(). This also means that algorithms from header <algorithm> can be applied to the array (see also section about algorithms in the following chapter).

```cpp
#include <array>
#include <algorithm>

using MyTypeArray = std::array<MyType, 10>;
MyTypeArray array;

void doSomethingWithEachElement(const MyType& element) {
  // ...
}

std::for_each(std::cbegin(array), std::cend(array), doSomethingWithEachElement);
```

NON-MEMBER std::begin( ) AND std::end( ) [C++11/14]

Every C++ Standard Library container has a `begin()` respectively `cbegin()` and an `end()` respectively `cend()` member function to retrieve iterators respectively const-iterators for that container.

C++11 has introduced free non-member functions for that purpose: `std::begin(<container>)` and `std::end(<container>)`. With C++14 the still missing functions `std::cbegin(<container>)`, `std::cend(<container>)`, `std::rbegin(<container>)`, and `std::rend(<container>)` have been added. Instead of using the member functions, it is now recommended to use these non-member functions (all defined in header `<iterator>`) to get iterators respectively const-iterators for a container, like this:

```cpp
#include <vector>

std::vector<AnyType> aVector;
auto iter = std::begin(aVector); // ...instead of 'auto iter = aVector.begin();'
```

The reason is that those free functions allow a more flexible and generic programming style. For instance, many user-defined containers don't have a `begin()` and `end()` member function, which makes them impossible to use with the Standard Library algorithms (see section about algorithms in Chapter 5) or any other user-defined template function that requires iterators. The non-member functions to retrieve iterators are extensible in the sense of that they can be overloaded for any type of sequence, including old C-style-arrays. In other words: Non-STL-compatible (custom) containers can be retrofitted with iterator capabilities.

For instance, assume that you have to deal with a C-style array of integers, like this one:

```cpp
int fibonacci[] = { 1, 1, 2, 3, 5, 8, 13, 21, 34, 55, 89, 144 };
```

This type of array can now be retrofitted with an Standard Library-compliant Iterator interface. For C-style arrays, such functions are already provided in the Standard Library, so you do not have to program them yourself. They look more or less like this:

```cpp
template <typename Type, std::size_t size>
Type* begin(Type (&element)[size]) {
    return &element[0];
}

template <typename Type, std::size_t size>
Type* end(Type (&element)[size]) {
    return &element[0] + size;
}
```

To insert all elements of the array into an output stream, for example, to print them on standard output, we can now write:

```cpp
int main() {
  for (auto it = begin(fibonacci); it != end(fibonacci); ++it) {
    std::cout << *it << ", ";
  }
  std::cout << std::endl;
  return 0;
}
```

Providing overloaded `begin()` and `end()` functions for custom container types, or old C-style arrays, enables the application of all Standard Library algorithms to these types.

Furthermore, `std::array` can access elements including bound checks with the help of member function `std::array::at(size_type n)`. If the given index is out of bounds, an exception of type `std::out_of_bounds` is thrown.

Use C++ casts Instead of Old C-Style Casts

Before a false impression emerges, I would first like to state an important warning:

Warning   Type casts are basically bad and should be avoided whereever possible! They are a trustworthy indication that there must be, albeit only a relatively tiny, design problem.

However, if a type cast cannot be avoided in a certain situation, then under no circumstances should you use a C-style-cast:

```cpp
double d { 3.1415 };
int i = (int)d;
```

In this case, the double is demoted to an integer. This explicit conversion is accompanied with a loss of precision since the decimal places of the floating-point number are thrown away. The explicit conversion with the C-style cast says something like this: "The programmer who wrote this line of code was been aware about the consequences."

Well, this is certainly better than an implicit type conversion. Nevertheless, instead using old C-style casts, you should use C++ casts for explicit type conversions, like this:

```cpp
int i = static_cast<int>(d);
```

The simple explanation for this advice is: C++ style casts are checked by the compiler during compile time! C-style casts are not checked this way and thus they can fail at runtime, which may cause ugly bugs or application crashes. For instance, an improvident used C-style cast can cause a corrupted stack, like in the following case.

```cpp
int32_t i { 200 };                  // Reserves and uses 4 byte memory
int64_t* pointerToI = (int64_t*)&i; // Pointer points to 8 byte

*pointerToI = 9223372036854775807;  // Can cause run-time error through stack corruption
```

Obviously, in this case it is possible to write a 64-bit value into a memory area that is only 32 bits in size. The problem is that the compiler cannot draw our attention to this potentially dangerous piece of code. The compiler translates this code, even with very conservative settings (g++ -std=c++17 -pedantic -pedantic-errors -Wall -Wextra -Werror -Wconversion), without complaints. This can lead to very insidious errors during program execution.

Now let's see what will happen if we use a C++ static_cast on the 2nd line instead of the old and bad C-style cast:

```cpp
int64_t* pointerToI = static_cast<int64_t*>(&i); // Pointer points to 8 byte
```

The compiler is now able to spot the problematic conversion and reports a corresponding error message:

```
error: invalid static_cast from type 'int32_t* {aka int*}' to type 'int64_t* {aka long int*}'
```

Another reason why you should use C++ casts instead of old C-style casts is that C-style casts are very hard to spot in a program. Neither can they be discovered easily by the developer, nor can they be searched conveniently using an ordinary editor or word processor. In contrast, it is very easy to search for terms such as static_cast<>, const_cast<>, or dynamic_cast<>.

At a glance, here are all advices regarding type conversions for a modern and well-designed C++ program:

1. **Try to avoid type conversions (casts) under all circumstances.** Instead, try to eliminate the underlying design error that forces you to use the conversion.

2. If an explicitely type conversion cannot be avoided, **use solely C++ style casts** (static_cast<> or const_cast<>), because these casts are checked by the compiler. **Never use old and bad C-style casts.**

3. Notice that dynamic_cast<> should also never be used **because it is considered bad design.** The need of a dynamic_cast<> is a reliable indication that something is wrong within a specialization hierarchy (This topic will be deeper in Chapter 6 about Object Orientation).

4. **Under all circumstances, never use** reinterpret_cast<>. This kind of type conversion marks an unsafe, non-portable, and implementation-dependent cast. Its long and inconvenient name is a broad hint to make you think about what you're currently doing.

Avoid Macros

Maybe one of the severest legacies of the C language is macros. A macro is a piece of code that can be identified by a name. If the so-called preprocessor finds the name of a macro in the program's source code while compiling, the name is replaced by its related code fragment.

One kind of macros is object-like macros that are often used to give symbolic names to numeric constants, like in the following example.

Listing 4-31. Two examples of object-like macros

```
#define BUFFER_SIZE 1024
#define PI 3.14159265358979
```

Other typical examples for macros are the following ones:

Listing 4-32. Two examples of function-like macros

```
#define MIN(a,b) (((a)<(b))?(a):(b))
#define MAX(a,b) (((a)>(b))?(a):(b))
```

MIN resp. MAX compares two values and returns the smaller respectively larger one. Such macros are called function-like macros. Although these macros look almost like functions, they are not. The C preprocessor performs merely a substitution of the name by the related code fragment (In fact, it is a textual find-and-replace operation).

Macros are potentially dangerous. They often do not behave as expected and can have unwanted side effects. For instance, let's assume that you have defined a macro like this one:

```
#define DANGEROUS 1024+1024
```

And somewhere in your code you write this:

```
int value = DANGEROUS * 2;
```

Probably someone expects that the variable value contains 4096, but actually it would be 3072. Remember the order of mathematical operations that tells us that division respectively multiplication, left to right, should happen first.

Another example of unexpected side effects due to using a macro is the usage of 'MAX' in the following way:

```
int maximum = MAX(12, value++);
```

The preprocessor will generate the following:

```
int maximum = (((12)>(value++))?(12):(value++));
```

As it can easily be seen now, the post-increment operation on value will be performed twice. This was certainly not the intention of the developer who had written the above piece of code.

Don't use macros anymore! At least since C++11, they are almost obsolete. With some very rare exceptions, macros are simply no longer necessary and should no longer be used in a modern C++ program. Maybe the introduction of so-called *Reflection* (i.e., the ability that the program can examine, introspect, and modify its own structure and behavior at runtime) as a possible part of a future C++ standard can help to get rid of macros entirely. But until the time has come, macros are still currently needed for some special purposes, for example, when using a Unit Test or Logging framework.

Instead of object-like macros, use constant expressions to define constants:

```
constexpr int HARMLESS = 1024 + 1024;
```

And instead of function-like macros, simply use true functions, for example, the function templates `std::min` or `std::max` which are defined in header `<algorithm>` (see also the section about the `<algorithm>` header in the following chapter):

```
#include <algorithm>
// ...
int maximum = std::max(12, value++);
```

CHAPTER 5

Advanced Concepts of Modern C++

In Chapters 3 and 4 we discussed the basic principles and practices that build a solid foundation for clean and modern C++ code. With these principles and rules in mind, a developer can raise the internal C++ code quality of a software project and, thus often, its external quality, significantly. The code becomes more understandable, more maintainable, easier extensible, less susceptible to bugs, and this leads to a better life for any software crafter, because it is more fun to work with a sound code base like that. And in Chapter 2 we also learned that, above all, a well-maintained suite of well-crafted Unit Tests can further improve the quality of the software as well as the development efficiency.

But can we do better? Of course, we can.

As I've already explained in this book's introduction, the good old dinosaur C++ has experienced some considerable improvements during the last years. The language standard C++11 (short for ISO/IEC 14882:2011), but also the following standards C++14 (which was just a small extension over C++11), and the newest version C++17 (which has reached the final ISO balloting process in June 2017), have made a modern, flexible, and efficient development tool out of the already somewhat dusty programming language. Some of the new introduced concepts through these standards, like move semantics, are virtually a paradigm shift.

I have already used some of the features of these C++ standards in the previous chapters and mostly explained in side bars. Now it is time to dive deeper in some of them and to explore how they can support us to write exceptionally sound and modern C++ code. Of course it is not possible to discuss all language features of the newer C++ standards completely here. That would go far beyond the scope of this book, leaving aside the fact that this is covered by numerous other books. Therefore, I have selected a few topics that I believe support the writing of clean C++ code very well.

Managing Resources

Managing resources is a bread-and-butter business for software developers. A multitude of miscellaneous resources must be regularly allocated, used, and returned after usage. These include the following:

- Memory (either on the stack or on the heap);

- File handles that are required to access files (read/write) on hard disk or other media;

- Network connections (e.g., to a server, a database, etc.);

- Threads, locks, timers, and transactions;

- Other operational system resources, like GDI handles on Windows Operating Systems. (The abbreviation GDI stands for *Graphics Device Interface*. GDI is a core operating system component of Microsoft Windows and is responsible for representing graphical objects.)

© Stephan Roth 2017
S. Roth, *Clean C++*, DOI 10.1007/978-1-4842-2793-0_5

The proper handling of resources can be a tricky task. Consider the following example:

Listing 5-1. Dealing with a resource that was allocated on the heap

```cpp
void doSomething() {
  ResourceType* resource = new ResourceType();
  try {
    // ...do something with resource...
    resource->foo();
  } catch (...) {
    delete resource;
    throw;
  }
  delete resource;
}
```

What's the problem here? Perhaps you've noticed the two identical delete statements. The catch-all exception handling mechanism introduces at least two possible paths in our program. This also means that we have to ensure that the resource is freed in two places. Under normal circumstances such catch-all exception handlers are frowned upon. But in this case, we have no other chance than to catch all possible occurring exceptions here just because we must free the resource first, before we throw the exception object farther to treat it elsewhere (e.g., at the call site of the function).

And in this simplified example we have only two paths. In real programs, significantly more execution paths can exist. The probability that one delete is forgotten is much higher. And any forgotten delete will result in a dangerous resource leakage.

■ **Warning**   Do not underestimate resource leaks! Resource leaks are a **serious problem**, particularly for long-lived processes, and for processes that rapidly allocate many resources without deallocating them after usage. If an operating system has a lack of resources, this can lead to critical system states. Furthermore, resource leaks can be a security issue, because they can be exploited by assaulters for denial-of-service attacks.

The simplest solution for our small sample above could be that we allocate the resource on the stack, instead of allocating it on the heap:

Listing 5-2. Much easier: Dealing with a resource on the stack

```cpp
void doSomething() {
  ResourceType resource;

  // ...do something with resource...
  resource.foo();

}
```

With this change the resource is safely removed in any case. But sometimes it is not possible to allocate everything on the stack, as we've already discussed in the section "Don't Pass or Return 0 (NULL, nullptr)" in Chapter 4. What about file handles, OS resources, etc.?

The central question is this: **How can we guarantee that allocated resources are always freed?**

Resource Acquisition Is Initialization (RAII)

Resource Acquisition Is Initialization (RAII) is an idiom (see Chapter 9 about idioms) that can help to cope with resources in a safe way. The idiom is also known as *Constructor Acquires, Destructor Releases* (CADRe) and *Scope-based Resource Management* (SBRM).

RAII takes advantage of the symmetry of a class by its constructor and its corresponding destructor. We can allocate a resource in the constructor of a class, and we can deallocate it in the destructor. If we create such class as a template, it can be used for different types of resources.

Listing 5-3. A very simple class template that can manage several types of resources

```cpp
template <typename RESTYPE>
class ScopedResource final {
public:
  ScopedResource() { managedResource = new RESTYPE(); }
  ~ScopedResource() { delete managedResource; }

  RESTYPE* operator->() const { return managedResource; }

private:
  RESTYPE* managedResource;
};
```

Now we can use the class template ScopedResource as follows:

Listing 5-4. Using ScopedResource to manage an instance of ResourceType

```cpp
#include "ScopedResource.h"
#include "ResourceType.h"

void doSomething() {

  ScopedResource<ResourceType> resource;

  try {
    // ...do something with resource...
    resource->foo();
  } catch (...) {
    throw;
  }
}
```

As it can be easily seen, no new or delete is required. If resource runs out of scope, which can happen at various points in this method, the wrapped instance of type ResourceType is deleted automatically through the destructor of ScopedResource.

But there is usually no need to reinvent the wheel and to implement such a wrapper, which is also called a smart pointer, by you.

Smart Pointers

Since C++11, the Standard Library offers different, efficient smart-pointer-implementations for easy use. These pointers have been developed over a long period within the well-known Boost library project before they were introduced into the C++ Standard, and can be regarded as foolproof as possible. Smart pointers reduce the likelihood of memory leaks. Furthermore, they are designed to be thread-safe.

This section provides a brief overview.

Unique Ownership with std::unique_ptr<T>

The class template std::unique_ptr<T> (defined in header <memory>) manages a pointer to an object of type T. As the name suggests, this smart pointer provides unique ownership, that is, an object can be owned by only one instance of std::unique_ptr<T> at a time, which is the main difference of the std::shared_ptr<T>, which is explained below. This also means that copy construction and copy assignment are not allowed.

Its use is pretty simple:

```cpp
#include <memory>

class ResourceType {
  //...
};

//...
std::unique_ptr<ResourceType> resource1 { std::make_unique<ResourceType>() };
// ... or shorter with type deduction ...
auto resource2 { std::make_unique<ResourceType>() };
```

After this construction, resource can be used very much like a regular pointer to an instance of ResourceType. (std::make_unique<T> is explained below in section "Avoid new and delete"). For example, you can use the * and -> operator for dereferencing:

```cpp
resource->foo();
```

Of course, if resource runs out of scope, the contained instance of type ResourceType is freed safely. But the best part is that resource can be easily put into containers, for example, in a std::vector:

```cpp
#include "ResourceType.h"
#include <memory>
#include <vector>

using ResourceTypePtr = std::unique_ptr<ResourceType>;
using ResourceVector = std::vector<ResourceTypePtr>;

//...

ResourceTypePtr resource { std::make_unique<ResourceType>() };
ResourceVector aCollectionOfResources;
aCollectionOfResources.push_back(std::move(resource));
// IMPORTANT: At this point, the instance of 'resource' is empty!
```

Please note that we ensure that std::vector::push_back() calls the move constructor respectively move assignment operator of std::unique_ptr<T> (see section about move semantics in the next chapter). As a consequence, resource does not manage an object anymore and is denoted as empty.

■ **Caution** **Do not use** `std::auto_ptr<T>` **anymore in your code!** With the publishing of the C++11 standard, `std::auto_ptr<T>` has been marked as "deprecated" and should no longer be used. **With the newest standard C++17, this smart-pointer class template is now finally removed from the language!** The implementation of this smart pointer did not support rvalue-references and move semantics (see section about move semantics later in this chapter), and can't be stored inside Standard Library containers. `std::unique_ptr<T>` is the appropriate replacement.

As already mentioned, copy construction of `std::unique_ptr<T>` is not allowed. However, the exclusive ownership of the managed resource can be transferred to another instance of `std::unique_ptr<T>` using move semantics (we will discuss move semantics in detail in a later section) in the following way:

```
std::unique_ptr<ResourceType> pointer1 = std::make_unique<ResourceType>();
std::unique_ptr<ResourceType> pointer2; // pointer2 owns nothing yet

pointer2 = std::move(pointer1); // Now pointer1 is empty, pointer2 is the new owner
```

Shared Ownership with std::shared_ptr<T>

Instances of class template `std::shared_ptr<T>` (defined in header `<memory>`) can take ownership of a resource of type T, and can share this ownership with other instances of `std::shared_ptr<T>`. In other words, the ownership for a **single** instance of type T, and thus the responsibility for its deletion, can be taken over by **many** shared owners.

`std::shared_ptr<T>` provides something like simple limited garbage collector functionality. The smart pointer's implementation has a reference counter that monitors how many pointer instances owning the shared object still exist. It releases the managed resource if the last instance of the pointer is destroyed.

Figure 5-1 shows an UML object diagram depicting a situation in a running system where three instances (`client1`, `client2`, and `client3`) are sharing the same resource (`:Resource`) using three smart pointer instances.

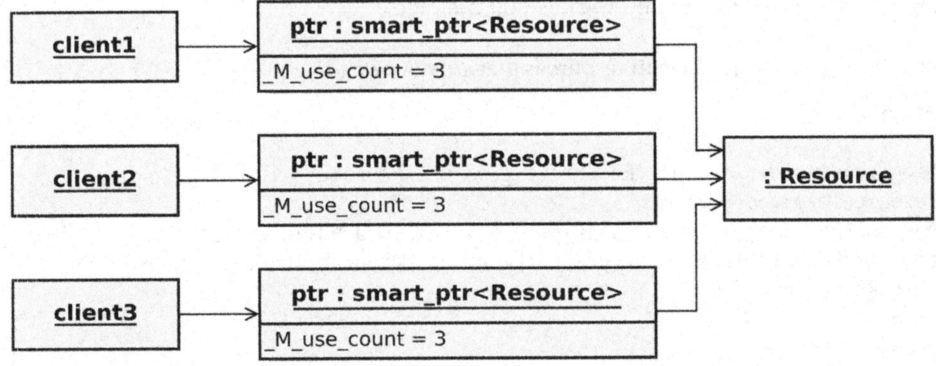

Figure 5-1. An object diagram depicting how three clients are sharing one resource through smart pointers

In contrast to the previously discussed `std::unique_ptr<T>`, `std::shared_ptr<T>` is of course copy-constructible as expected. But you can enforce that the managed resource is moved by using `std::move<T>`:

```
std::shared_ptr<ResourceType> pointer1 = std::make_shared<ResourceType>();
std::shared_ptr<ResourceType> pointer2;

pointer2 = std::move(pointer1); // The reference count does not get modified, pointer1 is empty
```

In this case, the reference counter is not modified, but you must be careful using the variable `pointer1` after the move, because it is empty, that is, it holds a `nullptr`. Move semantics and the utility function `std::move<T>` are discussed in a later section.

No Ownership, but Secure Access with std::weak_ptr<T>

Sometimes it is necessary to have a non-owning pointer to a resource that is owned by one or more shared pointers. At first you might say, "OK, but what's the problem? I simply can obtain the raw pointer from an instance of `std::shared_ptr<T>` at any time by calling its `get()` member function."

Listing 5-5. Retrieving the regular pointer from an instance of std::shared_ptr<T>

```
std::shared_ptr<ResourceType> resource = std::make_shared<ResourceType>();
// ...
ResourceType* rawPointerToResource = resource.get();
```

Watch your step! This could be dangerous. What will happen if the last instance of `std::shared_ptr<ResourceType>` gets destroyed somewhere in your program and this raw pointer is still in usage somewhere? The raw pointer will point to No-Man's-Land and using it can cause serious problems (remember my warning about undefined behavior in the previous chapter). You have absolutely no chance to determine that the raw pointer points to a valid address of a resource, or to an arbitrary location in memory.

If you need a pointer to the resource without having ownership, you should use `std::weak_ptr<T>` (defined in header `<memory>`), which has no influence on the resource's lifetime. `std::weak_ptr<T>` merely "observes" the managed resource and can be interrogated that it is valid.

Listing 5-6. Using std::weak_ptr<T> to deal with resources that are not owned

```
01  #include <memory>
02
03  void doSomething(const std::weak_ptr<ResourceType>& weakResource) {
04    if (! weakResource.expired()) {
05      // Now we know that weakResource contains a pointer to a valid object
06      std::shared_ptr<ResourceType> sharedResource = weakResource.lock();
07      // Use sharedResource...
08    }
09  }
10
11  int main() {
12    auto sharedResource(std::make_shared<ResourceType>());
13    std::weak_ptr<ResourceType> weakResource(sharedResource);
```

```
14
15    doSomething(weakResource);
16    sharedResource.reset(); // Deletes the managed instance of ResourceType
17    doSomething(weakResource);
18
19    return 0;
20  }
```

As you can see on line 4 in the code example above, we can interrogate the weak pointer object if it manages a valid resource. This is done by calling its expired() member function. std::weak_ptr<T> does not provide dereference operators, like *, or ->. If we want to use the resource, we first must call the lock() function (see line no. 6) to obtain a shared pointer object from it.

You are maybe asking yourself now what the use cases of this smart pointer type are. Why is it necessary, because I could readily also take a std::shared_ptr<T> everywhere a resource is needed?

First of all, with std::shared_ptr<T> and std::weak_ptr<T>, you are able to distinguish between owners of a resource and users of a resource in a software design. Not every software unit that requires a resource just for a certain and time-limited task wants to become its owner. As we can see in the function doSomething() in the example above, sometimes it is sufficient just to "promote" a weak pointer to a strong pointer just for a limited amount of time.

A good example would be an object cache that for the purpose of performance efficiency keeps recently accessed objects in memory for a certain amount of time. The objects in the cache are held with std::shared_ptr<T> instances, together with a last-used timestamp. Periodically, a kind of garbage collector process is running, that scans the cache and decides to destroy those objects that have not been used for a defined time span.

At those places where the cached objects are used, instances of std::weak_ptr<T> are used to hold non-owning pointers to these objects. If the expired() member function of those std::weak_ptr<T> instances returns true, the garbage collector process has already cleared the objects from the cache. In the other case, the std::weak_ptr<T>::lock() function can be used to retrieve a std::shared_ptr<T> from it. Now the object can be safely used, even if the Garbage Collector process gets active. Either the process evaluates the usage counter of the std::shared_ptr<T> and ascertains that the object has currently at least one user outside the cache. As a consequence the objects lifetime is extended. Or the process deletes the object from the cache, which does not interfere with its users.

Another example is to deal with circular dependencies. For instance, if you have a class A that needs a pointer to another class B, and vice versa, you will end up with a circular dependency. If you use std::shared_ptr<T> to point to the respective other class as shown in the following code example, you can end up with a memory leak. The reason for this is that the usage counter in the respective shared pointer instance will never count down to 0. Thus, the objects will never be deleted.

Listing 5-7. The problem with circular dependencies caused through a thoughtless use of std::shared_ptr<T>

```cpp
#include <memory>

class B; // Forward declaration

class A {
public:
  void setB(std::shared_ptr<B>& pointerToB) {
    myPointerToB = pointerToB;
  }
```

```cpp
private:
  std::shared_ptr<B> myPointerToB;
};

class B {
public:
  void setA(std::shared_ptr<A>& pointerToA) {
    myPointerToA = pointerToA;
  }

private:
  std::shared_ptr<A> myPointerToA;
};

int main() {
  { // Curly braces build a scope
    auto pointerToA = std::make_shared<A>();
    auto pointerToB = std::make_shared<B>();
    pointerToA->setB(pointerToB);
    pointerToB->setA(pointerToA);
  }
  // At this point, respectively one instance of A and B is "lost in space" (memory leak)

  return 0;
}
```

If the `std::shared_ptr<T>` member variables in the classes are replaced by non-owning weak pointers (`std::weak_ptr<T>`) to the respective other class, the issue with the memory leak is solved.

Listing 5-8. Circular dependencies implemented in the right way with std::weak_ptr<T>

```cpp
class B; // Forward declaration

class A {
public:
  void setB(std::shared_ptr<B>& pointerToB) {
    myPointerToB = pointerToB;
  }

private:
  std::weak_ptr<B> myPointerToB;
};

class B {
public:
  void setA(std::shared_ptr<A>& pointerToA) {
    myPointerToA = pointerToA;
  }

private:
  std::weak_ptr<A> myPointerToA;
};
// ...
```

Basically, circular dependencies are bad design in application code and should be avoided whenever possible. There might be a few exceptions in low-level libraries, where circular dependencies cause no serious issues. But apart from that, you should follow the *Acyclic Dependency Principle* that is discussed in a dedicated section in Chapter 6.

Avoid Explicit New and Delete

In a modern C++ program, when writing application code you should avoid calling new and delete explicitly. Why? Well, the simple and short explanation is this: new and delete increase complexity.

The more detailed answer is this: every time when it is inevitable to call new and delete, one has to deal with an exceptional, non-default situation, a situation that requires special treatment. To understand what these exceptional cases are, instead let's take a look on the default cases – the situations any C++ developer should strive for.

Explicit calls of new and/or delete can be avoided through the following measures:

- **Use allocations on the stack wherever possible.** Allocations on the stack are simple (remember KISS principle discussed in Chapter 3) and safe. It's impossible to leak any of that memory that was allocated on the stack. The resource will be destroyed once it goes out of scope. You can even return the object from a function by value, thus transferring its contents to the calling function.

- **To allocate a resource on the heap, use "make functions."** Use std::make_unique<T> or std::make_shared<T> to instantiate the resource and wrap it immediately into a manager object that takes care of the resource, a smart pointer.

- **Use containers (Standard Library, Boost, or others) wherever appropriate.** Container manages the storage space for its elements. Instead, in the case of self-developed data structures and sequences, you are forced to implement the entire storage management on your own, which can be a complex and error-prone task.

- **Provide wrappers for resources from proprietary third-party libraries** that require a specific memory management (see next section).

Managing Proprietary Resources

As already mentioned in the introduction to this section about resource management, sometimes other resources need to be managed that are not allocated respectively deallocated on the heap using the default new or delete operator. Examples for such kind of resources are opened files from a file system, a dynamically loaded module (e.g., a Dynamic Link Library (DLL) on Windows operating systems), or platform-specific objects of a graphical user interface (e.g., Windows, Buttons, Text input fields, etc.).

Often these kinds of resources are managed through something that is called a *handle*. A handle is an abstract and unique reference to an operational system resource. On Windows, the data type HANDLE is used to define such handles. In fact, this data type is defined as follows in header WinNT.h, a C-style header file that defines various Win32 API macros and types:

```cpp
typedef void *HANDLE;
```

For instance, if you want to access a running Windows process with a certain process ID, you can retrieve a handle to this process using the Win32 API function OpenProcess().

```cpp
#include <windows.h>
// ...
const DWORD processId = 4711;
HANDLE processHandle = OpenProcess(PROCESS_ALL_ACCESS, FALSE, processId);
```

After you are finished with the handle, you have to close it by using the `CloseHandle()` function:

```
BOOL success = CloseHandle(processHandle);
```

Hence, we have symmetry similar to operator new and its corresponding operator delete. It should therefore also be possible to take advantage of the RAII idiom and to use smart pointers for such resources. First, we just have to exchange the default deleter (which calls delete) by a custom deleter that calls CloseHandle():

```
#include <windows.h> // Windows API declarations

class Win32HandleCloser {
public:
  void operator()(HANDLE handle) const {
    if (handle != INVALID_HANDLE_VALUE) {
      CloseHandle(handle);
    }
  }
};
```

Be careful! If you now define a type alias by writing something like the following, the std::shared_ptr<T> will manage something that is of type void**, because HANDLE is already defined as a void-pointer:

```
using Win32SharedHandle = std::shared_ptr<HANDLE>; // Caution!
```

Therefore, smart pointers for Win32 HANDLE must be defined as follows:

```
using Win32SharedHandle = std::shared_ptr<void>;
using Win32WeakHandle = std::weak_ptr<void>;
```

Note It is not allowed to define a std::unique_ptr<void> in C++! It is because std::shared_ptr<T> implements type-erasure, while std::unique_ptr<T> does not. If a class supports type-erasure, it means that it can store objects of an arbitrary type, and destruct them correctly.

If you want to use the shared handle, you have to pay attention that you pass an instance of the custom deleter Win32HandleCloser as a parameter during construction:

```
const DWORD processId = 4711;
Win32SharedHandle processHandle { OpenProcess(PROCESS_ALL_ACCESS, FALSE, processId),
  Win32HandleCloser() };
```

We Like to Move It

If someone would ask me which C++11 feature has probably the most profound impact on how modern C++ programs will be written now and in the future, I would clearly nominate *move semantics*. I have already discussed C++ move semantics briefly in Chapter 4, in the section about strategies to avoid regular pointers. But I think that they are so important that I want to deepen this language feature here.

What Are Move Semantics?

In many former cases where the old C++ language forced us to use a copy constructor, we actually did not really want to create a deep copy of an object. Instead, we simply wanted to "move the object's payload." An object's payload is nothing else than the embedded data that the object carries around with it, so nothing else than other objects, or member variables of primitive types like int.

These cases in former times where we had to copy an object instead of moving it were, for example, the following:

- The returning of a local object instance as a return value from a function or method. To prevent the copy construction in these cases prior C++11, pointers were frequently used.

- Inserting an object into a std::vector or other containers.

- The implementation of the std::swap<T> template function.

In many of the before-mentioned situations, it is unnecessary to keep the source object intact, that is, to create a deep, and in terms of runtime efficiency often costly copy so that the source objects remains usable.

C++11 has introduced a language feature that has made the moving of an object's embedded data a first-class operation. In addition to the copy constructor and copy assignment operator, the class's developer can now implement *move constructors* and *move assignment operators* (we will see later why he actually should **not** do that!). The move operations are usually very efficient. In contrast to a real copy operation, the source object's data is just handed over to the target object, and the argument (the source object) of the operation is put into a kind of "empty" or initial state.

The following example shows an arbitrary class that explicitly implements both types of semantics: copy constructor (line no. 6) and assignment operator (line no. 8), as well as move constructor (line no. 7) and assignment operator (line no. 9).

Listing 5-9. An example class that explicitly declares special member functions for copy and move

```
01  #include <string>
02
03  class Clazz {
04  public:
05    Clazz() noexcept;                         // Default constructor
06    Clazz(const Clazz& other);                // Copy constructor
07    Clazz(Clazz&& other) noexcept;            // Move constructor
08    Clazz& operator=(const Clazz& other);     // Copy assignment operator
09    Clazz& operator=(Clazz&& other) noexcept; // Move assignment operator
10    virtual ~Clazz() noexcept;                // Destructor
11
12  private:
13    // ...
14  };
```

As we will see later in the section "The Rule of Zero," it should be a major goal of any C++ developer to **not** declare and define such constructors and assignment operators explicitly.

The move semantics are closely related to something that is called *rvalue references* (see next section). The constructor or assignment operator of a class is called a "move constructor" respectively "move assignment operator," when it takes an *rvalue reference* as a parameter. An rvalue reference is marked through the double ampersand operator (&&). For better distinction, the ordinary reference with its single ampersand (&) is now also called an *lvalue reference*.

The Matter with Those lvalues and rvalues

The so-called *lvalue* and *rvalue* are historically terms (inherited from language C), because lvalues could usually appear on the left-hand side of an assignment expression, whereas rvalues could usually appear on the right-hand side of an assignment expression. In my opinion, a much better explanation for lvalue is that it is a **locator value**. This makes it clear that an lvalue represents an object that occupies a location in memory (i.e., it has an accessible and identifiable memory address).

In contrast, rvalues are all those objects in an expression that are not lvalues. It is a temporary object, or subobject thereof. Hence, it is not possible to assign anything to an rvalue.

Although these definitions come from the old C world, and C++11 still has introduced more categories (*xvalue*, *glvalue*, and *prvalue*) to enable move semantics, they are pretty good for everyday use.

The simplest form of an lvalue expression is a variable declaration:

```
Type var1;
```

The expression var1 is an lvalue of type Type. The following declarations represent lvalues too:

```
Type* pointer;
Type& reference;
Type& function();
```

An lvalue can be the left operand of an assignment operation, like the integer-variable theAnswerToAllQuestions in this example:

```
int theAnswerToAllQuestions = 42;
```

Also the assignment of a memory address to a pointer makes clear that the pointer is an lvalue:

```
Type* pointerToVar1 = &var1;
```

The literal "42" instead is an rvalue. It doesn't represent an identifiable location in memory, so it is not possible to assign anything to it (of course, rvalues also occupy memory in the data section on the stack, but this memory is allocated temporarily and released immediately after completion of the assignment operation):

```
int number = 23; // Works, because 'number' is an lvalue
42 = number; // Compiler error: lvalue required as left operand of assignment
```

You don't believe that function() on the third line from the above generic examples is an lvalue? It is! You can write the following (without doubt, some kind of weird) piece of code and the compiler will compile it without complaints:

```
int theAnswerToAllQuestions = 42;

int& function() {
  return theAnswerToAllQuestions;
}

int main() {
  function() = 23; // Works!
  return 0;
}
```

rvalue References

As already mentioned above, C++11 move semantics are closely related to something that is called rvalue references. These rvalue references now make it possible to address the memory location of rvalues. In the following example, temporary memory is assigned to an rvalue reference and thus makes it "permanent." You can even retrieve a pointer pointing to this location and manipulate the memory referenced by the rvalue reference using this pointer.

```cpp
int&& rvalueReference = 25 + 17;
int* pointerToRvalueReference = &rvalueReference;
*pointerToRvalueReference = 23;
```

By introducing rvalue references, these can of course also appear as parameters in functions or methods. Table 5-1 shows the possibilities.

Table 5-1. *Different function respectively method signatures, and their allowed parameter kinds*

Function/method signature	Allowed parameter kinds
`void function(Type param)` `void X::method(Type param)`	Both **lvalues and rvalues** can be passed as parameters.

`void function(Type& param)`
`void function(const Type& param)`
`void X::method(Type& param)`
`void X::method(const Type& param)`
	Only **lvalues** can be passed as parameters.

`void function(Type&& param)` `void X::method(Type&& param)`	Only **rvalues** can be passed as parameters.

Table 5-2 shows the situation for return types of a function or method and what is permitted for the function's/method's return statement:

Table 5-2. *Possible kinds of return types of functions respectively parameters*

Function/method signature	Possible data types returned by the return statement
`int function()` `int X::method()`	`[const] int`, `[const] int&`, or `[const] int&&`.
`int& function()` `int& X::method()`	Non-const `int` or `int&`.
`int&& function()` `int&& X::method()`	Literals (e.g., `return 42`), or a rvalue reference (obtained with `std::move()`) to an object with a lifetime longer than the function's respective method's scope.

Although, of course, rvalue references are allowed to be used for parameters in any function or method, their predestined field of application is in move constructors and move assignment operators.

Listing 5-10. A class that explicitly defines both copy- and move semantics

```cpp
#include <utility> // std::move<T>

class Clazz {
public:
  Clazz() = default;
```

```cpp
  Clazz(const Clazz& other) {
    // Classical copy construction for lvalues
  }

  Clazz(Clazz&& other) noexcept {
    // Move constructor for rvalues: moves content from 'other' to this
  }
  Clazz& operator=(const Clazz& other) {
    // Classical copy assignment for lvalues
    return *this;
  }

  Clazz& operator=(Clazz&& other) noexcept {
    // Move assignment for rvalues: moves content from 'other' to this
    return *this;
  }
  // ...
};

int main() {
  Clazz anObject;
  Clazz anotherObject1(anObject);              // Calls copy constructor
  Clazz anotherObject2(std::move(anObject));   // Calls move constructor
  anObject = anotherObject1;                   // Calls copy assignment operator
  anotherObject2 = std::move(anObject);        // Calls move assignment operator
  return 0;
}
```

Don't Enforce Move Everywhere

Maybe you've noticed the use of the helper function `std::move<T>()` (defined in header `<utility>`) in the code example above to force the compiler to use move semantics.

First of all, the name of this small helper function is misleading. `std::move<T>()` doesn't move anything. It is more or less a cast that produces an rvalue reference to an object of type `T`.

In most cases, it is not necessary to do that. Under normal circumstances, the selection between the copy and the move versions of constructors or assignment operators is done automatically at compile time through overload resolution. The compiler ascertains whether it is confronted with an lvalue or an rvalue, and then selects the best fitting constructor or assignment operator accordingly. The container classes of the C++ Standard Library also take into account the level of exception-safety that is guaranteed by the move operations (we will discuss this topic in more detail later in the section "Prevention Is Better Than Aftercare").

Note this especially – don't write code like this:

Listing 5-11. An improper use of std::move()

```cpp
#include <string>
#include <utility>
#include <vector>

using StringVector = std::vector<std::string>;
```

```
StringVector createVectorOfStrings() {
  StringVector result;
  // ...do something that the vector is filled with many strings...
  return std::move(result); // Bad and unnecessary, just write "return result;"!
}
```

Using `std::move<T>()` with the return statement is not only completely unnecessary, because the compiler already knows that the variable is a candidate to be moved out of the function (since C++11, move semantics is supported by all Standard Library containers as well as by many other classes of the Standard Library, like `std::string`). A possibly even worse impact could be that it can interfere with the RVO (*Return Value Optimization*), also known as *Copy elision*, which is performed by nearly all compilers nowadays. RVO respective Copy elision allows compilers to optimize out a costly copy construction when returning values from a function or method.

Think always about the important principle from Chapter 3: **Be careful with optimizations!** Don't mess up your code with `std::move<T>()` statements everywhere, just because you think that you can be smarter than your compiler with the optimization of your code. You are not! The readability of your code will suffer with all those `std::move<T>()` everywhere, and your compiler might not be able to perform its optimization strategies properly.

The Rule of Zero

As an experienced C++ developer you may already know the *Rule of Three* respectively the *Rule of Five*. The Rule of Three [Koenig01], originally coined by Marshall Cline in 1991, states that if a class defines a destructor explicitly, it should almost always define a copy constructor and a copy assignment operator. With the advent of C++11 this rule was extended and became the Rule of Five, because the move constructor and the move assignment operator has been added to the language, and also these two special member functions must be defined as well if a class defines a destructor.

The reason why the Rule of Three and respectively the Rule of Five were good pieces of advice for a long time in C++ class design, and are subtle errors that can occur when developers are not considering them, as demonstrated with the following intentionally bad code example.

Listing 5-12. An improper implementation of a string class

```cpp
#include <cstring>

class MyString {
public:
  explicit MyString(const std::size_t sizeOfString) : data { new char[sizeOfString] } { }
  MyString(const char* const charArray, const std::size_t sizeOfArray) {
    data = new char[sizeOfArray];
    strcpy(data, charArray);
  }
  virtual ~MyString() { delete[] data; };

  char& operator[](const std::size_t index) {
    return data[index];
  }
  const char& operator[](const std::size_t index) const {
    return data[index];
  }
  // ...

private:
  char* data;
};
```

This is indeed a very amateurish implemented string class with some flaws, for example, a missing check that not a `nullptr` is passed into the initialization constructor, and totally ignoring the fact that strings usually could grow and shrink. Of course, no one has to implement a string class herself nowadays, and thus reinvent the wheel. With `std::string`, a bullet-proofed string class is available in the C++ Standard Library. On the basis of the above example, however, it is very easy to demonstrate why adhering to the Rule of Five is important.

In order that the memory allocated by the initialization constructors for the internal string representation is freed safely, an explicit destructor must be defined and has to be implemented to do this. In the above class, however, the Rule of Five is violated and the explicit copy/move constructors, as well as the copy/move assignment operators, are missing.

Now, let's assume that we're using class `MyString` in the following way:

```cpp
int main() {
  MyString aString("Test", 4);
  MyString anotherString { aString }; // Uh oh! :-(
  return 0;
}
```

Due to the fact that our `MyString` class does not explicitly define a copy or move constructor, the compiler will synthesize these special member functions, that is, the compiler will generate a default copy constructor respectively and a default move constructor. And these default implementations only create a flat copy of the member variables of the source object. In our case, the address value stored in the character pointer `data` is copied, but not the area in memory where this pointer is pointing to.

That means the following: after the automatically generated default copy constructor has been called to create `anotherString`, both instances of `MyString` are sharing the same data, as it can easily be seen in a Debugger's Variables View shown in Figure 5-2.

Name	Type	Value
▼ aString	MyString	{...}
▶ ➡ data	char *	0x555555768c20 "Test"
▼ anotherString	MyString	{...}
▶ ➡ data	char *	0x555555768c20 "Test"

Figure 5-2. Both character pointers are pointing to the same memory address

This will result in double deletion of the internal data if the string objects are destroyed, and thus can cause critical issues, like segmentation faults or undefined behavior.

Under normal circumstances, there is no reason to define an explicit destructor for a class. Every time when you are compelled to define a destructor, this is a noticeable exception, because it indicates that you need to do something special with resources at the end of the lifetime of an object that requires considerable effort. A non-trivial destructor is usually required to deallocate resources, for example, memory on the heap. As a consequence, you also need to define explicit copy/move constructors and copy/move assignment operators in order to handle these resources correctly while copying or moving. That's what the Rule of Five implies.

There are different approaches to deal with the above-described problem. For instance, we can provide explicit copy/move constructors and also copy/move assignment operators to handle the allocated memory correctly, for example, by creating a deep copy of the memory area the pointer is pointing to. Another approach would be to prohibit copying and moving, and prevent the compiler from generating default versions of these functions. This can be done since C++11 by deleting these special member functions so that any use of a deleted function is ill formed, that is, the program will not compile.

Listing 5-13. A modified MyString class that explicitely deletes copy constructor and copy assignment operator

```cpp
class MyString {
public:
  explicit MyString(const std::size_t sizeOfString) : data { new char[sizeOfString] } { }
  MyString(const char* const charArray, const int sizeOfArray) {
    data = new char[sizeOfArray];
    strcpy(data, charArray);
  }
  virtual ~MyString() { delete[] data; };
  MyString(const MyString&) = delete;
  MyString& operator=(const MyString&) = delete;
  // ...
};
```

The problem is that by deleting the special member functions, the class has now a very limited area of use. For instance, MyString cannot be used in a std::vector now, because std::vector requires that its element type T is copy-assignable and copy-constructible.

OK, it's time now to choose a different approach and to think differently. What we have to do is get rid of the destructor that frees the allocated resource. If this succeeds, it is also not necessary, according to the Rule of Five, to provide the other special member functions explicitly. So here we go:

Listing 5-14. Replacing the char-pointer by a vector of char makes an explicit destructor superfluous

```cpp
#include <vector>

class MyString {
public:
  explicit MyString(const std::size_t sizeOfString) {
    data.resize(sizeOfString, ' ');
  }

  MyString(const char* const charArray, const int sizeOfArray) : MyString(sizeOfArray) {
    if (charArray != nullptr) {
      for (int index = 0; index < sizeOfArray; index++) {
        data[index] = charArray[index];
      }
    }
  }

  char& operator[](const std::size_t index) {
    return data[index];
  }
```

```cpp
const char& operator[](const std::size_t index) const {
  return data[index];
}
// ...

private:
  std::vector<char> data;
};
```

Once again, a remark: I know that this is an impractical and amateurish implementation of a self-made string, which is not necessary nowadays, but it is for demonstration purposes only.

What has changed now? Well, we've replaced the private member of type char* by a std::vector with element type char. Thus, we do not need an explicit destructor anymore, because we have nothing to do if an object of our type MyString is destroyed. There is no need to deallocate any resource. As a result, the compiler-generated special member functions, like copy/move constructor or copy/move assignment operator, does the right things automatically if they are used, and we do not have to define them explicitly. And that's good news, because we've followed the KISS principle (see Chapter 3).

And that leads us to the Rule of Zero! The Rule of Zero was coined by R. Martinho Fernandes in a blog post in 2012 [Fernandes12]. The rule was also promoted by ISO standard committee member Prof. Peter Sommerlad, Director *IFS Institute for Software* at the *HSR Hochschule für Technik Rapperswil* (Switzerland), in a conference talk on *Meeting C++ 2013* [Sommerlad13]. Here is what the rule says:

Write your classes in a way that you do not need to declare/define neither a destructor, nor a copy/move constructor or copy/move assignment operator. Use C++ smart pointers and standard library classes and containers for managing resources.

In other words, the Rule of Zero states that your classes should be designed in a way so that the compiler-generated member functions for copying, moving, and destruction automatically do the right things. This makes your classes easier to understand (think always of the KISS principle from Chapter 3), less error prone, and better maintainable. The principle behind it is this: doing more by writing less code.

The Compiler Is Your Colleague

As I have already written elsewhere, the advent of the C++11 language standard has fundamentally changed the way how modern and clean C++ programs will be designed nowadays. Styles, patterns, and idioms that programmers are using while writing modern C++ code are totally different than before. Besides the fact that the newer C++ standards offer many useful new features to write C++ code that is well maintainable, understandable, efficient, and testable, something else has still changed: **the role of the compiler!**

In former times the compiler was just a tool to translate the source code into executable machine instructions (object code) for a computer; but now it is increasingly becoming a tool to support the developer on different levels. The three guiding principles for working with a C++ compiler nowadays are the following:

- Everything that can be done at compile time should also be done at compile time.

- Everything that can be checked at compile time should also be checked at compile time.

- Everything the compiler can know about a program should also be determined by the compiler.

In former chapters and sections, we've already experienced in some spots how the compiler can support us. For instance, in the section about move semantics, we've seen that modern C++ compilers nowadays are able to perform manifold sophisticated optimizations (e.g., copy elision) about we do not have to care about anymore. In the following sections, I'll show you how the compiler can support us developers and make many things much easier for us.

Automatic Type Deduction

Do you remember the meaning of the C++ keyword auto before C++11? I'm pretty sure that it was probably the least-known and used keyword in the language. Maybe you remember that auto in C++98 or C++03 was a so-called storage class specifier and has been used to define that a local variable has "automatic duration," that is, the variable is created at the point of definition, and destroyed when the block it was part of is exited. Since C++11, all variables have automatic duration per default unless otherwise specified. Thus, the previous semantics of auto was getting useless, and the keyword got a completely new meaning.

Nowadays, auto is used for *automatic type deduction*, sometimes also called *type inference*. If it is used as a type specifier for a variable, it specifies that the type of the variable that is being declared will be automatically deduced (or inferred) from its initializer, like in the following examples:

```cpp
auto theAnswerToAllQuestions = 42;
auto iter = begin(myMap);
const auto gravitationalAccelerationOnEarth = 9.80665;
constexpr auto sum = 10 + 20 + 12;
auto strings = { "The", "big", "brown", "fox", "jumps", "over", "the", "lazy", "dog" };
auto numberOfStrings = strings.size();
```

ARGUMENT DEPENDENT NAME LOOKUP (ADL)

Argument Dependent (Name) Lookup (short: ADL), also known as *Koenig Lookup* (named after the American computer scientist Andrew Koenig), is a compiler technique to look up for an unqualified function name (that is, a function name without a prefixed namespace qualifier) depending on the types of the arguments passed to the function at its call site.

Suppose you have a std::map<K, T> (defined in header <map>) like the following one:

```cpp
#include <map>
#include <string>
std::map<unsigned int, std::string> words;
```

Due to ADL, it is not necessary to specify the namespace std if you use the begin() or end() function to retrieve an iterator from the container. You can simply write:

```cpp
auto wordIterator = begin(words);
```

The compiler does not just look at local scope, but also the namespaces that contain the argument's type (in this case, the namespace of map<T>, which is std). Thus, in the above example, the compiler finds a fitting begin() function for maps in the std-namespace.

In some cases you need to explicitly define the namespace, for example, if you want to use std::begin() and std::end() with a simple C-style array.

On first sight, using `auto` instead of a concrete type seems to be a convenience feature. Developers are no longer forced to remember a type's name. They simply write `auto`, `const auto`, `auto&` (for references), or `const auto&` (for const references), and the compiler is doing the rest, because it knows the type of the assigned value. Automatic type deduction can of course also be used in conjunction with `constexpr` (see section about computations at compile time).

Please do not be afraid to use `auto` (or `auto&` respectively `const auto&`) as much as possible. The code is still statically typed, and the types of the variables are clearly defined. For instance, the type of the variable `strings` from the above example is `std::initializer_list<const char*>`, the type of `numberOfStrings` is `std::initializer_list<const char*>::size_type`.

STD::INITIALIZER_LIST<T> [C++11]

In former days (prior C++11), if we wanted to initialize a Standard Library container using literals, we had to do the following:

```cpp
std::vector<int> integerSequence;
integerSequence.push_back(14);
integerSequence.push_back(33);
integerSequence.push_back(69);
// ...and so on...
```

Since C++11, we can simply do it this way:

```cpp
std::vector<int> integerSequence { 14, 33, 69, 104, 222, 534 };
```

The reason for this is that `std::vector<T>` has an overloaded constructor that accepts a so-called initializer list as a parameter. An initializer list is an object of type `std::initializer_list<T>` (defined in header `<initializer_list>`).

An instance of type `std::initializer_list<T>` is automatically constructed when you use a list of comma-separated literals that are surrounded with a pair of curly braces, a so-called *braced-init-list*. You can equip your own classes with constructors that can accept initializer lists, as shown in this example:

```cpp
#include <string>
#include <vector>

using WordList = std::vector<std::string>;

class LexicalRepository {
public:
  explicit LexicalRepository(const std::initializer_list<const char*>& words) {
    wordList.insert(begin(wordList), begin(words), end(words));
  }
  // ...

private:
  WordList wordList;
};
```

```cpp
int main() {
  LexicalRepository repo { "The", "big", "brown", "fox", "jumps", "over",
  "the", "lazy", "dog" };
  // ...
  return 0;
}
```

Note: This initializer list should not be confused with a class of its member initializer list!

Since C++14, also automatic return type deduction for functions is supported. This is especially helpful when a return type has a difficult-to-remember or unutterable name, which is often the case when dealing with complex non-standard data types as return types.

```cpp
auto function() {
  std::vector<std::map<std::pair<int, double>, int>> returnValue;
  // ...fill 'returnValue' with data...
  return returnValue;
}
```

We haven't discussed lambda functions until now (they will be discussed in detail in Chapter 7), but C++11 and higher lets you store lambda expressions in named variables:

```cpp
auto square = [](int x) { return x * x; };
```

Maybe you're wondering now this: well, in Chapter 4 the author told us that an expressive and good naming is important for the readability of the code and should be a major goal for every professional programmer. The same author now promotes the usage of the keyword auto, which makes it more difficult to recognize the type of a variable quickly just by reading the code. Isn't that a contradiction?

My clear answer is this: no, quite the contrary! Apart from a few exceptions, auto can raise the readability of the code. Let's look at the following two alternatives of a variable assignment:

Listing 5-15. Which one of the following two versions would you prefer?

```cpp
// 1st version: without auto
std::shared_ptr<controller::CreateMonthlyInvoicesController> createMonthlyInvoicesController =
  std::make_shared<controller::CreateMonthlyInvoicesController>();

// 2nd version: with auto:
auto createMonthlyInvoicesController =
  std::make_shared<controller::CreateMonthlyInvoicesController>();
```

From my point of view, the version using auto is easier to read. There is no need to repeat the type explicitly, because it is pretty clear from its initializer of what type createMonthlyInvoicesController will be. By the way, repeating the explicit type would also be a kind of violation of the DRY principle (see Chapter 3). And if you think of the above lambda expression named square, whose type is a unique, unnamed non-union class type, how can such type be explicitly defined?

So, here is my advice:

If it doesn't obscure the intent of your code, use auto wherever possible!

Computations during Compile Time

Fans of High Performance Computing (HPC), but also developers of embedded software and programmers who prefer to use static, constant tables to separate data and code, want to compute as much as possible at compile time. The reasons for this are very easy to comprehend: everything that can be computed or evaluated at compile time does not have to be computed or evaluated at runtime. In other words: the computation of as much as possible at compile time is low-hanging fruits to raise the runtime efficiency of your program. This advantage is sometimes accompanied by a drawback, which is the more or less increasing time that it takes to compile our code.

Since C++11 there is the `constexpr` (constant expression) specifier to define that it is possible to evaluate the value of a function or a variable at compile time. And with the subsequent standard C++14, some of the stringent restrictions for `constexpr` were lifted that existed before. For instance, a `constexpr`-specified function was allowed to have exactly one `return`-statement only. This restriction has been abolished since C++14.

One of the simplest examples is that a variable's value is calculated from literals by arithmetic operations at compile time, like this:

```cpp
constexpr int theAnswerToAllQuestions = 10 + 20 + 12;
```

The variable `theAnswerToAllQuestions` is also a constant as if it has been declared with `const`; thus you cannot manipulate it during runtime:

```cpp
int main() {
  // ...
  theAnswerToAllQuestions = 23; // Compiler error: assignment of read-only variable!
  return 0;
}
```

There are also `constexpr` functions:

```cpp
constexpr int multiply(const int multiplier, const int multiplicand) {
  return multiplier * multiplicand;
}
```

Such functions can be called at compile time, but they are also used like ordinary functions with non-const arguments at runtime. This is already necessary for the reason to test those functions with the help of Unit Tests (see Chapter 2).

```cpp
constexpr int theAnswerToAllQuestions = multiply(7, 6);
```

Unsurprisingly, also `constexpr` specified functions can be called recursively, as shown in the following example of a function to calculate factorials.

Listing 5-16. Calculating the factorial of a non-negative integer 'n' at compile time

```cpp
01  #include <iostream>
02
03  constexpr unsigned long long factorial(const unsigned short n) {
04      return n > 1 ? n * factorial(n - 1) : 1;
05  }
06
07  int main() {
08      unsigned short number = 6;
09      auto result1 = factorial(number);
10      constexpr auto result2 = factorial(10);
11
12      std::cout << "result1: " << result1 << ", result2: " << result2 << std::endl;
13      return 0;
14  }
```

The previous example already works under C++11. The `factorial()` function consists of only one statement, and recursion was allowed from the beginning in `constexpr` functions. The `main()` function contains two calls of the `factorial()` function. It is worth it to take a closer look at these two function calls.

The first call on line no. 9 uses the variable `number` as the argument for the function's parameter `n`, and its result is assigned to a non-const variable `result1`. The second function call on line no. 10 uses a number literal as the argument, and its result is assigned to a variable with a `constexpr` specifier. The difference between these two function calls at runtime can best be seen in the disassembled object code. Figure 5-3 shows the object code at our key spot in the Disassembly Window of Eclipse CDT.

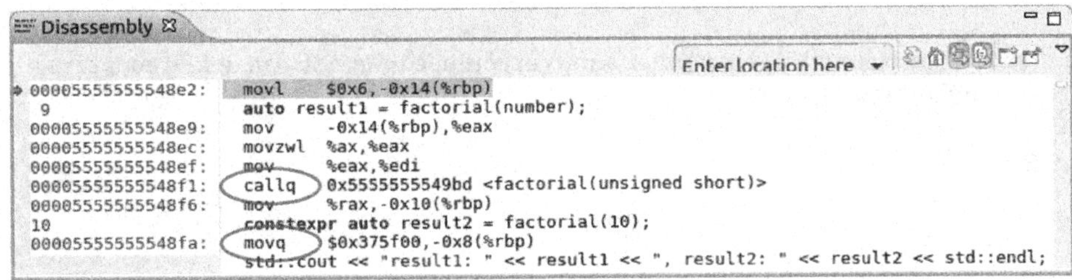

Figure 5-3. *The disassembled object code*

The first function call on line no. 9 results in five machine instructions. The 4th of these instructions (callq) is the jump to the function `factorial()` at memory address 0x5555555549bd. In other words, it is obvious that the function is called at runtime. In contrast, we see that the second call of `factorial()` at line no. 10 results in just one simple machine instruction. The `movq` instruction copies a quadword from the source operand to the destination operand. There is no costly function call at runtime. The result of `factorial(10)`, which is 0x375f00 in hexadecimal and respectively 3,628,800 in decimal, has been calculated at compile time and is available like a constant in the object code.

As I have already written earlier, some restrictions for `contexpr` specified functions in C++11 have been repealed since C++14. For instance, a `constexpr` specified function can now have more than one return statement, it can have conditionals like `if-else`-branches, local variables of "literal" type, or loops. Basically, almost all C++ statements are allowed if they do not presuppose or require something that is only available in the context of a run time environment, for example, allocating memory on the heap, or throwing exceptions.

Variable Templates

I think it is less surprising that constexpr can also be used in templates, as shown in the following example.

Listing 5-17. A variable template for mathematical constant pi

```cpp
template <typename T>
constexpr T pi = T(3.1415926535897932384626433L);
```

This is known as a *variable template* and is a good and flexible alternative to the archaic style of constant definitions by using #define for macros (see section "Avoid Macros" in Chapter 4). Depending on its usage context during template instantiation, the mathematical constant pi is typed as float, double, or long double.

Listing 5-18. Calculating a circles circumference at compile time using variable template 'pi'

```cpp
template <typename T>
constexpr T computeCircumference(const T radius) {
  return 2 * radius * pi<T>;
}

int main() {
  const long double radius { 10.0L };
  constexpr long double circumference = computeCircumference(radius);
  std::cout << circumference << std::endl;
  return 0;
}
```

Last but not least, you can also use classes in computations at compile time. You can define constexpr constructors and member functions for classes.

Listing 5-19. Rectangle is a constexpr class

```cpp
#include <iostream>
#include <cmath>

class Rectangle {
public:
  constexpr Rectangle() = delete;
  constexpr Rectangle(const double width, const double height) :
    width { width }, height { height } { }
  constexpr double getWidth() const { return width; }
  constexpr double getHeight() const { return height; }
  constexpr double getArea() const { return width * height; }
  constexpr double getLengthOfDiagonal() const {
    return std::sqrt(std::pow(width, 2.0) + std::pow(height, 2.0));
  }

private:
  double width;
  double height;
};
```

```cpp
int main() {
  constexpr Rectangle americanFootballPlayingField { 48.76, 110.0 };
  constexpr double area = americanFootballPlayingField.getArea();
  constexpr double diagonal = americanFootballPlayingField.getLengthOfDiagonal();

  std::cout << "The area of an American Football playing field is " <<
      area << "m^2 and the length of its diagonal is " << diagonal <<
      "m." << std::endl;
  return 0;
}
```

Also constexpr classes can be used both, at compile time and at runtime. In contrast to ordinary classes, however, it is not allowed to define virtual member functions (there is no polymorphism at compile time), and a constexpr class must not have an explicitly defined destructor.

Note The above code example could fail to compile on some C++ compilers. By today's standards, the C++ standard does not specify common mathematical functions from the numerics library (header <cmath>) as constexpr, like std::sqrt() and std::pow(). Compiler implementations are free to do it anyway, but it's not mandatorily required.

However, how should these computations at compile time have been judged from a Clean Code perspective? Is it basically a good idea to add constexpr to anything that can possibly have it?

Well, my opinion is that constexpr does not reduce the readability of the code. The specifier is always in front of variables and constants definitions, respectively in front of function or method declarations. Hence, it does not disturb so much. On the other hand, if I definitely know that something will never be evaluated at compile time, I should also renounce the specifier.

Don't Allow Undefined Behavior

In C++ (and in some other programming languages too) the language specification does not define the behavior in any possible situation. In some places the specification says that the behavior of a certain operation is undefined under certain circumstances. In such a kind of situation you cannot predict what will happen, because the behavior of the program depends on compiler implementation, the underlying operating system, or special optimization switches. That's really bad! The program may either crash or silently generate incorrect results.

Here is an example of undefined behavior, an incorrect use of a smart pointer:

```cpp
const std::size_t NUMBER_OF_STRINGS { 100 };
std::shared_ptr<std::string> arrayOfStrings(new std::string[NUMBER_OF_STRINGS]>);
```

Let's assume that this std::shared_ptr<T> object is the last one pointing to the string array resource and runs out of scope somewhere, what will happen?

Answer: The destructor of std::shared_ptr<T> decrements the number of shared owners and the counter reaches zero. As a consequence, the resource managed by the smart pointer (the array of std::string) is destroyed by calling its destructor. But it will do it wrong, because when you allocate the managed resource using new[] you need to call the array form delete[], and not delete, to free the resource, and the default deleter of std::shared_ptr<T> use delete.

Deleting an array with delete instead of delete[ ] results in undefined behavior. It is not specified what happens. Maybe it results in a memory leak, but that's just a guess.

■ **Caution**   Avoid undefined behavior! It is a bad mistake and ends up with programs that silently misbehave.

There are several solutions to let the smart pointer delete the string array correctly. For example, you can provide a custom deleter as a function-like object (also known as "Functor," see Chapter 7):

```cpp
template< typename Type >
struct CustomArrayDeleter
{
  void operator()(Type const* pointer)
  {
    delete [] pointer;
  }
};
```

Now you can use your own deleter as follows:

```cpp
const std::size_t NUMBER_OF_STRINGS { 100 };
std::shared_ptr<std::string> arrayOfStrings(new std::string[NUMBER_OF_STRINGS], CustomArrayD
eleter<std::string>());
```

In C++11 there is a default deleter for array types defined in header <memory>:

```cpp
const std::size_t NUMBER_OF_STRINGS { 100 };
std::shared_ptr<std::string> arrayOfStrings(new std::string[NUMBER_OF_STRINGS],
  std::default_delete<std::string[]>());
```

Of course it should be taken into consideration, depending on the requirements to satisfy, whether the usage of a std::vector is not always the best solution to implement an "array of things."

Type-Rich Programming

Don't trust names.

Trust types.

Types don't lie.

Types are your friends!

—Mario Fusco (@mariofusco), April 13, 2016, on Twitter

On September 23, 1999, NASA lost its *Mars Climate Orbiter I*, a robotic space probe, after a 10-month journey to the fourth planet of our Solar System. As the spacecraft went into orbital insertion, the transfer of important data failed between the propulsion team at *Lockheed Martin Astronautics* in Colorado, and the NASA mission navigation team in Pasadena (California). This error pushed the spacecraft too close to the atmosphere of Mars where it burned immediately.

Figure 5-4. *Artist's rendering of the Mars Climate Orbiter (Author: NASA/JPL/Corby Waste; License: Public Domain)*

The cause for the failed data transfer was that the NASA mission navigation team used the *International System of Units* (SI), while Lockheed Martin's navigation software used English units (*Imperial Measurement System*). The software used by the mission navigation team has sent values in pound-force-seconds (lbf·s), but the Orbiter's navigation software expected values in newton-seconds (N·s). NASA's total financial loss was 328 million in U.S. dollars. The lifetime work of around 200 good spacecraft engineers were destroyed in a few seconds.

This failure is not a typical example of a simple software bug. Both systems for themselves may have worked correctly. But it reveals an interesting aspect in software development. It seems that communication and coordination problems between both engineering teams to be the elementary reason for this failure. It is obvious: neither were there joint system tests with both subsystems, nor the interfaces between both subsystems had been properly designed.

> *People sometimes make errors. The problem here was not the error, it was the failure of NASA's systems engineering, and the checks and balances in our processes to detect the error. That's why we lost the spacecraft.*
>
> —Dr. Edward Weiler, NASA Associate Administrator for Space Science [JPL99]

In fact, I don't know any detail about the Mars Climate Orbiter's system software. But according to the examination report of the failure, I've understood that one piece of software produced results in an "English system" unit, while the other piece of software that used those results expected them to be in metric units.

I think everybody knows C++ member function declarations that look like the one in the following class:

```cpp
class SpacecraftTrajectoryControl {
public:
  void applyMomentumToSpacecraftBody(const double impulseValue);
};
```

What does the double stand for? Of what unit is the value that is expected by the member function named applyMomentumToSpacecraftBody? Is it a value measured in newton (N), newton-second (N·s), pound-force-second (lbf·s), or any other unit? In fact we don't know it. The double can be anything. It is, of course, a type, but it is not a semantic type. Maybe it has been documented somewhere, or we could give the parameter a more meaningful and verbose name like impulseValueInNewtonSeconds, which would be better than nothing. But even the best documentation or parameter name cannot guarantee that a client of this class passes a value of an incorrect unit to this member function.

Can we do it better? Of course we can.

What we really want to have for defining an interface properly, and rich of semantics, is something like this:

```cpp
class SpacecraftTrajectoryControl {
public:
  void applyMomentumToSpacecraftBody(const Momentum& impulseValue);
};
```

In mechanics, Momentum is measured in newton-second (Ns). One newton-second (1 Ns) is the force of one Newton (which is 1 kg m/s^2 in SI base units) acting on a body (a physical object) for one second.

To use a type like Momentum instead of the unspecific floating-point type double, we must introduce that type first. In a first step we define a template that can be used to represent physical quantities on the base of the MKS system of units. The abbreviation MKS stands for meter (length), kilogram (mass), and seconds (time). These three fundamental units can be used to express any given physical measurement.

Listing 5-20. A class template to represent MKS units

```cpp
template <int M, int K, int S>
struct MksUnit {
  enum { metre = M, kilogram = K, second = S};
};
```

Furthermore, we need a class template for the representation of values:

Listing 5-21. A class template to represent values of MKS units

```cpp
template <typename MksUnit>
class Value {
private:
  long double magnitude{ 0.0 };

public:
  explicit Value(const long double magnitude) : magnitude(magnitude) {}
  long double getMagnitude() const {
    return magnitude;
  }
};
```

Next we can use both class templates to define type aliases for concrete physical quantities. Here are some examples:

```cpp
using DimensionlessQuantity = Value<MksUnit<0, 0, 0>>;
using Length = Value<MksUnit<1, 0, 0>>;
using Area = Value<MksUnit<2, 0, 0>>;
using Volume = Value<MksUnit<3, 0, 0>>;
using Mass = Value<MksUnit<0, 1, 0>>;
using Time = Value<MksUnit<0, 0, 1>>;
using Speed = Value<MksUnit<1, 0, -1>>;
using Acceleration = Value<MksUnit<1, 0, -2>>;
using Frequency = Value<MksUnit<0, 0, -1>>;
using Force = Value<MksUnit<1, 1, -2>>;
using Pressure = Value<MksUnit<-1, 1, -2>>;
// ... etc. ...
```

Now it is also possible to define the Momentum, which is required as the parameter type for our applyMomentumToSpacecraftBody member function:

```cpp
using Momentum = Value<MksUnit<1, 1, -1>>;
```

After we've introduced the type alias Momentum, the following code will not compile, because there is no suitable constructor to convert from double to Value<MksUnit<1,1,-1>>:

```cpp
SpacecraftTrajectoryControl control;
const double someValue = 13.75;
control.applyMomentumToSpacecraftBody(someValue); // Compile-time error!
```

Even the next example will lead to compile-time errors, because a variable of type Force must not be used like a Momentum, and an implicit conversion between these different dimensions must be prevented:

```cpp
SpacecraftTrajectoryControl control;
Force force { 13.75 };
control.applyMomentumToSpacecraftBody(force); // Compile-time error!
```

But this will work fine:

```cpp
SpacecraftTrajectoryControl control;
Momentum momentum { 13.75 };
control.applyMomentumToSpacecraftBody(momentum);
```

The units can also be used for the definition of constants. For this purpose, we need to slightly modify the class template Value. We add the keyword constexpr (see section "Computations during Compile Time" in Chapter 4) to the initialization constructor and the getMagnitude() member function. This allows us not only to create compile-time constants of Value that don't have to be initialized during runtime. As we will see later, we are also able to perform computations with our physical values during compile time now.

```cpp
template <typename MksUnit>
class Value {
public:
  constexpr explicit Value(const long double magnitude) noexcept : magnitude { magnitude } {}
```

```cpp
  constexpr long double getMagnitude() const noexcept {
    return magnitude;
  }

private:
  long double magnitude { 0.0 };
};
```

Thereafter, constants of different physical units can be defined as in the following example:

```cpp
constexpr Acceleration gravitationalAccelerationOnEarth { 9.80665 };
constexpr Pressure standardPressureOnSeaLevel { 1013.25 };
constexpr Speed speedOfLight { 299792458.0 };
constexpr Frequency concertPitchA { 440.0 };
constexpr Mass neutronMass { 1.6749286e-27 };
```

Furthermore, computations between units are possible if the necessary operators are implemented. For instance, these are the addition, subtraction, multiply, and the division operator templates to perform different calculations with two values of different MKS units:

```cpp
template <int M, int K, int S>
constexpr Value<MksUnit<M, K, S>> operator+
  (const Value<MksUnit<M, K, S>>& lhs, const Value<MksUnit<M, K, S>>& rhs) noexcept {
  return Value<MksUnit<M, K, S>>(lhs.getMagnitude() + rhs.getMagnitude());
}

template <int M, int K, int S>
constexpr Value<MksUnit<M, K, S>> operator-
  (const Value<MksUnit<M, K, S>>& lhs, const Value<MksUnit<M, K, S>>& rhs) noexcept {
  return Value<MksUnit<M, K, S>>(lhs.getMagnitude() - rhs.getMagnitude());
}

template <int M1, int K1, int S1, int M2, int K2, int S2>
constexpr Value<MksUnit<M1 + M2, K1 + K2, S1 + S2>> operator*
  (const Value<MksUnit<M1, K1, S1>>& lhs, const Value<MksUnit<M2, K2, S2>>& rhs) noexcept {
  return Value<MksUnit<M1 + M2, K1 + K2, S1 + S2>>(lhs.getMagnitude() * rhs.getMagnitude());
}

template <int M1, int K1, int S1, int M2, int K2, int S2>
constexpr Value<MksUnit<M1 - M2, K1 - K2, S1 - S2>> operator/
  (const Value<MksUnit<M1, K1, S1>>& lhs, const Value<MksUnit<M2, K2, S2>>& rhs) noexcept {
  return Value<MksUnit<M1 - M2, K1 - K2, S1 - S2>>(lhs.getMagnitude() / rhs.getMagnitude());
}
```

Now you will be able to write something like this:

```cpp
constexpr Momentum impulseValueForCourseCorrection = Force { 30.0 } * Time { 3.0 };
SpacecraftTrajectoryControl control;
control.applyMomentumToSpacecraftBody(impulseValueForCourseCorrection);
```

That's obviously a significant improvement over a multiplication of two meaningless `double` and assigning its result to another meaningless `double`. It's pretty expressive. And it's safer, because you will not be able to assign the result of the multiplication to something different than a variable of type `Momentum`.

And the best part is this: **the type safety is ensured during compile time!** There is no overhead during runtime, because a C++11 (and higher)-compliant compiler can perform all necessary type compatibility checks.

Let us go one step further. Would it not be very convenient, and intuitive, if we could write something like the following?

```cpp
constexpr Acceleration gravitationalAccelerationOnEarth = 9.80665_ms2;
```

Even that is possible with modern C++. Since C++11 we can provide custom suffixes for literals by defining special functions – so-called *literal operators* – for them:

```cpp
constexpr Force operator"" _N(long double magnitude) {
  return Force(magnitude);
}

constexpr Acceleration operator"" _ms2(long double magnitude) {
  return Acceleration(magnitude);
}

constexpr Time operator"" _s(long double magnitude) {
  return Time(magnitude);
}

constexpr Momentum operator"" _Ns(long double magnitude) {
  return Momentum(magnitude);
}

// ...more literal operators here...
```

USER-DEFINED LITERALS [C++11]

Basically, a literal is a compile-time constant whose value is specified in the source file. Since C++11, developers can produce objects of user-defined types by defining user-defined suffixes for literals. For instance, if a constant should be initialized with a literal of U.S.-$ 145.67, this can be done by writing the following expression:

```cpp
constexpr Money amount = 145.67_USD;
```

In this case, "_USD" is the user-defined suffix for floating-point literals that represent money amounts. So that such a user-defined literal can be used, a function that is known as *literal operator* must be defined:

```cpp
constexpr Money operator"" _USD (const long double amount) {
  return Money(amount);
}
```

Once we've defined user-defined literals for our physical units, we can work with them in the following manner:

```
Force force = 30.0_N;
Time time = 3.0_s;
Momentum momentum = force * time;
```

This notation is not only familiar to physicists and other scientists. It is even safer. With type-rich programming and user-defined literals you are protected against assigning a literal expressing a value of seconds to a variable of type Force.

```
Force force1 = 3.0; // Compile-time error!
Force force2 = 3.0_s; // Compile-time error!
Force force3 = 3.0_N; // Works!
```

It is, of course, also possible to use user-defined literals together with automatic type deduction and/or constant expressions:

```
auto force = 3.0_N;
constexpr auto acceleration = 100.0_ms2;
```

That's pretty convenient and quite elegant, isn't it? So, here is my advice for public interface design:

Create interfaces (APIs) that are strongly typed.

With other words: you should largely avoid general, low-level built-in types, like int, double, or – at worst – void*, in public interfaces respectively APIs. Such non-semantic types are dangerous under certain circumstances, because they can represent just about anything.

Tip There are already some template-based libraries available that provide types for physical quantities, including all SI units. A well-known example is Boost.Units (part of Boost since version 1.36.0; see `http://www.boost.org`).

Know Your Libraries

Have you ever heard of the "Not invented here" (NIH) syndrome? It is an organizational anti-pattern. The NIH syndrome is a derogatory term for a stance in many development organizations that describes the ignoring of existing knowledge or tried-and-tested solutions based on their place of origin. It is a form of "reinventing the wheel," that is, reimplementing something (a library or a framework) that is already available somewhere of pretty high quality. The reasoning behind this attitude is often the belief that in-house developments must be better in several aspects. They are often mistakenly regarded as cheaper, more secure, more flexible, and more controllable than existing and well-established solutions.

In fact, only a few companies succeed in developing a truly equivalent, or even better alternative, to a solution that already exists on the market. Often, the enormous effort of such developments does not justify the low benefit. And not infrequently is the self-developed library or framework clearly worse in quality compared to existing and mature solutions that already exist for years.

Over the past decades, many excellent libraries and frameworks have emerged in the C++ environment. These solutions had the chance to mature over a long time, and have been used successfully in tens of thousands of projects. There is no need to reinvent the wheel. Good software craftspeople should know about these libraries. It is not required to know every tiny detail about these libraries and their APIs. It is just good to know, however, that there are already tried-and-tested solutions for certain fields of application, which are worth looking at to take into a narrower selection for your software development project.

Take Advantage of <algorithm>

If you want to improve the code quality in your organization, replace all your coding guidelines with one goal: No raw loops!

—Sean Parent, Principal software architect with Adobe, at CppCon 2013

Fiddling with collections of elements is everyday activity in programming. Regardless of whether we are dealing with collections of measurement data, with e-mails, strings, records from a database, or other elements, software must filter them, sort them, delete them, manipulate them, and more.

In many programs we can find "raw loops" (e.g., hand-crafted `for`-loops or `while`-loops) for visiting some or all elements in a container, or sequence, in order to do something with them. A simple example is to reverse an order of integers that are stored in a `std::vector` this way:

```cpp
#include <vector>

std::vector<int> integers { 2, 5, 8, 22, 45, 67, 99 };

// ...somewhere in the program:
std::size_t leftIndex = 0;
std::size_t rightIndex = integers.size() - 1;

while (leftIndex < rightIndex) {
  int buffer = integers[rightIndex];
  integers[rightIndex] = integers[leftIndex];
  integers[leftIndex] = buffer;
  ++leftIndex;
  --rightIndex;
}
```

Basically this code will work. But it has several disadvantages. It is difficult to see immediately what this piece of code is doing (in fact, the first three lines inside the while-loop could be substituted by `std::swap` from header `<utility>`). Furthermore, writing code this way is very tedious and error prone. Just imagine that, for any reason, we violate the boundaries of the vector and try to access an element at a position out of range. Unlike member function `std::vector::at()`, `std::vector::operator[]` does not raise a `std::out_of_range` exception then. It will lead to undefined behavior.

The C++ standard library provides more than 100 useful algorithms that can be applied to containers or sequences for searching, counting, and manipulating elements. They are collected in the header `<algorithm>`.

For example, to reverse the order of elements in any kind of Standard Library container, for example, in a `std::vector`, we can simply use `std::reverse`:

```cpp
#include <algorithm>
#include <vector>

std::vector<int> integers = { 2, 5, 8, 22, 45, 67, 99 };
// ...somewhere in the program:
std::reverse(std::begin(integers), std::end(integers));
// The content of 'integers' is now: 99, 67, 45, 22, 8, 5, 2
```

Unlike our self-written solution before, this code is not only much more compact, less error prone, and easier to read. Since `std::reverse` is a function template (like all other algorithms too), it is universally applicable to all Standard Library sequence containers, associative containers, unordered associative containers, `std::string`, and also primitive arrays (which, by the way, should not be used anymore in a modern C++ program; see section "Prefer Standard Library Containers over Simple C-Style Arrays" in Chapter 4).

Listing 5-22. Applying std::reverse to a C-style array and a string

```cpp
#include <algorithm>
#include <string>

// Works, but primitive arrays should not be used in a modern C++ program
int integers[] = { 2, 5, 8, 22, 45, 67, 99 };
std::reverse(std::begin(integers), std::end(integers));

std::string text { "The big brown fox jumps over the lazy dog!" };
std::reverse(std::begin(text), std::end(text));
// Content of 'text' is now: "!god yzal eht revo spmuj xof nworb gib ehT"
```

The reverse algorithm can be applied, of course, also to sub-ranges of a container or sequence:

Listing 5-23. Only a sub-area of the string is reversed

```cpp
std::string text { "The big brown fox jumps over the lazy dog!" };
std::reverse(std::begin(text) + 13, std::end(text) - 9);
// Content of 'text' is now: "The big brown eht revo spmuj xof lazy dog!"
```

Easier Parallelization of Algorithms Since C++17

Your free lunch will soon be over.

—Herb Sutter [Sutter05]

The above quote, which was addressed to software developers all over the world, is taken from an article published by Herb Sutter, member of the ISO C++ standardization committee at that time, in 2005. It was at a time when the clock rates of processors stopped increasing from year to year. In other words, serial-processing speed has reached a physical limit. Instead, processors were increasingly equipped with more cores. This development in processor architectures leads to a heavy consequence: developers can no longer take advantage of ever-increasing processor performance by clock rates – the "free lunch" that Herb was talking about – but they will be forced to develop massively multithreaded programs as a way to better utilize modern multi-core processors. As a result, developers and software architects now need to consider parallelization in their software architecture and design.

Before the advent of C++11, the C++ standard supported only single-threaded programming, and you have to use third-party libraries (e.g., *Boost.Thread*) or compiler extensions (e.g., *Open Multi-Processing* (OpenMP)) to parallelize your programs. Since C++11, the so-called *Thread Support Library* is available to support multithreaded and parallel programming. This extension of the Standard Library has introduced threads, mutual exclusions, condition variables, and futures.

Parallelizing a section of code requires good problem knowledge and must be considered in the software design accordingly. Otherwise, subtle errors caused by race conditions can occur that could be very difficult to debug. Especially for the algorithms of the standard library, which often have to operate on containers that are filled with a huge amount of objects, the parallelization should be simplified for developers in order to exploit today's modern multi-core processors.

Starting with C++17, parts of the Standard Library have been redesigned according to the *Technical Specification for C++ Extensions for Parallelism* (ISO/IEC TS 19570:2015), also known as the *Parallelism TS* (TS = technical specification) in short. In other words, with C++17 these extensions became part of the mainline ISO C++ standard. Their main goal is to relieve developers a bit from the complex task to fiddle around with those low-level language features from the Thread Support Library, such as `std::thread`, `std::mutex`, etc.

In fact that means that 69 well-known algorithms were overloaded and are now also available in one or more versions accepting an extra template parameter for parallelization called `ExecutionPolicy` (see sidebar). Some of these algorithms are, for instance, `std::for_each`, `std::transform`, `std::copy_if`, or `std::sort`. Furthermore, seven new algorithms have been added that can also be parallelized, like `std::reduce`, `std::exclusive_scan` or `std::transform_reduce`. These new algorithms are particularly useful in functional programming, which is why I will discuss them later in Chapter 7.

EXECUTION POLICIES [C++17]

A majority of algorithm templates from header `<algorithm>` have been overloaded and are now also available in a parallelizable version. For example, in addition to the already existing template for the function `std::find`, another version has been defined that takes an additional template parameter to specify the execution policy:

```
// Standard (single-threaded) version:
template< class InputIt, class T >
InputIt find( InputIt first, InputIt last, const T& value );
// Additional version with user-definable execution policy (since C++17):
template< class ExecutionPolicy, class ForwardIt, class T >
ForwardIt find(ExecutionPolicy&& policy, ForwardIt first, ForwardIt last, const T& value);
```

The three standard policy tags that are available for the template parameter `ExecutionPolicy` are:

- `std::execution::seq` – An execution policy type that defines that a parallel algorithm's execution may be sequentially. Hence, it is more or less the same as you would use the single-threaded standard version of the algorithm template function without an execution policy.

- `std::execution::par` – An execution policy type that defines that a parallel algorithm's execution may be parallelized. It permits the implementation to execute the algorithm on multiple threads. **Important:** The parallel algorithms do not automatically protect against critical data races or deadlocks! You are responsible to ensure that no data race conditions can occur while executing the function.

- `std::execution::par_unseq` – An execution policy type that defines that a parallel algorithm's execution may be vectorized and parallelized. Vectorization takes advantage of the SIMD (*Single Instruction, Multiple Data*) command set of modern CPU's. SIMD means that a processor can perform the same operation on multiple data points simultaneously.

Of course, it makes absolutely no sense to sort a small vector with a few elements in parallel. The overhead for thread management would be much higher than the gain on performance. Thus, an execution policy can also be selected dynamically during runtime, for example, by taking the size of the vector into consideration. **Unfortunately, the dynamic execution policy has not yet been accepted for the C++17 standard. It is now planned for the upcoming C++20 standard.**

A full discussion of all available algorithms is way beyond the scope of this book. But after this short introduction to header `<algorithm>` and the new possibilities of parallelization with C++17, let's take a look at a few examples of what can be done with algorithms.

Sorting and Output of a Container

The following example uses two templates from header `<algorithm>`: `std::sort` and `std::for_each`. Internally, `std::sort` is using the quicksort algorithm. By default, the comparisons inside `std::sort` are performed with the `operator<` function of the elements. This means that if you want to sort a sequence of instances of one of your own classes, you have to ensure that `operator<` is properly implemented on that type.

Listing 5-24. Sorting a vector of strings and printing them on stdout

```cpp
#include <algorithm>
#include <iostream>
#include <string>
#include <vector>

void printCommaSeparated(const std::string& text) {
  std::cout << text << ", ";
}

int main() {
  std::vector<std::string> names = { "Peter", "Harry", "Julia", "Marc", "Antonio", "Glenn" };
  std::sort(std::begin(names), std::end(names));
  std::for_each(std::begin(names), std::end(names), printCommaSeparated);
  return 0;
}
```

Comparing Two Sequences

The following example compares two sequences of strings using std::equal.

Listing 5-25. Comparing two sequences of strings

```cpp
#include <algorithm>
#include <iostream>
#include <string>
#include <vector>

int main() {
  const std::vector<std::string> names1 { "Peter", "Harry", "Julia", "Marc", "Antonio",
    "Glenn" };
  const std::vector<std::string> names2 { "Peter", "Harry", "Julia", "John", "Antonio",
    "Glenn" };

  const bool isEqual = std::equal(std::begin(names1), std::end(names1), std::begin(names2),
  std::end(names2));

  if (isEqual) {
    std::cout << "The contents of both sequences are equal.\n";
  } else {
    std::cout << "The contents of both sequences differ.\n";
  }
  return 0;
}
```

Per default, std::equal compares elements using operator==. But you can define "equalness" as you want. The standard comparison can be replaced by a custom comparison operation:

Listing 5-26. Comparing two sequences of strings using a custom predicate function

```cpp
#include <algorithm>
#include <iostream>
#include <string>
#include <vector>

bool compareFirstThreeCharactersOnly(const std::string& string1,
                                     const std::string& string2) {
  return (string1.compare(0, 3, string2, 0, 3) == 0);
}

int main() {
  const std::vector<std::string> names1 { "Peter", "Harry", "Julia", "Marc", "Antonio",
    "Glenn" };
  const std::vector<std::string> names2 { "Peter", "Harold", "Julia", "Maria", "Antonio",
    "Glenn" };
```

```cpp
const bool isEqual = std::equal(std::begin(names1), std::end(names1), std::begin(names2),
  std::end(names2), compareFirstThreeCharactersOnly);

if (isEqual) {
  std::cout << "The first three characters of all strings in both sequences are equal.\n";
} else {
  std::cout << "The first three characters of all strings in both sequences differ.\n";
}
return 0;
}
```

If no reusability is required for the comparison function compareFirstThreeCharactersOnly(), the above line in which the comparison takes place can also be implemented using a lambda expression (We discuss lamda expressions in more detail in Chapter 7), like this:

```cpp
// Compare just the first three characters of every string to ascertain equalness:
const bool isEqual =
  std::equal(std::begin(names1), std::end(names1), std::begin(names2), std::end(names2),
    [](const auto& string1, const auto& string2) {
      return (string1.compare(0, 3, string2, 0, 3) == 0);
  });
```

This alternative may appear more compact, but it does not necessarily contribute to the readability of the code. The explicit function compareFirstThreeCharactersOnly() has a semantic name that expresses very clear **what** is compared (not the How; see section "Use Intention-Revealing Names" in Chapter 4). What exactly is compared cannot necessarily be seen at first sight from the version with the lambda expression. Always keep in mind that the readability of our code should be one of our first goals. Also, always keep in mind that source code comments are basically a code smell and not suitable to explain hard-to-read code (remember the section about Comments in Chapter 4).

Take Advantage of Boost

I can't give a broad introduction into the famous Boost library (http://www.boost.org, distributed under the *Boost Software License*, Version 1.0) here. The library (in fact, it is a library of libraries) is too big and too powerful, and discussing it in detail is beyond the scope of this book. Furthermore, there are numerous good books and tutorials about Boost.

But I think that it is very important to know about this library and its content. Many problems and challenges that C++ developers are facing in their daily work can be pretty well solved with libraries from Boost.

Beyond that, Boost is a kind of "incubator" for several libraries that are sometimes accepted to become part of the C++ language standard, if they have a certain level of maturity. Be careful: that does not necessarily mean that they are fully compatible! For instance, std::thread (part of the standard since C++11) is partially equal to Boost.Thread, but there are some differences. For example, the Boost implementation supports thread cancellation, C++11 threads do not. On the other hand, C++11 supports std::async, but Boost does not.

From my perspective, it is worth it to know the libraries from Boost, and to remember when you have a suitable problem that can be properly solved by them.

More Libraries That You Should Know About

Apart from Standard Library containers, `<algorithm>`, and Boost, there are some more libraries out there that you might take into consideration when writing your code. Here is a – certainly incomplete – list of libraries, which are worth looking at when you are confronted with a certain suitable problem:

- **Date and time utilities** (`<chrono>`): Since C++11, the language provides a collection of types to represent clocks, time points, and durations. For instance, you can represent time intervals with the help of `std::chrono::duration`. And with `std::chrono::system_clock`, a system-wide real time clock is available. You can use the library since C++11 by just including the `<chrono>` header.

- **Regular expressions library** (`<regex>`): Since C++11, a regular expressions library is available that can be used to perform pattern matching within strings. Also the replacement of text within a string based on regular expressions is supported. You can use the library since C++11 by just including the `<regex>` header.

- **Filesystem library** (`<filesystem>`): Since C++17, the Filesystem library has become part of the standard. Before it became part of the mainline C++ standard, it has been a Technical Specification (ISO/IEC TS 18822:2015). The operational system independent library provides various facilities for performing operations on file systems and their components. With the help of `<filesystem>` you can create directories, copy files, iterate over directory entries, retrieve the size of a file, etc. You can use the library since C++17 by just including the `<filesystem>` header.

■ **Tip**   TIf you are currently still not working according to the latest C++17 standard, *Boost.Filesystem* could be an alternative.

- **Range-v3**: A range library for C++11/14/17 written by Eric Niebler, member of the ISO C++ Standardization Committee. Range-v3 is a header-only library that simplifies the dealing with containers of the C++ Standard Library or containers from other libraries (e.g., Boost). With the help of this library you can get rid of the sometimes a bit tricky juggling with iterators in various situations. For instance, instead of writing `std::sort(std::begin(container), std::end(container))`, you can simply write `ranges::sort(container)`.
Range-v3 is available on GitHub, URL: `https://github.com/ericniebler/range-v3`. The documentation can be found here: `https://ericniebler.github.io/range-v3/`.

- **Concurrent Data Structures (libcds)**: A mostly header-only C++ template library written by Max Khizhinsky, providing lock-free algorithms and concurrent data structure implementations for parallel high performance computing. The library is written on C++11 and published under a BSD license. libcds and its documentation can be found on SourceForge, URL: `http://libcds.sourceforge.net`.

Proper Exception and Error Handling

Maybe you have already heard the term *cross-cutting concerns*. This expression includes all those things that are difficult to address through a modularization concept and therefore require special treatment by software architecture and design. One of these typical cross-cutting concerns is *Security*. If you have to take care of Data Security and Access Restrictions in your software system, because it is demanded by certain quality requirements, it is a sensitive topic that pervades the whole system. You have to deal with it nearly everywhere, in virtually every component.

Another cross-cutting concern is *Transaction Handling*. Especially in software applications that use databases, you have to ensure that a so-called Transaction, which is a coherent series of single operations, must succeed or fail as a complete unit; it can never be only partially complete.

And as another example, also *Logging* is a cross-cutting concern. Logging is typically needed everywhere in a software system. Sometimes the domain-specific and productive code is littered with log statements, which is detrimental to the readability and understandability of the code.

If the software architecture did not take care of these cross-cutting concerns, this could lead to inconsistent solutions. For instance, two different logging frameworks could be used in the same project, because two development teams working on the same system decided to choose different frameworks.

The exception and error handling is another cross-cutting concern. Dealing with errors and unpredictable exceptions that require special responses and treatments is mandatory in every software system. And, of course, the system-wide error handling strategies should be uniform and consistent. Hence, it is very important that those people that are responsible for the software's architecture have to design and develop an error-handling strategy quite early in the project.

Well, but what are the principles that guide us in developing a good error handling strategy? When is it justified to throw an exception? How do I deal with thrown exceptions? And for what purposes should exceptions never be used? What are the alternatives?

The following sections present some rules, guidelines, and principles that help C++ programmers to design and implement a good error handling strategy.

Prevention Is Better Than Aftercare

A fundamentally good basic strategy for dealing with errors and exceptions is to generally avoid them. The reason for this is obvious: everything that cannot happen does not have to be treated.

Maybe you will say now: "Well, this is a truism. Of course it is much better to avoid errors or exceptions, but sometimes it is not possible to prevent them." You're right, it sounds banal at first glance. And yes, especially when using third-party libraries, accessing databases, or accessing an external system, unforeseeable things can happen. But for your own code, meaning the things that you can design as you want, you can take appropriate measures to avoid exceptions as far as possible.

David Abrahams, an American programmer, former ISO C++ standardization committee member, and a founding member of Boost C++ Libraries created an understanding of what is called *exception-safety* and presented them in a paper [Abrahams98] in 1998. The set of contractual guidelines formulated in this paper, which are also known as the "Abrahams Guarantees," had a significant influence on the design of the C++ Standard Library and how this library deals with exceptions. But these guidelines are not only relevant for low-level library implementers. They can also be considered by software developers that are writing the application code on higher abstraction levels.

Exception-safety is part of the interface design. An interface (API) does not only consist of function signatures, that is, a function's parameters and return types. Also the exceptions that might be thrown if a function is invoked are part of its interface. Furthermore, there are three more aspects that must be considered:

- **Precondition:** A precondition is a condition that must always be true before a function or a class's method is invoked. If a precondition is violated, no guarantee can be given that the function call leads to the expected result: the function call may succeed, may fail, can cause unwanted side effects, or show undefined behavior.

- **Invariant:** An invariant is a condition that must always be true during the execution of a function or method. In other words, it is a condition that is true at the beginning and at the end of a function's execution. A special form of an invariant in object-orientation is a *class invariant*. If such an invariant is violated, the object (instance) of the class is left behind in an incorrect and inconsistent state after a method call.

- **Postcondition:** A postcondition is a condition that must always be true immediately after the execution of a function or method. If a postcondition is violated, an error must have occurred during execution of the function or method.

The idea behind exception-safety is that functions, or a class and its methods, give their clients a kind of promise, or a guarantee, about invariants, postconditions, and about exceptions that might be thrown or not thrown. There are four levels of exception-safety. In the following subsections I discuss them shortly in increasing order of safety.

No Exception-Safety

With this lowest level of exception-safety – literally, no exception-safety – absolutely nothing is guaranteed. Any occurring exception can have disastrous consequences. For instance, invariants and postconditions of the called function or method are violated, and a portion of your code, for example, an object, is possibly left behind in a corrupted state.

I think that there is no doubt about that the code written by you should **never ever offer this inadequate level of exception-safety!** Just pretend that there is no such thing as "no exception-safety." That's all; there's nothing more to say about that.

Basic Exception-Safety

The *basic exception-safety* guarantee is the guarantee that any piece of code should offer at least. It is also the exception-safety level that can be achieved with relatively little implementation effort. This level guarantees the following:

- If an exception is thrown during a function or method call, it is ensured that no resources are leaked! This guarantee includes memory resources as well as other resources. This can be achieved by applying RAII Pattern (see section about RAII and Smart Pointers).

- If an exception is thrown during a function or method call, all invariants are preserved.

- If an exception is thrown during a function or method call, there will be no corruption of data or memory afterwards, and all objects are in a healthy and consistent state. However, it is **not** guaranteed that the data content is the same as before the function or method has been called.

The strict rule is this:

Design your code, especially your classes, such that they guarantee at least the basic exception-safety. This should always be the default exception-safety level!

It is important to know that the C++ standard library expects all user types to give always at least the basic exception guarantee.

Strong Exception-Safety

The *strong exception-safety* guarantees everything that is also guaranteed by the basic exception-safety level, but ensures additionally that in case of an exception the content of the data is recovered exactly to the same as before the function or method has been called. In other words, with this exception-safety level we get commit or rol lback semantics like in transaction handling on databases.

It is easy to comprehend that this exception-safety level leads to a higher implementation effort and can be costly at runtime. An example of this additional effort is the so-called *copy-and-swap* idiom that must be used to ensure strong exception-safety for copy assignment.

Equipping your whole code with strong exception-safety without any good reasons would violate the principles KISS and YAGNI (see Chapter 3). Hence, the guideline regarding this is the following:

Issue the strong exception-safety guarantee for your code only if it is absolutely required.

Of course, if there are certain quality requirements regarding data integrity and data correctness that have to be satisfied, you have to provide the rollback mechanism that is guaranteed through strong exception-safety.

The No-Throw Guarantee

This is the highest exception-safety level, also known as *failure transparency*. Simply speaking, this level means that as a caller of a function or method you don't have to worry about exceptions. The function or method call will succeed. **Always!** It will never throw an exception, because everything is properly handled internally. There will never be violated invariants and postconditions.

This is the all-round carefree package of exception-safety, but it is sometimes very difficult or even impossible to achieve, especially in C++. For instance, if you use any kind of dynamic memory allocation inside a function, like operator new, either directly or indirectly (e.g., via std::make_shared<T>), you have absolutely no chance anymore to end up with a successfully processed function after an exception was encountered.

Here are the cases where the no-throw guarantee is either absolutely mandatory or at least explicitly advised:

- **Destructors of classes must guarantee to be no-throw under all circumstances!**
  The reason is that, among other situations, destructors are also called while stack unwinding after an exception has been encountered. It would be fatal if another exception would occur during stack unwinding, because the program would terminate immediately.
  As a consequence, any operation inside a destructor that deals with allocated resources and tries to close them, like opened files or allocated memory on the heap, must not throw.

- **Move operations** (move constructors and move assignment operators; see earlier section about move semantics) **should guarantee to be no-throw.** If a move operation throws an exception, the probability is enormously high that the move has not taken place. Hence, it should be avoided at all costs that implementations of move operations allocate resources via resource allocation techniques that can throw exceptions. Furthermore, it is important to give the no-throw guarantee for types that are intended to be used with the C++ standard library containers. If the move constructor for an element type in a container doesn't give a no-throw guarantee (i.e., the move constructor is not declared with the noexcept specifier, see sidebar below), then the container will prefer using the copy operations rather than the move operations.

- **Default constructors should be preferably no-throw.** Basically, throwing an exception in a constructor is not desirable, but it is the best way to deal with constructor failures. A "half-constructed object" does highly likely violate invariants. And an object in a corrupt state that violates its class invariants is useless and dangerous. Therefore, there is nothing speaking against throwing an exception in a default constructor when it is unavoidable. However, it is a good design strategy to largely avoid it. Default constructors should be simple. If a default constructor can throw, it is probably doing too many complex things. Hence, when designing a class, you should try to avoid exceptions in the default constructor.

- **A swap function must guarantee to be no-throw under all circumstances!** An expertly implemented swap() function should not allocate any resources (e.g., memory) using memory allocation techniques that potentially can throw exceptions. It would be fatal if swap() can throw, because it can end up with an inconsistent state. And the best way of writing an exception safe operator=() is by using a non-throwing swap() function for its implementation.

NOEXCEPT SPECIFIER AND OPERATOR [C++11]

Prior C++11, there was the throw keyword that could be in a function's declaration. It was used to list all exception types in a comma-separated list that a function might directly or indirectly throw, known as the *dynamic exception specification*. **The usage of** throw(exceptionType, exceptionType, ...) **is deprecated since C++11 and has now been finally removed from the standard with C++17!** What is still available, but also marked as deprecated since C++11 is the throw() specifier without an exception type list. Its semantics are now the same as the noexcept(true) specifier.

The noexcept specifier in a function's signature declares that the function may not throw any exceptions. The same is valid for noexcept(true), which is just a synonym for noexcept. Instead, a function that is declared with noexcept(false) is potentially throwing, that is, it may throw exceptions. Here are some examples:

```
void nonThrowingFunction() noexcept;
void anotherNonThrowingFunction() noexcept(true);
void aPotentiallyThrowingFunction() noexcept(false);
```

There are two good reasons for the use of noexcept: First, exceptions that a function or method could throw (or not) are parts of the function's interface. It is about semantics, and helps a developer who's reading the code to know what might happen and what not might happen. noexcept tells developers that they can safely use this function in their own non-throwing functions. Hence, the presence of noexcept is somewhat akin to const.

Second, it can be used by the compiler for optimizations. noexcept potentially allows a compiler to compile the function without adding the runtime overhead that was formerly required by the removed throw(...), that is, the object code that was necessary to call std::unexpected() when an exception that was not listed was thrown.

For template implementers there is also a noexcept operator, which performs a compile-time check that returns true if the expression is declared to not throw any exceptions:

```
constexpr auto isNotThrowing = noexcept(nonThrowingFunction());
```

Note: Also constexpr functions (see section "Computations during Compile Time") can throw when evaluated at runtime, so you may also need noexcept for some of those.

An Exception Is an Exception – Literally!

In Chapter 4 we discussed in the section "Do Not Pass or Return 0 (NULL, nullptr)" that you should not return `nullptr` as a return value from a function. As a code example we have had a small function that should perform a lookup for a customer by name, which of course leads to no result if this customer cannot be found. Someone could now come up with the idea that we could throw an exception for a non-found customer, as shown in the following code example.

```cpp
#include "Customer.h"
#include <string>
#include <exception>

class CustomerNotFoundException : public std::exception {
  virtual const char* what() const noexcept override {
    return "Customer not found!";
  }
};

// ...

Customer CustomerService::findCustomerByName(const std::string& name) const noexcept(false)
{
  // Code that searches the customer by name...
  // ...and if the customer could not be found:
  throw CustomerNotFoundException();
}
```

And now let's take a look at the invocation site of this function:

```cpp
Customer customer;
try {
  customer = findCustomerByName("Non-existing name");
} catch (const CustomerNotFoundException& ex) {
  // ...
}
// ...
```

At first sight, this seems to look like a feasible solution. If we have to avoid returning `nullptr` from the function, we can throw a `CustomerNotFoundException` instead. At the invocation site we are now able to distinguish between the happy case and the bad case with the help of a `try-catch`-construct.

In fact, it is a really bad solution! Not finding a customer just because its name does not exist is definitely no exceptional case. These are things that will happen normally. What has been done in the above example is an abuse of exceptions. Exceptions are not there to control the normal program flow. **Exceptions should be reserved for what's truly exceptional!**

What does "truly exceptional" mean? Well, it means that there is nothing you can do about it, and you cannot really handle that exception. For instance, let's assume that you are confronted with a `std::bad_alloc` exception, which means that there was a failure to allocate memory. How should the program continue now? What was the root cause for this problem? Has the underlying hardware system a lack of memory? Well, then we have a really serious problem! Is there any meaningful way to recover from this serious exception and resume the program's execution? Can we still take responsibility for that the program simply continues running as if nothing had happened?

These questions cannot be answered easily. Perhaps the real trigger for this problem was a dangling pointer, which has been used inexpertly millions of instructions before we've encountered the `std::bad_alloc` exception. All of this can seldom be reproduced at the time of the exception.

Here is my advice:

Throw exceptions only in very exceptional cases. Do not misuse exceptions to control the normal program flow.

Maybe you will ask yourself now: "Well, it is bad to use `nullptr` respectively NULL as a return value, and exceptions are also undesired … what should I do now instead?" In section "Special Case Object (Null Object)" in Chapter 9 about Design Patterns, I will present a feasible solution to handle these cases in a proper way.

If You Can't Recover, Get Out Quickly

If you are confronted with an exception from which you cannot recover, it is often the best approach to log the exception (if possible), or to generate a crash dump file for later analyzing purposes, and to terminate the program immediately. A good example where a quick termination can be the best reaction is a failed memory allocation. If a system is lack of memory, well, what should you do then in the context of your program?

The principle behind this strict handling strategy for some critical exceptions and errors is called "Dead Programs Tell No Lies" and is described in the book *Pragmatic Programmer* [Hunt99].

Nothing is worse than to continue after a serious error as if nothing had happened, and to produce, for example, tens of thousands of erroneous bookings, or to send the lift for the hundredth time from the cellar to the top floor and back. Instead, get out before too much consequential damage occurs.

Define User-Specific Exception Types

Although you can throw whatever you want in C++, like an `int` or a `const char*`, I would not recommend it. Exceptions are caught by its types; hence it is a very good idea to create your custom exception classes for certain, mostly domain-specific, exceptions. As I've already explained in Chapter 4, a good naming is crucial for the readability and the maintainability of the code, and also exception types should have good names. And also further principles, which are valid for designing of the "normal" program code, are of course also valid for exception types (we will discuss these principles in detail in the Chapter 6 about object-orientation).

To provide your own exception type, you can simply create your own class and derive it from `std::exception` (defined in header `<stdexcept>`):

```cpp
#include <stdexcept>

class MyCustomException : public std::exception {
  virtual const char* what() const noexcept override {
    return "Provide some details about what was going wrong here!";
  }
};
```

By overriding the virtual what() member function inherited from std::exception, we can provide some information to the caller about what went wrong. Furthermore, deriving our own exception class from std::exception will make it catchable by a generic catch-clause (which, by the way, should only be regarded as the very last possibility to catch an exception), like this one:

```cpp
#include <iostream>

// ...
try {
  doSomethingThatThrows();
} catch (const std::exception& ex) {
  std::cerr << ex.what() << std::endl;
}
```

Basically, exception classes should have a simple design, but if you want to provide more details about the cause of the exception, you can also write more sophisticated classes, like the following:

Listing 5-27. A custom exception class for divisions by zero

```cpp
class DivisionByZeroException : public std::exception {
public:
  DivisionByZeroException() = delete;
  explicit DivisionByZeroException(const int dividend) {
    buildErrorMessage(dividend);
  }

  virtual const char* what() const noexcept override {
    return errorMessage.c_str();
  }

private:
  void buildErrorMessage(const int dividend) {
    errorMessage = "A division with dividend = ";
    errorMessage += std::to0_string(dividend);
    errorMessage += ", and divisor = 0, is not allowed (Division by Zero)!";
  }

  std::string errorMessage;
};
```

Please note, that due to its implementation, the private member function buildErrorMessage() can only guarantee strong exception-safety, that is, it may throw due to the use of std::string::operator+=()! Hence, also the initialization constructor cannot give the no-throw guarantee. That's the reason why exception classes generally should have a pretty simple design.

Here is a small usage example of our DivisionByZeroException class:

```cpp
int divide(const int dividend, const int divisor) {
  if (divisor == 0) {
    throw DivisionByZeroException(dividend);
  }
  return dividend / divisor;
}
```

```cpp
int main() {
  try {
    divide(10, 0);
  } catch (const DivisionByZeroException& ex) {
    std::cerr << ex.what() << std::endl;
    return 1;
  }
  return 0;
}
```

Throw by Value, Catch by const Reference

Sometimes I've seen that exception objects are allocated on the heap with the help of new, and thrown as a pointer, like in this example:

```cpp
try
{
  CFile f(_T("M_Cause_File.dat"), CFile::modeWrite);
  // If "M_Cause_File.dat" does not exist, the constructor of CFile throws an exception
  // this way: throw new CFileException()
}
catch(CFileException* e)
{
  if( e->m_cause == CFileException::fileNotFound)
    TRACE(_T("ERROR: File not found\n"));
  e->Delete();
}
```

Perhaps you have recognized this C++ coding style: throwing and catching of exceptions in this manner can be found in the good old MFC (Microsoft Foundation Classes) library galore. And it is important that you don't forget to call the Delete() member function at the end of the catch-clause; otherwise you can say "Hello!" to memory leaks.

Well, throwing exceptions with new and catching them as a pointer is possible in C++, but it is bad design. **Don't do it!** If you forget to delete the exception object, it will result in a memory leak. Throw always the exception object by value, and catch them by const reference, as it can be seen in all the examples before.

Pay Attention to the Correct Order of Catch-Clauses

If you provide more than one catch-clause after a try block, for example to distinguish between different types of exceptions, it is important that you take care about the correct order. Catch-clauses are evaluated in the order they appear. This means that the catch-clauses for the more specific exception types must come first. In the following example, exception classes DivisionByZeroException and CommunicationInterruptedException are both derived from std::exception.

Listing 5-28. The more specific exceptions must be handled first

```cpp
try {
  doSomethingThatCanThrowSeveralExceptions();
} catch (const DivisionByZeroException& ex) {
  // ...
} catch (const CommunicationInterruptedException& ex) {
  // ...
} catch (const std::exception& ex) {
  // Handle all other exceptions here that are derived from std::exception
} catch (...) {
  // The rest...
}
```

The reason is obvious, I think: let's assume that the catch-clause for the general std::exception would be the first one, what would happen? The more specific ones below would never get a chance because they are "hidden" by the more general one. Therefore, developers must pay attention to put them in the correct order.

CHAPTER 6

Object Orientation

The historical roots of object orientation (OO) can be found in the late 1950s. The Norwegian computer scientists Kristen Nygaard and Ole-Johan Dahl carried out simulation calculations for the development and construction of Norway's first nuclear reactor at the military research institute *Norwegian Defense Research Establishment* (NDRE). While developing the simulation programs, the two scientists noted that the procedural programming languages used for that task were not well suited for the complexity of the problems to be addressed. Dahl and Nygaard felt the need for suitable possibilities in those languages to abstract and reproduce the structures, concepts, and processes of the real world.

In 1960, Nygaard moved to the *Norwegian Computing Center* (NCC) that had been established in Oslo two years before. Three years later, Ole-Johan Dahl also joined the NCC. At this private, independent, and nonprofit research foundation, the two scientists developed first ideas and concepts for an – from today's point of view – object-oriented programming language. Nygaard and Dahl were looking for a language that is suitable for all domains and less specialized for certain fields of application, like, for instance, *Fortran* for numeric computations and linear algebra; or *COBOL,* which is designed especially for business use.

The result of their research activities was finally the programming language *Simula-67*, an extension of the procedural programming language *ALGOL 60*. The new language introduced classes, subclassing, objects, instance variables, virtual methods, and even a garbage collector. Simula-67 is considered the first object-oriented programming language and has influenced many other of the following programming languages, for example, the full object-oriented programming language Smalltalk, which was designed by Alan Kay and his team in the early 1970s.

While the Danish computer scientist Bjarne Stroustrup worked on his PhD thesis *Communication and Control in Distributed Computer Systems* at University of Cambridge in late 1970, he used Simula-67 and found it pretty useful, but far too slow for practical use. So he began to search for possibilities to combine the object-oriented concepts of data abstraction from Simula-67 with the high efficiency of low-level programming languages. The most efficient programming language at that time was C, which had been developed by the American computer scientist Dennis Ritchie at *Bell Telephone Laboratories* in the early 1970s. Stroustrup, who joined the *Computer Science Research Center* of the *Bell Telephone Laboratories* in 1979, began to add object-oriented features, like classes, inheritance, strong type checking, and many other things to the C language and named it "C with Classes." In 1983, the name of the language was changed to C++, a word creation by Stroustrups associate Rick Mascitti, whereby the ++ was inspired by the post-increment operator of the language.

In the following decades, object orientation became the dominant programming paradigm.

Object-Oriented Thinking

There is a very important point that we need to bear in mind. Just because there are several programming languages available on the market supporting object-oriented concepts, there is absolutely no guarantee that developers using these languages will produce an object-oriented software design automatically. Especially

© Stephan Roth 2017
S. Roth, *Clean C++*, DOI 10.1007/978-1-4842-2793-0_6

those developers who have worked with procedural languages for a long time often have difficulties with the transition to that programming paradigm. Object orientation is not a simple concept to grasp. It requires that developers view the world in a new way.

Dr. Alan Curtis Kay, who developed object-oriented programming language Smalltalk with some colleagues at *Xerox PARC* in the early 1970s, is well known as one of the fathers of the term "object orientation." In a documented discussion via E-Mail with the German university lecturer Dipl.-Ing. Stefan Ram from *Freie Universität Berlin* from the year 2003, Kay explained what makes object orientation for him:

> *I thought of objects being like biological cells and/or individual computers on a network, only able to communicate with messages (so messaging came at the very beginning – it took a while to see how to do messaging in a programming language efficiently enough to be useful). (...) OOP to me means only messaging, local retention and protection and hiding of state-process, and extreme late-binding of all things.*

> —Dr. Alan Curtis Kay, American computer scientist, July 23, 2003 [Ram03]

A biological cell can be defined as the smallest structural and functional unit of all organisms. They are often called the "building blocks of life." Alan Kay considered software in the same way a biologist sees complex, living organisms. This perspective of Alan Kay should not be surprising, because he has a bachelor's degree in mathematics and molecular biology.

Alan Kay's cells are what we call objects in OO. An object can be considered a "thing" that has structure and behavior. A biological cell has a membrane that surrounds and encapsulates it. This can also be applied to objects in object orientation. An object should be well encapsulated and offers its services through well-defined interfaces.

In addition, Alan Kay emphasized that "messaging" plays a central role for him in object orientation. However, he does not define exactly what he means by that. Is calling a method named foo() on an object the same as sending a message named "foo" to that object? Or had Alan Kay a message passing infrastructure in mind, such as *CORBA* (Common Object Request Broker Architecture) and similar technologies? Dr. Kay is also a mathematician, so he could also mean a prominent mathematical model of message passing named *Actor model*, which is very popular in concurrent computation.

In any case and whatever Alan Kay had in mind when he talked about messaging, I consider this view interesting and, by and large, applicable to explain the typical structure of an object-oriented program on an abstract level. But Mr. Kay's elucidations are definitely not sufficient enough to answer the following important questions:

- How do I find and form the "cells" (objects)?

- How do I design the public available interface of those cells?

- How do I govern who can communicate with whom (dependencies)?

Object orientation (OO) is primarily a mindset, and less a matter of the language used. And it can also be abused and misapplied.

I've seen many programs written in C++, or in a pure OO-language like Java, where classes are used, but these classes only have constituted large namespaces wrapping a procedural program. Or slightly sarcastically expressed: Fortran-like programs can be written in nearly any programming language, obviously. On the other hand, every developer who has internalized object-oriented thinking will be able to develop software with an object-oriented design even in languages like ANSI-C, Assembler, or using shell scripts.

Abstraction – the Key to Master Complexity

The basic idea behind OO is that we are modeling things and concepts from relevant parts of our domain in our software. Thereby we confine ourselves only to those things that must be represented in our software system to satisfy stakeholder needs, also known as requirements. The abstraction is the most important tool to model these things and concepts in an appropriate manner. We do not want to model a reproduction of the entire real world. We only need an excerpt from the real world, reduced to the details that are relevant to realize the system's use cases.

For instance, if we want to represent a customer in a bookstore system, it is highly probable and of absolutely no interest which blood group a customer has. On the other hand, for a software system from the medical domain, the blood group of a human can be an important detail.

For me, object orientation is all about data abstraction, responsibilities, modularization, and also about divide and conquer. If I have to boil it down, I would say that OO is about **the mastery of complexity**. Let me explain with a small example.

Consider a car. A car is a composition of several parts, for example, body, engine, gears, wheels, seats, etc. Each of these parts itself consists also of smaller parts. Take for instance the car's engine (let's assume that it is a combustion engine, and not an electric motor). The engine consists of the cylinder block, the gasoline ignition pump, the driving shaft, the cam shaft, pistons, an engine control unit (ECU), a coolant subsystem, etc. The coolant subsystem again consists of a heat exchanger, coolant pump, coolant reservoir, fan, thermostat, and the heater core. The decomposition of the car can theoretically be continued to the smallest screw. And every identified subsystem or part has a well-defined responsibility. But only all parts together, and assembled in the right way, build a car that provides the services that drivers expect.

Complex software systems can be considered in the same way. They can be decomposed hierarchically into coarse to-fine-grained modules. That helps to cope with the system's complexity, provides more flexibility, and fosters reusability, maintainability, and testability. Guiding principles for doing this decomposition are mainly the following:

- Information hiding (see the eponymous section in Chapter 3),

- Strong cohesion (see the eponymous section in Chapter 3),

- Loose coupling (see the eponymous section in Chapter 3), and

- Single Responsibility Principle (SRP; see the eponymous section later in this chapter).

Principles for Good Class Design

The widespread and well-known mechanism for the formation of the previously described modules in object-oriented languages is the concept of a class. Classes are considered as encapsulated software modules that combine structural features (synonyms: attributes, data members, fields) and behavioral features (synonyms: member functions, methods, operations) together into one cohesive unit.

In programming languages with object-oriented facilities like C++, classes are the next higher structuring concept above functions. They are often described as the blueprints of the objects (synonym: instances). That's reason enough to investigate the concept of classes further. In this chapter I give several important clues for designing and writing good classes in C++.

Keep Classes Small

In my career as a software developer, I have seen many classes that were very large. Many thousands of lines of code were no rarity. On closer inspection I've noticed that these large classes often were only used as namespaces for a more or less procedural program, whose developers commonly did not understand object orientation.

I think that the problems with such large classes are obvious. If classes contain several thousand lines of code, they are difficult to understand, and their maintainability and testability is usually bad, not to mention reusability. And according to several studies, large classes generally contain a higher number of defects.

THE GOD CLASS ANTI-PATTERN

In many systems, there are exceptionally large classes with many attributes and several hundred operations. The names of these classes often end with "…Controller," "…Manager," or "…Helpers." Developers often argue that somewhere in the system must be one central instance that pulls the strings and coordinates everything. The results of this way of thinking are such giant classes with very poor cohesion (see section about strong cohesion in Chapter 3). They are like a convenience store that offers a colorful palette of goods.

Such classes are called *God Classes*, *God Objects*, or sometimes also *The Blob* (*The Blob* is a 1958 American horror/science-fiction film about an alien amoeba that eats the citizens of a village). This is a so-called Anti-Pattern, a synonym for what is perceived as bad design. A God Class is an untamable beast, horrible to maintain, difficult to understand, not testable, error prone, and has also a huge amount of dependencies to other classes. During the life cycle of the system, such classes are getting bigger and bigger. This makes the problems worse.

What has been proven as a good rule for a function's size (see section "Let Them be Small" in Chapter 4), which seems to be also good advice for the size of classes: **Classes should be small!**

If small size is an objective in class design, then the immediate next question is this: How small?

For functions, I've given a number of lines of code in Chapter 4. Wouldn't it be even possible to define a number of lines for classes that would be perceived as good, or proper?

In *The ThoughtWorks® Anthology* [ThoughtWorks08], Jeff Bay contributed an essay entitled "Object Calisthenics: 9 steps to better software design today" that advises no more than 50 lines of code for a single class.

An upper limit of about 50 lines seems to be out of the question for many developers. It appears that they feel a kind of unexplainable resistance against the creation of classes. They often argue as follows: "Not more than 50 lines? But that will result in a huge amount of tiny little classes, with just a few members and functions." And then they will surely conjure up an example that is irreducible to classes of such a small size.

I'm convinced that those developers are totally wrong. I'm pretty sure that every software system can be decomposed into such small elementary building blocks.

Yes, if classes are to be small, you will have more of them. But that's OO! In object-oriented software development, a class is an equally natural language element such as a function, or a variable. In other words: Do not be afraid to create small classes. Small classes are much easier to use, to understand, and to test.

Nonetheless, that leads to a fundamental question: Is the definition of an upper limit for lines of code basically the right way? I think that the metric of lines of code (LOC) can be a helpful indicator. Too many LOC's are a smell. You can take a careful look at classes with more than 50 lines. But it is not necessarily the case that many lines of code are always a problem. A much better criterion is the amount of responsibilities of a class.

Single Responsibility Principle (SRP)

The *Single Responsibility Principle* (SRP) states that each software unit – and these include, among others, components, classes, and functions – should have only one single and well-defined responsibility.

SRP is based on the general principle of cohesion that I've discussed in Chapter 3. If a class has a well-defined responsibility, normally as well its cohesion is strong.

But what exactly is a responsibility? In literature we can often find the explanation that there must only be one reason to change the class. And a frequently mentioned example is that this rule is violated when the class needs to be changed due to new or changed requirements for different aspects of the system.

These aspects can be, for example, device driver and UI. If the same class must be changed, either because the interface of the device driver has changed, or a new requirement regarding the graphical user interface has to be implemented, then this class has obviously too many responsibilities.

Another type of aspects relates to the system's domain. If the same class must be changed, either because there are new requirements regarding the customer management, or there are new requirements regarding the invoicing, then this class has too many responsibilities.

Classes that follow the SRP are usually small and have few dependencies. They are clear, easy to understand, and can be tested easily.

Responsibility is a much better criterion than the amount of lines of code of a class. There can be classes with 100, 200, or even 500 lines, and it can be perfectly OK if those classes do not violate the Single Responsibility Principle. Nonetheless, a high LOC count can be an indicator. It is a clue that says: "You should take a look on these classes! Maybe everything is fine, but maybe they are so big because they have too many responsibilities."

Open-Closed Principle (OCP)

All systems change during their life cycles. This must be borne in mind when developing systems expected to last longer than the first version.

—Ivar Jacobson, Swedish computer scientist, 1992

Another important guideline for any kind of software unit, but especially for class design, is the *Open-Closed Principle* (OCP). It states that software entities (modules, classes, functions, etc.) should be open for extension, but closed for modification.

It is a simple fact that software systems will evolve over time. Constantly new requirements must be satisfied, and existing requirements must be changed according to customer needs or technology progress. These extensions should be made not only in an elegant manner and with as little effort as possible. They should be especially made in such a way that existing code does not need to be changed. It would be fatal if any new requirement would lead to a cascade of changes and adjustments in existing and well-tested parts of the software.

One way to support this principle in object orientation is the concept of inheritance. With inheritance it is possible to add new functionality to a class without modifying that class. Furthermore there are many object-oriented design patterns that are fostering OCP, such as Strategy, or Decorator (see Chapter 9 about Design Patterns).

In the section about Loose Coupling in Chapter 3 we have already discussed a design that supports OCP very well (see Figure 3-6). There we have de-coupled a switch and a lamp through an interface. Through this step, the design is closed against modification but pleasantly open for extensions. We can add more switchable devices easily, and we don't need to touch classes Switch, Lamp, and the interface Switchable. And as you can imagine easily, another advantage of such design is that it is very easy now to provide a Test Double (e.g., a mock object) for testing purposes (see section about Test Doubles (Fake Objects) in Chapter 2).

Liskov Substitution Principle (LSP)

Basically the Liskov Substitution Principle states that you cannot create an octopus by extending a dog with four additional fake legs.

—Mario Fusco (@mariofusco), September 15, 2013, on Twitter

The object-oriented key concepts of inheritance and polymorphism seem relatively simple at first glance. Inheritance is a taxonomical concept that should be used to build a specialization hierarchy of types, that is, subtypes are derived from a more general type. Polymorphism means in general, that one single interface is provided as an access possibility to objects of different types.

So far, so good. But sometimes you get into situations where a subtype does not really wants to fit into a type hierarchy. Let us discuss a very popular example that is often used to illustrate the problem.

The Square-Rectangle Dilemma

Suppose that we are developing a class library with primitive types of shapes for drawing on a canvas, for example, a `Circle`, a `Rectangle`, a `Triangle`, and a `TextLabel`. Visualized as an UML class diagram, this library might look like Figure 6-1.

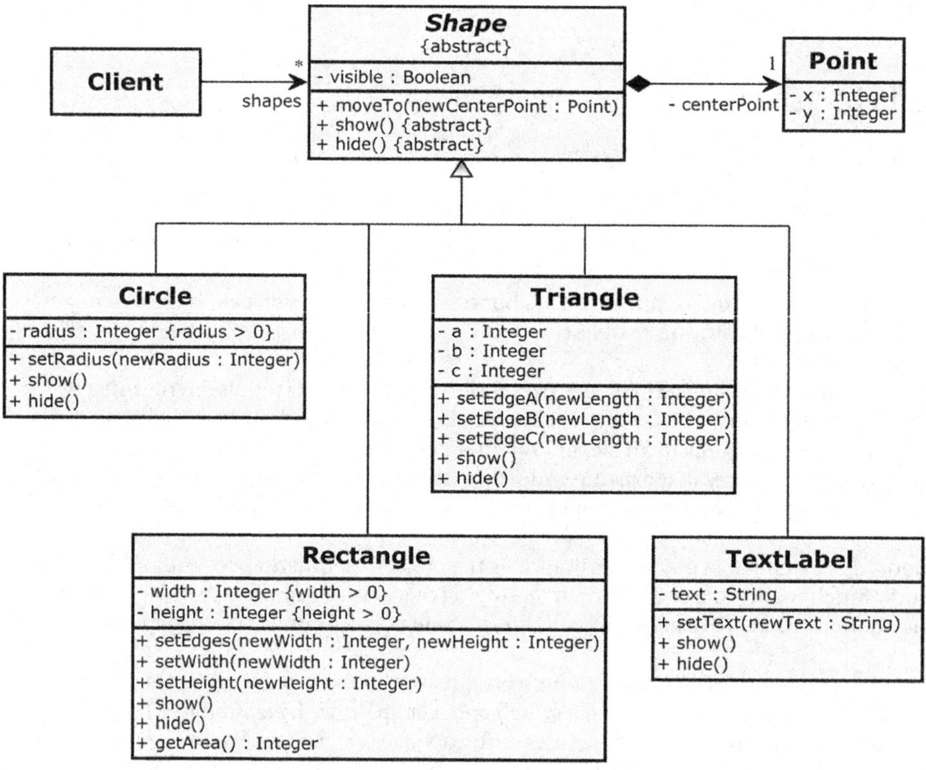

Figure 6-1. *A class library of different shapes*

138

The abstract base class Shape has attributes and operations that are the same for all specific shapes. For example, it is the same for all shapes how they can be moved from one position to another position on the canvas. However, the Shape cannot know how specific shapes can be shown (synonym: drawn) or hidden (synonym: erased). Therefore these operations are abstract, that is, they cannot be (fully) implemented in Shape.

In C++, an implementation of the abstract class Shape (and the class Point that is required by Shape) might look like this:

Listing 6-1. This is what the two classes Point and Shape look like

```cpp
class Point final {
public:
  Point() : x { 5 }, y { 5 } { }
  Point(const unsigned int initialX, const unsigned int initialY) :
    x { initialX }, y { initialY } { }
  void setCoordinates(const unsigned int newX, const unsigned int newY) {
    x = newX;
    y = newY;
  }
  // ...more member functions here...

private:
  unsigned int x;
  unsigned int y;
};

class Shape {
public:
  Shape() : isVisible { false } { }
  virtual ~Shape() = default;
  void moveTo(const Point& newCenterPoint) {
    hide();
    centerPoint = newCenterPoint;
    show();
  }
  virtual void show() = 0;
  virtual void hide() = 0;
  // ...

private:
  Point centerPoint;
  bool isVisible;
};

void Shape::show() {
  isVisible = true;
}

void Shape::hide() {
  isVisible = false;
}
```

FINAL SPECIFIER [C++11]

The `final` specifier, available since C++11, can be used in two ways.

On the one hand, you can use this specifier to avoid individual virtual member functions being overridden in derived classes, like in this example:

```cpp
class AbstractBaseClass {
public:
  virtual void doSomething() = 0;
};

class Derived1 : public AbstractBaseClass {
public:
  virtual void doSomething() final {
    //...
  }
};

class Derived2 : public Derived1 {
public:
  virtual void doSomething() override { // Causes a compiler error!
    //...
  }
};
```

In addition, you can also mark a complete class as `final`, like the class `Point` in our Shape library. This ensures that a developer cannot use such a class as a base class for inheritance.

```cpp
class NotDerivable final {
  // ...
};
```

Of all concrete classes from the Shapes library we can take an exemplary look into one class, the `Rectangle`:

Listing 6-2. The important parts of class Rectangle

```cpp
class Rectangle : public Shape {
public:
  Rectangle() : width { 2 }, height { 1 } { }
  Rectangle(const unsigned int initialWidth, const unsigned int initialHeight) :
    width { initialWidth }, height { initialHeight } { }

  virtual void show() override {
    Shape::show();
    // ...code to show a rectangle here...
  }
```

```cpp
  virtual void hide() override {
    Shape::hide();
    // ...code to hide a rectangle here...
  }

  void setWidth(const unsigned int newWidth) {
    width = newWidth;
  }

  void setHeight(const unsigned int newHeight) {
    height = newHeight;
  }

  void setEdges(const unsigned int newWidth, const unsigned int newHeight) {
    width = newWidth;
    height = newHeight;
  }

  unsigned long long getArea() const {
    return static_cast<unsigned long long>(width) * height;
  }
  // ...

private:
  unsigned int width;
  unsigned int height;
};
```

The client code wants to use all shapes in a similar fashion, no matter which particular instance (Rectangle, Circle, etc.) it is confronted with. For instance, all shapes should be shown on a canvas at one blow, which can be achieved using the following code:

```cpp
#include "Shapes.h" // Circle, Rectangle, etc.
#include <memory>
#include <vector>

using ShapePtr = std::shared_ptr<Shape>;
using ShapeCollection = std::vector<ShapePtr>;

void showAllShapes(const ShapeCollection& shapes) {
  for (auto& shape : shapes) {
    shape->show();
  }
}

int main() {

  ShapeCollection shapes;
  shapes.push_back(std::make_shared<Circle>());
  shapes.push_back(std::make_shared<Rectangle>());
  shapes.push_back(std::make_shared<TextLabel>());
```

```
// ...etc...

showAllShapes(shapes);
  return 0;
}
```

And now let's assume that users formulate a new requirement for our library: **they want to have a square!**

Probably everyone is immediately reminded of his geometry lessons in elementary school. At that time also your teacher maybe has said that a square is a special kind of rectangle that has four sides of equal length and four equal angles (90-degree angles). Thus, a first obvious solution seems to be that we derive a new class Square from Rectangle, as depicted in Figure 6-2.

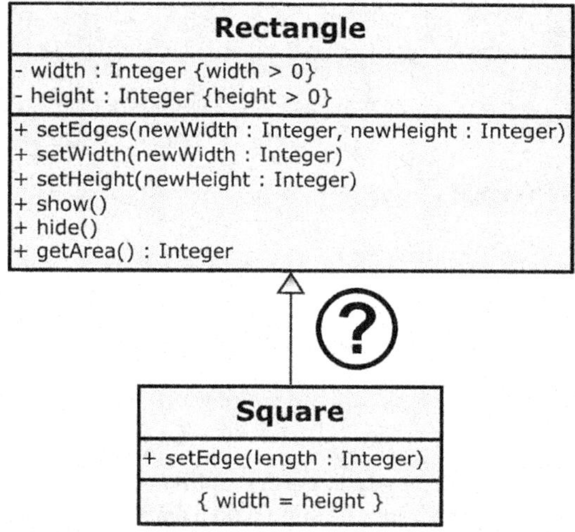

Figure 6-2. Deriving a Square from class Rectangle – a good idea?

At first glance, this seems to be a feasible solution. The Square inherits the interface and the implementation of Rectangle. This is good to avoid code duplication (see the DRY principle we've discussed in Chapter 3), because the Square can easily reuse the behavior that is implemented in Rectangle.

And a square just has to fulfill one additional and simple requirement that is shown in the UML diagram above as a constraint in class Square: {width = height}. This constraint means that an instance of type Square ensures in all circumstances that its edges are always of the same length.

And so we first implement our Square by deriving it from our Rectangle:

```
class Square : public Rectangle {
public:
  //...
};
```

But in fact, it is not a good solution!

Please note that the Square inherits all operations of the Rectangle. That means that we can do the following with an instance of Square:

```cpp
Square square;
square.setHeight(10);    // Err...changing only the height of a square?!
square.setEdges(10, 20); // Uh oh!
```

First of all it would be very puzzling for users of Square that it provides a setter with two parameters (remember Principle of Least Astonishment in Chapter 3). They think: Why are there two parameters? Which parameter is used to set the length of all edges? Must I maybe put both parameters to the same value? What happens if I don't?

The situation is even more dramatic when we do the following:

```cpp
std::unique_ptr<Rectangle> rectangle = std::make_unique<Square>();
// ...and somewhere else in the code...
rectangle->setEdges(10, 20);
```

In this case, the client code uses a setter that makes sense. Both edges of a rectangle can be manipulated independently. That's not a surprise; it's exactly the expectation. However, the result may be weird. The instance of type Square would de facto not be a square after such a call anymore, because it has two different edge lengths. So we have once again committed a violation of the Principle of Least Astonishment, and much worse: violated the Square's class invariant.

However, one could now argue that we can declare setEdges(), setWidth(), and setHeight() as virtual in class Rectangle and override these member functions in class Square with an alternative implementation, which throws an exception in case of unsolicited use. Furthermore, we provide a new member function setEdge() in class Square instead, as follows:

Listing 6-3. A really bad implementation of Square that tries to "erase" unwanted inherited features

```cpp
#include <stdexcept>
// ...

class IllegalOperationCall : public std::logic_error
{
public:
explicit IllegalOperationCall(const std::string& message) : logic_error(message) { }
virtual ~IllegalOperationCall() { }
};

class Square : public Rectangle {
public:
Square() : Rectangle { 5, 5 } { }
explicit Square(const unsigned int edgeLength) : Rectangle { edgeLength, edgeLength } { }

virtual void setEdges([[maybe_unused]] const unsigned int newWidth,
                      [[maybe_unused]] const unsigned int newHeight) override {
  throw IllegalOperationCall { ILLEGAL_OPERATION_MSG };
}

virtual void setWidth([[maybe_unused]] const unsigned int newWidth) override {
  throw IllegalOperationCall { ILLEGAL_OPERATION_MSG };
}
```

```cpp
virtual void setHeight([[maybe_unused]] const unsigned int newHeight) override {
  throw IllegalOperationCall { ILLEGAL_OPERATION_MSG };
}

void setEdge(const unsigned int length) {
  Rectangle::setEdges(length, length);
}

private:
static const constexpr char* const ILLEGAL_OPERATION_MSG { "Unsolicited call of a
prohibited "
    "operation on an instance of class Square!" };
};
```

Well, I think it's obvious that that would be a terribly bad design. It violates a fundamental principle of object orientation, that a derived class must not delete inherited properties of their base class. It is definitely not a solution to our problem. First, the new setter setEdge() would not be visible if we want to use an instance of Square as a Rectangle. Furthermore, all the other setters throw an exception if they are used – this is really abysmal! It ruined object orientation.

So, what's the fundamental problem here? Why does the obviously sensible derivation of a class Square from a Rectangle cause so many difficulties?

The explanation is this: Deriving Square from Rectangle violates an important principle in object-oriented software design – the **Liskov Substitution Principle** (LSP)!

Barbara Liskov, an American computer scientist who is an institute professor at the *Massachusetts Institute of Technology* (MIT), and Jeannette Wing, who was the President's Professor of Computer Science at *Carnegie Mellon University* until 2013, formulated the principle in a 1994 paper as follows:

> *Let q(x) be a property provable about objects x of type T. Then q(y) should be provable for objects y of type S, where S is a subtype of T.*
>
> —Barbara Liskov, Jeanette Wing [Liskov94]

Well, that's not necessarily a definition for everyday use. Robert C. Martin formulated this principle in an article in 1996 as follows:

> *Functions that use pointers or references to base classes must be able to use objects of derived classes without knowing it.*
>
> —Robert C. Martin [Martin96]

In fact that means the following: Derived types must be completely substitutable for their base types. In our example this is not possible. An instance of type Square cannot substitute a Rectangle. The reason for that lies in the constraint {width = height} (a so-called class invariant) that would be enforced by the Square, but the Rectangle cannot fulfill that constraint.

The Liskov Substitution Principle stipulates the following rules for type respectively class hierarchies:

- The preconditions (see also section "Prevention Is Better Than Aftercare" in Chapter 5 about preconditions) of a base class cannot be strengthened in a derived subclass.

- Postconditions (see also section "Prevention Is Better Than Aftercare" in Chapter 5) of a base class cannot be weakened in a derived subclass.

- All invariants of a base class must not be changed or violated through a derived subclass.

- The History constraint (a.k.a. the "History rule"): The (internal) state of objects should only be changed by method calls at their public interface (encapsulation). Since derived classes may introduce new attributes and methods that do not exist in the base class, the introduction of these methods may allow state changes in objects of the derived class that are not allowed in the base class. The so-called History constraint prohibits this. For instance, if the base class is designed to be the blueprint for an immutable object (see Chapter 9 about immutable classes), the derived class should not invalidate this property of immutability with the help of newly introduced member functions.

The interpretation of the generalization relationship (the arrow between Square and Rectangle) in the class diagram above (Figure 6-2) is often translated with "...IS A...": Square IS A Rectangle. But that could be misleading. In Mathematics it may be possible to say that a square is a special kind of rectangle, but in programming it is not!

To deal with this problem, the client has to know with which specific type he's working. Some developers might now say, "No problem, this can be done by using *Run-Time Type Information* (RTTI)."

RUN-TIME TYPE INFORMATION (RTTI)

The term Run-Time Type Information (sometimes also Run-Time Type Identification) denotes a C++ mechanism to access information about an object's data type at runtime. The general concept behind RTTI is called *type introspection* and is available also in other programming languages, like Java.

In C++, the typeid operator (defined in header <typeinfo>) and dynamic_cast<T> (see section about C++ casts in Chapter 4) belong to RTTI. For instance, to determine the class of an object at runtime, you can write:

```cpp
const std::type_info& typeInformationAboutObject = typeid(instance);
```

The const reference of type std::type_info (also defined in header <typeinfo>) now holds information about the object's class, for example, the class's name. Since C++11, a hash code is also available (std::type_info::hash_code()), which is identical for the std::type_info objects referring to the same type.

It is important to know that RTTI is available only for classes that are polymorphic, that is, for classes that have at least one virtual function, either directly or through inheritance. In addition, RTTI can be turned on or off on some compilers. For example, when using the gcc (GNU Compiler Collection), RTTI can be disabled by using the -fno-rtti option.

Listing 6-4. Just another "hack": Using RTTI to distinguish between different types of shape during runtime

```cpp
using ShapePtr = std::shared_ptr<Shape>;
using ShapeCollection = std::vector<ShapePtr>;
//...

void resizeAllShapes(const ShapeCollection& shapes) {
  try {
    for (const auto& shape : shapes) {
      const auto rawPointerToShape = shape.get();
      if (typeid(*rawPointerToShape) == typeid(Rectangle)) {
        Rectangle* rectangle = dynamic_cast<Rectangle*>(rawPointerToShape);
        rectangle->setEdges(10, 20);
        // Do more Rectangle-specific things here...
      } else if (typeid(*rawPointerToShape) == typeid(Square)) {
        Square* square = dynamic_cast<Square*>(rawPointerToShape);
        square->setEdge(10);
      } else {
        // ...
      }
    }
  } catch (const std::bad_typeid& ex) {
    // Attempted a typeid of NULL pointer!
  }
}
```

Don't do this! This cannot, and it should not, be the appropriate solution, especially not in a clean and modern C++ program. Many of the benefits of object orientation, such as dynamic polymorphism, are counteracted.

■ **Caution**   Whenever you are compelled to use RTTI in your program to distinguish between different types, it is a distinct "design smell," that is, an obvious indicator for a bad object-oriented software design!

In addition, our code will be heavily polluted with lousy if-else constructs and the readability will go down the drain. And as if this wasn't enough, the try-catch construct also makes it clear that something could go wrong.

But what can we do?

First of all, we should take another careful look on what a square really is.

From a pure mathematical point of view a square can be regarded as a rectangle with equal edge lengths. So far, so good. But this definition cannot be directly transferred into an object-oriented type hierarchy. **A square is not a subtype of a rectangle!**

Instead, having a square shape is merely a special state of a rectangle. If a rectangle has identical edge lengths, which is solely a state of the rectangle, then we usually give such particular rectangle a special name in our natural language: we then speak about a Square!

That means that we just need to add an inspector method to our class Rectangle to query its state, allowing us to waive an explicit class Square. According to the KISS principle (see Chapter 3), this solution might be completely sufficient to satisfy the new requirement. Furthermore, we can provide a convenient setter method to clients for setting both edge lengths equally.

Listing 6-5. A simple solution without an explicit class Square

```
class Rectangle : public Shape {
public:
  // ...
  void setEdgesToEqualLength(const unsigned int newLength) {
    setEdges(newLength, newLength);
  }

  bool isSquare() const {
    return width == height;
  }
  //...
};
```

Favor Composition over Inheritance

But what can we do if an explicit class Square is uncompromisingly required, for example, because someone demands it? Well, if that is the case, then we should never ever inherit from Rectangle, but from class Shape, as depicted in Figure 6-3. In order not to violate the DRY principle, we then use an instance of class Rectangle for the Square's internal implementation.

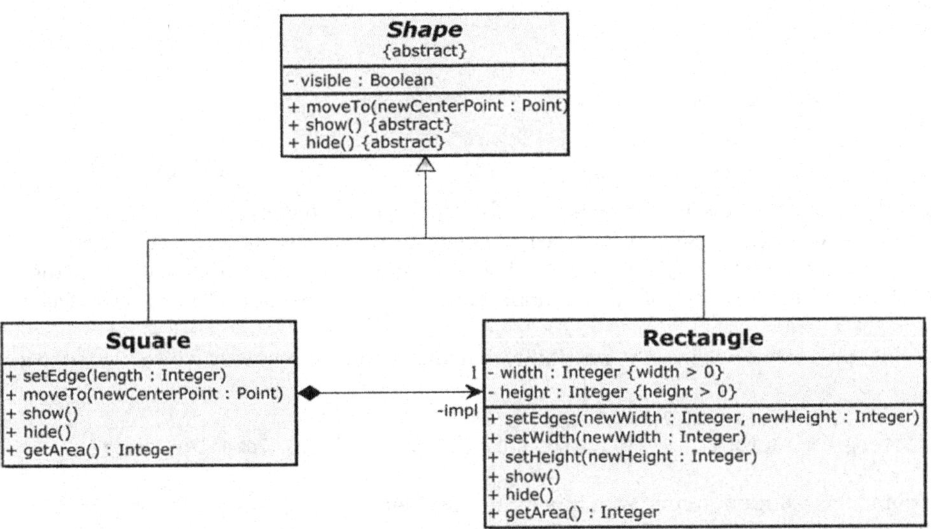

Figure 6-3. *The Square uses and delegates to an embedded instance of Rectangle*

Expressed in source code, the implementation of this class Square would look like this:

Listing 6-6. The Square delegates all method calls to an embedded instance of Rectangle

```
class Square : public Shape {
public:
  Square() {
    impl.setEdges(5, 5);
  }
```

```cpp
  explicit Square(const unsigned int edgeLength) {
    impl.setEdges(edgeLength, edgeLength);
  }

  void setEdge
(const unsigned int length) {
    impl.setEdges(length, length);
  }

  virtual void moveTo(const Point& newCenterPoint) override {
    impl.moveTo(newCenterPoint);
  }

  virtual void show() override {
    impl.show();
  }

  virtual void hide() override {
    impl.hide();
  }

  unsigned lomg longgetArea() const {
    return impl.getArea();
  }

private:
  Rectangle impl;
};
```

Perhaps you've noticed that the moveTo() method was also overwritten. To this end, the moveTo() method must also be made virtual in the Shape class. We must override it, because the moveTo() inherited from Shape operates on the centerPoint of the base class Shape, and not on the embedded instance of the Rectangle used. This is one small drawback of this solution: some parts inherited from the base class Shape lie fallow.

Obviously, with this solution we will lose the possibility that an instance of Square can be assigned to a Rectangle:

```cpp
std::unique_ptr<Rectangle> rectangle = std::make_unique<Square>(); // Compiler error!
```

The principle behind this solution to cope with inheritance problems in OO is called "Favor Composition over Inheritance" (FCoI), sometimes also named "Favor Delegation over Inheritance." For the reuse of functionality, object-oriented programming basically has two options: inheritance ("white box reuse") and composition or delegation ("black box reuse"). It is sometimes better to treat another type in a way as it would be a black box, that is, to use it only through its well-defined public interface, instead of deriving a subtype from this type. Reuse by composition/delegation fosters a looser coupling between classes than reuse by inheritance.

Interface Segregation Principle (ISP)

We already know interfaces as a way to foster loose coupling between classes. In a previous section about the Open-Closed Principle we've seen that interfaces are a way to have an extension and variation point in the code. An interface is like a contract: classes may request services through this contract, which may be offered by other classes that fulfill the contract.

But what problems can arise when these contracts become too extensive, that is, if an interface becomes too broad or "fat"? The consequences can be best be demonstrated with an example. Assume that we have the following interface:

Listing 6-7. An interface for Birds

```cpp
class Bird {
public:
  virtual ~Bird() = default;

  virtual void fly() = 0;
  virtual void eat() = 0;
  virtual void run() = 0;
  virtual void tweet() = 0;
};
```

This interface is implemented by several concrete birds, for example, by a `Sparrow`.

Listing 6-8. The class Sparrow overrides and implements all pure virtual member functions of Bird

```cpp
class Sparrow : public Bird {
public:
  virtual void fly() override {
    //...
  }
  virtual void eat() override {
    //...
  }
  virtual void run() override {
    //...
  }
  virtual void tweet() override {
    //...
  }
};
```

So far, so good. And now assume that we have another concrete `Bird`: a `Penguin`.

Listing 6-9. The class Penguin

```cpp
class Penguin : public Bird {
public:
  virtual void fly() override {
    // ???
  }
  //...
};
```

Although a penguin is unequivocal a bird, he cannot fly. Although our interface is relatively small, because it declares only four simple member functions, these declared services cannot, obviously, be offered by each bird species.

The *Interface Segregation Principle* (ISP) states that an interface should not be bloated with member functions that are not required by implementing classes, or that these classes are unable to implement in a meaningful way. In our example above, the class Penguin is not able to provide a meaningful implementation for Bird::fly(), but Penguin is enforced to overwrite that member function.

The Interface Segregation Principle says that we should segregate a "fat interface" into smaller and highly cohesive interfaces. The resulting small interfaces are also referred to as *role interfaces*.

Listing 6-10. The three role interfaces as a better alternative to the broad Bird interface

```cpp
class Lifeform {
public:
  virtual void eat() = 0;
  virtual void move() = 0;
};

class Flyable {
public:
  virtual void fly() = 0;
};

class Audible {
public:
  virtual void makeSound() = 0;
};
```

These small role interfaces can now be combined very flexibly. This means that the implementing classes only need to provide a meaningful functionality for those declared member functions, which they are able to implement in a sensible manner.

Listing 6-11. The classes Sparrow and Penguin respectively implement the relevant interfaces

```cpp
class Sparrow : public Lifeform, public Flyable, public Audible {
  //...
};

class Penguin : public Lifeform, public Audible {
  //...
};
```

Acyclic Dependency Principle

Sometimes there is the need for two classes to "know" each other. For example, let's assume that we're developing a web shop. So that certain use cases can be implemented, the class representing a customer in this web shop must know its related account. For other use cases it is necessary that the account can access its owner, which is a customer.

In UML, this mutual relationship looks like that in Figure 6-4.

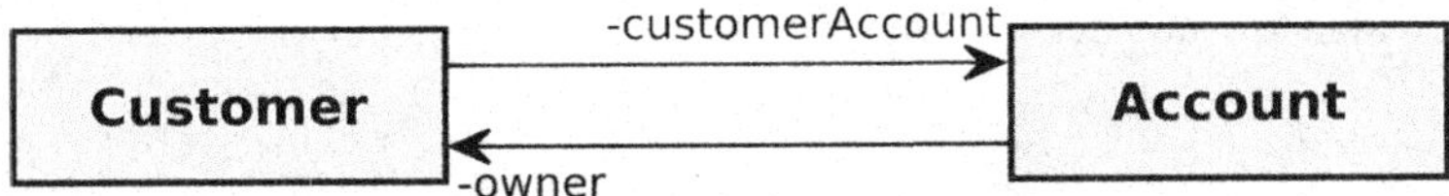

Figure 6-4. *The association relationships between class Customer and class Account*

This is known as a circular dependency. Both classes, either directly or indirectly, depend on each other. And in this case, there are only two classes. Circular dependencies can also occur with several software units involved.

Let's look at how that circular dependency shown in Figure 6-4 can be implemented in C++.

What definitely would not work in C++ is the following:

Listing 6-12. The content of file Customer.h

```
#ifndef CUSTOMER_H_
#define CUSTOMER_H_

#include "Account.h"

class Customer {
// ...
private:
  Account customerAccount;
};

#endif
```

Listing 6-13. The content of file Account.h

```
#ifndef ACCOUNT_H_
#define ACCOUNT_H_

#include "Customer.h"

class Account {
private:
  Customer owner;
};

#endif
```

I think that the problem is obvious here. As soon as someone uses class Account, or class Customer, he would trigger a chain reaction while compiling. For example, the Account owns an instance of Customer who owns an instance of Account who owns an instance of Customer, and so on, and so on... Due to the strict processing order of C++ compilers, the above implementation will result in compiler errors.

These compiler errors can be avoided, for example, by using references or pointers in combination with forward declarations. A forward declaration is the declaration of an identifier (e.g., of a type, like a class) without defining the full structure of that identifier. Therefore such types are sometimes also called incomplete types. Hence, they can only be used for pointers or references, but not for an instance member variable, because the compiler knows nothing about its size.

Listing 6-14. The modified Customer with a forward-declared Account

```cpp
#ifndef CUSTOMER_H_
#define CUSTOMER_H_

class Account;

class Customer {
public:
  // ...
  void setAccount(Account* account) {
    customerAccount = account;
  }
  // ...
private:
  Account* customerAccount;
};

#endif
```

Listing 6-15. The modified Account with a forward-declared Customer

```cpp
ifndef ACCOUNT_H_
#define ACCOUNT_H_

class Customer;

class Account {
public:
  //...
  void setOwner(Customer* customer) {
    owner = customer;
  }
  //...
private:
  Customer* owner;
};

#endif
```

Hand on heart: do you feel a little bit unwell with this solution? If yes, it's for good reasons! The compiler errors are gone, but this "fix" produces a bad gut feeling. Let's look how both classes are used:

Listing 6-16. Creating the instances of Customer and Account, and wiring them circularly together

```cpp
#include "Account.h"
#include "Customer.h"
// ...
  Account* account = new Account { };
  Customer* customer = new Customer { };
  account->setOwner(customer);
  customer->setAccount(account);
// ...
```

I'm sure that a serious problem is obvious: what happens if, for example, the instance of Account will be deleted, but the instance of Customer still exists? Well, the instance of Customer will contain a dangling pointer then, that is, a pointer to No-Man's Land! Using or dereferencing such a pointer can cause serious issues, like undefined behavior, or application crashes.

Forward declarations are pretty useful for certain things, but using them to deal with circular dependencies is a really bad practice. It is a creepy workaround that is supposed to conceal a fundamental design problem.

The problem is the circular dependency itself. This is bad design. The two classes Customer and Account cannot be separated. Thus, they cannot be used independently of one another, nor are they testable independently of one another. This makes Unit Testing considerably more difficult.

And the problem is getting even worse if we have the situation depicted in Figure 6-5.

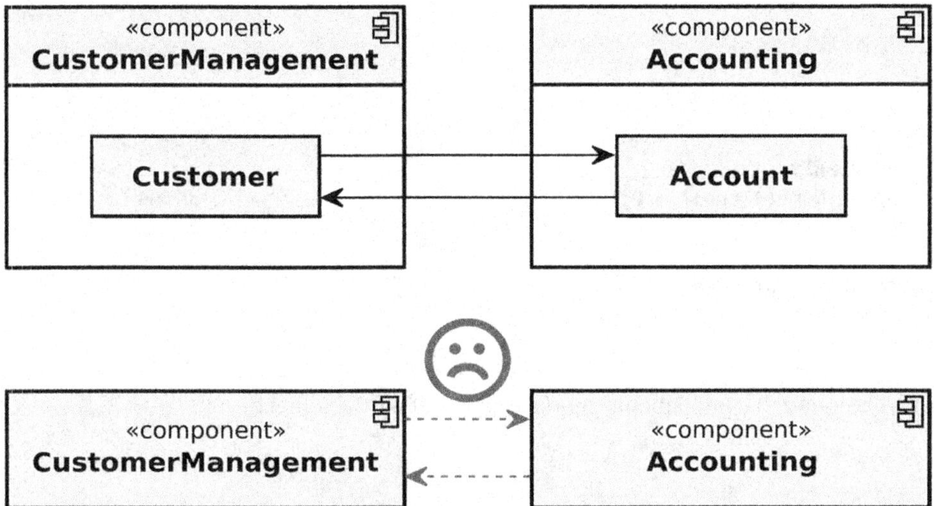

Figure 6-5. *The impact of circular dependencies between classes in different components*

Our classes Customer and Account are each located in different components. Perhaps there are many more classes in each of these components, but these two classes have a circular dependency. The consequence is that this circular dependency has also a negative impact on the architectural level. The circular dependency on class level leads to a circular dependency on component level. CustomerManagement and Accounting are tightly coupled (remember the section about Loose Coupling in Chapter 3) and cannot be (re)used independently. And of course, also, an independent component test is not possible anymore. The modularization on architecture level has been practically reduced to absurdity.

The *Acyclic Dependency Principle* states that the dependency graph of components or classes should have no cycles. Circular dependencies are a bad form of tight coupling and should be avoided at all costs.

Don't sweat it! It is **always** possible to break a circular dependency, and the following section will show how to avoid, respectively, breaking them.

Dependency Inversion Principle (DIP)

In the previous section we experienced that circular dependencies are bad and should be avoided under all circumstances. And as with many other problems with unwanted dependencies, too, the concept of the interface (in C++, interfaces are simulated using abstract classes) is our friend to deal with such troubles like in the previous case.

The goal should therefore be to break the circular dependency without losing the necessary possibility that class Customer can access Account and vice versa.

The first step is that we no longer allow one of the two classes to have direct access to the other class. Instead we allow such an access only via an interface. Basically it does not matter from which one of both classes (Customer or Account) the interface is extracted. I've decided to extract an interface named Owner from Customer. Exemplary, the Owner interface declares just one pure virtual member function that must be overridden by classes that implements this interface.

Listing 6-17. An exemplary implementation of the new interface Owner (File: Owner.h)

```cpp
#ifndef OWNER_H_
#define OWNER_H_

#include <memory>
#include <string>

class Owner {
public:
  virtual ~Owner() = default;
  virtual std::string getName() const = 0;
};


using OwnerPtr = std::shared_ptr<Owner>;


#endif
```

Listing 6-18. The class Customer that implements interface Owner (File: Customer.h)

```cpp
#ifndef CUSTOMER_H_
#define CUSTOMER_H_

#include "Owner.h"
#include "Account.h"

class Customer : public Owner {
public:
  void setAccount(AccountPtr account) {
    customerAccount = account;
  }

  virtual std::string getName() const override {
    // return the Customer's name here...
  }
  // ...

private:
  AccountPtr customerAccount;
  // ...
};

using CustomerPtr = std::shared_ptr<Customer>;

#endif
```

As it can easily be seen from the above shown source code of class Customer, the Customer still knows its Account. But when we take a look now into the changed implementation of class Account, there is no dependency to Customer anymore:

Listing 6-19. The changed implementation of class Account (File: Account.h)

```cpp
#ifndef ACCOUNT_H_
#define ACCOUNT_H_

#include "Owner.h"

class Account {
public:
  void setOwner(OwnerPtr owner) {
    this->owner = owner;
  }
  //...

private:
  OwnerPtr owner;
};

using AccountPtr = std::shared_ptr<Account>;

#endif
```

Depicted as an UML class diagram, the changed design on class level is as shown in Figure 6-6.

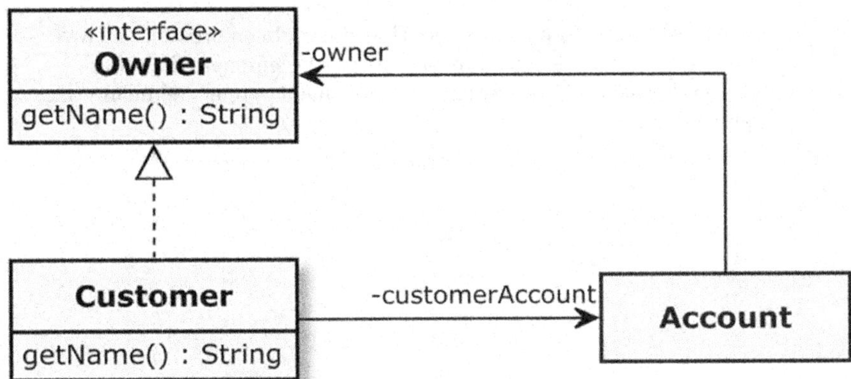

Figure 6-6. *The introduction of the interface has eliminated the circular dependency on class level*

Excellent! With this first step in the redesign we have now achieved that there are no more circular dependencies on class level. Now the class Account knows absolutely nothing anymore about the class Customer. But how does the situation look like when we climb up onto the component level as depicted in Figure 6-7?

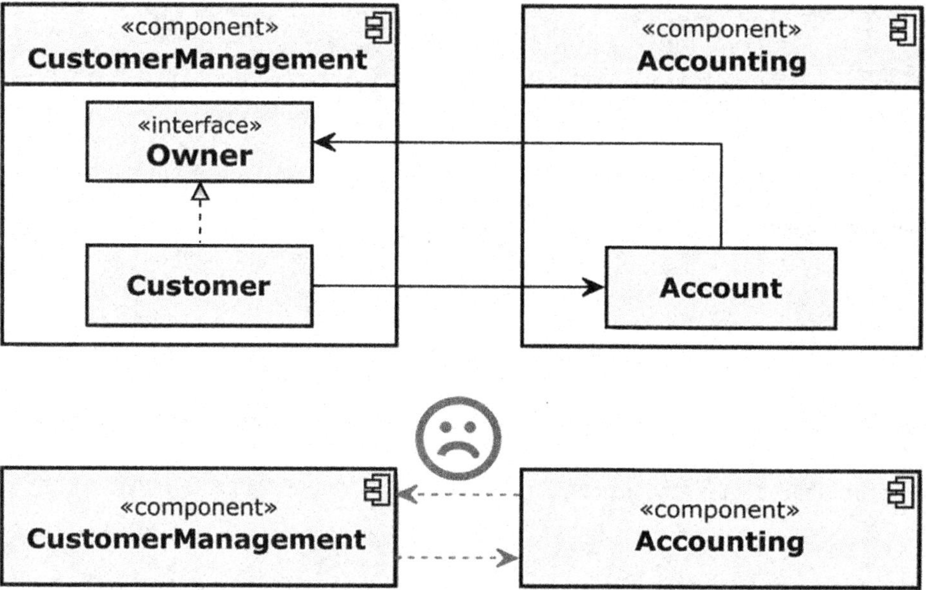

Figure 6-7. *The circular dependency between the components is still there*

Unfortunately, the circular dependency between the components has not yet been broken. The two association relationships still go from one element in the one component to one element in the other component. However, the step to achieve this goal is blindingly easy: we only need to relocate the interface Owner into the other component as depicted in Figure 6-8.

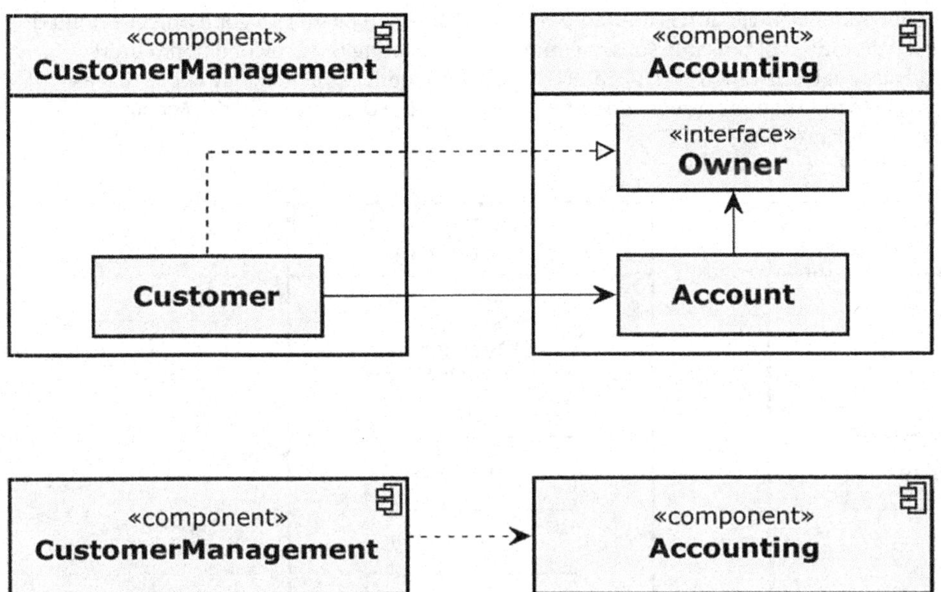

Figure 6-8. *Relocating the interface also fixes the circular dependency problem on an architecture level*

Great! Now the circular dependencies between the components have disappeared. The Accounting component is no longer dependent on the CustomerManagement, and as a result the quality of the modularization has been significantly improved. Furthermore, the Accounting component can now be tested independently.

In fact, the bad dependency between both components was not really literally eliminated. On the contrary, through the introduction of the interface Owner, we have even gotten one dependency more on class level. **What we really had done was to invert the dependency.**

The *Dependency Inversion Principle* (DIP) is an object-oriented design principle to decouple software modules. The principle states that the basis of an object-oriented design is not the special properties of concrete software modules. Instead, their common features should be consolidated in a shared used abstraction (e.g., an interface). Robert C. Martin a.k.a. "Uncle Bob" formulated the principle as follows:

A. High-level modules should not depend on low-level modules. Both should depend on abstractions.

B. Abstractions should not depend on details. Details should depend on abstractions.

—Robert C. Martin [Martin03]

■ **Note**   The terms "high-level modules" and "low-level modules" in this quote can be misleading. They refer not necessarily to their conceptual position within a layered architecture. A high-level module in this particular case is a software module that requires external services from another module, the so-called low-level module. High-level modules are those where an action is invoked, low-level modules are the ones where the action is performed. In some cases, these two categories of modules may also be located on different levels of a software architecture (e.g., layers), or as in our example in different components.

The principle of dependency inversion is fundamental for what is perceived as a good object-oriented design. It fosters the development of reusable software modules by defining the provided and required external services solely through abstractions (e.g., interfaces). Consistently applied to our above discussed case, we would also have to redesign the direct dependency between the `Customer` and the `Account` accordingly, as depicted in Figure 6-9.

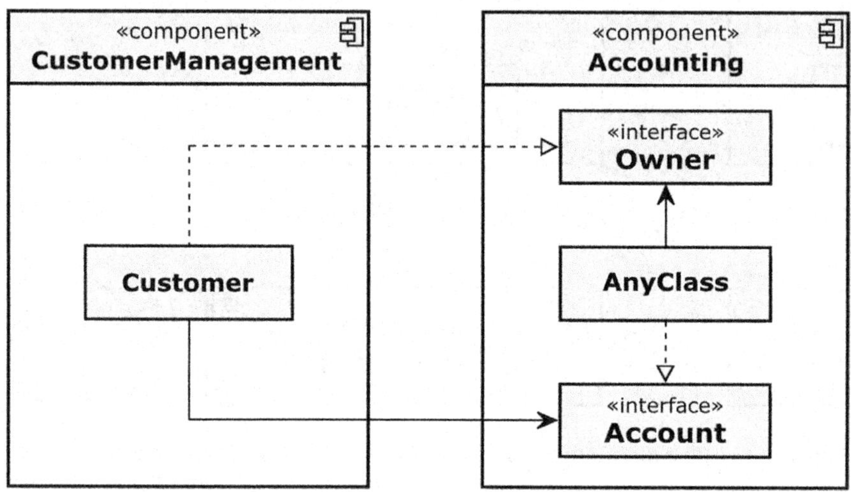

Figure 6-9. *Dependency Inversion Principle applied*

The classes in both components are solely dependent on abstractions. Therefore, it is no longer important to the client of the `Accounting` component which class requires the `Owner` interface or provides the `Account` interface (remember the section about Information Hiding in Chapter 3) – I have insinuated this circumstance by introducing a class that is named `AnyClass`, which implements `Account` and uses `Owner`.

For instance, if we have to change or replace the `Customer` class now, for example, because we want to mount the `Accounting` against a test fixture for component testing, then nothing has to be changed in class `AnyClass` to achieve it. This also applies to the reverse case.

The Dependency Inversion Principle allows software developers to design dependencies between modules purposefully, that is, to define in which direction dependencies are pointing. You want to inverse the dependency between the components, that is, `Accounting` should be dependent on `CustomerManagement`? No problem: simply relocate both interfaces from `Accounting` to the `CustomerManagement` and the dependency is turning around. Bad dependencies, which reduce the maintainability and the testability of the code, can be elegantly redesigned and reduced.

Don't Talk to Strangers (Law of Demeter)

Do you remember the car I talked about earlier in this chapter? I described this car as a composition of several parts, for example, body, engine, gears, and so on. And I have explained that these parts can again consist of parts, which for themselves can also consist of several parts, etc. This leads to a hierarchical top-down decomposition of a car. And of course, a car can have a driver that wants to use it.

Visualized as an UML class diagram, an excerpt from the car's decomposition can look like what is shown in Figure 6-10.

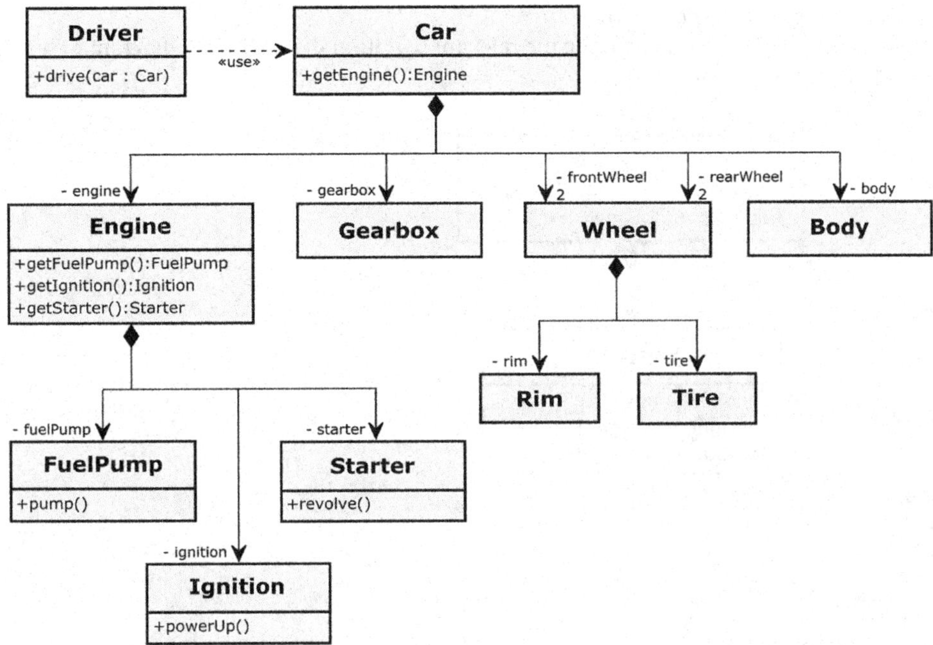

Figure 6-10. *The hierarchical decomposition of a simple car*

According to the Single Responsibility Principle discussed in Chapter 5, everything is fine, because every single class has a well-defined responsibility.

Now let's assume that the driver wants to drive the car. This could be implemented as follows in the class Driver:

Listing 6-20. An excerpt from the implementation of class Driver

```cpp
class Driver {
public:
// ...
  void drive(Car& car) const {
    Engine& engine = car.getEngine();
    FuelPump& fuelPump = engine.getFuelPump();
    fuelPump.pump();
    Ignition& ignition = engine.getIgnition();
    ignition.powerUp();
    Starter& starter = engine.getStarter();
    starter.revolve();
  }
// ...
};
```

What is the problem here? Well, would you expect as a driver of a car that you have to take directly access to your car's engine, to turn on the fuel pump, turn on the ignition system, and let revolve the starter? I go even further: are you even interested in the fact that your car consists of these parts if you just want to drive it?!

I'm pretty sure your clear answer would be: **No!**

And now let's take a look on Figure 6-11, depicting the relevant part from the UML class diagram to see what impact this implementation has on the design.

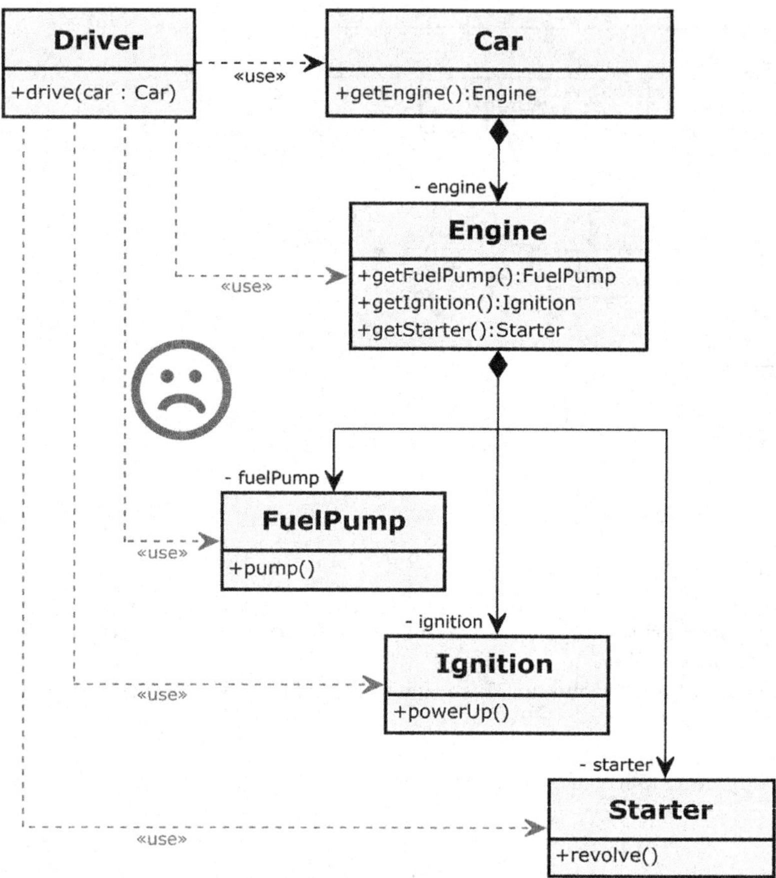

Figure 6-11. *The bad dependencies of class Driver*

As it can easily be seen in the diagram above, the class Driver has many awkward dependencies. The Driver is not only dependent from Engine. The class has also several dependency relationships to parts of the Engine. It is easy to imagine that this has some disadvantageous consequences.

What would happen, for example, if the combustion engine would be replaced by an electric power train? An electric drive doesn't have a fuel pump, an ignition system, and a starter. Thus, the consequences would be that the implementation of the class Driver has to be adapted. This violates the Open-Closed Principle (see earlier section). Furthermore, all public getters that expose the innards of the Car and the Engine to their environment are violating the Information Hiding Principle (see Chapter 3).

Essentially, the above software design violates the *Law of Demeter* (LoD), also known as the *Principle of Least Knowledge*. The Law of Demeter can be regarded as a principle that says something like "Don't talk to strangers", or "Only talk to your immediate neighbors." This principle states that you should do shy programming, and the goal is to govern the communication structure within an object-oriented design.

The Law of Demeter postulates the following rules:

- A member function is allowed to call other member functions in its own class scope directly.

- A member function is allowed to call member functions on member variables that are in its class scope directly.

- If a member function has parameters, the member function is allowed to call the member functions of these parameters directly.

- If a member function creates local objects, the member function is allowed to call member functions on those local objects.

If one of these four aforementioned kinds of member function calls returns an object that is structurally farther distant than the immediate neighbors of the class, **it is forbidden to call a member function on those objects.**

WHY THIS RULE IS NAMED LAW OF DEMETER

The name of this principle goes back to the *Demeter Project* about Aspect-Oriented Software Development, where these rules were formulated and strictly applied. The Demeter Project was a research project in the late 1980s with a main focus on making software easier to maintain and easier to expand through adaptive programming. The Law of Demeter was discovered and proposed by Ian M. Holland and Karl Lieberherr who worked in that project. In Greek mythology, Demeter is the sister of Zeus and the goddess of agriculture.

So, what is now the solution in our example to get rid of the bad dependencies? Quite simply, we should ask ourselves: what does a driver really want to do? The answer is easy: he wants to start the car!

```cpp
class Driver {
public:
// ...
  void drive(Car& car) const {
    car.start();
  }
// ...
};
```

And what does the car do with this start command? Also quite simple: it delegates this method call to its engine.

```cpp
class Car {
public:
// ...
  void start() {
    engine.start();
  }
// ...
private:
  Engine engine;
};
```

And last but not least, the engine knows how it can execute the start process by calling the appropriate member functions in the correct order on its parts, which are its immediate neighbors in the software design.

```cpp
class Engine {
public:
// ...
  void start() {
    fuelPump.pump();
    ignition.powerUp();
    starter.revolve();
  }
// ...
private:
  FuelPump fuelPump;
  Ignition ignition;
  Starter starter;
};
```

The positive effect of these changes on the object-oriented design can be very clearly seen in the class diagram that is depicted in Figure 6-12.

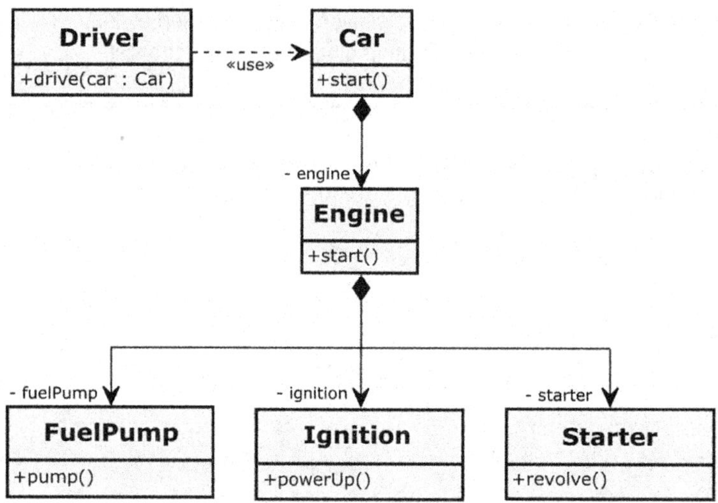

Figure 6-12. *Less dependencies after the application of the Law of Demeter*

The annoying dependencies of the driver to the car's parts are vanished. Instead, the driver can start the car, regardless of the internal structure of the car. The class Driver doesn't know anymore that there is an Engine, a FuelPump, etc. All those bad public getter functions, which had revealed the innards of the car or the engine to all other classes, are gone. This also means that changes to the Engine and its parts have only very local impacts and will not result in cascading changes straight through the whole design.

Following the Law of Demeter when designing software can reduce the number of dependencies significantly. This leads to loose coupling, and fosters both the Information Hiding Principle and the Open-Closed Principle. As with many other principles and rules, too, there may be some justified exceptions where a developer must vary from this principle for very good reasons.

Avoid Anemic Classes

In several projects I've seen classes that looked as follows:

Listing 6-21. A class without functionality that serves only as a bucket for a bunch of data

```cpp
class Customer {
public:
  void setId(const unsigned int id);
  unsigned int getId() const;
  void setForename(const std::string& forename);
  std::string getForename() const;
  void setSurname(const std::string& surname);
  std::string getSurname() const;
  //...more setters/getters here...

private:
  unsigned int id;
  std::string forename;
  std::string surname;
  // ...more attributes here...
};
```

This domain class, representing a customer in an arbitrary software system, does not contain any logic. The logic is in a different place, even that logic which represents exclusive functionality for the `Customer`, that is, operating only on attributes of the `Customer`.

Programmers who did this are using objects as bags for a bunch of data. This is just procedural programming with data structures, and it has nothing to do with object orientation. Also all those setters/ getters are totally foolish and violate the Information Hiding principle severely – actually we could use a simple C-structure (Keyword: `struct`) here.

Such classes are called *anemic classes* and should be avoided at all costs. They can often be found in a software design that is an Anti-Pattern that has been called *Anemic Domain Model* by Martin Fowler [Fowler03]. It is the exact opposite of the basic idea of object-oriented design, which is to combine data and the functionality that works with the data together into cohesive units.

As long as you do not violate the Law of Demeter, you should insert logic also into (domain) classes, if this logic is operating on attributes of that class or collaborates only with the immediate neighbors of the class.

Tell, Don't Ask!

The principle *Tell, Don't Ask* has some similarities with the previously discussed Law of Demeter. This principle is the "declaration of war" to all those public get-methods, which reveals something about the internal state of an object. Also Tell Don't Ask fosters encapsulation, strengthened Information Hiding (see Chapter 3), but first and foremost this principle is about strong cohesion.

Let's examine a small example. Let's assume that the member function `Engine::start()` from the previous example is implemented as follows:

Listing 6-22. A possible, but not recommendable implementation of the Engine::start() member function

```cpp
class Engine {
public:
// ...
  void start() {
    if (! fuelPump.isRunning()) {
```

```cpp
      fuelPump.powerUp();
      if (fuelPump.getFuelPressure() < NORMAL_FUEL_PRESSURE) {
        fuelPump.setFuelPressure(NORMAL_FUEL_PRESSURE);
      }
    }
    if (! ignition.isPoweredUp()) {
      ignition.powerUp();
    }
    if (! starter.isRotating()) {
      starter.revolve();
    }
    if (engine.hasStarted()) {
      starter.openClutchToEngine();
      starter.stop();
    }
  }
// ...
private:
  FuelPump fuelPump;
  Ignition ignition;
  Starter starter;
  static const unsigned int NORMAL_FUEL_PRESSURE { 120 };
};
```

As it is easy to see, the `start()` method of the class `Engine` queries many states from its parts and
responds accordingly. Furthermore, the `Engine` checks the fuel pressure of the fuel pump and adjusts it if
it is too low. This also means that the `Engine` must know the value for the normal fuel pressure. Due to the
numerous if branches, the cyclomatic complexity is high.

The principle Tell Don't Ask reminds us that we should not ask an object to release information about
its internal state and to decide outside of this object what to do, if this object would be able to decide it on its
own. Basically, this principle reminds us that in Object Orientation, data, and the operations operating on
these data, are to be combined to cohesive units.

If we apply this principle to our example, the `Engine::start()` method would only tell its parts what
they should do:

Listing 6-23. Delegating of stages of the starting procedure to the responsible parts of the engine

```cpp
class Engine {
public:
// ...
  void start() {
    fuelPump.pump();
    ignition.powerUp();
    starter.revolve();
  }
// ...
private:
  FuelPump fuelPump;
  Ignition ignition;
  Starter starter;
};
```

The parts can decide for themselves how they want to execute this command, because they have the knowledge about it, for example, the `FuelPump` can do all the things what it has to do to build up fuel pressure:

Listing 6-24. An excerpt from the FuelPump class

```cpp
class FuelPump {
public:
// ...
  void pump() {
    if (! isRunning) {
      powerUp();
      setNormalFuelPressure();
    }
  }
// ...

private:
  void powerUp() {
    //...
  }

  void setNormalFuelPressure() {
    if (pressure != NORMAL_FUEL_PRESSURE) {
      pressure = NORMAL_FUEL_PRESSURE;
    }
  }

  bool isRunning;
  unsigned int pressure;
  static const unsigned int NORMAL_FUEL_PRESSURE { 120 };
};
```

Of course, not all getters are inherently bad. Sometimes it is necessary to retrieve information from an object, for example, if this information should be displayed on a graphical user interface.

Avoid Static Class Members

I can well imagine that many readers are wondering now: what the heck is wrong with static member variables and, respectively, static member functions?

Well, perhaps you still remember the God Class Anti-Pattern I've described in the earlier section on small classes. There I've described that utility classes typically tend to become such huge "God Classes." In addition, these utility classes usually also consist of many static member functions, often even without exception. The quiet comprehensible justification for this is: why should I force users of the utility class to create an instance of it? And because such classes offer a colorful assortment of different functions for different purpose, which is a sign of weak cohesion by the way, I have created a special pattern name for these cluttered things: the **Junk Shop Anti-Pattern**. According to the online encyclopedia *Wikipedia*, a junk shop is a retail outlet similar to a thrift store that offers a broad assortment of mostly used goods at cheap prices.

Listing 6-25. Excerpt from some utility class

```cpp
class JunkShop {
public:
  // ...many public utility functions...
  static int oneOfManyUtilityFunctions(int param);
  // ...more public utility functions...
};
```

Listing 6-26. Another class that uses the Utility class

```cpp
#include "JunkShop.h"

class Client {
  // ...
  void doSomething() {
    // ...
    y = JunkShop::oneOfManyUtilityFunctions(x);
    // ...
  }
};
```

The first problem is that your code becomes hard-wired with all those static helper functions in these "Junk Shops." As it can easily be seen from the example above, such static functions from utility classes are used somewhere in the implementation of another software module. Hence, there is no easy way to replace this function call with something else. But in Unit testing (see Chapter 2), this is exactly what you want to do.

Furthermore, static member functions foster a procedural programming style. Using them in conjunction with static variables reduces object- orientation to absurdity. Sharing the same state across all instances of a class with the help of a static member variable is intrinsically not OOP, because it breaks encapsulation, because an object is no longer in complete control of its state.

Of course, C++ is not a pure object-oriented programming language like Java or C#, and it is basically not forbidden to write procedural code in C++. But when you want to do that, you should be honest to yourself and consequently use simple free-standing procedures, respectively functions, global variables, and namespaces.

My advice is to avoid static member variables respectively and member functions largely.

One exception from this rule are private constants of a class, because they are read-only and do not represent an object's state. Another exception are factory methods, that is, static member functions that create instances of an object, usually instances of the class type that serves also as the namespace of the static member function.

CHAPTER 7

Functional Programming

For several years, a programming paradigm experienced a renaissance, which is often viewed as a kind of counterdraft to object orientation. The talk is about Functional Programming.

One of the first functional programming languages was *Lisp* (The uppercase "LISP" is an older spelling, because the name of the language is an abbreviation for "LISt Processing"), which was designed by the American computer scientist and cognitive scientist John McCarthy in 1958 at the Massachusetts Institute of Technology (MIT). McCarthy also coined the term "artificial intelligence" (AI), and he used Lisp as the programming language for AI applications. Lisp is based on the so-called *Lambda Calculus* (λ calculus), a formal model that was introduced in the 1930s by the American mathematician Alonzo Church (see following sidebar).

In fact, Lisp is a family of computer programming languages. Various dialects of Lisp have emerged in the past. For instance, everyone who has ever used one member of the famous Emacs text editor family, for example, *GNU Emacs* or *X Emacs*, knows the dialect *Emacs Lisp* that is used as a scripting language for extension and automation.

Noteworthy functional programming languages, which have been developed past Lisp, were, among others:

- *Scheme*: a Lisp dialect with static binding that was developed in the 1970s at the MIT Artificial Intelligence Laboratory (AI Lab).

- *Miranda*: the first purely and lazy functional language that was commercially supported.

- *Haskell*: a general-purpose, purely functional programming language named after the American logician and mathematician Haskell Brooks Curry.

- *Erlang*: developed by the Swedish telecommunication company Ericsson with a main focus on building massive scalable and high reliable real-time software systems.

- *F#* (pronounced *F sharp*): A multiparadigm programming language and a member of the Microsoft .NET Framework. The main paradigm of F# is functional programming, but it allows the developer to switch also to the imperative/object-oriented world of the .NET ecosystem.

- *Clojure*: a modern dialect of the Lisp programming language created by Rich Hickey. Clojure is pure functional and runs on the Java™ virtual machine and the *Common Language Runtime* (CLR; the runtime environment of the Microsoft .NET framework).

© Stephan Roth 2017
S. Roth, *Clean C++*, DOI 10.1007/978-1-4842-2793-0_7

THE LAMBDA CALCULUS

It is difficult to find a painless introduction into the Lambda Calculus. Many essays on this subject are very scientifically written and require a good knowledge of mathematics and logic. And even I will not try to explain the Lambda Calculus here, because it is not the main focus of this book to do this. But you can find countless explanations on the Internet; just ask the search engine of your trust, and you will get hundreds of hits.

Only that much: The Lambda Calculus can be regarded as the simplest and smallest programming language that is even possible. It consists only of two parts: **one single function definition scheme** and **one single transformation rule**. These two components are sufficient to have a generic model for the formal description of functional programming languages, like LISP, Haskell, Clojure, etc.

As of today, functional programming languages are still not as widely used as their imperative relatives, for example like the object-oriented ones, but they increase in dissemination. Examples are *JavaScript* and *Scala*, which admittedly are both multiparadigm languages (i.e., they are not purely functional), but which became increasingly popular, especially in web development, among others because of their functional programming capabilities.

This is reason enough to dive deeper into this topic and to explore what this style of programming is all about, and what modern C++ has to offer in this direction.

What Is Functional Programming?

It is difficult to find a generally accepted definition for Functional Programming (sometimes abbreviated FP). Often, one reads that Functional Programming is a programming style in which the whole program is built up exclusively from pure functions. This immediately raises the question: what is meant by "pure function" in this context? Well, we will address this question in the following section. Basically it is however correct: the foundations for functional programming are functions in their mathematical sense. Programs are built by a composition of functions, and the evaluation of functions and function chains.

Just like Object Orientation (see Chapter 6), also Functional Programming is a programming paradigm. That means that it is a way of thinking about software construction. However, the Functional Programming paradigm is also often defined by all those positive properties that are attributed to it. These properties, which are regarded as advantageous compared to other programming paradigms, especially object orientation, are the following:

- **No side effects by avoiding a (globally) shared mutable state.** In pure Functional Programming, a function call does not have any side effect. This important property of pure functions is discussed in detail in the following section, "What Is a Function?"

- **Immutable data and objects.** In pure Functional Programming, all data is immutable, that is, once a data structure has been created it can never be changed. Instead, if we apply a function to a data structure, a new data structure is created as a result that is either a new one, or a variant of the old one. As a pleasant consequence, immutable data has the great advantage to be thread-safe.

- **Function composition and higher-order functions.** In Functional Programming, functions can be treated like data. You can store a function in a variable. You can pass a function as an argument to other functions. Functions can be returned as results from other functions. Functions can be easily chained. In other words: functions are *first-class citizens* of the language.

- **Better and easier parallelization.** Concurrency is basically hard. A software designer must pay attention to a lot of things in a multithreaded environment that she usually does not have to worry about when there is only one single thread of execution. And finding bugs in such a program can be very painful. But if calls of a functions never have any side effects, if there are no global states, and if we deal solely with immutable data structures, it is much easier to make a piece of software parallel. Instead, with imperative languages, like object-oriented ones, and its often mutable states, you need locking and synchronization mechanisms to protect data from being simultaneously accessed and manipulated by several threads (see section "The Power of Immutability" in Chapter 9 on how to create an immutable class respectively object in C++).

- **Easy to test.** If pure functions have all the positive properties mentioned above, they are also very easy to test. It is not necessary to consider global mutable states or other side effects in the test cases.

We will see that programming in a functional style in C++ cannot fully ensure all of these positive aspects automatically. For instance, if we need an immutable data type, we have to design it that way, as explained in Chapter 9. But now let's dive deeper into this topic and let us discuss the central question: what is a function in Functional Programming?

What Is a Function?

In software development we can find many things that are named "function." For instance, some of the features that a software application offers to its users are often also called the program's functions. In C++, the methods of a class are sometimes called member functions. The subroutines of a computer program are generally considered as functions. No doubt, these examples are also "functions" after a sort, but not the functions that we deal with in Functional Programming.

When we talk about functions in Functional Programming, we are talking about **true mathematical functions**. That means that we consider a function as a relation between a set of input parameters and a set of permissible output parameters, whereby each set of input parameters is related to exactly one set of output parameters. Depicted as a simple and general formula, a function is an expression as shown in Figure 7-1.

$$y = f(x)$$

Figure 7-1. *The function f maps x to y*

This simple formula defines the basic pattern of any function. It expresses that the value of y depends on, and solely on, the value of x. And another important point is that for the same values of x, also the value of y is always the same! In other words, the function f maps any possible value of x to exactly one unique value of y. In mathematics and computer programming, this is also known as *referential transparency*.

REFERENTIAL TRANSPARENCY

An essential advantage that is often mentioned in conjunction with Functional Programming is that pure functions are always referentially transparent.

The term "Referential Transparency" has its origin in analytical philosophy, which is an umbrella term for certain philosophical movements that are evolved since the beginning of the 20th century. Analytical philosophy is based on a tradition that initially operated mainly with ideal languages (formal logics) or by analyzing the everyday language of everyday use. The term "Referential Transparency" is ascribed to the American philosopher and logician Willard Van Orman Quine (1908 – 2000).

If a function is referentially transparent, it means that anytime we call the function with the same input values, we will always receive the same output. A function written in a truly functional language, which evaluates an expression and returns its value, does nothing else. In other words, we are theoretically able to substitute the function call directly with its result value, and this change will not have any impact. This enables us to chain together functions as if they are black boxes.

Referential transparency leads us directly to the concept of pure function.

Pure vs. Impure Functions

Here is a simple example of a pure function in C++:

Listing 7-1. A simple example of a pure function in C++

```cpp
double square(const double value) noexcept {
  return value * value;
};
```

As it can easily be seen, the output value of `square()` depends solely on the argument value that is passed to the function, so calling `square()` twice with the same argument value will produce the same result each time. We have no side effects, because if any call of this function is completed, it does not leave any "dirt" behind that can influence subsequent calls of `square()`. Such functions, which are completely independent of an outside state, which are not having any side effects, and which will produce always the same output for same inputs – in concreto: which are referentially transparent – are called **pure functions**.

In contrast, imperative programming paradigms, such as procedural or object-oriented programming, do not provide this guarantee of side-effect freeness, as the following example shows:

Listing 7-2. An example demonstrating that member functions of classes can cause side effects

```cpp
#include <iostream>

class Clazz {
public:
  int functionWithSideEffect(const int value) noexcept {
    return value * value + someKindOfMutualState++;
  }

private:
  int someKindOfMutualState { 0 };
};
```

```cpp
int main() {
  Clazz instanceOfClazz { };
  std::cout << instanceOfClazz.functionWithSideEffect(3) << std::endl; // Output: "9"
  std::cout << instanceOfClazz.functionWithSideEffect(3) << std::endl; // Output: "10"
  std::cout << instanceOfClazz.functionWithSideEffect(3) << std::endl; // Output: "11"
  return 0;
}
```

In this case, every call of the member function with the telling name `Clazz::functionWithSideEffect()` will alter an internal state of the instance of class `Clazz`. As a consequence, every call of this member function returns a different result, although the given argument for the function's parameter is always the same. You can have similar effects in procedural programming with global variables that are manipulated by procedures. Functions, that can produce different outputs even if they are called always with the same arguments, are called **impure functions**. Another clear indicator that a function is an impure function is when it makes sense to call it without using its return value. If you can do that, this function must have any kind of side effect.

In a single-threaded execution environment, global states may cause few problems and pain. But now imagine that you have a multithreaded execution environment, where several threads are running, calling functions in a non-deterministic order? In such an environment, global states, or object-wide states of instances, are often problematic and can cause unpredictable behavior or subtle errors.

Functional Programming in Modern C++

Believe it or not, but Functional Programming has always been a part of C++! With this multiparadigm language, you were always able to program in a functional style, even with C++98. The reason why I can claim this with best conscience is the existence of the known *Template Metaprogramming* (TMP) since the beginning of C++ (TMP is, by the way, a very complicated subject and thus a challenge for many, even well-skilled and experienced developers).

Functional Programming with C++ Templates

What is known to many C++ developers is that Template Metaprogramming is a technique in which so-called templates are used by a compiler to generate C++ source code in a step before the compiler translates source code to object code. What many programmers may not be aware of is the fact that Template Metaprogramming is functional programming, and that it is Turing Complete.

TURING COMPLETENESS

The term Turing Complete, named after the well-known English computer scientist, mathematician, logician, and cryptanalyst Alan Turing (1912 – 1954), is often used to define what makes a language a "real" programming language. A programming language is characterized as Turing Complete, if you can solve any possible problem with it that can be theoretically computed by a Turing Machine. A Turing Machine is an abstract and theoretical machine invented by Alan Turing that serves as an idealized model for computations.

In practice, no computer system is really Turing Complete. The reason is that ideal Turing Completeness requires unlimited memory and unbounded recursions, what today's computer systems cannot offer. Hence, some systems approximate Turing completeness by modeling unbounded memory, but restricted by a physical limitation in the underlying hardware.

As a proof, we will calculate the greatest common divisor (GCD) of two integers using TMP only. The GCD of two integers, which are both not zero, is the largest positive integer that divides both of the given integers.

Listing 7-3. Calculating the greatest common divisor using template metaprogramming

```
01  #include <iostream>
02
03  template< unsigned int x, unsigned int y >
04  struct GreatestCommonDivisor {
05    static const unsigned int result = GreatestCommonDivisor< y, x % y >::result;
06  };
07
08  template< unsigned int x >
09  struct GreatestCommonDivisor< x, 0 > {
10    static const unsigned int result = x;
11  };
12
13  int main() {
14    std::cout << "The GCD of 40 and 10 is: " << GreatestCommonDivisor<40u, 10u>::result <<
15      std::endl;
16    std::cout << "The GCD of 366 and 60 is: " << GreatestCommonDivisor<366u, 60u>::result <<
17      std::endl;
18    return 0;
19  }
```

This is the output that our program generates:

```
The GCD of 40 and 10 is: 10
The GCD of 366 and 60 is: 6
```

What is remarkable about this style of calculating the GCD at compile time using templates is that it is real functional programming. The two class templates used are completely free of states. There are no *mutable variables*, meaning that no variable can change its value once it has been initialized. During template instantiation, a recursive process is initiated that stops when the specialized class template on line 9 - 11 comes into play. And, as already mentioned above, we have Turing Completeness in template metaprogramming, meaning that any conceivable computation can be done at compile time using this technique.

Well, Template Metaprogramming is undoubtedly a powerful tool, but also has some disadvantages. Particularly the readability and understandability of the code can suffer drastically if a great deal of Template Metaprogramming is used. The syntax and idioms of TMP are difficult to understand, not to mention those extensive and often cryptic error messages when something goes wrong. And, of course, the compile time also increases with an extensive use of Template Metaprogramming. Therefore, TMP is certainly a proper way of designing and developing generic libraries (see C++ Standard Library), but should only be used in modern and well-crafted application code if this kind of generic programming is required (e.g., to minimize code duplication).

By the way, since C++11 it is no longer necessary to use template metaprogramming for computations at compile time. With the help of constant expressions (`constexpr`; see section about computations during compile time in Chapter 5) the GCD can easily be implemented as a usual recursive function, like in the following example:

Listing 7-4. A GCD function using recursion that can be evaluated at compile time

```cpp
constexpr unsigned int greatestCommonDivisor(const unsigned int x,
                                             const unsigned int y) noexcept {
  return y == 0 ? x : greatestCommonDivisor(y, x % y);
}
```

By the way, the mathematical algorithm behind this is called *Euclidean algorithm,* or *Euclid's algorithm,* named after the ancient Greek mathematician Euclid.

And with C++17 the numeric algorithm `std::gcd()` has become part of the C++ Standard Library (defined in header <numeric>), hence it is not necessary anymore to implement it on your own.

Listing 7-5. Using function std::gcd from header <numeric>

```cpp
#include <iostream>
#include <numeric>

int main() {
  constexpr auto result = std::gcd(40, 10);
  std::cout << "The GCD of 40 and 10 is: " << result << std::endl;
  return 0;
}
```

Function-Like Objects (Functors)

What was always possible in C++ from the very beginning is the definition and use of so-called *Function-like Objects,* also known as *Functors* (another synonym is *Functionals*) in short. Technically speaking, a Functor is more or less just a class that defines the parenthesis operator, that is, the `operator()`. After the instantiation of these classes, they can then be pretty much used like functions.

Depending on whether the `operator()` has none, one, or two parameters, the Functor is called *Generator, Unary Function,* or *Binary Function.* Let's look at a Generator first.

Generator

As the name "Generator" reveals, this type of Functor is used to produce something.

Listing 7-6. An example of a Generator, a functor that is called with no argument

```cpp
class IncreasingNumberGenerator {
public:
  int operator()() noexcept { return number++; }

private:
  int number { 0 };
};
```

The working principle is quite simple: every time IncreasingNumberGenerator::operator() is called, the actual value of the member variable number is returned to the caller, and then the value of this member variable is increased by 1. The following usage example prints a sequence of the numbers 0 to 2 on standard output:

```cpp
int main() {
  IncreasingNumberGenerator numberGenerator { };
  std::cout << numberGenerator() << std::endl;
  std::cout << numberGenerator() << std::endl;
  std::cout << numberGenerator() << std::endl;
  return 0;
}
```

Remember the quote from Sean Parent that I've presented in the section on algorithms in Chapter 5: no raw loops! To fill a std::vector<T> with a certain amount of increasing values, we should not implement an own handcrafted loop. Instead, we can use std::generate defined in header <algorithm>, a function template that assigns each element in a certain range a value generated by a given Generator object. Hence, we can write the following simple and well-readable code to fill a vector with an increasing number sequence using our IncreasingNumberGenerator:

Listing 7-7. Filling a vector with an increasing number sequence using std::generate

```cpp
#include <algorithm>
#include <vector>

using Numbers = std::vector<int>;

int main() {
  const std::size_t AMOUNT_OF_NUMBERS { 100 };
  Numbers numbers(AMOUNT_OF_NUMBERS);
  std::generate(std::begin(numbers), std::end(numbers), IncreasingNumberGenerator());
  // ...now 'numbers' contain values from 0 to 99...
  return 0;
}
```

As one can easily imagine, these kinds of Functors do **not** fulfill the strict requirements for pure functions. Generators do commonly have a mutable state, that is, when operator() is called, these Functors usually have some side effect. In our case, the mutable state is represented by the private member variable IncreasingNumberGenerator::number, which is incremented after each call of the parenthesis operator.

■ **Tip**   The header <numeric> already contains a function template std::iota(), named after the functional symbol ι (Iota) from programming language APL, which is not a generator functor, but it can be used to fill a container with an ascending sequence of values in an elegant way.

Another example of a function-like object of type Generator is the following random number generator functor template. This Functor encapsulates all the stuff that is necessary for the initialization and usage of a pseudorandom number generator (PRNG) based on the so-called *Mersenne Twister* algorithm (defined in header <random>).

Listing 7-8. A generator functor class template, encapsulating a pseudorandom number generator

```cpp
#include <random>

template <typename NUMTYPE>
class RandomNumberGenerator {
public:
  RandomNumberGenerator() {
    mersenneTwisterEngine.seed(randomDevice());
  }

  NUMTYPE operator()() {
    return distribution(mersenneTwisterEngine);
  }

private:
  std::random_device randomDevice;
  std::uniform_int_distribution<NUMTYPE> distribution;
  std::mt19937_64 mersenneTwisterEngine;
};
```

And this is how the Functor RandomNumberGenerator could then be used:

Listing 7-9. Filling a vector with 100 random numbers

```cpp
#include "RandomGenerator.h"
#include <algorithm>
#include <functional>
#include <iostream>
#include <vector>

using Numbers = std::vector<short>;
const std::size_t AMOUNT_OF_NUMBERS { 100 };

Numbers createVectorFilledWithRandomNumbers() {
  RandomNumberGenerator<short> randomNumberGenerator { };
  Numbers randomNumbers(AMOUNT_OF_NUMBERS);
  std::generate(begin(randomNumbers), end(randomNumbers), std::ref(randomNumberGenerator));
  return randomNumbers;
}

void printNumbersOnStdOut(const Numbers& randomNumbers) {
  for (const auto& number : randomNumbers) {
    std::cout << number << std::endl;
  }
}

int main() {
  Numbers randomNumbers = createVectorFilledWithRandomNumbers();
  printNumbersOnStdOut(randomNumbers);
  return 0;
}
```

Unary Function

Next, let's look at an example of a unary function-like object, which is a Functor whose paranthesis operator has one parameter.

Listing 7-10. An example for a unary functor

```cpp
class ToSquare {
public:
  constexpr int operator()(const int value) const noexcept { return value * value; }
};
```

As its name suggests, this Functor squares the values passed to it in the parenthesis operator. The `operator()` is declared as `const`, which is an indicator that it behaves like a pure function, that is, a call will have no side effects. This does not necessarily always have to be the case, because, of course, also a unary Functor can have private member variables, and thus a mutable state.

With the `ToSquare` Functor, we can now extend the above example and apply it to the vector with the ascending integer sequence.

Listing 7-11. All 100 numbers in a vector are squared

```cpp
#include <algorithm>
#include <vector>

using Numbers = std::vector<int>;

int main() {
  const std::size_t AMOUNT_OF_NUMBERS = 100;
  Numbers numbers(AMOUNT_OF_NUMBERS);
  std::generate(std::begin(numbers), std::end(numbers), IncreasingNumberGenerator());
  std::transform(std::begin(numbers), std::end(numbers), std::begin(numbers), ToSquare());
  // ...
  return 0;
}
```

The used algorithm `std::transform` (defined in header `<algorithm>`) applies the given function or function object to a range (defined by the first two parameters) and stores the result in another range (defined by the third parameter). In our case, both ranges are the same.

Predicates

A special kind of Functors is *Predicates*. A unary Functor is called a *Unary Predicate* if it has one parameter and a Boolean return value indicating the result `true` or `false` of some test, like in the following example:

Listing 7-12. An example for a Predicate

```cpp
class IsAnOddNumber {
public:
  constexpr bool operator()(const int value) const noexcept { return (value % 2) != 0; }
};
```

This Predicate can now be applied to our number sequence using the `std::remove_if` algorithm to get rid of all odd numbers. The problem is that the name of this algorithm is misleading. Actually, it doesn't remove anything. Any element, that doesn't match to the Predicate (in our case all even numbers), are moved to the beginning of the container so that the elements to be removed are at the end. Afterwards `std::remove_if` returns an iterator pointing to the beginning of the range to be removed. This iterator can be used by the `std::vector::erase()` member function to truly eliminate the unwanted elements from the vector. This, by the way, very efficient technique is called the *Erase-remove idiom*.

Listing 7-13. All odd numbers from the vector are deleted using the Erase-remove idiom

```cpp
#include <algorithm>
#include <vector>

using Numbers = std::vector<int>;

int main() {
  const std::size_t AMOUNT_OF_NUMBERS = 100;
  Numbers numbers(AMOUNT_OF_NUMBERS);
  std::generate(std::begin(numbers), std::end(numbers), IncreasingNumberGenerator());
  std::transform(std::begin(numbers), std::end(numbers), std::begin(numbers), ToSquare());
  numbers.erase(std::remove_if(std::begin(numbers), std::end(numbers), IsAnOddNumber()),
    std::end(numbers));
  // ...
  return 0;
}
```

In order to be able to use a Functor in a more flexible and generic way, it is usually implemented as a class template. Therefore, we can refactor our unary functor `IsAnOddNumber` into a class template so that it can be used with all integral types, such as `short`, `int`, `unsigned int`, etc. And since C++11, the language provides so-called *Type Traits* (defined in header `<type_traits>`), we can ensure that the template is used solely with integral types, as shown in the following example:

Listing 7-14. Ensuring that the template parameter is an integral data type

```cpp
#include <type_traits>

template <typename INTTYPE>
class IsAnOddNumber {
public:
  static_assert(std::is_integral<INTTYPE>::value,
    "IsAnOddNumber requires an integer type for its template parameter INTTYPE!");
  constexpr bool operator()(const INTTYPE value) const noexcept { return (value % 2) != 0; }
};
```

Since C++11, the language provides `static_assert()`, an assertion check that is performed at compile time. In our case, `static_assert()` is used to check during template instantiation that the template parameter INTTYPE is of an integral type using the type trait `std::is_integral<T>`. The location within the body of the `main()` function, where the predicate is used (the erase-remove construct), has now to be adjusted a little bit:

```cpp
// ...
numbers.erase(std::remove_if(std::begin(numbers), std::end(numbers),
  IsAnOddNumber<Numbers::value_type>()), std::end(numbers));
// ...
```

If we now inadvertently use the template with a non-integral data type, such as `double`, we get a compelling error message from the compiler:

```
[...]
../src/Functors.h: In instantiation of 'class IsAnOddNumber<double>':
../src/Main.cpp:13:94:   required from here
../src/Functors.h:42:3: error: static assertion failed: IsAnOddNumber requires an integer
type for its template parameter INTTYPE!
[...]
```

TYPE TRAITS

Templates are the foundation of generic programming. The containers from the C++ Standard Library, but also iterators and algorithms, are outstanding examples of very flexible generic programming using C++'s template concept. But from a technical point of view, however, just a simple textual find-and-replace procedure takes place if a template is instantiated with template arguments. For instance, if a template parameter is named T, every occurrence of T is replaced by the data type that is passed in as template argument during template instantiation.

The problem is this: not every data type is suitable for the instantiation of each template. For instance, if you have defined a mathematical operation as a C++ Functor template so that it can be used for different numeric data types (short, int, double, etc.), it absolutely doesn't make sense to instantiate this template with std::string.

The C++ Standard library header <type_traits> (available since C++11) provides a comprehensive collection of checks to retrieve information about the types passed in as template arguments at compile time. In other words, with the help of type traits you are able to define compiler-verifiable requirements that template arguments must fulfill.

For example, you can ensure that the type that is used for template instantiation must be copy-constructible combined with the no-throw exception-safety guarantee (see section "The No-Throw Guarantee" in Chapter 5) by using the type trait std::is_nothrow_copy_constructible<T>.

```cpp
template <typename T>
class Clazz {
  static_assert(std::is_nothrow_copy_constructible<T>::value,
    "The given type for T must be copy-constructible and may not throw!");
  // ...
};
```

Type traits can not only be used in conjunction with static_assert() to abort compilation with an error message. They can, for example, also be used for an idiom that is called *SFINAE* (Substitution failure is not an error) that is discussed in more detail in the section about Idioms in Chapter 9.

Last but not least, let's take a look at the Binary Functor.

Binary Functors

As already mentioned above, a Binary Functor is a function-like object that takes two parameters. If such a Functor operates on its two parameters to perform some calculation (e.g., addition) and returns the result of this operation, it is called a *Binary Operator*. If such a Functor has a Boolean return value as a result of some test, as shown in the following example, it is called a *Binary Predicate*.

Listing 7-15. An example for a binary predicate that compares its two parameters

```cpp
class IsGreaterOrEqual {
public:
  bool operator()(const auto& value1, const auto& value2) const noexcept {
    return value1 >= value2;
  }
};
```

■ **Note** Until C++11, it was a good practice that functors, depending on their number of parameters, were derived from the templates `std::unary_function` respectively `std::binary_function` (both defined in header `<functional>`). **These templates have been labelled as deprecated with C++11, and are removed from the Standard Library with the recent C++17 standard.**

Binders and Function Wrappers

A next development step in terms of Functional Programming in C++ was made with the publication of the draft C++ Technical Report 1 (TR 1) in 2005, which is the common name for the standard ISO/IEC TR 19768:2007 *C++ Library Extensions*. The TR 1 specifies a series of extensions to the C++ Standard library, including, among other things, extensions for Functional Programming. This technical report was the library extension proposal for the later C++11 standard, and in fact, 12 of the 13 proposed libraries (with slight modifications) also made it into the new language standard that was published in 2011.

In terms of Functional Programming, the TR 1 introduced the two function templates `std::bind` and `std::function`, which are defined in the library header `<functional>`.

The function template `std::bind` is a binder wrapper for functions and its arguments. You can take a function (or a function pointer, or a Functor), and "bind" actual values to one or all of the function's parameters. In other words, you can create new function-like objects from existing functions or Functors. Let's start with a simple example:

Listing 7-16. Using std::bind to wrap binary function multiply()

```cpp
#include <functional>
#include <iostream>

constexpr double multiply(const double multiplicand, const double multiplier) noexcept {
  return multiplicand * multiplier;
}
```

```cpp
int main() {
  const auto result1 = multiply(10.0, 5.0);
  auto boundMultiplyFunctor = std::bind(multiply, 10.0, 5.0);
  const auto result2 = boundMultiplyFunctor();

  std::cout << "result1 = " << result1 << ", result2 = " << result2 << std::endl;
  return 0;
}
```

In this example, the `multiply()` function is wrapped, together with two floating-point number literals (`10.0` and `5.0`), using `std::bind`. The number literals represent the actual parameters that are bound to the two function arguments `multiplicand` and `multiplier`. As a result, we get a new function-like object that is stored in the variable `boundMultiplyFunctor`. It can then be called like an ordinary Functor using the parenthesis operator.

Maybe you will ask yourself now: Nice, but I don't get it. What's the purpose of that? What is the practical benefit of the binder function template?

Well, `std::bind` allows something that is known as *partial application* (or *partial function application*) in programming. Partial application is a process in which only a subset of the function parameters is bound to values or variables, whereas the other part is not yet bound. The unbound parameters are replaced by the placeholders `_1`, `_2`, `_3`, and so on, which are defined in the namespace `std::placeholders`.

Listing 7-17. An example of partial function application

```cpp
#include <functional>
#include <iostream>

constexpr double multiply(const double multiplicand, const double multiplier) noexcept {
  return multiplicand * multiplier;
}

int main() {
  using namespace std::placeholders;

  auto multiplyWith10 = std::bind(multiply, _1, 10.0);
  std::cout << "result = " << multiplyWith10(5.0) << std::endl;
  return 0;
}
```

In the above example, the second parameter of the `multiply()` function is bound to the floating-point number literal `10.0`, but the first parameter is bound to a placeholder. The function-like object, which is the return value of `std::bind()`, is stored in the variable `multiplyWith10`. This variable can now be used like a function, but we only need to pass one parameter: the value that is to be multiplied by `10.0`.

Partial function application is an adaptation technique that allows us to use a function or a Functor in various situations, where we need their functionality, but where we are only able to supply some but not all of the arguments. In addition, with the help of the placeholders, the order of the functions parameters can be adapted to the order that client code expects. For example, the position of the `multiplicand` and the `multiplier` in the parameter list can be interchanged by mapping them to a new function-like object in the following way:

```cpp
auto multiplyWithExchangedParameterPosition = std::bind(multiply, _2, _1);
```

In our case with the multiply() function, this is obviously senseless (remember the commutative property of multiplication), because the new function object will produce exactly the same results as the original multiply() function, but in other situations an adaptation of the order of the parameters can improve the usability of a function. Partial function application is a tool for interface adaptation.

By the way, especially in conjunction with functions as return parameters, the automatic type deduction with its keyword auto (see section "Automatic Type Deduction" in Chapter 5) can provide valuable services, because if we inspect what the GCC compiler returns from the above call of std::bind(), it is an object of the following complex type:

```
std::_Bind_helper<bool0,double (&)(double, double),const _Placeholder<int2> &,
const _Placeholder<int1> &>::type
```

Terrifying, isn't it? Writing down such a type explicitly in source code is not only a little helpful, but apart from that the readability of the code also suffers considerably. Thanks to the keyword auto it is not necessary to define these types explicitly. But in those rare cases, where you must do it, the class template std::function comes into play, which is a general-purpose polymorphic function wrapper. This template can wrap an arbitrary callable object (an ordinary function, a Functor, a function pointer, etc.), and manages the memory used to store that object. For example, to wrap our multiplication function multiply() into a std::function object, the code looks as follows:

```
std::function<double(double, double)> multiplyFunc = multiply;
auto result = multiplyFunc(10.0, 5.0);
```

Now that we've discussed std::bind, std::function, and the technique of partial application, I have a possibly disappointing message for you: since C++ 11 and the introduction of lambda expressions, most of this template stuff from the C++ Standard Library is only seldomly required.

Lambda Expressions

With the advent of C++11, the language has been extended with a new and noteworthy feature: lambda expressions! Other frequently used terms for them are *lambda functions, function literals*, or just *lambdas*. Sometimes they are also called *Closures*, which is actually a general term from functional programming, and which, incidentally, is also not entirely correct.

CLOSURE

In imperative programming languages, we are accustomed to the fact that a variable is no longer available when the program execution leaves the scope within which the variable is defined. For instance, if a function is done and returns to its caller, all local variables of that function are removed from the call stack and deleted from memory.

On the other hand, in Functional Programming, we can build a Closure, which is a function object with a persistent local variable scope. In other words, Closures allow that a scope with some or all of its local variables is tied to a function, and that this scope object will persist as long as that function exists.

In C++, such Closures can be created with the help of lambda expressions due to its capture list in the lambda introducer. A Closure is not the same as a lambda expression, as well as an object (instance) in object orientation is not the same as its class.

What is special about lambda expressions is that they are usually implemented inline, that is, at the point of their application. This can sometimes improve the readability of the code, and compilers can apply their optimization strategies even more efficiently. Of course, also lambda functions can be treated as data, for example, stored in variables, or passed as a function argument to a so-called high-order function (see next section about this topic).

The basic structure of a lambda expression looks as follows:

```
[ capture list ](parameter list) -> return_type_declaration { lambda body }
```

Since this book is not a C++ language introduction, I will not explain all the basics about lambda expressions here. Even if you are seeing something like this for the first time, it should be relatively clear that the return type, the parameter list, and the lambda body are pretty much the same as with ordinary functions. What might seem unusual at first glance are two things. For example, a lambda expression has no name like an ordinary function or a function-like object. This is the reason why one speaks in this context also of *anonymous functions*. The other conspicuousness is the square bracket at the beginning, which is also called the *lambda introducer*. As the name suggests, the lambda introducer marks the beginning of a lambda expression. In addition, the introducer also optionally contains something that is called a *capture list*.

What this capture list makes so important is that here all the variables from the outside scope are listed, which should be available inside of the lambda body, and whether they should be captured by value (copying) or by reference. In other words, these are the closures of the lambda expression.

An example lambda expression is defined as follows:

```
[](const double multiplicand, const double multiplier) { return multiplicand * multiplier; }
```

This is our good old multiplication function as a lambda. The introducer has a blank capture list, which means that nothing from the surrounding scope is used. Also the return type is not specified in this case, because the compiler can easily deduce it.

By assigning the lambda expression to a variable, a corresponding runtime object is created, the so-called closure. And this is actually true: the compiler generates a functor class of an unspecified type from a lambda expression, which is instantiated at runtime and assigned to the variable. The captures in the capture list are converted into constructor parameters and member variables of the functor object. The parameters in the lambda's parameter list are turned into parameters for the functor's parenthesis operator (operator()).

Listing 7-18. Using the lambda expression to multiply two doubles

```cpp
#include <iostream>

int main() {
  auto multiply = [](const double multiplicand, const double multiplier) {
    return multiplicand * multiplier;
  };
  std::cout << multiply(10.0, 50.0) << std::endl;
  return 0;
}
```

However, the whole thing can be done shorter, because a lambda expression can be called directly at the place of its definition by appending parentheses with arguments behind the lambda body.

Listing 7-19. Defining and calling of a lambda expression in one go

```cpp
int main() {
  std::cout <<
    [](const double multiplicand, const double multiplier) {
      return multiplicand * multiplier;
    }(50.0, 10.0) << std::endl;
  return 0;
}
```

The previous example is, of course, for demonstration purposes only, since the use of a lambda in this style makes definitely no sense. The following example uses two lambda expressions. One is used by the algorithm `std::transform` to envelop the words in the string vector `quote` with angle brackets and store them in another vector named `result`. The other lambda expression is used by `std::for_each` to output the content of `result` on standard output.

Listing 7-20. Putting every single word in a list in angle brackets

```cpp
#include <algorithm>
#include <iostream>
#include <string>
#include <vector>

int main() {
  std::vector<std::string> quote { "That's", "one", "small", "step", "for", "a", "man,", "one",
    "giant", "leap", "for", "mankind." };
  std::vector<std::string> result;

  std::transform(begin(quote), end(quote), back_inserter(result),
    [](const std::string& word) { return "<" + word + ">"; });
  std::for_each(begin(result), end(result),
    [](const std::string& word) { std::cout << word << " "; });

  return 0;
}
```

The output of this small program is:

```
<That's> <one> <small> <step> <for> <a> <man,> <one> <giant> <leap> <for> <mankind.>
```

Generic Lambda Expressions (C++14)

With the publishing of C++14, lambda expressions have experienced some further improvements. Since C++14 it is allowed to use `auto` (see section about automatic type deduction in Chapter 5) as the return type of a function, or a lambda. In other words, the compiler will deduce the type. Such lambda expressions are called *generic lambda expressions*.

Here is an example:

Listing 7-21. Applying a generic lambda expression on values of different data type

```cpp
#include <complex>
#include <iostream>

int main() {
  auto square = [](const auto& value) noexcept { return value * value; };

  const auto result1 = square(12.56);
  const auto result2 = square(25u);
  const auto result3 = square(-6);
  const auto result4 = square(std::complex<double>(4.0, 2.5));

  std::cout << "result1 is " << result1 << "\n";
  std::cout << "result2 is " << result2 << "\n";
  std::cout << "result3 is " << result3 << "\n";
  std::cout << "result4 is " << result4 << std::endl;

  return 0;
}
```

The parameter type as well as the result type is derived automatically depending on the type of the concrete parameter (literal) when the function is compiled (in the previous example double, unsigned int, int, and a complex number of type std::complex<T>). Generalized lambdas are extremely useful in interaction with standard library algorithms, because they are universally applicable.

Higher-Order Functions

A central concept in Functional Programming is so-called *higher-order functions*. They are the pendant to first-class functions. A higher-order function is a function that takes one or more other functions as arguments, or they can return a function as a result. In C++, any callable object, for example, an instance of the std::function wrapper, a function pointer, a closure created from a lambda expression, a handcrafted Functor, and anything else that implements operator() can be passed as an argument to a higher-order function.

We can keep this introduction relatively short, because we have already seen and used several higher-order functions. Many of the algorithms (see section about algorithms in Chapter 5) in the C++ Standard Library are such kind of functions. Depending on their purpose, they take a Unary Operator, Unary Predicate, or Binary Operator to apply it to a container, or to a sub-range of elements in a container.

Of course, despite the fact that header <algorithm> and also header <numeric> provides a comprehensive selection of powerful higher-order functions for different purposes, you can also implement higher-order functions, respectively, or higher-order function templates by yourself, like in the following example:

Listing 7-22. An example for self-made higher-order functions

```cpp
#include <functional>
#include <iostream>
#include <vector>

template<typename CONTAINERTYPE, typename UNARYFUNCTIONTYPE>
```

```cpp
void myForEach(const CONTAINERTYPE& container, UNARYFUNCTIONTYPE unaryFunction) {
  for (const auto& element : container) {
    unaryFunction(element);
  }
}

template<typename CONTAINERTYPE, typename UNARYOPERATIONTYPE>
void myTransform(CONTAINERTYPE& container, UNARYOPERATIONTYPE unaryOperator) {
  for (auto& element : container) {
    element = unaryOperator(element);
  }
}

template<typename NUMBERTYPE>
class ToSquare {
public:
  NUMBERTYPE operator()(const NUMBERTYPE& number) const noexcept {
    return number * number;
  }
};

template<typename TYPE>
void printOnStdOut(const TYPE& thing) {
  std::cout << thing << ", ";
}

int main() {
  std::vector<int> numbers { 1, 2, 3, 4, 5, 6, 7, 8, 9, 10 };
  myTransform(numbers, ToSquare<int>());
  std::function<void(int)> printNumberOnStdOut = printOnStdOut<int>;
  myForEach(numbers, printNumberOnStdOut);
  return 0;
}
```

In this case, our two self-made higher-order function templates myTransform() and myForEach() are only applicable to entire containers because, unlike the standard library algorithms, they have no iterator interface. The crucial point, however, is that developers can provide custom higher-order functions that do not exist in the C++ standard library.

We will now look at three of these high-order functions in greater detail, because they play an important role in Functional Programming.

Map, Filter, and Reduce

Each serious functional programming language must provide at least three useful higher-order functions: *map*, *filter*, and *reduce* (synonym: *fold*). Even if they may have sometimes different names depending on the programming language, you can find this triumvirate in Haskell, Erlang, Clojure, JavaScript, Scala, and many other languages with functional programming capabilities. Hence, we can claim justifiably, that these three higher-order functions form a very common functional programming design pattern.

It should therefore hardly surprise you that these higher-order functions are also contained in the C++ standard library. And maybe you will also not be surprised that we have already used some of these functions.

Let's take a consecutive look at each of these functions.

Map

Map might be the easiest to understand of the three. With the help of this higher-order function, we can apply an operator function to each single element of a list. In C++, this function is provided by the standard library algorithm `std::transform` (defined in header `<algorithm>`) that you've already seen in some previous code examples.

Filter

Also filter is easy. As the name suggests, this higher-order function takes a Predicate (see section about Predicates earlier in this chapter) and a list, and it removes any element from the list that does not satisfy the Predicate's condition. In C++, this function is provided by the standard library algorithm `std::remove_if` (defined in header `<algorithm>`) that you've already seen in some previous code examples.

Nevertheless, here's another nice example for filter respectively `std::remove_if`. If you are suffering from a disease called "aibohphobia," which is a humorous term for the irrational fear of palindromes, you should filter out palindromes from word lists as follows:

Listing 7-23. Removing all palindromes from a vector of words

```cpp
#include <algorithm>
#include <iostream>
#include <string>
#include <vector>

class IsPalindrome {
public:
  bool operator()(const std::string& word) const {
    const auto middleOfWord = begin(word) + word.size() / 2;
    return std::equal(begin(word), middleOfWord, rbegin(word));
  }
};

int main() {
  std::vector<std::string> someWords { "dad", "hello", "radar", "vector", "deleveled", "foo",
    "bar", "racecar", "ROTOR", "", "C++", "aibohphobia" };
  someWords.erase(std::remove_if(begin(someWords), end(someWords), IsPalindrome()),
    end(someWords));
  std::for_each(begin(someWords), end(someWords), [](const auto& word) {
    std::cout << word << ",";
  });
  return 0;
}
```

The output of this program is:

```
hello,vector,foo,bar,C++,
```

Reduce (Fold)

Reduce (synonyms: Fold, Collapse, Aggregate) is the most powerful of the three higher-order functions and might be a bit hard to understand at first glance. Reduce respectively fold is a higher-order function to get a single result value by applying a binary operator on a list of values. In C++, this function is provided by the standard library algorithm `std::accumulate` (defined in header `<numeric>`). Some say that `std::accumulate` is the most powerful algorithm in the standard library.

To start with a simple example, you can easily get the sum of all integers in a vector this way:

Listing 7-24. Building the sum of all values in a vector using std::accumulate

```cpp
#include <numeric>
#include <iostream>
#include <vector>

int main() {
  std::vector<int> numbers { 12, 45, -102, 33, 78, -8, 100, 2017, -110 };

  const int sum = std::accumulate(begin(numbers), end(numbers), 0);
  std::cout << "The sum is: " << sum << std::endl;
  return 0;
}
```

Here the version of `std::accumulate` was used that does not expect an explicit binary operator in the parameter list. Using this version of the function, simply the sum of all values is calculated. Of course, you can provide an own binary operator, like in the following example through a lambda expression:

Listing 7-25. Finding the highest number in a vector using std::accumulate

```cpp
int main() {
  std::vector<int> numbers { 12, 45, -102, 33, 78, -8, 100, 2017, -110 };

  const int maxValue = std::accumulate(begin(numbers), end(numbers), 0,
    [](const int value1, const int value2) {
    return value1 > value2 ? value1 : value2;
  });
  std::cout << "The highest number is: " << maxValue << std::endl;
  return 0;
}
```

LEFT AND RIGHT FOLD

Functional programming often distinguishes between two ways to fold a list of elements: a *left fold* and a *right fold*.

If we combine the first element with the result of recursively combining the rest, this is called a right fold. Instead, if we combine the result of recursively combining all elements but the last one, with the last element, this operation is called a left fold.

If, for example, we take a list of values that are to be folded with a + operator to a sum, then the parentheses are as follows for a left fold operation: ((A + B) + C) + D. Instead, with a right fold, the parentheses would be set like this: A + (B + (C + D)). In the case of a simple associative + operation, the result does not make any difference whether it is formed with a left fold or a right fold. But in the case of non-associative binary functions, the order in which the elements are combined may influence the final result's value.

Also in C++, we can distinguish between a left fold and a right fold. If we use `std::accumulate` with normal iterators, we get a left fold:

```
std::accumulate(begin, end, init_value, binary_operator)
```

Instead, if we use `std::accumulate` with a reverse iterator, we get a right fold:

```
std::accumulate(rbegin, rend, init_value, binary_operator)
```

Fold Expressions in C++17

Starting with C++17, the language has gained an interesting new feature called *fold expressions*. C++17 fold expressions are implemented as so-called variadic templates (available since C++11), that is, as templates that can take a variable number of arguments in a type-safe way. This arbitrary number of arguments is held in a so-called *parameter pack*.

What has been added with C++17 is the possibility to reduce the parameter pack directly with the help of a binary operator, that is, to perform a folding. The general syntax of C++17 fold expressions are as follows:

```
( ... operator parampack )                          // left fold
( parampack operator ... )                          // right fold
( initvalue operator ... operator parampack )  // left fold with an init value
( parampack operator ... operator initvalue )  // right fold with an init value
```

Let's look at an example, a left fold with an init value:

Listing 7-26. An example for a left fold

```
#include <iostream>

template<typename... PACK>
int subtractFold(int minuend, PACK... subtrahends) {
  return (minuend - ... - subtrahends);
}

int main() {
  const int result = subtractFold(1000, 55, 12, 333, 1, 12);
  std::cout << "The result is: " << result << std::endl;
  return 0;
}
```

Note that a right fold cannot be used in this case due to the lack of associativity of operator-. Fold expressions are supported for 32 operators, including logical operators like ==, &&, and ||.

Here is another example that tests that a parameter pack contains at least one even number:

Listing 7-27. Checking whether a parameter pack contains an even value

```cpp
#include <iostream>

template <typename... TYPE>
bool containsEvenValue(const TYPE&... argument) {
  return ((argument % 2 == 0) || ...);
}

int main() {
  const bool result1 = containsEvenValue(10, 7, 11, 9, 33, 14);
  const bool result2 = containsEvenValue(17, 7, 11, 9, 33, 29);

  std::cout << std::boolalpha;
  std::cout << "result1 is " << result1 << "\n";
  std::cout << "result2 is " << result2 << std::endl;
  return 0;
}
```

The output of this program is:

```
result1 is true
result2 is false
```

Clean Code in Functional Programming

No doubt, the functional programming movement has not stopped before C++, and that's basically good. Many useful concepts have been incorporated into our somewhat aged programming language.

But code that is written in a functional style is not automatically good or clean code. The increasing popularity of functional programming languages during the last years could make you believe that functional code is per se better maintainable, better readable, better testable, and is less error prone than, for instance, object-oriented code. **But that's not true!** On the contrary, nifty elaborated functional code that is doing non-trivial things can be very difficult to understand.

Let's, for example, take a simple fold operation that is very similar to one of the previous examples:

```cpp
// Build the sum of all product prices
const Money sum = std::accumulate(begin(productPrices), end(productPrices), 0.0);
```

If you would read this without the explaining source code comment...is this intention revealing code? Please remember what we've learned in Chapter 4 about comments: Whenever you feel the urge to write a source code comment, you should first think about how to improve the code so that the comment becomes superfluous.

So, what we really want to read or respectively write is something like this:

```cpp
const Money totalPrice = buildSumOfAllPrices(productPrices);
```

So, let's first make a fundamental statement:

The principles of good software design still apply, regardless of the programming style you will use!

You prefer the functional programming style over OO? OK, but I'm sure that you will agree that KISS, DRY, and YAGNI (see Chapter 3) are also very good principles in functional programming! Do you think that you can ignore the Single Responsibility Principle (see Chapter 6) in functional programming? Forget it! If a function does more than one thing, it will lead to similar problems as in object orientation. And I think that I do not have to mention that good and expressive naming (see Chapter 4 about good names) is also enormously important for the understandability and maintainability of code in a functional environment. Always keep in mind, that developers spend much more time in reading code than writing code.

Thus, we can conclude that most design principles used by object-oriented software designers and programmers can also be used by functional programmers.

Personally I prefer a balanced mix of both programming styles. There are many design challenges that can be solved perfectly using object-oriented paradigms. Polymorphism is a great benefit of OO. I can take advantage of the Dependency Inversion Principle (see the eponymous section in Chapter 6), which allows me an inversion of source code and runtime dependencies.

Instead, complex mathematical computations can be better solved using a functional programming style. And if high and ambitious performance and efficiency requirements must be fulfilled, which will inevitably require a parallelization of certain tasks, functional programming can play out its trump card.

Regardless of whether you prefer to write software in an object-oriented way, or in a functional style, or in an appropriate mixture of both, you should always remember the following quote:

> *Always code as if the guy who ends up maintaining your code will be a violent psychopath who knows where you live.*

> —John F. Woods, 1991, in a post to the comp.lang.c++ newsgroup

CHAPTER 8

Test-Driven Development

Project Mercury ran with very short (half-day) iterations that were time boxed. The development team conducted a technical review of all changes, and, interestingly, applied the Extreme Programming practice of test-first development, planning and writing tests before each micro-increment.

—Craig Larman and Victor R. Basili, Iterative and Incremental Development:
A Brief History. IEEE, 2003

In the section "Unit Tests" (see Chapter 2) we have learned that a good suite of small and fast tests can ensure that our code works correctly. So far, so good. But what is so special about Test-Driven Development (TDD) and why does it justify an additional chapter in this book?

Especially in recent years, the discipline of Test-Driven Development has gained in popularity. TDD has become an important ingredient of the toolbox of software craftspeople. That's a little bit surprising, because the basic idea of Test First approaches is nothing new. *Project Mercury*, which is mentioned in the above quote, was the first human spaceflight program of the United States and was conducted under the direction of NASA **from 1958 through 1963**. Although what was practiced about 50 years ago as a Test-First approach certainly is not exactly the kind of TDD as we know it today, we can say that the basic idea was present quite early in professional software development.

But then it seems that this approach has fallen into oblivion for decades. In countless projects with billions of lines of code, the tests were postponed at the end of the development process. The sometimes devastating consequences of this right-shifting of the important tests in the project's schedules are known: if time is getting short in the project, the first things that are usually abandoned by the development team are the important tests.

With the increasing popularity of agile practices in software development and the coming up of a new method called *eXtreme Programming* (XP) at the beginning of the 2000s, Test-Driven Development was rediscovered. Kent Beck wrote his famous book *Test-Driven Development: By Example* [Beck02], and Test First approaches like TDD experienced a renaissance and became increasingly important tools in the toolbox of software craftspeople.

In this chapter, I will not only explain that although the term "Test" is included in Test-Driven Development, it is not primarily about quality assurance. TDD offers many more benefits than just a simple validation of the correctness of the code. Rather I will explain the differences of TDD to what is sometimes called *Plain Old Unit Testing* (POUT), followed by the discussion of the workflow of TDD in detail, supported by a detailed practical example showing how to do it in C++.

© Stephan Roth 2017
S. Roth, *Clean C++*, DOI 10.1007/978-1-4842-2793-0_8

The Drawbacks of Plain Old Unit Testing (POUT)

No doubt, as we've seen in Chapter 2 a suite of unit tests is basically a much better situation than having no tests in place. But in many projects the unit tests are written somehow parallel to the implementation of the code to be tested, sometimes even completely after finalization of the module to be developed. The activity diagram depicted in Figure 8-1 visualizes this process.

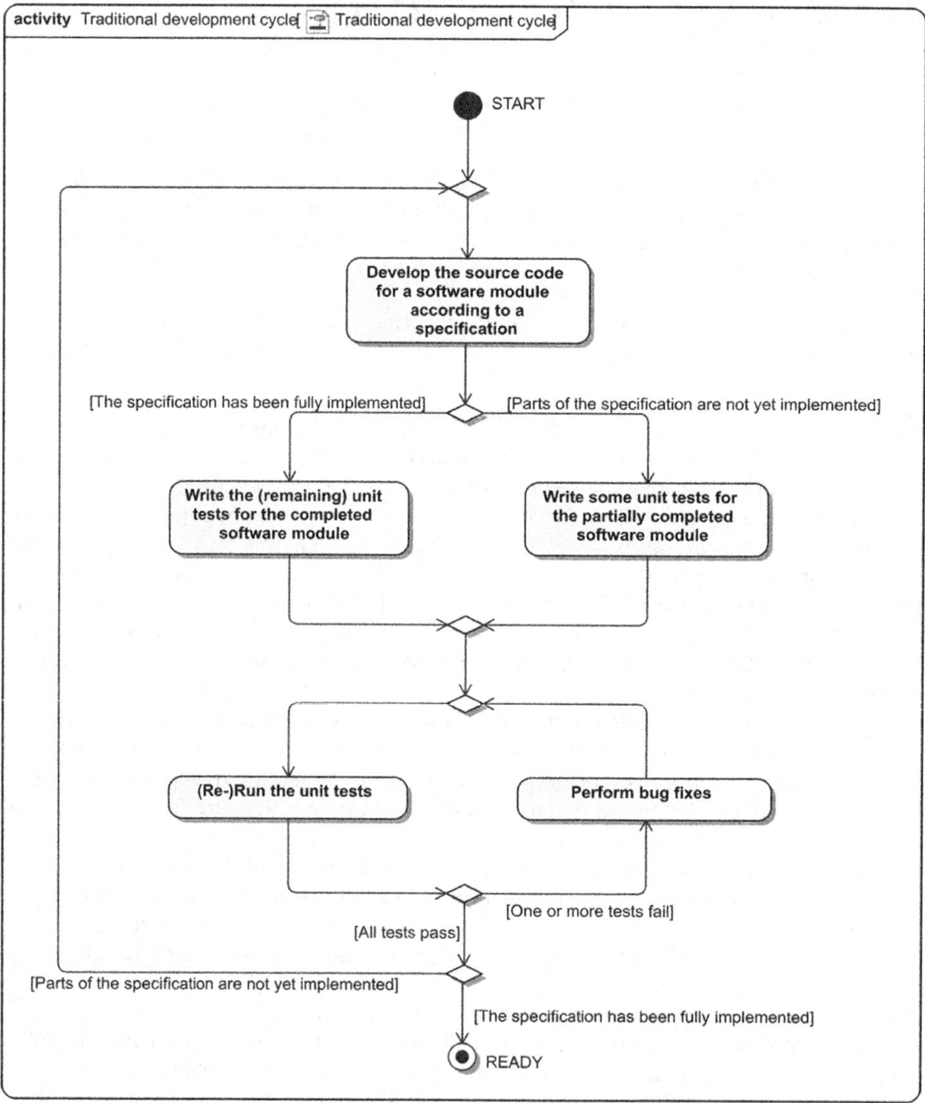

Figure 8-1. *The typical sequence in development with traditional unit testing*

This widespread approach is occasionally also referred to as Plain Old Unit Testing (POUT). Basically, POUT means that the software will be developed "Code First" and not Test First; for example, with this approach, unit tests are written always after the code to be tested has been written. And to many developers this order appears to be the only logical sequence. They argue that to test something, obviously the thing to be tested needs to have been built previously. And in some development organizations, this approach is even mistakenly named as "test-driven development," which is flat wrong.

Like I said, Plain Old Unit Testing is better than no unit testing. Nonetheless, this approach has a few disadvantages:

- There is no compulsion to write the unit tests afterwards. Once a feature works (...or seems to work), there is little motivation to retrofit the code with unit tests. It's no fun, and the temptation to move onto the next thing is just too great for many developers.

- The resulting code can be difficult to test. Often it is not so easy to retrofit existing code with unit tests, because little importance was attached to the testability of the code that was originated. This allowed tightly coupled code to emerge.

- It is not easy to reach pretty-high test coverage with retrofitted unit tests. The writing of unit tests after the code has the tendency that some issues or bugs can slip through.

Test-Driven Development as a Game Changer

Test-Driven Development (TDD) completely turns traditional development around. For developers who have not yet dealt with TDD, this approach represents a paradigm shift.

As a so-called Test First approach and in contrast to POUT, TDD does not allow that any production code is written before the associated test has been written. In other words: TDD means that we write the test for a new feature or function always **before** we write the corresponding production code. This is done strictly step by step: after each implemented test, just enough production code is written that the test will pass. And it is done as long as there are still unrealized requirements for the module to be developed.

At first glance, it seems to be paradoxical, and also a little bit absurd to write a unit test for something that does not yet exist. How can this work?

Don't worry, it works. After we have discussed the process behind TDD in detail in the next section, all doubts are hopefully eliminated.

The Workflow of TDD

When performing Test-Driven Development, the steps depicted in Figure 8-2 are run through repeatedly until all known requirements for the unit to develop are satisfied.

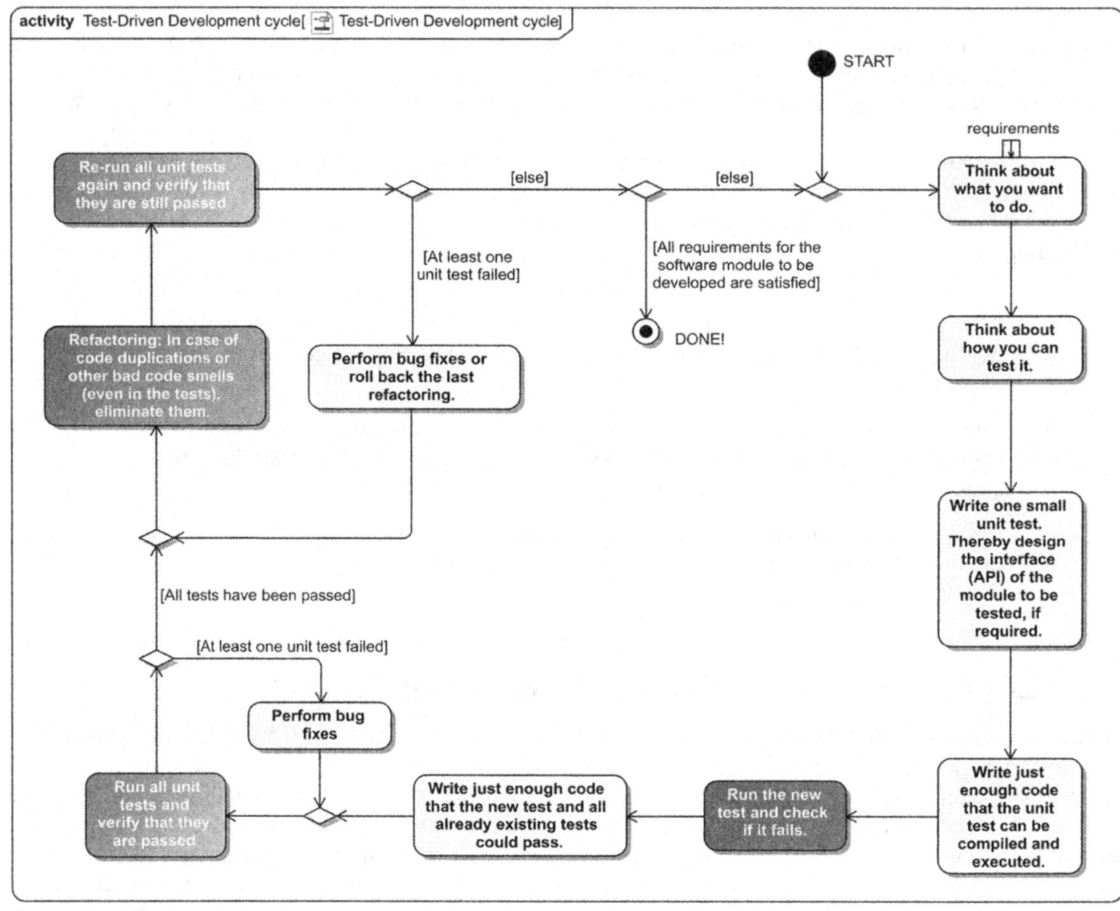

Figure 8-2. *The detailed workflow of TDD as an activity diagram*

First of all, it is remarkable that the first action after the initial node that is labeled with "START" is that the developer should think about what she wants to do. And we see a so-called *Input Pin* at the upper side of this action that accepts "requirements." Which requirements are meant here?

Well, first and foremost there are requirements that must be fulfilled by a software system. This applies both to the requirements of the business stakeholders on the top level regarding the whole system, as well as to the requirements residing on lower abstraction levels, that is, requirements for components, classes, and functions, which were derived from the business stakeholders requirements. With TDD and its Test First approach, requirements are nailed down firmly by unit tests – in fact, before the production code is written. In our case of a Test First approach for the development of units, that is, at the lowest level of the Test Pyramid (see Figure 2-1 in Chapter 2), of course the requirements at the lowest level are meant here.

Next, a test is to be written, whereby the public interface (API) is to be designed. This might be surprising, because in the first run through this cycle we still do not have written any production code. So, what interface can be designed here if we have a blank piece of paper?

Well, the simple answer is this: that "blank piece of paper" is exactly what we want to fill in now, but coming from a different perspective than usual. We now take the perspective of a future external client of the unit to be developed. We use a small test to define how we want to use the unit to be developed. In other words, this is the step that should lead to well-testable and thus also well-usable software units.

After we have written the appropriate lines in the test, we must, of course, also satisfy the compiler and provide the interface requested by the test.

Then immediately the next surprise: the newly written unit test must (initially) fail. Why?

Simple answer: we have to make sure that the test can fail at all. Even a unit test can itself be implemented wrong and, for example, always pass, no matter what we're doing in the production code. So we have to ensure that the newly written test is armed.

Now we are getting to the climax of this small workflow: we write just enough production code – and not a single line more! – that the new unit test (… and, if any, all previously existing tests) is passed! And it is very important to be disciplined at this point and not write more code than required (remember the KISS principle from Chapter 3). It's up to the developer to decide what is appropriate here in each situation. Sometimes a single line of code, or even just one statement, is sufficient; in other cases you need to call a library function. If the latter is the case, the time has now come to think about how to integrate and use this library, and especially how to be able to replace it with a Test Double (see section about Test Doubles (Mock Objects) in Chapter 2).

If we now run the unit tests and we have done everything right, the tests will pass.

Now we have reached a remarkable point in the process. **If the tests pass now, we always have 100% unit test coverage at this step.** Always! Not only 100% in the sense of a technical test coverage metric, such as function coverage, branch coverage, or statement coverage. No, much more important is, that we have 100% unit test coverage regarding the requirements that were already implemented at this point! And yes, at this point possibly there may be still some or many non-implemented requirements for the unit to be developed. This is OK, because we will go through the TDD cycle again and again until all requirements are satisfied. But for a subset of requirements that are already fulfilled at this point, we have 100% unit test coverage.

This fact gives us tremendous power! With this gapless safety net of unit tests, we are now able to carry out fearless refactorings. Code smells (e.g., duplicated code) or design issues can be fixed now. We do not need to be afraid to break functionality, because regularly executed unit tests will give us immediately feedback about that. And the pleasant thing is this: if one or more tests fail during the refactoring phase, the code change that had led to this was a very small one.

After the refactoring has been completed, we can now implement another requirement that has not yet been fulfilled by continuing the TDD cycle. If there are no more requirements, we are ready.

Figure 8-2 depicts the TDD cycle with many details. Boiled down to its three essential main steps as depicted in Figure 8-3, the TDD cycle is often referred to as "RED – GREEN – REFACTOR."

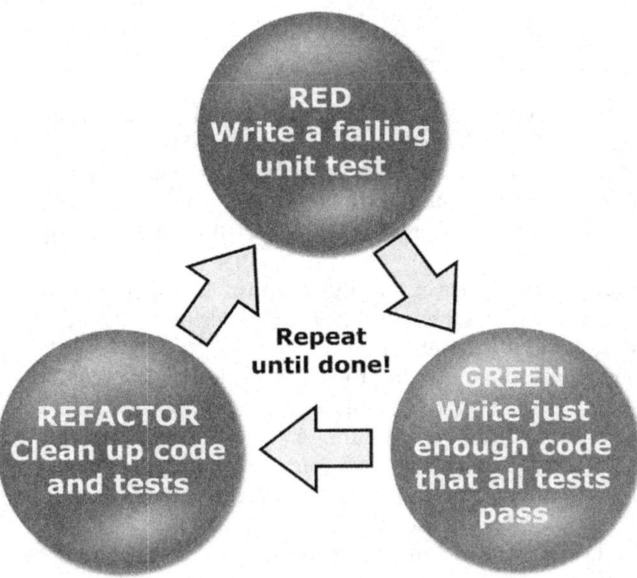

Figure 8-3. *The core workflow of TDD*

- **RED**: We write one failing unit test.

- **GREEN**: We write just enough production code that the new test and all previously written tests will pass.

- **REFACTOR**: Code duplication and other code smells are eliminated, both from the production code as well as from the unit tests.

The terms RED and GREEN refer to typical Unit Test Framework integrations that are available for a variety of IDE's, where tests that passed are displayed green, and tests that failed are shown in red.

UNCLE BOB'S THREE RULES OF TDD

In his great book *The Clean Coder* [Martin11], Robert C. Martin a.k.a. Uncle Bob recommends that we follow the three rules of TDD:

- You are not allowed to write any production code until you have first written a failing unit test.

- You are not allowed to write more of a unit test than is sufficient to fail – and not compiling is failing.

- You are not allowed to write more production code than is sufficient to pass the currently failing unit test.

Martin argues that the strict adherence of these three rules forces the developer to work in very short cycles. As a result, the developer will never be more than a few seconds or just a few minutes away from a comfortable situation where the code was correct and everything worked.

Enough of theory, I will now explain a complete development of a piece of software using TDD by a small example.

TDD by Example: The Roman Numerals Code Kata

The basic idea for what is nowadays called a Code Kata has first been described by Dave Thomas, one of the two authors of the remarkable book *The Pragmatic Programmer* [Hunt99]. Dave was of the opinion that developers should practice on small, not job-related code base repeatedly so that they can master their profession like a musician. He said that developers should constantly learn and improve themselves, and for that purpose they need practice sessions to apply the theory over and over again, using feedback to get better every time.

A code kata is a small exercise in programming, which serves exactly this purpose. The term kata is inherited from the martial arts. In far-eastern combatant sports they use katas to practice their basic moves over and over again. The goal is to bring the course of motion to perfection.

This kind of practice was devolved to software development. To improve their programming skills, developers should practice their craft with the help of small exercises. Katas became an important facet of the Software Craftsmanship movement. They can address different abilities a developer should have, for example, knowing the keyboard shortcuts of the IDE, learning a new programming language, focusing on certain design principles, or practicing TDD. On the Internet, several catalogues with suitable katas for different purposes exist, for example, the collection by Dave Thomas on http://codekata.com.

For our first steps with TDD we use a code kata with an algorithmic emphasis: the well-known Roman numerals code kata.

TDD KATA: CONVERT ARABIC NUMBERS TO ROMAN NUMERALS

The Romans wrote numbers using letters. For instance, they wrote "V" for the Arabic number 5.

Your task is to develop a piece of code using the Test-Driven Development (TDD) approach that translates the Arabic numbers between 1 and 3,999 into their respective Roman representation.

Numbers in the Roman system are represented by combinations of letters from the Latin alphabet. Roman numerals, as used today, are based on seven characters:

```
    1 ⇒ I
    5 ⇒ V
   10 ⇒ X
   50 ⇒ L
  100 ⇒ C
  500 ⇒ D
1,000 ⇒ M
```

Numbers are formed by combining characters together and adding the values. For instance, the Arabic number 12 is represented by "XII" (10 + 1 + 1). And the number 2017 is "MMXVII" in its Roman equivalent.

Exceptions are 4, 9, 40, 90, 400, and 900. To avoid that, four equal characters must be repeated in succession, the number 4, for instance, is not represented by "IIII", but "IV". This is known as subtractive notation, that is, the number that is represented by the preceding character I is subtracted from V (5 - 1 = 4). Another example is "CM," which is 900 (1,000 - 100).

By the way: The Romans had no equivalent for 0, furthermore they didn't know negative numbers.

Preparations

Before we can write our first test, we need to make some preparations and have to set up the test environment.

As the unit test framework for this kata I use *Google Test* (https://github.com/google/googletest), a platform-independent C++ unit test framework released under the *New BSD License*. Of course, any other C++ unit testing framework can be used for this kata as well.

It is also strongly recommended to use a version control system. Apart from a few exceptions, we will perform a commit to the version control system after each pass-through of the TDD cycle. This has the great advantage that we are able to walk back and to regress possibly wrong decisions.

Furthermore we have to think about how the source code files are to be organized. My suggestion for this kata is initially to start with just one file, the file that will take up all future unit tests: `ArabicToRomanNumeralsConverterTestCase.cpp`. Since TDD guides us incrementally through the formation process of a software unit, it is possible to decide later if additional files are required.

For a fundamental function check, we write a main function that initializes Google Test and runs all tests, and we write one simple unit test (named `PreparationsCompleted`) that always fails intentionally, as shown in the following code sample.

Listing 8-1. The initial content of ArabicToRomanNumeralsConverterTestCase.cpp

```cpp
#include <gtest/gtest.h>

int main(int argc, char** argv) {
  testing::InitGoogleTest(&argc, argv);
  return RUN_ALL_TESTS();
}


TEST(ArabicToRomanNumeralsConverterTestCase, PreparationsCompleted) {
  GTEST_FAIL();
}
```

After compiling and linking, we execute the resulting binary file to run the test. The output of our small program on standard output (stdout) should be as follows:

Listing 8-2. The output of the test run

```
[==========] Running 1 test from 1 test case.
[----------] Global test environment set-up.
[----------] 1 test from ArabicToRomanNumeralsConverterTestCase
[ RUN      ] ArabicToRomanNumeralsConverterTestCase.PreparationsCompleted
../ ArabicToRomanNumeralsConverterTestCase.cpp:9: Failure
Failed
[  FAILED  ] ArabicToRomanNumeralsConverterTestCase.PreparationsCompleted (0 ms)
[----------] 1 test from ArabicToRomanNumeralsConverterTestCase (2 ms total)

[----------] Global test environment tear-down
[==========] 1 test from 1 test case ran. (16 ms total)
[  PASSED  ] 0 tests.
[  FAILED  ] 1 test, listed below:
[  FAILED  ] ArabicToRomanNumeralsConverterTestCase.PreparationsCompleted

 1 FAILED TEST
```

As expected, the test fails. The output on stdout is pretty helpful to imagine what went wrong. It specifies the name of the failed tests, the file name, the line number, and the reason why the test failed. In this case, it is a failure that was enforced by a special Google Test macro.

If we now exchange the macro `GTEST_FAIL()` with the macro `GTEST_SUCCEED()` inside the test, after a recompilation the test should pass:

Listing 8-3. The output of the successful test run

```
[==========] Running 1 test from 1 test case.
[----------] Global test environment set-up.
[----------] 1 test from ArabicToRomanNumeralsConverterTestCase
[ RUN      ] ArabicToRomanNumeralsConverterTestCase.PreparationsCompleted
[       OK ] ArabicToRomanNumeralsConverterTestCase.PreparationsCompleted (0 ms)
[----------] 1 test from ArabicToRomanNumeralsConverterTestCase (0 ms total)

[----------] Global test environment tear-down
[==========] 1 test from 1 test case ran. (4 ms total)
[  PASSED  ] 1 test.
```

That's good, because now we know that everything is prepared properly and we can start with our kata.

The First Test

The first step is to decide which first small requirement we want to implement. Then we will write a failing test for it. For our example, we've decided to start with converting a single Arabic number into a Roman numeral: We want to convert the Arabic number 1 into an "I."

Hence, we take the already existing dummy test and convert it into a real unit test, which can prove the fulfillment of this small requirement. Thereby we also have to consider what the interface to the conversion function should look like.

Listing 8-4. The first test (irrelevant parts of the source code were omitted)

```cpp
TEST(ArabicToRomanNumeralsConverterTestCase, 1_isConvertedTo_I) {
  ASSERT_EQ("I", convertArabicNumberToRomanNumeral(1));
}
```

As you can see, we have decided for a simple function that takes an Arabic number as a parameter and has a string as a return value.

But the code cannot be compiled without compiler errors, because the function convertArabicNumberToRomanNumeral() does not yet exist. Let's remember the second of the three rules of TDD by Uncle Bob: "You are not allowed to write more of a unit test than is sufficient to fail – **and not compiling is failing.**"

That means that we now have to stop writing test code to write just enough production code that it can be compiled without errors. So we're going to create the conversion function now, and we'll even write that function directly into the source code file, which also contains the test. Of course, we are aware about the fact that it cannot remain this way.

Listing 8-5. The function stub satisfies the compiler

```cpp
#include <gtest/gtest.h>
#include <string>

int main(int argc, char** argv) {
  testing::InitGoogleTest(&argc, argv);
  return RUN_ALL_TESTS();
}

std::string convertArabicNumberToRomanNumeral(const unsigned int arabicNumber) {
  return "";
}

TEST(ArabicToRomanNumeralsConverterTestCase, 1_isConvertedTo_I) {
  ASSERT_EQ("I", convertArabicNumberToRomanNumeral(1));
}
```

Now the code can be compiled again without errors. And for the moment the function returns only an empty string.

In addition, we now have our first executable test, which must fail (RED), because the test expects an "I," but the function returns an empty string:

Listing 8-6. The output of Google Test after executing the deliberately failing unit test (RED)

```
[==========] Running 1 test from 1 test case.
[----------] Global test environment set-up.
[----------] 1 test from ArabicToRomanNumeralsConverterTestCase
[ RUN      ] ArabicToRomanNumeralsConverterTestCase.1_isConvertedTo_I
../ArabicToRomanNumeralsConverterTestCase.cpp:14: Failure
Value of: convertArabicNumberToRomanNumeral(1)
  Actual: ""
Expected: "I"
[  FAILED  ] ArabicToRomanNumeralsConverterTestCase.1_isConvertedTo_I (0 ms)
[----------] 1 test from ArabicToRomanNumeralsConverterTestCase (0 ms total)

[----------] Global test environment tear-down
[==========] 1 test from 1 test case ran. (6 ms total)
[  PASSED  ] 0 tests.
[  FAILED  ] 1 test, listed below:
[  FAILED  ] ArabicToRomanNumeralsConverterTestCase.1_isConvertedTo_I

 1 FAILED TEST
```

OK, that's what we've expected.

■ **Note**   Depending on the version of Google Test used, the output of the test framework may be slightly different than what is shown here.

Now we need to change the implementation of function convertArabicNumberToRomanNumeral() so that the test will pass. The rule is this: do the simplest thing that could possibly work. And what could be easier than returning an "I" from the function?

Listing 8-7. The changed function (irrelevant parts of the source code were omitted)

```cpp
std::string convertArabicNumberToRomanNumeral(const unsigned int arabicNumber) {
  return "I";
}
```

You will probably say, "Wait a minute! That's not an algorithm to convert Arabic numbers into their Roman equivalents. That's cheating!"

Of course, the algorithm isn't ready yet. You have to change your mind. The rules of TDD state that we should write the simplest bit of code that passes the current test. It is an incremental process, and we are just at the beginning.

```
[==========] Running 1 test from 1 test case.
[----------] Global test environment set-up.
[----------] 1 test from ArabicToRomanNumeralsConverterTestCase
[ RUN      ] ArabicToRomanNumeralsConverterTestCase.1_isConvertedTo_I
[       OK ] ArabicToRomanNumeralsConverterTestCase.1_isConvertedTo_I (0 ms)
[----------] 1 test from ArabicToRomanNumeralsConverterTestCase (0 ms total)

[----------] Global test environment tear-down
[==========] 1 test from 1 test case ran. (1 ms total)
[  PASSED  ] 1 test.
```

Excellent! The test passed (GREEN) and we can go to the refactoring step. Actually there is no need to refactor something yet, so we can just proceed with the next run-through the TDD cycle. But first we have to commit our changes to the source code repository.

The Second Test

For our second unit test we will take a 2, which has to be converted into "II."

```cpp
TEST(ArabicToRomanNumeralsConverterTestCase, 2_isConvertedTo_II) {
  ASSERT_EQ("II", convertArabicNumberToRomanNumeral(2));
}
```

Unsurprisingly, this test must fail (RED), because our function convertArabicNumberToRomanNumeral() returns always an "I." After we have verified that the test fails, we complement the implementation so that the test could pass. Once again, we do the simplest thing that could possibly work.

Listing 8-8. We add some code to pass the new test

```cpp
std::string convertArabicNumberToRomanNumeral(const unsigned int arabicNumber) {
  if (arabicNumber == 2) {
    return "II";
  }
  return "I";
}
```

Both tests pass (GREEN).

Should we refactor something now? Maybe not yet, but you might get a sneaking suspicion that we will need a refactoring soon. At the moment we continue with our third test...

The Third Test and the Tidying Afterwards

Unsurprisingly, our third test will test the conversion of the number 3:

```cpp
TEST(ArabicToRomanNumeralsConverterTestCase, 3_isConvertedTo_III) {
  ASSERT_EQ("III", convertArabicNumberToRomanNumeral(3));
}
```

Of course, this test will fail (RED). The code to pass this test, and all previously tests (GREEN), looks as follows:

```cpp
std::string convertArabicNumberToRomanNumeral(const unsigned int arabicNumber) {
  if (arabicNumber == 3) {
    return "III";
  }
  if (arabicNumber == 2) {
    return "II";
  }
  return "I";
}
```

The bad gut feeling about the emerging design, which we already had on the second test, was not unfounded. At least now we should be completely dissatisfied with the obvious code duplication. It's pretty evident that we cannot continue this path. An endless sequence of if-statements cannot be a solution, because we will end up with a horrible design. It's time for refactoring, and we can do it without fear, because 100% unit test coverage creates a comfortable feeling of safety!

If we take a look at the code inside function `convertArabicNumberToRomanNumeral()`, a pattern is recognizable. The Arabic number is like a counter of the I-characters of its Roman equivalent. In other words: as long as the number to be converted can be decremented by 1 before it reaches 0, an "I" is added to the Roman numeral string.

Well, this can be done in an elegant way using a while-loop and string concatenation, like this:

Listing 8-9. The conversion function after refactoring

```cpp
std::string convertArabicNumberToRomanNumeral(unsigned int arabicNumber) {
  std::string romanNumeral;
  while (arabicNumber >= 1) {
    romanNumeral += "I";
    arabicNumber--;
  }
  return romanNumeral;
}
```

That looks pretty good. We have removed code duplication and found a compact solution. We also had to remove the `const` declaration from parameter `arabicNumber` because we have to manipulate the Arabic number in the function. And the three existing unit tests are still passed.

We can proceed to the next test. Of course you can also continue with the 5, but I decided for "10-is-X." I have the hope that the group of ten will reveal a similar pattern as 1, 2, and 3. The Arabic number 5 will, of course, be treated later.

Listing 8-10. The 4th unit test

```cpp
TEST(ArabicToRomanNumeralsConverterTestCase, 10_isConvertedTo_X) {
  ASSERT_EQ("X", convertArabicNumberToRomanNumeral(10));
}
```

Well, it shouldn't surprise anyone that this test fails (RED). Here is what Google Test writes on stdout about this new test:

```
[ RUN      ] ArabicToRomanNumeralsConverterTestCase.10_isConvertedTo_X
../ArabicToRomanNumeralsConverterTestCase.cpp:31: Failure
Value of: convertArabicNumberToRomanNumeral(10)
  Actual: "IIIIIIIIII"
Expected: "X"
[  FAILED  ] ArabicToRomanNumeralsConverterTestCase.10_isConvertedTo_X (0 ms)
```

The test fails, because 10 is not "IIIIIIIIII," but "X." However, if we see the output of Google Test, we could get an idea. Maybe the same approach that we've used for the Arabic numbers 1, 2. and 3, could be used also for 10, 20, and 30?

STOP! Well, that's imaginable, but we should not yet create something for the future without unit tests that lead us to such a solution. We would not work test-driven anymore, if we implement the production code for 20 and 30 in one go with the code for 10. So, we do again the simplest thing that could possibly work.

Listing 8-11. The conversion function can now also convert 10

```cpp
std::string convertArabicNumberToRomanNumeral(unsigned int arabicNumber) {
  if (arabicNumber == 10) {
    return "X";
  } else {
    std::string romanNumeral;
    while (arabicNumber >= 1) {
      romanNumeral += "I";
      arabicNumber--;
    }
    return romanNumeral;
  }
}
```

OK, the test and all previous tests are passed (GREEN). We can stepwise add a test for the Arabic number 20, and then for 30. After we've run through the TDD cycle for both cases, our conversion function looks as follows:

Listing 8-12. The result during the 6th TDD-cycle before refactoring

```cpp
std::string convertArabicNumberToRomanNumeral(unsigned int arabicNumber) {
  if (arabicNumber == 10) {
    return "X";
  } else if (arabicNumber == 20) {
    return "XX";
  } else if (arabicNumber == 30) {
    return "XXX";
  } else {
    std::string romanNumeral;
    while (arabicNumber >= 1) {
      romanNumeral += "I";
      arabicNumber--;
    }
    return romanNumeral;
  }
}
```

At least now a refactoring is urgently required. The emerged code has some bad smells, like some redundancies and a high cyclomatic complexity. However, our suspicion has also been confirmed that the processing of the numbers 10, 20, and 30 follows a similar pattern to processing the numbers 1, 2, and 3. Let's try it:

Listing 8-13. After the refactoring all if-else-decisions are gone

```cpp
std::string convertArabicNumberToRomanNumeral(unsigned int arabicNumber) {
  std::string romanNumeral;
  while (arabicNumber >= 10) {
    romanNumeral += "X";
    arabicNumber -= 10;
  }
  while (arabicNumber >= 1) {
```

```
    romanNumeral += "I";
    arabicNumber--;
  }
  return romanNumeral;
}
```

Excellent, all tests passed immediately! It seems that we are on the right track.

We must, however, have the goal in mind of the refactoring step in the TDD cycle. Further up in this section you can read the following: Code duplication and other code smells are eliminated, both from the production code **as well as from the unit tests**.

We should take a critical look at our test code. Currently it looks like this:

Listing 8-14. The emerged unit tests have a lot of code duplications

```
TEST(ArabicToRomanNumeralsConverterTestCase, 1_isConvertedTo_I) {
  ASSERT_EQ("I", convertArabicNumberToRomanNumeral(1));
}

TEST(ArabicToRomanNumeralsConverterTestCase, 2_isConvertedTo_II) {
  ASSERT_EQ("II", convertArabicNumberToRomanNumeral(2));
}

TEST(ArabicToRomanNumeralsConverterTestCase, 3_isConvertedTo_III) {
  ASSERT_EQ("III", convertArabicNumberToRomanNumeral(3));
}

TEST(ArabicToRomanNumeralsConverterTestCase, 10_isConvertedTo_X) {
  ASSERT_EQ("X", convertArabicNumberToRomanNumeral(10));
}

TEST(ArabicToRomanNumeralsConverterTestCase, 20_isConvertedTo_XX) {
  ASSERT_EQ("XX", convertArabicNumberToRomanNumeral(20));
}

TEST(ArabicToRomanNumeralsConverterTestCase, 30_isConvertedTo_XXX) {
  ASSERT_EQ("XXX", convertArabicNumberToRomanNumeral(30));
}
```

Please remember what I wrote about test code quality in Chapter 2: the quality of the test code must be as high as the quality of the production code. In other words, our tests need to be refactored, because they contain a lot of duplication and should be designed more elegantly. Furthermore we want to increase their readability and maintainability. But what can we do?

Take a look at the six tests above. The verification in the tests is always the same and could be read more generally as: "Assert that Arabic number <x> is converted to the Roman numeral <string>."

A solution could be to provide a dedicated assertion (also known as *custom assertion* or *custom matcher*) for that purpose, which can be read in the same way as the sentence above:

```
assertThat(x).isConvertedToRomanNumeral("string");
```

More Sophisticated Tests with a Custom Assertion

To implement our custom assertion, we first of all write a unit test that fails, but different to the unit tests we've written before:

```
TEST(ArabicToRomanNumeralsConverterTestCase, 33_isConvertedTo_XXXIII) {
  assertThat(33).isConvertedToRomanNumeral("XXXII");
}
```

The probability is very high that the conversion of 33 already works. Therefore, we force the test to fail (RED) by specifying an intentional wrong result as the expected value ("XXXII"). But this new test fails also due to another reason: the compiler cannot compile the unit test without errors. A function named assertThat does not exist yet, equally there is no isConvertedToRomanNumeral. Always remember Robert C. Martin's second rule of TDD (see above): "You are not allowed to write more of a unit test than is sufficient to fail – **and not compiling is failing.**"

So we must first satisfy the compiler by writing the custom assertion. This will consist of two parts:

- A free assertThat(<parameter>) function, returning one instance of a custom assertion class.

- The custom assertion class that contains the real assertion method, verifying one or various properties of the tested object.

Listing 8-15. A custom assertion for Roman numerals

```
class RomanNumeralAssert {
public:
  RomanNumeralAssert() = delete;
  explicit RomanNumeralAssert(const unsigned int arabicNumber) :
      arabicNumberToConvert(arabicNumber) { }
  void isConvertedToRomanNumeral(const std::string& expectedRomanNumeral) const {
    ASSERT_EQ(expectedRomanNumeral, convertArabicNumberToRomanNumeral(arabicNumberToConvert));
  }

private:
  const unsigned int arabicNumberToConvert;
};

RomanNumeralAssert assertThat(const unsigned int arabicNumber) {
  RomanNumeralAssert assert { arabicNumber };
  return assert;
}
```

▪ **Note**   Instead of a free function assertThat, a static and public class method can also be used in the assertion class. This can be necessary when you're facing namespace violations, for example, clashes of identical function names. Of course, then the namespace name must be prepended when using the class method: RomanNumeralAssert::assertThat(33).isConvertedToRomanNumeral("XXXIII");

Now the code can be compiled without errors, but the new test will fail as expected during execution.

Listing 8-16. An excerpt from the output of Google-Test on stdout

```
[ RUN      ] ArabicToRomanNumeralsConverterTestCase.33_isConvertedTo_XXXIII
../ArabicToRomanNumeralsConverterTestCase.cpp:30: Failure
Value of: convertArabicNumberToRomanNumeral(arabicNumberToConvert)
  Actual: "XXXIII"
Expected: expectedRomanNumeral
Which is: "XXXII"
[  FAILED  ] ArabicToRomanNumeralsConverterTestCase.33_isConvertedTo_XXXIII (0 ms)
```

So we need to modify the test and correct the Roman numeral that we expect as the result.

Listing 8-17. Our Custom Asserter allows a more compact spelling of the test code

```
TEST(ArabicToRomanNumeralsConverterTestCase, 33_isConvertedTo_XXXIII) {
  assertThat(33).isConvertedToRomanNumeral("XXXIII");
}
```

Now we can sum up all previous tests into a single one.

Listing 8-18. All checks can be elegantly pooled in one test function

```
TEST(ArabicToRomanNumeralsConverterTestCase, conversionOfArabicNumbersToRomanNumerals_Works)
{
  assertThat(1).isConvertedToRomanNumeral("I");
  assertThat(2).isConvertedToRomanNumeral("II");
  assertThat(3).isConvertedToRomanNumeral("III");
  assertThat(10).isConvertedToRomanNumeral("X");
  assertThat(20).isConvertedToRomanNumeral("XX");
  assertThat(30).isConvertedToRomanNumeral("XXX");
  assertThat(33).isConvertedToRomanNumeral("XXXIII");
}
```

Take a look at our test code now: redundancy-free, clean, and easily readable. The directness of our self-made assertion is quite elegant. And it is blindingly easy to add more tests now, because we have just to write a single line of code for every new test.

You might complain that this refactoring also has a small disadvantage. The name of the test method is now less specific than the name of all test methods prior to the refactoring (see section Unit Test Names in Chapter 2). Can we tolerate these small drawbacks? I think yes. We've made a compromise here: This little disadvantage is compensated by the benefits in terms of maintainability and extensibility of our tests.

Now we can continue the TDD cycle and implement the production code successively for the following three tests:

```
assertThat(100).isConvertedToRomanNumeral("C");
assertThat(200).isConvertedToRomanNumeral("CC");
assertThat(300).isConvertedToRomanNumeral("CCC");
```

After three iterations the code will look like this prior to the refactoring step:

Listing 8-19. Our conversion function in the 9th TDD cycle before refactoring

```cpp
std::string convertArabicNumberToRomanNumeral(unsigned int arabicNumber) {
  std::string romanNumeral;
  if (arabicNumber == 100) {
    romanNumeral = "C";
  } else if (arabicNumber == 200) {
    romanNumeral = "CC";
  } else if (arabicNumber == 300) {
    romanNumeral = "CCC";
  } else {
    while (arabicNumber >= 10) {
      romanNumeral += "X";
      arabicNumber -= 10;
    }
    while (arabicNumber >= 1) {
      romanNumeral += "I";
      arabicNumber--;
    }
  }
  return romanNumeral;
}
```

And again the same pattern emerges as before with 1, 2, 3; and 10, 20, and 30. We can also use a similar loop for the hundreds:

Listing 8-20. The emerging pattern, as well as which parts of the code are variable and which are identical, is clearly recognizable

```cpp
std::string convertArabicNumberToRomanNumeral(unsigned int arabicNumber) {
  std::string romanNumeral;
  while (arabicNumber >= 100) {
    romanNumeral += "C";
    arabicNumber -= 100;
  }
  while (arabicNumber >= 10) {
    romanNumeral += "X";
    arabicNumber -= 10;
  }
  while (arabicNumber >= 1) {
    romanNumeral += "I";
    arabicNumber--;
  }
  return romanNumeral;
}
```

It's Time to Clean Up Again

At this point we should take once again a critical look at our code. If we continue like this, the code will contain many code duplications, because the three while-statements are looking very similar. We can, however, take advantage of these similarities by abstracting the code parts that are equal in all three while-loops.

It's refactoring time! The only code parts that are different in all three while-loops are the Arabic number and its corresponding Roman numeral. The idea is to separate these variable parts from the rest of the loop.

In a first step, we introduce a struct that maps Arabic numbers to its Roman equivalent. In addition, we need an array (we will use std::array from the C++ Standard Library here) of that struct. Initially we will only add one element to the array that allocates letter "C" to the number 100.

Listing 8-21. Introducing an array that holds mappings between Arabic numbers and their Roman equivalent

```cpp
struct ArabicToRomanMapping {
  unsigned int arabicNumber;
  std::string romanNumeral;
};

const std::size_t numberOfMappings = 1;
using ArabicToRomanMappings = std::array<ArabicToRomanMapping, numberOfMappings>;

const ArabicToRomanMappings arabicToRomanMappings = {
  { 100, "C" }
};
```

After these preparations, we modify the first while-loop in the conversion function to verify if the basic idea will work.

Listing 8-22. Replacing the literals with entries from the new array

```cpp
std::string convertArabicNumberToRomanNumeral(unsigned int arabicNumber) {
  std::string romanNumeral;
  while (arabicNumber >= arabicToRomanMappings[0].arabicNumber) {
    romanNumeral += arabicToRomanMappings[0].romanNumeral;
    arabicNumber -= arabicToRomanMappings[0].arabicNumber;
  }
  while (arabicNumber >= 10) {
    romanNumeral += "X";
    arabicNumber -= 10;
  }
  while (arabicNumber >= 1) {
    romanNumeral += "I";
    arabicNumber--;
  }
  return romanNumeral;
}
```

All tests pass. So we can continue to fill the array with the mappings "10-is-X," and "1-is-I" (don't forget to adjust the array size accordingly!).

Listing 8-23. Again a pattern emerges: the obvious code redundancy can be eliminated by a loop

```cpp
const std::size_t numberOfMappings { 3 };
// ...
const ArabicToRomanMappings arabicToRomanMappings = { {
  { 100, "C" },
  {  10, "X" },
  {   1, "I" }
} };
```

```cpp
std::string convertArabicNumberToRomanNumeral(unsigned int arabicNumber) {
  std::string romanNumeral;
  while (arabicNumber >= arabicToRomanMappings[0].arabicNumber) {
    romanNumeral += arabicToRomanMappings[0].romanNumeral;
    arabicNumber -= arabicToRomanMappings[0].arabicNumber;
  }
  while (arabicNumber >= arabicToRomanMappings[1].arabicNumber) {
    romanNumeral += arabicToRomanMappings[1].romanNumeral;
    arabicNumber -= arabicToRomanMappings[1].arabicNumber;
  }
  while (arabicNumber >= arabicToRomanMappings[2].arabicNumber) {
    romanNumeral += arabicToRomanMappings[2].romanNumeral;
    arabicNumber -= arabicToRomanMappings[2].arabicNumber;
  }
  return romanNumeral;
}
```

And again, all tests are passed. Excellent! But there is still a lot of duplicated code, so we have to continue our refactoring. The good news is that we can now see that the only difference in all three while-loops is just the array index. This means that we can get along with just one while-loop if we would iterate through the array.

Listing 8-24. Through the range based for-loop, the DRY principle is no more violated

```cpp
std::string convertArabicNumberToRomanNumeral(unsigned int arabicNumber) {
  std::string romanNumeral;
  for (const auto& mapping : arabicToRomanMappings) {
    while (arabicNumber >= mapping.arabicNumber) {
      romanNumeral += mapping.romanNumeral;
      arabicNumber -= mapping.arabicNumber;
    }
  }
  return romanNumeral;
}
```

All tests pass. Wow, that's great! Just take a look at this compact and well-readable piece of code. More mappings of Arabic numbers to their Roman equivalents can now be supported by adding them to the array. We will try this for 1,000, which must be converted into an "M." Here is our next test:

```cpp
assertThat(1000).isConvertedToRomanNumeral("M");
```

The test failed as expected. By adding another element for "1000-is-M" to the array, the new test, and of course all previously tests, should pass.

```cpp
const ArabicToRomanMappings arabicToRomanMappings = { {
    { 1000, "M" },
    {  100, "C" },
    {   10, "X" },
    {    1, "I" }
} };
```

A successful test run after this small change confirms our assumption: it works! That was quite easy. We can add more tests now, for example, for 2,000 and 3,000. And even 3,333 should work immediately:

```
assertThat(2000).isConvertedToRomanNumeral("MM");
assertThat(3000).isConvertedToRomanNumeral("MMM");
assertThat(3333).isConvertedToRomanNumeral("MMMCCCXXXIII");
```

Good. Our code works even with these cases. However, there are some Roman numerals that have not yet been implemented. For example the 5 that has to be converted to "V."

```
assertThat(5).isConvertedToRomanNumeral("V");
```

As expected, this test fails. The interesting question is the following: what should we do now that the test gets passed? Maybe you think about a special treatment of this case. But is this really a special case, or can we treat this conversion in the same way as the previous and already implemented conversions?

Probably the simplest thing that could possibly work is to just add a new element at the correct index to our array? Well, maybe it's worth it to try it out...

```
const ArabicToRomanMappings arabicToRomanMappings = { {
    { 1000, "M" },
    {  100, "C" },
    {   10, "X" },
    {    5, "V" },
    {    1, "I" }
} };
```

Our assumption was true: All tests are passed! Even Arabic numbers like 6 and 37 should be converted correctly now to their Roman equivalent. We verify that by adding assertions for these cases:

```
   assertThat(6).isConvertedToRomanNumeral("VI");
//...
   assertThat(37).isConvertedToRomanNumeral("XXXVII");
```

Approaching the Finish Line

And it comes as no surprise that we can use basically the same approach for "50-is-L" and "500-is-D."

Next we need to deal with the implementation of the so-called subtraction notation, for example, the Arabic number 4 has to be converted to the Roman numeral "IV." How could we implement these special cases elegantly?

Well, after a short consideration it becomes obvious that these cases are nothing really special! Ultimately, it is of course not forbidden to add a mapping rule to our array where the string contains two instead of one character. For instance, we can just add a new "4-is-IV" entry to the arabicToRomanMappings array. Maybe you will say, "Isn't that a hack?" No, I don't think so. It is pragmatic and easy, without making things unnecessarily complicated.

Therefore, we first add a new test that will fail:

```
assertThat(4).isConvertedToRomanNumeral("IV");
```

For the new test to be passed, we add the corresponding mapping rule for 4 (see the penultimate entry in the array):

```cpp
const ArabicToRomanMappings arabicToRomanMappings = { {
    { 1000, "M"  },
    {  500, "D"  },
    {  100, "C"  },
    {   50, "L"  },
    {   10, "X"  },
    {    5, "V"  },
    {    4, "IV" },
    {    1, "I"  }
} };
```

After we've executed all tests and verified that they passed, we can be certain that our solution also works for 4! Hence, we can repeat that pattern for "9-is-IX," "40-is-XL," "90-is-XC," and so on. The schema is always the same, so I do not show the resulting source code here (the final result with the complete code is shown below), but I think it's not hard to comprehend.

Done!

The interesting question is this: When do we know that we are done? That the piece of software that we have to implement is finished? That we can discontinue running through the TDD cycle? Do we really have to test all the numbers from 1 up to 3999 each by a unit test to know that we're done?

The simple answer: **If all requirements on our piece of code have been successfully implemented, and we do not find a new unit test that would lead to new production code, we are done!**

And that is exactly the case right now for our TDD kata. We could still add many more assertions to the test method; the test would be passed each time without the necessity to change the production code. This is the way TDD "speaks" to us: "Hey, dude, you're done!"

The result looks like the following:

Listing 8-25. This version has been checked-in at GitHub (URL see below) with the commit message "Done."

```cpp
#include <gtest/gtest.h>
#include <string>
#include <array>

int main(int argc, char** argv) {
  testing::InitGoogleTest(&argc, argv);
  return RUN_ALL_TESTS();
}

struct ArabicToRomanMapping {
  unsigned int arabicNumber;
  std::string romanNumeral;
};

const std::size_t numberOfMappings { 13 };
using ArabicToRomanMappings = std::array<ArabicToRomanMapping, numberOfMappings>;
```

```cpp
const ArabicToRomanMappings arabicToRomanMappings = { {
    { 1000, "M"  },
    {  900, "CM" },
    {  500, "D"  },
    {  400, "CD" },
    {  100, "C"  },
    {   90, "XC" },
    {   50, "L"  },
    {   40, "XL" },
    {   10, "X"  },
    {    9, "IX" },
    {    5, "V"  },
    {    4, "IV" },
    {    1, "I"  }
} };

std::string convertArabicNumberToRomanNumeral(unsigned int arabicNumber) {
  std::string romanNumeral;
  for (const auto& mapping : arabicToRomanMappings) {
    while (arabicNumber >= mapping.arabicNumber) {
      romanNumeral += mapping.romanNumeral;
      arabicNumber -= mapping.arabicNumber;
    }
  }
  return romanNumeral;
}

// Test code starts here...

class RomanNumeralAssert {
public:
  RomanNumeralAssert() = delete;
  explicit RomanNumeralAssert(const unsigned int arabicNumber) :
      arabicNumberToConvert(arabicNumber) { }
  void isConvertedToRomanNumeral(const std::string& expectedRomanNumeral) const {
    ASSERT_EQ(expectedRomanNumeral, convertArabicNumberToRomanNumeral(arabicNumberToConvert));
  }

private:
  const unsigned int arabicNumberToConvert;
};

RomanNumeralAssert assertThat(const unsigned int arabicNumber) {
  return RomanNumeralAssert { arabicNumber };
}

TEST(ArabicToRomanNumeralsConverterTestCase, conversionOfArabicNumbersToRomanNumerals_Works)
{
  assertThat(1).isConvertedToRomanNumeral("I");
  assertThat(2).isConvertedToRomanNumeral("II");
  assertThat(3).isConvertedToRomanNumeral("III");
```

```
  assertThat(4).isConvertedToRomanNumeral("IV");
  assertThat(5).isConvertedToRomanNumeral("V");
  assertThat(6).isConvertedToRomanNumeral("VI");
  assertThat(9).isConvertedToRomanNumeral("IX");
  assertThat(10).isConvertedToRomanNumeral("X");
  assertThat(20).isConvertedToRomanNumeral("XX");
  assertThat(30).isConvertedToRomanNumeral("XXX");
  assertThat(33).isConvertedToRomanNumeral("XXXIII");
  assertThat(37).isConvertedToRomanNumeral("XXXVII");
  assertThat(50).isConvertedToRomanNumeral("L");
  assertThat(99).isConvertedToRomanNumeral("XCIX");
  assertThat(100).isConvertedToRomanNumeral("C");
  assertThat(200).isConvertedToRomanNumeral("CC");
  assertThat(300).isConvertedToRomanNumeral("CCC");
  assertThat(499).isConvertedToRomanNumeral("CDXCIX");
  assertThat(500).isConvertedToRomanNumeral("D");
  assertThat(1000).isConvertedToRomanNumeral("M");
  assertThat(2000).isConvertedToRomanNumeral("MM");
  assertThat(2017).isConvertedToRomanNumeral("MMXVII");
  assertThat(3000).isConvertedToRomanNumeral("MMM");
  assertThat(3333).isConvertedToRomanNumeral("MMMCCCXXXIII");
  assertThat(3999).isConvertedToRomanNumeral("MMMCMXCIX");
}
```

■ **Info**   The source code of the completed Roman Numerals Kata, including its version history, can be found on GitHub at: `https://github.com/clean-cpp/book-samples/`.

Wait! However, there is still one really important step to be taken: we must separate the production code from the test code. We used the file `ArabicToRomanNumeralsConverterTestCase.cpp` all the time like our workbench, but now the time has come that the software crafter has to remove his finished piece of work from the vise. In other words, the production code has now to be moved into a different, still-to-be created new file; but of course the unit tests should still be able to test the code.

During this last refactoring step, some design decisions can be made. For example, does it remain with a free-standing conversion function, or should the conversion method and the array be wrapped into a new class? I would clearly favor the latter (embedding the code in a class) because it is toward an object-oriented design, and it is easier to hide implementation details with the help of encapsulation.

No matter how the production code will be provided and be integrated in its usage environment (this depends on the purpose), our gapless unit test coverage makes it unlikely that thereby something will go wrong.

The Advantages of TDD

Test-Driven Development is primarily a tool and technique for incremental design and development of a software component. That's why the acronym TDD is also often referred to as "Test-Driven Design." It's one way, of course not the only way, to think through your requirements or design before your write the production code.

The significant advantages of TDD are the following:

- **TDD, if done right, forces you to take small steps when writing software.** The approach ensures that you always have to write just a few lines of production code to reach the comfortable state again where everything works. This also means that you are at most a few lines of code away from a situation where everything still has worked. This is the main difference to the traditional approach of producing and changing a lot of production code beforehand, which goes hand in hand with the drawback that the software sometimes cannot be compiled and executed without errors for hours or days.

- **TDD establishes a very fast feedback loop.** Developers must always know if they are still working on a correct system. Therefore it is important for them that they have a fast feedback loop to know in a split second that everything works correctly. Complex system and integration tests, especially if they are still carried out manually, are not capable of this and are much too slow (remember the Test Pyramid in Chapter 2).

- **Creating a unit test first helps a developer to really consider what needs to be done.** In other words, TDD ensures that code is not simply hacked down from the brain into the keyboard. That's good, because code that was written this way is often error prone, difficult to read, and sometimes even superfluous. Many developers are usually going faster than their true capacity to deliver good work. TDD is a way to slow the developers down in a positive sense. Don't worry, managers, it is good that your developers slow down, because this will soon be rewarded with a noticeable increase in quality and speed in the development process when the high test coverage reveals its positive effect.

- **With TDD a gapless specification arises in the form of executable code.** Specifications written in natural language with a text processing program of an Office suite, for example, are not executable – they are "dead artifacts."

- **The developer deals much more consciously and responsibly with dependencies.** If another software component or even an external system (for example, a database) is required, this dependency can be defined due to an abstraction (interface) and replaced by a test double (a.k.a. mock object) for the test. The resulting software modules (e.g., classes) are smaller, loosely coupled, and contain only the code necessary to pass the tests.

- **The emerging production code with TDD will have 100% unit test coverage by default.** If TDD was performed correctly, there should not be a single line of production code that was not motivated by a previously written unit test.

Test-Driven Development can be a driver and enabler for a good and sustainable software design. As with many other tools and methods, the practice of TDD cannot guarantee a good design. It is not a silver bullet for design issues. The design decisions are still taken by the developer and not by the tool. At the least, TDD is a helpful approach to avoid what might be perceived as bad design. Many developers who use TDD in their daily work can confirm that it is extremely hard to produce or tolerate bad and messy code with this approach.

And there is no doubt about when a developer has finished implementing all required functionalities: if all unit tests are green, it means that all requirements on the unit are satisfied and the job is done! And an enjoyable side effect is that it's done in high quality.

In addition, the TDD workflow also drives the design of the unit to be developed, especially its interface. With TDD and Test First, the API's design and implementation are guided by its test cases. Anyone who has ever tried to write unit tests for legacy code knows how difficult that could be. These systems are typically built "Code First." Many inconvenient dependencies and a bad API design complicate testing in such systems. And if a software unit is hard to test, it is also hard to (re-)use. With other words: TDD gives an early feedback on a software unit's usability, that is, how simple that piece of software can be integrated and used in its planned execution environment.

When We Should Not Use TDD

The final question is this: should we develop every piece of code of a system using a test first approach?

My clear answer is **No!**

No doubt: Test-Driven Development is a great practice to guide the design and implementation of a piece of software. Theoretically, it would even be possible to develop almost all parts of a software system this way. And as a kind of positive side effect, the emerging code is 100% tested by default.

But some parts of a project are so simple, small, or less complex, that it doesn't justify this approach. If you can write your code quickly off the cuff, because complexity and risks are low, then of course you can do that. Examples of such situations are pure data classes without functionality (which is, by the way, a smell, but for other reasons; see section about anemic classes in Chapter 6), or simple glue code that just couples together with two modules.

Furthermore, prototyping can be a very difficult task with TDD. When you enter new territory, or you should develop software in a very innovative environment without domain experience, you're sometimes not sure what road you're going to take to a solution. Writing unit tests first in projects with very volatile and fuzzy requirements can be an extremely challenging task. Sometimes it may be better to write down a first rudimentary solution easily and quickly then, and to ensure its quality in a later step with the help of retrofitted Unit Tests.

Another big challenge, for which TDD won't help, is getting a good architecture. TDD does not replace the necessary reflecting on the coarse-grained structures (subsystems, components, ...) of your software system. If you are faced with fundamental decisions about frameworks, libraries, technologies, or architecture patterns, TDD will not help you.

For anything else I strongly recommend TDD. This approach can save a lot of time, headaches, and false starts when you must develop a software unit, like a class, in C++.

For anything that is more complex than just a few lines of code, software craftsmen can test-drive code as fast as other developers can write code without tests, if not faster.

—Sandro Mancuso

■ **Tip**   If you want to dive deeper into Test-Driven Development with C++, I recommend the excellent book *Modern C++ Programming with Test-Driven Development* [Langr13] by Jeff Langr. Jeff's book offers much deeper insights into TDD and gives you hands-on lessons in the challenges and rewards of doing TDD in C++.

CHAPTER 9

Design Patterns and Idioms

Good craftspeople can draw on a wealth of experience and knowledge. Once they've found a good solution for a certain problem, they take this solution into their repertoire to apply it in the future to a similar problem. Ideally, they transform their solution into something that is known as a *canonical form* and document it, both for themselves and for others.

> ## CANONICAL FORM
>
> The term Canonical Form in this context describes a representation of something that is reduced to the simplest and most significant form without losing generality. Related to design patterns, the canonical form of a pattern describes its most basic elements: name, context, problem, forces, solution, examples, drawbacks, etc.

This is also true for software developers. Experienced developers can draw on a wealth of sample solutions for constantly recurring design problems in software. They share their knowledge with others and make it reusable for similar problems. The principle behind this: **Don't reinvent the wheel!**

In 1995, a much-noticed and widely acclaimed book was published. Its four authors, namely Erich Gamma, Richard Helm, Ralph Johnson, and John Vlissides, also known as the *Gang of Four* (GoF), introduced the principle of design patterns into software development and presented a catalogue of 23 object-oriented design patterns. Its title is *Design Patterns: Elements of Reusable Object-Oriented Software* [Gamma95] and can be regarded until today as one of the most important works in the software development domain.

Some people believe that Gamma et al. had invented all the design patterns that are described in their book. But that's not true. Design patterns are not invented, but they can be found. The authors have examined software systems that were well made regarding flexibility, maintainability, and extendibility. They found the cause of these positive characteristics and described them in a canonical form.

After the book of the Gang of Four had appeared, it was thought that there would be a flood of pattern books in the following years. But this did not happen. Indeed, in the following years there were a few other important books on the subject pattern, such as *Pattern-Oriented Software Architecture* (also known under the acronym "POSA") [Busch96] or *Patterns of Enterprise Application Architecture* [Fowler02] about architectural patterns, but the expected huge mass stayed out.

Design Principles vs. Design Patterns

In the previous chapters, we have discussed a lot of design principles. But how are these principles related to design patterns? What is more important?

© Stephan Roth 2017
S. Roth, *Clean C++*, DOI 10.1007/978-1-4842-2793-0_9

Well, let's assume just hypothetically that perhaps one day object orientation will become totally unpopular, and Functional Programming (see Chapter 7) will be the dominating programming paradigm. Are principles like KISS, DRY, YAGNI, Single Responsibility Principle, Open-Closed Principle, Information Hiding, etc., becoming invalid then and thus worthless? The clear answer is **no!**

A principle is a fundamental "truth" or "law" that serves as the foundation for decisions. Therefore, a principle is in most cases independent from a certain programming paradigm or technology. The KISS principle (see Chapter 3), for instance, is a very universal principle. No matter if you are programming in an object-oriented or a functional style, or using different languages like C++, C#, Java, or Erlang, trying to do something as simple as possible is always a worthwhile attitude!

In contrast, a design pattern is a solution for a concrete design problem in a certain context. Especially those ones that are described in the famous Design Pattern book of the Gang of Four are closely associated to object orientation. Therefore, principles are more long lasting and more important. You can find a design pattern for a certain programming problem by yourself, if you have internalized the principles.

Decisions and patterns give people solutions; principles help them design their own.

—Eoin Woods in a keynote on the
Joint Working IEEE/IFIP Conference on Software Architecture 2009 (WICSA2009)

Some Patterns, and When to Use Them

In addition to the 23 design patterns described in the book of the Gang of Four, there are of course more patterns. Some patterns are often being found in development projects, while others are more or less rare or exotic. The following sections discusses some of the in my opinion most important design patterns. Those who solve very often occurring design problems and which a developer should at least have heard before.

By the way, we have already used a few design patterns in the previous chapters, some even relatively intense, but we have just not mentioned or noticed it. Just a slight hint: In the book of the Gang of Four [Gamma95] you can find a design pattern that is called... *Iterator*!

Before we continue with the discussion of individual design patterns, a warning must be pointed out here:

 Warning   Don't exaggerate it with the usage of design patterns! No doubt, design patterns are cool and sometimes even fascinating. But an overplayed use of them, especially if there are no good reasons to justify it, can have catastrophic consequences. Your software design will suffer from useless overengineering. Always remember KISS and YAGNI (see Chapter 3).

But now let's take a look at a few patterns.

Dependency Injection (DI)

Dependency Injection is a key element of agile architecture.

—Ward Cunningham, paraphrased from the
"Agile and Traditional Development" panel discussion
at Pacific NW Software Quality Conference (PNSQC) 2004

The fact that I start the section about specific design patterns with one that is not mentioned in the famous book of the Gang of Four has weighty reasons, of course. I am convinced that Dependency Injection is by far the most important pattern that can help software developers to significantly improve a software design. This pattern can be regarded quite rightly as a game changer.

Before we dive deeper into Dependency Injection, I first want to reckon with another pattern that is detrimental to good software design: the Singleton!

The Singleton Anti-Pattern

I'm pretty sure that you know the design pattern named *Singleton*. It is, on first sight, a simple and widespread pattern, not only in the C++ domain (we shall see soon that its alleged simplicity can be deceptive). Some code bases are even littered with Singletons. This pattern is, for instance, often used for so-called Loggers (objects for logging purposes), for database connections, for central user management, or to represent things from the physical world (e.g., hardware, such as USB or printer interfaces). In addition, Factories and those so-called Utility Classes are often implemented as Singletons. The latter are a code smell for themselves, because they are a sign of weak cohesion (see Chapter 3).

The authors of *Design Patterns* have been regularly asked by journalists when they would revise their book and publish a new edition. And their regular answer was that they would not see any reason for this, because the contents of the book are still largely valid. In an interview with the online journal *InformIT*, however, they allowed themselves to give a more detailed answer. Here is a small excerpt from the entire interview, which reveals an interesting opinion of Gamma about Singletons (Larry O'Brien was the interviewer, and Erich Gamma gives the answer):

> *[...]*
>
> **Larry:** *How would you refactor "Design Patterns"?*
>
> **Erich:** *We did this exercise in 2005. Here are some notes from our session. We have found that the object-oriented design principles and most of the patterns haven't changed since then. (...)*
>
> *When discussing which patterns to drop, we found that we still love them all. (Not really— I'm in favor of dropping Singleton. Its use is almost always a design smell.)*
>
> —Design Patterns 15 Years Later: An Interview with Erich Gamma,
> Richard Helm, and Ralph Johnson, 2009 [InformIT09]

So, why did Erich Gamma say that the Singleton Pattern is almost always a design smell? What's wrong with it?

To answer this, let us first look at what goals are to be achieved by means of Singletons. What requirements can be fulfilled with this pattern? Here is the mission statement of the Singleton pattern from the GoF book:

> *Ensure a class only has one instance, and provide a global point of access to it.*
>
> —Erich Gamma et. al., *Design Patterns* [Gamma95]

This statement contains two conspicuous aspects. On the one hand, the mission of this pattern is to control and manage the whole life cycle of its one-and-only instance. In accordance with the principle of Separation of Concerns, the management of the life cycle of an object should be independent and separated from its domain-specific business logic. In a Singleton, these two concerns are basically not separated.

On the other hand, a global access to this instance is provided, so that every other object in the application can use it. Already this speech about a "global point of access" in the context of object orientation appears fishy and should raise red flags.

Let us first look at a general implementation style of a Singleton in C++, the so-called *Meyers' Singleton*, named after Scott Meyers, the author of the *Effective C++* book [Meyers05]:

Listing 9-1. An implementation of Meyers' Singleton in modern C++

```cpp
#ifndef SINGLETON_H_
#define SINGLETON_H_

class Singleton final {
public:
  static Singleton& getInstance() {
    static Singleton theInstance { };
    return theInstance;
  }

  int doSomething() {
    return 42;
  }

  // ...more member functions doing more or less useful things here...

private:
  Singleton() = default;
  Singleton(const Singleton&) = delete;
  Singleton(Singleton&&) = delete;
  Singleton& operator=(const Singleton&) = delete;
  Singleton& operator=(Singleton&&) = delete;
  // ...
};

#endif
```

One of the main advantages of this implementation style of a Singleton is that since C++11, the construction process of the one-and-only instance using a static variable inside getInstance() is thread-safe per default (see § 6.7 in [ISO11]). Be careful, because that does not automatically mean that all the other member functions of the Singleton are thread-safe too! The latter must be ensured by the developer.

In source code, the use of such a global singleton instance looks typically like this:

Listing 9-2. An excerpt from the implementation of an arbitrary class that uses the Singleton

```cpp
001  #include "AnySingletonUser.h"
002  #include "Singleton.h"
003  #include <string>
004
...  // ...
024
025  void AnySingletonUser::aMemberFunction() {
...      // ...
040    std::string result = Singleton::getInstance().doThis();
```

```
...     // ...
050  }
051
...     // ...
089
090  void AnySingletonUser::anotherMemberFunction() {
...     //...
098    int result = Singleton::getInstance().doThat();
...     //...
104    double value = Singleton::getInstance().doSomethingMore();
...     //...
110  }
111  // ...
```

I think now it becomes clear what one of the main problems with Singletons is. Due to their global visibility and accessibility, they are simply used anywhere inside the implementation of other classes. That means that in the software design, all the dependencies to this Singleton are hidden inside the code. You cannot see these dependencies by examining the interfaces of your classes, that is, their attributes and methods.

And the class AnySingletonUser exemplified above is only representative for perhaps hundreds of classes within a large code base, many of which also use the Singleton at different places. In other words: **A Singleton in OO is like a global variable in procedural programming.** You can use this global object everywhere, and you cannot see that usage in the interface of the using class, but only in its implementation.

This has a significant negative impact on the dependency situation in a project, as depicted in Figure 9-1.

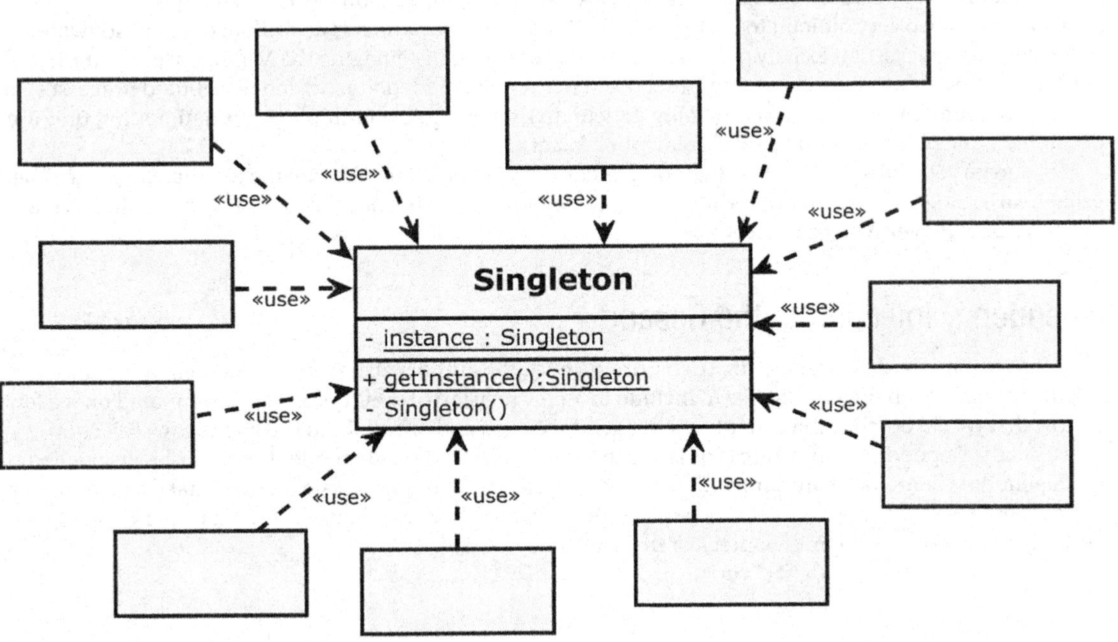

Figure 9-1. Loved by everyone: the Singleton!

■ **Note**   Perhaps you are wondering when looking at Figure 9-1 that there is a private member variable `instance` inside the Singleton class, which cannot be found in this form in Meyers's recommended implementation. Well, UML is programming language agnostic, that is, as a multipurpose modeling language it does not know about C++, Java, or other OO languages. In fact, also in Meyers's Singleton there is a variable that holds the one-and-only instance, but there is not a graphical notation for a variable with static storage duration in UML, because this feature is proprietary in C++. Therefore, I chose the way to represent this variable as a private static member. This makes the representation also compatible with the nowadays no longer recommended Singleton implementation described in the GoF book [Gamma95].

I think it's easy to imagine that all these dependencies will have major drawbacks regarding reusability, maintainablility, and testability. All those anonymous client classes of the Singleton are tightly coupled to it (remember the good property of loose coupling we've discussed in Chapter 3).

As a consequence, we completely forfeit the possibility to take advantage of polymorphism to supply an alternative implementation. Just think about unit testing. How can it succeed at all to implement a real unit test, if something is used inside the implementation of the class to be tested that cannot be replaced easily by a Test Double (a.k.a. Mock Object; see section about Test Doubles in Chapter 2)?

And remember all the rules for good unit tests we've discussed in Chapter 2, especially unit-test independence. A global object like a Singleton holds sometimes a mutable state. How can the independence of tests be ensured, if many or nearly all classes in a code base are dependent on one single object that has a life cycle that ends with the termination of the program, and that possibly holds a state that is shared between them?!

Another disadvantage of Singletons is that if they have to be changed due to new or changing requirements, this change could trigger a cascade of changes in all dependent classes. All the dependencies visible in Figure 9-1 and pointing to the Singleton are potential propagation paths for changes.

Finally, it is also very difficult to ensure in a distributed system, which is an ordinary case in software architecture nowadays, that exactly one instance of a class exists. Just imagine the Microservices pattern, where a complex software system is composed from many small, independent, and distributed processes. In such an environment, Singletons are not only difficult to protect against multiple instantiations, but they are also problematic because of the tight coupling they foster.

So, maybe you will ask now: "OK, I've got it, Singletons are bad, but what are the alternatives to it?" The perhaps surprisingly simple answer, which of course requires some further explanations, is this: **Just create one, and inject it everywhere its needed!**

Dependency Injection to the Rescue

In the abovementioned interview with Erich Gamma et al. the authors also made a statement about those design patterns, which they would like to include in a new revision of their book. They nominated only a few patterns that would possibly make it into their legendary work and one of them is Dependency Injection.

Basically, Dependency Injection (DI) is a technique in which the independent service objects needed by a dependent client object are supplied from outside. The client object does not have to take care about its required service objects itself, or actively request the service objects, for example, from a Factory (see Factory pattern later in this chapter), or from a Service Locator.

The intent behind DI could be formulated as follows:

Decouple components from their required services in such a way that the components do not have to know the names of these services, nor how they have to be procured.

Let's look at a specific example, the Logger already mentioned above, for example, a service class, which offers the possibility to write log entries. Such Loggers have often been implemented as Singletons. Hence, every client of the Logger is dependent on that global Singleton object, as depicted in Figure 9-2.

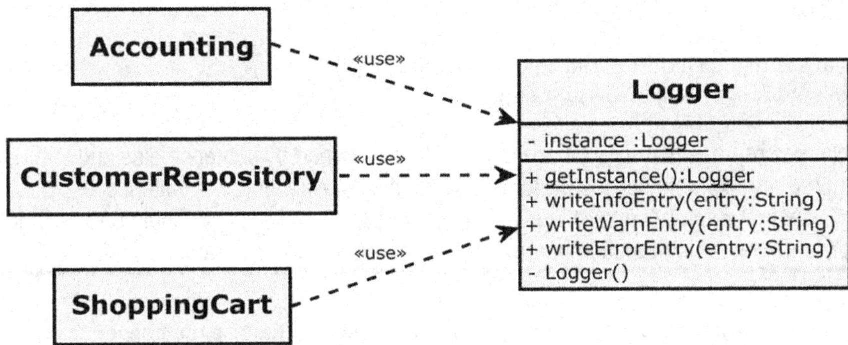

Figure 9-2. *Three domain-specific classes of a web shop are dependent on the Logger singleton*

This is how the Logger singleton class might look in source code (only the relevant parts are shown):

Listing 9-3. The Logger implemented as a Singleton

```cpp
#include <string_view>

class Logger final {
public:
  static Logger& getInstance() {
    static Logger theLogger { };
    return theLogger;
  }

  void writeInfoEntry(std::string_view entry) {
    // ...
  }

  void writeWarnEntry(std::string_view entry) {
    // ...
  }

  void writeErrorEntry(std::string_view entry) {
    // ...
  }
};
```

---

std::string_view [C++17]

Since C++17, there is a new class available in the C++ language standard: `std :: string_view` (defined in header `<string_view>`). Objects of this class are very performant proxies (Proxy is, by the way, also a design pattern) of a string, which are cheap to construct (there is no memory allocation for raw string data) and thus also cheap to copy.

And another nice feature is: `std::string_view` can also serve as an adapter for C-style strings (`char*`), character arrays, and even for proprietary string implementations from different frameworks such as `CString` (MFC) or `QString` (Qt):

```cpp
CString aString("I'm a string object of the MFC type CString");
std::string_view viewOnCString { (LPCTSTR)aString };
```

Therefore, it is the ideal class to represent strings whose data is already owned by someone else and if read-only access is required, for example, for the duration of a function's execution. For instance, instead of the widespread constant references to `std::string`, now `std::string_view` should be used as a replacement for read-only string function parameters in a modern C++ program.

We now just pick out for demonstration purposes one of those many classes that use the Logger Singleton in their implementation to write log entries, the class `CustomerRepository`:

Listing 9-4. An excerpt from class CustomerRepository

```cpp
#include "Customer.h"
#include "Identifier.h"
#include "Logger.h"

class CustomerRepository {
public:
  //...
  Customer findCustomerById(const Identifier& customerId) {
    Logger::getInstance().writeInfoEntry("Starting to search for a customer specified by a
      given unique identifier...");
    // ...
  }
  // ...
};
```

In order to get rid of the Singleton and to be able to replace the Logger object with a Test Double during unit tests, we must first apply the Dependency Inversion Principle (DIP; see Chapter 6). This means that we first have to introduce an abstraction (an interface), and make both the `CustomerRepository` and the concrete Logger dependent from that interface, as depicted in Figure 9-3.

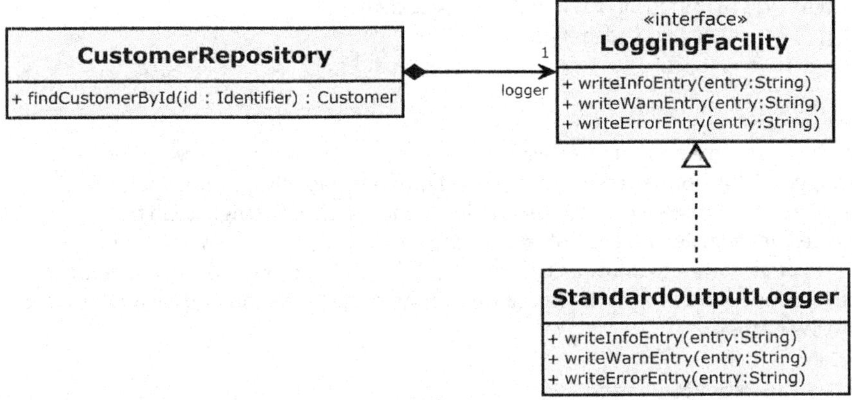

Figure 9-3. *Decoupling through the applied Dependency Inversion Principle*

This is how the newly introduced interface LoggingFacility looks like in source code:

Listing 9-5. The LoggingFacility interface

```cpp
#include <memory>
#include <string_view>

class LoggingFacility {
public:
  virtual ~LoggingFacility() = default;
  virtual void writeInfoEntry(std::string_view entry) = 0;
  virtual void writeWarnEntry(std::string_view entry) = 0;
  virtual void writeErrorEntry(std::string_view entry) = 0;
};

using Logger = std::shared_ptr<LoggingFacility>;
```

The StandardOutputLogger is one example for a specific Logger class that implements the LoggingFacility interface and writes the log on standard output, as its name suggests:

Listing 9-6. One possible implementation of a LoggingFacility: the StandardOutputLogger

```cpp
#include "LoggingFacility.h"
#include <iostream>

class StandardOutputLogger : public LoggingFacility {
public:
  virtual void writeInfoEntry(std::string_view entry) override {
    std::cout << "[INFO] " << entry << std::endl;
  }

  virtual void writeWarnEntry(std::string_view entry) override {
    std::cout << "[WARNING] " << entry << std::endl;
  }
```

```
  virtual void writeErrorEntry(std::string_view entry) override {
    std::cout << "[ERROR] " << entry << std::endl;
  }
};
```

Next we need to modify the CustomerRepository class. First, we create a new member variable of the smart pointer type alias Logger. This pointer instance is passed into the class via an initialization constructor. In other words, we allow an instance of a class that implements the LoggingFacility interface **to be injected into** the CustomerRepository object during construction. We also delete the default constructor, because we do not want to allow a CustomerRepository to be created without a logger. Furthermore, we remove the direct dependency in the implementation to the Singleton and instead use the smart pointer Logger to write log entries.

Listing 9-7. The modified class Customer Repository

```
#include "Customer.h"
#include "Identifier.h"
#include "LoggingFacility.h"

class CustomerRepository {
public:
  CustomerRepository() = delete;
  explicit CustomerRepository(const Logger& loggingService) : logger { loggingService } { }
  //...

  Customer findCustomerById(const Identifier& customerId) {
    logger->writeInfoEntry("Starting to search for a customer specified by a given unique
    identifier...");
    // ...
  }
  // ...

private:
  // ...
  Logger logger;
};
```

As a consequence of this refactoring, we have now achieved that the CustomerRepository class is no longer dependent on a specific logger. Instead, the CustomerRepository simply has a dependency on an abstraction (interface) that is now explicitly visible in the class and its interface, because it is represented by a member variable and a constructor parameter. That means that the CustomerRepository class now accepts service objects for logging purposes that are passed in from outside, like this:

Listing 9-8. The Logger object is injected into the instance of CustomerRepository

```
Logger logger = std::make_shared<StandardOutputLogger>();
CustomerRepository customerRepository { logger };
```

This design change has significantly positive effects. A loose coupling is promoted, and the client object CustomerRepository can now be configured with various service objects that provide logging functionality, as it can be seen in the following UML class diagram (Figure 9-4):

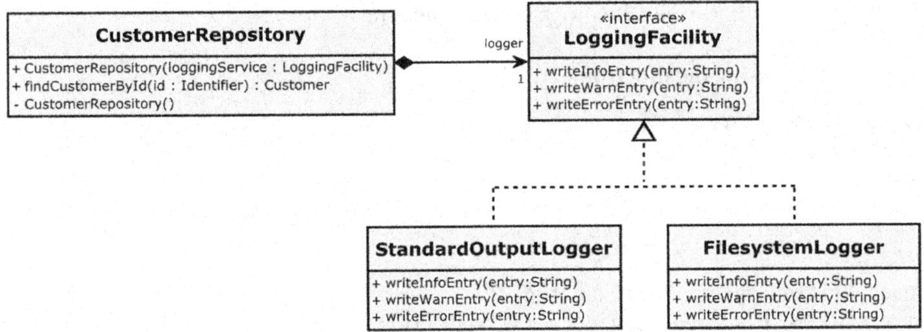

Figure 9-4. *Class CustomerRepository can be supplied with specific logging implementations via its constructor*

Also the testability of the `CustomerRepository` class has been significantly improved. There are no hidden dependencies to Singletons anymore. Now we can easy replace a real Logging service by a mock object (see Chapter 2 about Unit Tests and Test Doubles). We can equip the mock object with spy methods, for example, to check inside the unit test which data would leave our `CustomerRepository` object via the `LoggingFacility` interface.

Listing 9-9. A test double (mock object) for Unit-Testing of classes that have a dependency on LoggingFacility

```cpp
namespace test {

#include "../src/LoggingFacility.h"
#include <string>

class LoggingFacilityMock : public LoggingFacility {
public:
  virtual void writeInfoEntry(std::string_view entry) override {
    recentlyWrittenLogEntry = entry;
  }

  virtual void writeWarnEntry(std::string_view entry) override {
    recentlyWrittenLogEntry = entry;
  }

  virtual void writeErrorEntry(std::string_view entry) override {
    recentlyWrittenLogEntry = entry;
  }

  std::string_view getRecentlyWrittenLogEntry() const {
    return recentlyWrittenLogEntry;
  }

private:
  std::string recentlyWrittenLogEntry;
};

using MockLogger = std::shared_ptr<LoggingFacilityMock>;

}
```

And in this exemplary unit test you can see the mock object in action:

Listing 9-10. An example unit test using the mock object

```cpp
#include "../src/CustomerRepository.h"
#include "LoggingFacilityMock.h"
#include <gtest/gtest.h>

namespace test {

TEST(CustomerTestCase, WrittenLogEntryIsAsExpected) {
  MockLogger logger = std::make_shared<LoggingFacilityMock>();
  CustomerRepository customerRepositoryToTest { logger };
  Identifier customerId { 1234 };

  customerRepositoryToTest.findCustomerById(customerId);

  ASSERT_EQ("Starting to search for a customer specified by a given unique identifier...",
    logger->getRecentlyWrittenLogEntry());}

}
```

In the previous example, I presented Dependency Injection as a pattern to remove annoying Singletons, but of course this is only one of many applications. Basically, a good object-oriented software design should ensure that the involved modules or components are as loosely coupled as possible, and Dependency Injection is the key to this goal. By consistently applying this pattern, a software design will emerge that has a very flexible plug-in architecture. And as a kind of positive side effect, this technique results in highly testable objects.

The responsibility for object creation and linking is removed from the objects themselves and is centralized in an infrastructure component, the so-called *Assembler*, or *Injector*. This component (see Figure 9-5) usually operates at program startup and processes something like a "construction plan" (e.g., a configuration file) for the whole software system, that is, it instantiates the objects and services in the correct order and injects the services into the objects that needs them.

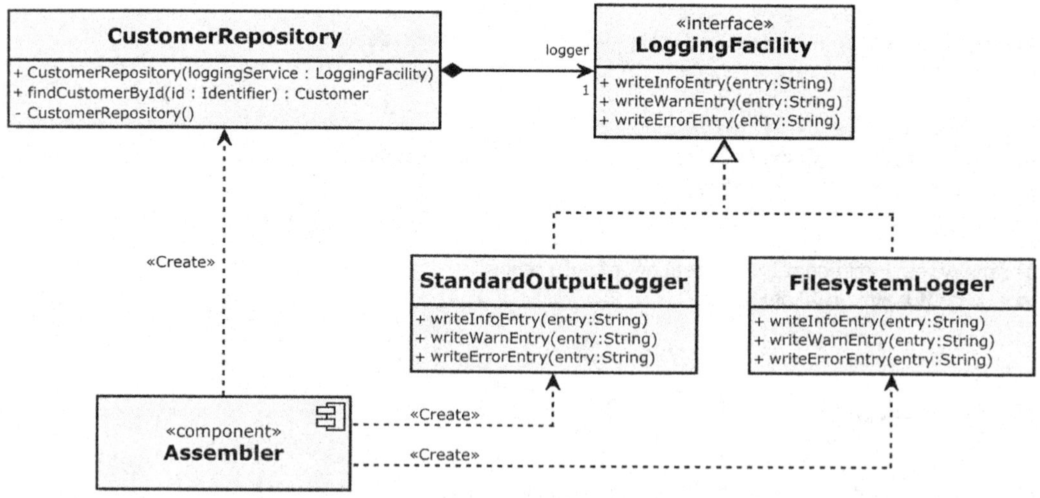

Figure 9-5. *The Assembler is responsible for object creation and injection*

Please, pay attention to the pleasant dependency situation. The direction of the creation dependencies (dashed arrows with stereotype «Create») leads away from the `Assembler` to the other modules (classes). In other words, no class in this design "knows" that such an infrastructure element like an `Assembler` exists (That's not completely correct, because at least one other element in the software system knows about the existence of this component, because the assemble process must be triggered by someone, usually at program start).

Somewhere within the `Assembler` component, something like the following lines of code could possibly be found:

Listing 9-11. Parts of the implementation of the Assembler could look like this

```cpp
// ...
Logger loggingServiceToInject = std::make_shared<StandardOutputLogger>();
auto customerRepository = std::make_shared<CustomerRepository>(loggingServiceToInject);
// ...
```

This DI technique is called *constructor injection*, because the service object to be injected is passed as an argument to an initialization constructor of the client object. The advantage of constructor injection is that the client object gets completely initialized during its construction and is immediately usable then.

But what do we do if service objects are to be injected into client objects while the program is running, for instance, if a client object is only occasionally created during program execution, or the specific logger should be exchanged at runtime? Then the client object must provide a setter for the service object, as in the following example:

Listing 9-12. The class Customer provides a setter to inject a Logger

```cpp
#include "Address.h"
#include "LoggingFacility.h"

class Customer {
public:
  Customer() = default;

  void setLoggingService(const Logger& loggingService) {
    logger = loggingService;
  }

  //...

private:
  Address address;
  Logger logger;
};
```

This DI technique is called *setter injection*. And, of course, it is also possible to combine constructor injection and setter injection.

Dependency Injection is a design pattern that makes a software design loosely coupled and eminently configurable. It allows the creation of different product configurations for different customers or intended purposes of a software product. It greatly increases the testability of a software system, since it enables to inject mock objects very easily. Therefore, this pattern should not be ignored when designing any serious software system. If you want to dive deeper into this pattern, I recommend to read the trend-setting blog article "Inversion of Control Containers and the Dependency Injection pattern" written by Martin Fowler [Fowler04].

In practice, often Dependency Injection frameworks are used, which are available as both commercial and open source solutions.

Adapter

I'm sure the Adapter (synonym: Wrapper) is one of the most commonly used design patterns. The reason for this is that the adaptation of incompatible interfaces is certainly a case that's often necessary in software development, for instance, if a module developed by another team has to be integrated, or when using third-party libraries.

Here is the mission statement of the Adapter pattern:

> *Convert the interface of a class into another interface clients expect. Adapter lets classes work together that couldn't otherwise because of incompatible interfaces.*

> —Erich Gamma et. al., *Design Patterns* [Gamma95]

Let's develop further the example from the previous section about Dependency Injection. Let's assume that we want to use *BoostLog v2* (see http://www.boost.org) for logging purposes, but we want to keep a usage of this third-party library exchangeable with other logging approaches and technologies.

The solution is simple: we just have to provide another implementation of the LoggingFacility interface, which adapts the interface of BoostLog to the interface that we want, as depicted in Figure 9-6.

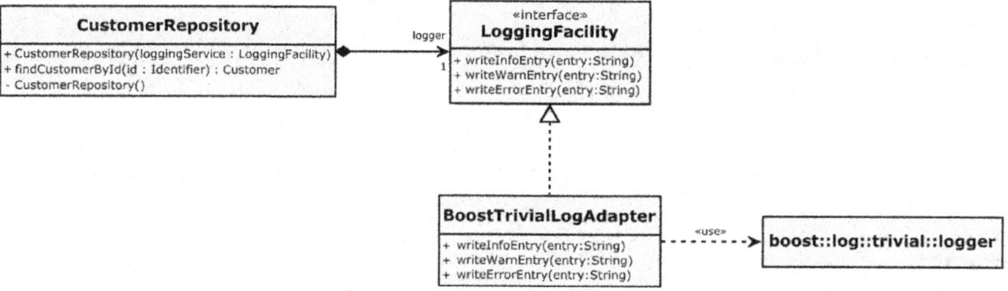

Figure 9-6. *An adapter for a Boost logging solution*

In source code, our additional implementation of the LoggingFacility interface BoostTrivialLog Adapter looks as follows:

Listing 9-13. The Adapter for Boost.Log is just another implementation of LoggingFacility

```cpp
#include "LoggingFacility.h"
#include <boost/log/trivial.hpp>

class BoostTrivialLogAdapter : public LoggingFacility {
public:
  virtual void writeInfoEntry(std::string_view entry) override {
    BOOST_LOG_TRIVIAL(info) << entry;
  }
```

```cpp
  virtual void writeWarnEntry(std::string_view entry) override {
    BOOST_LOG_TRIVIAL(warn) << entry;
  }

  virtual void writeErrorEntry(std::string_view entry) override {
    BOOST_LOG_TRIVIAL(error) << entry;
  }
};
```

The advantages are obvious: through the Adapter pattern, there is now exactly one class in my entire software system that has a dependency to the third-party logging solution. This also means that our code is not contaminated with proprietary logging statements, like `BOOST_LOG_TRIVIAL()`. And because this Adapter class is just another implementation of the `LoggingFacility` interface, I can also use Dependency Injection (see previous section) to inject instances – or just exactly the same instance – of this class into all client objects that want to use it.

Adapters can facilitate a broad range of adaptation and conversion possibilities for incompatible interfaces. This ranges from simple adaptations, such as operations names and data type conversions, right up to supporting an entire different set of operations. In our case above, a call of a member function with a string parameter is converted into a call of the insertion operator for streams.

Interface adaptations are of course easier if the interfaces to be adapted are similar. If the interfaces are very different, an Adapter can also become a very complex piece of code.

Strategy

If we remember the Open-Closed Principle (OCP) described in Chapter 6 as a guideline for an extensible object-oriented design, the Strategy design pattern may be considered as the "celebrity gig" of this important principle. Here is the mission statement of this pattern:

> *Define a family of algorithms, encapsulate each one, and make them interchangeable. Strategy lets the algorithm vary independently from clients that use it.*
>
> —Erich Gamma et. al., *Design Patterns* [Gamma95]

Doing things in different ways is a common requirement in software design. Just think of sorting algorithms for lists. There are various sorting algorithms that have different characteristics regarding the time complexity (number of operations required) and the space complexity (additional required storage space in addition to the input list). Examples are Bubble-Sort, Quick-Sort, Merge-Sort, Insert-Sort, and Heap-Sort.

For instance, Bubble-Sort is the least complex one and it is very efficient regarding memory consumption, but also one of the slowest sorting algorithms. In contrast, Quick-Sort is a fast and efficient sorting algorithm that is easy to implement through its recursive structure and does not require additional memory, but it is very inefficient with presorted and inverted lists. With the help of the Strategy pattern, a simple exchange of the sorting algorithm can be implemented, for example, depending on the properties of the list to be sorted.

Let's consider another example. Assume that we want to have a textual representation of an instance of a class `Customer` in an arbitrary business IT system. A stakeholder requirement states that the textual representation shall be formatted in various output formats: as plain text, as XML (Extensible Markup Language), and as JSON (JavaScript Object Notation).

OK, first of all let's introduce an abstraction for our various formatting strategies, the abstract class
Formatter:

Listing 9-14. The abstract Formatter contains everything that all specific formatter classes have in common

```cpp
#include <memory>
#include <string>
#include <string_view>
#include <sstream>

class Formatter {
public:
  virtual ~Formatter() = default;

  Formatter& withCustomerId(std::string_view customerId) {
    this->customerId = customerId;
    return *this;
  }

  Formatter& withForename(std::string_view forename) {
    this->forename = forename;
    return *this;
  }

  Formatter& withSurname(std::string_view surname) {
    this->surname = surname;
    return *this;
  }

  Formatter& withStreet(std::string_view street) {
    this->street = street;
    return *this;
  }

  Formatter& withZipCode(std::string_view zipCode) {
    this->zipCode = zipCode;
    return *this;
  }

  Formatter& withCity(std::string_view city) {
    this->city = city;
    return *this;
  }

  virtual std::string format() const = 0;

protected:
  std::string customerId { "000000" };
  std::string forename { "n/a" };
  std::string surname { "n/a" };
  std::string street { "n/a" };
```

```cpp
  std::string zipCode { "n/a" };
  std::string city { "n/a" };n
};
```

```cpp
using FormatterPtr = std::unique_ptr<Formatter>;
```

The three specific formatters that provide the formatting styles that are requested by the stakeholders are as follows:

Listing 9-15. The three specific formatters override the pure virtual format() member function of Formatter

```cpp
#include "Formatter.h"

class PlainTextFormatter : public Formatter {
public:
  virtual std::string format() const override {
    std::stringstream formattedString { };
    formattedString << "[" << customerId << "]: "
      << forename << " " << surname << ", "
      << street << ", " << zipCode << " "
      << city << ".";
    return formattedString.str();
  }
};

class XmlFormatter : public Formatter {
public:
  virtual std::string format() const override {
    std::stringstream formattedString { };
    formattedString <<
      "<customer id=\"" << customerId << "\">\n" <<
      "  <forename>" << forename << "</forename>\n" <<
      "  <surname>" << surname << "</surname>\n" <<
      "  <street>" << street << "</street>\n" <<
      "  <zipcode>" << zipCode << "</zipcode>\n" <<
      "  <city>"  << city << "</city>\n" <<
      "</customer>\n";
    return formattedString.str();
  }
};

class JsonFormatter : public Formatter {
public:
  virtual std::string format() const override {
    std::stringstream formattedString { };
    formattedString <<
      "{\n" <<
      "  \"CustomerId : \"" << customerId << END_OF_PROPERTY <<
      "  \"Forename: \"" << forename << END_OF_PROPERTY <<
      "  \"Surname: \"" << surname << END_OF_PROPERTY <<
      "  \"Street: \"" << street << END_OF_PROPERTY <<
```

```cpp
      "  \"ZIP code: \"" << zipCode << END_OF_PROPERTY <<
      "  \"City: \"" << city << "\"\n" <<
      "}\n";
    return formattedString.str();
  }

private:
  static constexpr const char* const END_OF_PROPERTY { "\",\n" };
};
```

As it can be seen clearly here, the OCP is particularly well supported. As soon as a new output format is required, only another specialization of the abstract class Formatter has to be implemented. Modifications to the already existing formatters are not required.

Listing 9-16. This is how the passed-in formatter object is used inside the member function getAsFormattedString()

```cpp
#include "Address.h"
#include "CustomerId.h"
#include "Formatter.h"

class Customer {
public:
  // ...
  std::string getAsFormattedString(const FormatterPtr& formatter) const {
    return formatter->
    withCustomerId(customerId.toString()).
    withForename(forename).
    withSurname(surname).
    withStreet(address.getStreet()).
    withZipCode(address.getZipCodeAsString()).
    withCity(address.getCity()).
    format();
  }
  // ...

private:
  CustomerId customerId;
  std::string forename;
  std::string surname;
  Address address;
};
```

The member function Customer::getAsFormattedString() has a parameter that expects a unique pointer to a formatter object. This parameter can be used to control the format of the string that can be retrieved through this member function, or in other words: the member function Customer::getAsFormatted String() can be supplied with a formatting strategy.

By the way: perhaps you've noticed the special design of the public interface of the Formatter with its numerous chained with...() member functions. Here also another design pattern has been used, which is called *Fluent Interface.* In object-oriented programming, a Fluent Interface is a style to design APIs in a way that the readability of the code is close to that of ordinary written prose. In the previous chapter about Test-Driven Development (Chapter 8), we have already seen such an interface. There we've introduced a custom assertion (see section "More sophisticated tests with a custom assertion") to write more elegant and better readable tests. In our case here, the trick is that every `with...()` member function is self-referential, that is, the new context for calling a member function on the Formatter is equivalent to the previous context, unless when the final `format()` function is called.

As usual, here is also a graphical visualization of the class structure of our code example, a UML class diagram (Figure 9-7):

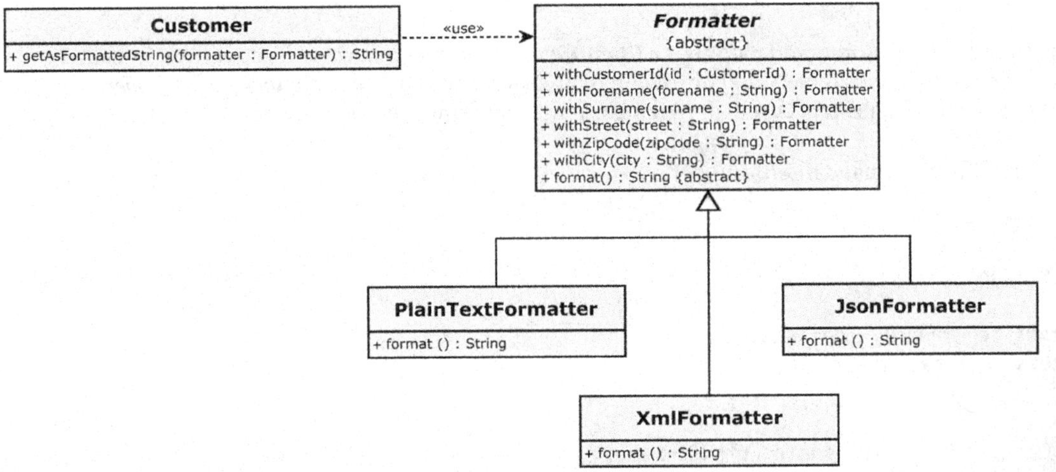

Figure 9-7. *An abstract Formatting strategy and its three concrete Formatting strategies*

As it is easy to see, the Strategy pattern in this example ensures that the caller of member function `Customer::getAsFormattedString()` can configure the output format as it wants. You want to support another output format? No problem: thanks to the excellent support of the Open-Closed Principle, another concrete formatting strategy can be easily added. The other formatting strategies, as well as the class `Customer`, remain completely unaffected by this extension.

Command

Software systems usually have to perform a variety of actions due to the reception of instructions. Users of text processing software, for example, issue a variety of commands by interacting with the software's user interface. They want to open a document, save a document, print a document, copy a piece of text, paste a copied piece of text, etc. This general pattern is also observable in other domains. For example, in the financial world, there could be orders from a customer to his securities dealer to buy shares, sell shares, etc. And in a more technical domain like manufacturing, commands are used to control industrial facilities and machines.

When implementing software systems that are controlled by commands, it is important to ensure that the request for an action is separated from the object which actually performs the action. The guiding principle behind this is loose coupling (see Chapter 3) and Separation of Concerns.

A good analogy is a restaurant. In a restaurant, the waiter accepts the customer's order, but she is not responsible for the cooking of the food. That is a task for the restaurant's kitchen. Actually, it is even transparent for the customer how the food is prepared. Maybe the restaurant prepares the food itself, but the food might also be delivered from somewhere else.

In object-oriented software development there is a behavioral pattern named *Command* (synonym: *Action*) that fosters this kind of decoupling. Its mission statement is as follows:

> *Encapsulate a request as an object, thereby letting you parameterize clients with different requests, queue or log requests, and support undoable operations.*

> —Erich Gamma et. al., *Design Patterns* [Gamma95]

A good example for the Command pattern is a Client/Server architecture, where a client – the so-called *Invoker* – sends commands that should be executed on a server, which is referred to as the *Receiver*.

Let's start with the abstract Command, which is a simple and small interface that looks as follows:

Listing 9-17. The Command interface

```cpp
#include <memory>

class Command {
public:
  virtual ~Command() = default;
  virtual void execute() = 0;
};

using CommandPtr = std::shared_ptr<Command>;
```

We've also introduced a type alias (CommandPtr) for a smart pointer to commands.

This abstract Command interface can now be implemented by various concrete commands. Let us first take a look at a very simple command, the output of the string "Hello World!":

Listing 9-18. A first and very simple implementation of a concrete Command

```cpp
#include <iostream>

class HelloWorldOutputCommand : public Command {
public:
  virtual void execute() override {
    std::cout << "Hello World!" << "\n";
  }
};
```

Next, we need the element that accepts and executes the commands. This element is called Receiver in the general description of this design pattern. In our case it is a class named Server that plays this role:

Listing 9-19. The Command receiver

```cpp
#include "Command.h"

class Server {
public:
  void acceptCommand(const CommandPtr& command) {
    command->execute();
  }
};
```

Currently, this class contains only one simple public member function that can accept and execute commands.

Finally, we need the so-called Invoker, which is the class `Client` in our Client/Server architecture:

Listing 9-20. The Client sends commands to the Server

```cpp
class Client {
public:
  void run() {
    Server theServer { };
    CommandPtr helloWorldOutputCommand = std::make_shared<HelloWorldOutputCommand>();
    theServer.acceptCommand(helloWorldOutputCommand);
  }
};
```

Inside the `main()` function we find the following simple code:

Listing 9-21. The main() function

```cpp
#include "Client.h"

int main() {
  Client client { };
  client.run();
  return 0;
}
```

If this program is now being compiled and executed, the output "Hello World!" will appear on stdout. Well, at first sight, this may seem not very exciting, but what we have achieved through the command pattern is that the origination and sending off of the command is decoupled from its execution. We can now handle command objects as well as other objects.

Since this design pattern supports the Open-Closed Principle (OCP; see Chapter 6) very well, it is also very easy to add new commands with negligible minor modifications of existing code. For instance, if we want to force the Server to wait for a certain amount of time, we can just add the following new command:

Listing 9-22. Another concrete command that instructs the server to wait

```cpp
#include "Command.h"
#include <chrono>
#include <thread>

class WaitCommand : public Command {
public:
  explicit WaitCommand(const unsigned int durationInMilliseconds) noexcept :
    durationInMilliseconds{durationInMilliseconds} { };

  virtual void execute() override {
    std::chrono::milliseconds dur(durationInMilliseconds);
    std::this_thread::sleep_for(dur);
  }

private:
  unsigned int durationInMilliseconds { 1000 };
};
```

Now we can use the new `WaitCommand` like this:

Listing 9-23. Our new WaitCommand in use

```cpp
class Client {
public:
  void run() {
    Server theServer { };
    const unsigned int SERVER_DELAY_TIMESPAN { 3000 };

    CommandPtr waitCommand = std::make_shared<WaitCommand>(SERVER_DELAY_TIMESPAN);
    theServer.acceptCommand(waitCommand);

    CommandPtr helloWorldOutputCommand = std::make_shared<HelloWorldOutputCommand>();
    theServer.acceptCommand(helloWorldOutputCommand);
  }
};
```

In order to get an overview of the structure that has been originated so far, Figure 9-8 depicts a corresponding UML class diagram:

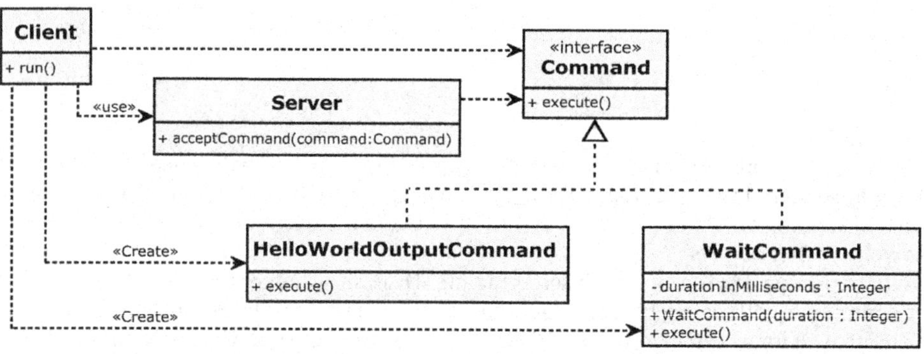

Figure 9-8. *The Server just knows the Command interface, but not any concrete command*

As it can be seen in this example, we can parameterize commands with values. Since the signature of the pure virtual `execute()` member function is specified as parameterless by the `Command` interface, the parameterization is done with the help of an initialization constructor. Furthermore, we didn't have to change anything in the class `Server`, because it was able to treat and execute the new command immediately.

The Command pattern provides manifold possibilities of applications. For example, commands can be queued. This also supports an asynchronous execution of the commands: the Invoker sends off the command and can then do other things immediately, but the command is executed by the Receiver at a later time.

However, something is missing! In the above quoted mission statement of the Command pattern, you can read something about "...support undoable operations." Well, the following section is dedicated to that topic.

Command Processor

In our small example of a Client/Server architecture from the previous section, I cheated a bit. In reality, a server would not execute the commands in that manner as I have demonstrated above. The command objects that are arriving at the server would be distributed to the internal parts of the server that are responsible for the execution of the command. This can, for example, be done with the help of another pattern that is called *Chain of Responsibility* (this pattern is not described in this book).

Let's consider another and a bit more complex example. Assume that we have a drawing program. Users of this program can draw many different shapes, for instance, circles and rectangles. For this purpose, corresponding menus are available in the program's user interface via that these drawing operations can be invoked. I'm pretty sure that you've guessed it: the well-skilled software developers of this program implemented the Command pattern to perform these drawing operations. A stakeholder requirement, however, states that a user of the program can also undo drawing operations.

To fulfill this requirement, we need, first of all, undoable commands.

Listing 9-24. The UndoableCommand interface is created by combining Command and Revertable

```cpp
#include <memory>

class Command {
public:
  virtual ~Command() = default;
  virtual void execute() = 0;
};

class Revertable {
public:
  virtual ~Revertable() = default;
  virtual void undo() = 0;
};

class UndoableCommand : public Command, public Revertable { };

using CommandPtr = std::shared_ptr<UndoableCommand>;
```

According to the Interface Segregation Principle (ISP; see Chapter 6) we've added another interface Revertable that supports Undo functionality. This new interface can be combined with the existing Command interface using inheritance to an UndoableCommand.

As an example for many, different undoable drawing commands, I just show the concrete command for the circle here:

Listing 9-25. An undoable command for drawing circles

```cpp
#include "Command.h"
#include "DrawingProcessor.h"
#include "Point.h"

class DrawCircleCommand : public UndoableCommand {
public:
  DrawCircleCommand(DrawingProcessor& receiver, const Point& centerPoint,
    const double radius) noexcept :
    receiver { receiver }, centerPoint { centerPoint }, radius { radius } { }
```

```cpp
  virtual void execute() override {
    receiver.drawCircle(centerPoint, radius);
  }

  virtual void undo() override {
    receiver.eraseCircle(centerPoint, radius);
  }

private:
  DrawingProcessor& receiver;
  const Point centerPoint;
  const double radius;
};
```

It is easy to imagine that the commands for drawing a rectangle and other shapes look very similar. The executing receiver of the command is a class named DrawingProcessor, which is the element that performs the drawing operations. A reference to this object is passed along with other arguments during the construction of the command (see initialization constructor). At this place I show only a small excerpt of the presumably complex class DrawingProcessor, because it does not play an important role for the understanding of the pattern:

Listing 9-26. The DrawingProcessor is the element that will perform the drawing operations

```cpp
class DrawingProcessor {
public:
  void drawCircle(const Point& centerPoint, const double radius) {
    // Instructions to draw a circle on the screen...
  };

  void eraseCircle(const Point& centerPoint, const double radius) {
    // Instructions to erase a circle from the screen...
  };

  // ...
};
```

Now we come to the centerpiece of this pattern, the CommandProcessor:

Listing 9-27. The class CommandProcessor manages a stack of undoable command objects

```cpp
#include <stack>

class CommandProcessor {
public:
  void execute(const CommandPtr& command) {
    command->execute();
    commandHistory.push(command);
  }
```

```cpp
  void undoLastCommand() {
    if (commandHistory.empty()) {
      return;
    }
    commandHistory.top()->undo();
    commandHistory.pop();
  }

private:
  std::stack<std::shared_ptr<Revertable>> commandHistory;
};
```

The CommandProcessor class (which is by the way not thread-safe when using the above implementation) contains a std::stack<T> (defined in header <stack>), which is an abstract data type that operates as a LIFO (Last-In First-Out). After an execution of a command has been triggered by the CommandProcessor::execute() member function, the command object is stored on the commandHistory stack. When calling the CommandProcessor::undoLastCommand() member function, the last command stored on the stack is undone and then removed from the top of the stack.

Also the undo operation can now be modeled as a command object. In this case, the command receiver is, of course, the CommandProcessor itself:

Listing 9-28. The UndoCommand prompts the CommandProcessor to perform an undo

```cpp
#include "Command.h"
#include "CommandProcessor.h"

class UndoCommand : public UndoableCommand {
public:
  explicit UndoCommand(CommandProcessor& receiver) noexcept :
      receiver { receiver } { }

  virtual void execute() override {
    receiver.undoLastCommand();
  }

  virtual void undo() override {
    // Intentionally left blank, because an undo should not be undone.
  }

private:
  CommandProcessor& receiver;
};
```

Lost the overview? OK, it's once again time for a "big picture" in the form of a UML class diagram (Figure 9-9).

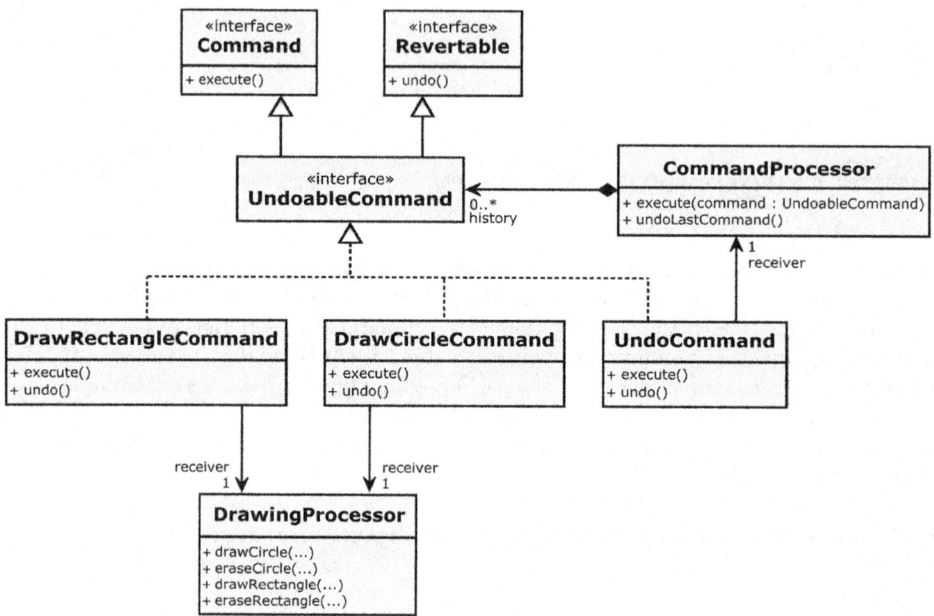

Figure 9-9. *The CommandProcessor (on the right) executes the Commands he receives and manages a command history*

When using the command pattern in practice, you're often confronted with the need to be able to compose a more complex command from several simple commands or to record and replay commands (scripting). In order to be able to implement such requirements in an elegant manner, the following design pattern is suitable.

Composite

A data structure widely used in Computer Science is that of a tree. Trees can be found everywhere. For instance, the hierarchical organization of a file system on a data media (e.g., a hard disk) conforms to that of a tree. The project browser of an Integrated Development Environment (IDE) has usually a tree structure. In compiler design, the abstract syntax tree (AST), is, as the name suggests, a tree representation of the abstract syntactic structure of the source code that is usually the result of the syntax analysis phase of a compiler.

The object-oriented blueprint for a tree-like data structure is called the *Composite* pattern. This pattern has the following intent:

> *Compose objects into tree structures to represent part-whole hierarchies. Composite lets clients treat individual objects and compositions of objects uniformly.*

> —Erich Gamma et. al., *Design Patterns* [Gamma95]

Our previous example from the sections Command and Command Processor should be extended by the possibility that we can build composite commands, and that commands can be recorded and replayed. So we add a new class to the previous design, a CompositeCommand:

Listing 9-29. A new concrete UndoableCommand that manages a list of commands

```cpp
#include "Command.h"
#include <vector>

class CompositeCommand : public UndoableCommand {
public:
  void addCommand(CommandPtr& command) {
    commands.push_back(command);
  }

  virtual void execute() override {
    for (const auto& command : commands) {
      command->execute();
    }
  }

  virtual void undo() override {
    for (const auto& command : commands) {
      command->undo();
    }
  }

private:
  std::vector<CommandPtr> commands;
};
```

The composite command has a member function addCommand(), which allows you to add commands to an instance of CompositeCommand. Since the class CompositeCommand also implements the UndoableCommand interface, its instances can be treated like ordinary commands. In other words, it is also possible to assemble composite commands with other composite commands hierarchically. Through the recursive structure of the Composite pattern, you are able to generate command trees.

The following UML class diagram (Figure 9-10) depicts the extended design.

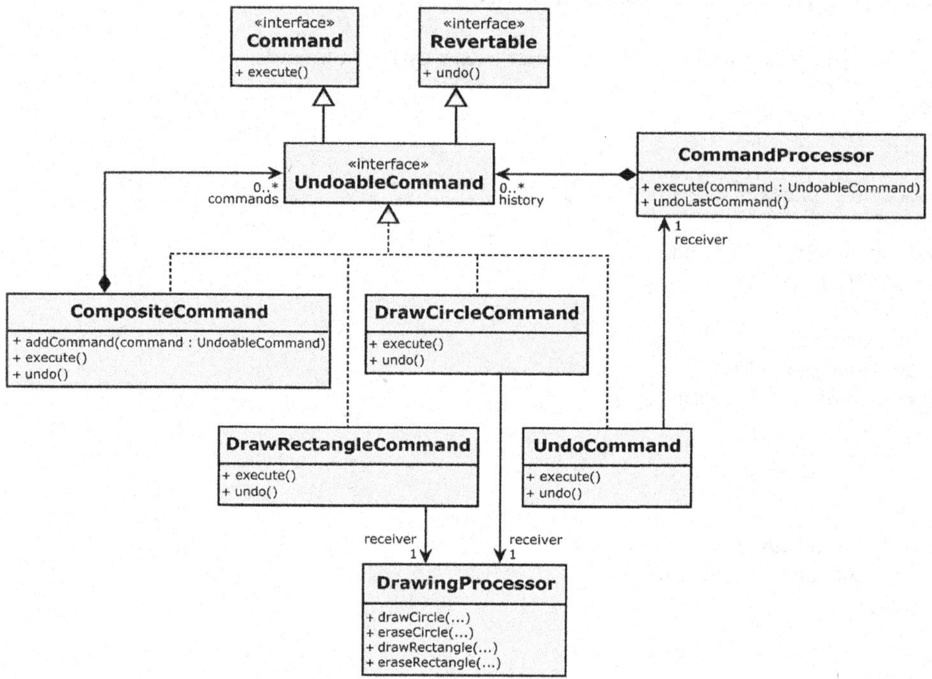

Figure 9-10. *With the added CompositeCommand (on the left), commands can now be scripted*

The newly added class CompositeCommand can now be used, for example, as a macro recorder in order to record and replay command sequences:

Listing 9-30. Our new CompositeCommand in action as a Macro Recorder

```cpp
int main() {
  CommandProcessor commandProcessor { };
  DrawingProcessor drawingProcessor { };

  auto macroRecorder = std::make_shared<CompositeCommand>();

  Point circleCenterPoint { 20, 20 };
  CommandPtr drawCircleCommand = std::make_shared<DrawCircleCommand>(drawingProcessor,
  circleCenterPoint, 10);
  commandProcessor.execute(drawCircleCommand);
  macroRecorder->addCommand(drawCircleCommand);

  Point rectangleCenterPoint { 30, 10 };
  CommandPtr drawRectangleCommand = std::make_shared<DrawRectangleCommand>(drawingProcessor,
  rectangleCenterPoint, 5, 8);
  commandProcessor.execute(drawRectangleCommand);
  macroRecorder->addCommand(drawRectangleCommand);
```

```
commandProcessor.execute(macroRecorder);

CommandPtr undoCommand = std::make_shared<UndoCommand>(commandProcessor);
commandProcessor.execute(undoCommand);

    return 0;
}
```

With the help of the Composite pattern, it is now very easy to assemble complex command sequences from simple commands (the latter are referred to as "leafs" in the canonical form). Since the `CompositeCommand` also implements the `UndoableCommand` interface, they can be used exactly like the simple commands. This greatly simplifies the usage through client code.

On closer inspection there is a small disadvantage. You may have noticed that an access to the member function `CompositeCommand::addCommand()` is only possible if you use an instance (`macroRecorder`) of the concrete type `CompositeCommand` (see source code above). This member function is not available via the interface `UndoableCommand`. In other words, the promised equal treatment (remember the pattern's intent) of composites and leafs is not given here!

If you take a look at the general Composite pattern in [Gamma95], then you'll see that the administrative functions for managing child elements are declared in the abstraction. In our case, however, this would mean that we would have to declare an `addCommand()` in the interface `UndoableCommand` (Which would be a violation of the ISP, by the way). The fatal consequence would be that the leaf elements would have to override `addCommand()`, and must provide a meaningful implementation for this member function. This is not possible! What shall happen, please, what doesn't violate the Principle of Least Astonishment (see Chapter 3), if we add a command to an instance of `DrawCircleCommand`?

If we would do that, it would be a violation of the Liskov Substitution Principle (LSP; see Chapter 6). Therefore it is better to make a tradeoff in our case and to do without the equal treatment of composites and leafs.

Observer

A well-known architecture pattern for the structuring of software systems is *Model-View-Controller* (MVC). With the help of this architecture pattern, which is described in detail in the book *Pattern-Oriented Software Architecture* [Busch96], usually the presentation part (User Interface) of an application is structured. The principle behind it is Separation of Concerns (SoC). Among other things, the data to be displayed, which is held in the so-called model, is separated from the manifold visual representations (so-called views) of these data.

In MVC, the coupling between the views and the model should be as loose as possible. This loose coupling is usually realized with the *Observer* pattern. The Observer is a behavioral pattern that is described in [Gamma95] and it has the following intent:

> *Define a one-to-many dependency between objects so that when one object changes state, all its dependents are notified and updated automatically.*

> —Erich Gamma et. al., *Design Patterns* [Gamma95]

As usual, the pattern can best be explained using an example. Let's consider a spreadsheet application, which is a natural constituent of many office software suites. In such an application, the data can be displayed in a worksheet, in a pie chart graphic, and in many other presentation forms; the so-called views. Different views on the data can be created, and also closed again.

First of all we need an abstract element for the views that is called Observer.

Listing 9-31. The abstract Observer

```cpp
#include <memory>

class Observer {
public:
  virtual ~Observer() = default;
  virtual int getId() = 0;
  virtual void update() = 0;
};

using ObserverPtr = std::shared_ptr<Observer>;
```

The Observers observe a so-called Subject. For this purpose, they can be registered at the Subject, and they can also be deregistered.

Listing 9-32. Observers can be added to and removed from a so-called Subject

```cpp
#include "Observer.h"
#include <algorithm>
#include <vector>

class IsEqualTo final {
public:
  explicit IsEqualTo(const ObserverPtr& observer) :
    observer { observer } { }
  bool operator()(const ObserverPtr& observerToCompare) {
    return observerToCompare->getId() == observer->getId();
  }

private:
  ObserverPtr observer;
};

class Subject {
public:
  void addObserver(ObserverPtr& observerToAdd) {
    auto iter = std::find_if(begin(observers), end(observers),
        IsEqualTo(observerToAdd));
    if (iter == end(observers)) {
      observers.push_back(observerToAdd);
    }
  }

  void removeObserver(ObserverPtr& observerToRemove) {
    observers.erase(std::remove_if(begin(observers), end(observers),
        IsEqualTo(observerToRemove)), end(observers));
  }
```

```cpp
protected:
  void notifyAllObservers() const {
    for (const auto& observer : observers) {
      observer->update();
    }
  }

private:
  std::vector<ObserverPtr> observers;
};
```

In addition to the class Subject, a Functor named IsEqualTo is also defined (see Chapter 7 about Functors), which is used for comparisons when adding and removing observers. The Functor compares the IDs of the Observer. It would also be conceivable that it compares the memory addresses of the Observer instances. Then it would even be possible for several observers of the same type to register at the Subject.

The core is the notifyAllObservers() member function. It is protected since it is intended to be called by the concrete Subjects that are inherited from this one. This function iterates over all registered Observers and calls their update() member function.

Let's look at a concrete subject, the SpreadsheetModel.

Listing 9-33. The SpreadsheetModel is a concrete Subject

```cpp
#include "Subject.h"
#include <iostream>
#include <string_view>

class SpreadsheetModel : public Subject {
public:
  void changeCellValue(std::string_view column, const int row, const double value) {
    std::cout << "Cell [" << column << ", " << row << "] = " << value << std::endl;
    // Change value of a spreadsheet cell, and then...
    notifyAllObservers();
  }
};
```

This, of course, is only an absolute minimum of a SpreadsheetModel. It just serves to explain the functional principle of the pattern. The only thing you can do here is to call a member function that calls the inherited notifyAllObservers() function.

The three concrete observers in our example that implement the update() member function of the Observer interface are the three views TableView, BarChartView, and PieChartView.

Listing 9-34. Three concrete views implement the abstract Observer interface

```cpp
#include "Observer.h"
#include "SpreadsheetModel.h"

class TableView : public Observer {
public:
  explicit TableView(SpreadsheetModel& theModel) :
    model { theModel } { }
  virtual int getId() override {
    return 1;
  }
```

```cpp
  virtual void update() override {
    std::cout << "Update of TableView." << std::endl;
  }

private:
  SpreadsheetModel& model;
};

class BarChartView : public Observer {
public:
  explicit BarChartView(SpreadsheetModel& theModel) :
    model { theModel } { }
  virtual int getId() override {
    return 2;
  }

  virtual void update() override {
    std::cout << "Update of BarChartView." << std::endl;
  }

private:
  SpreadsheetModel& model;
};

class PieChartView : public Observer {
public:
  explicit PieChartView(SpreadsheetModel& theModel) :
    model { theModel } { }
  virtual int getId() override {
    return 3;
  }

  virtual void update() override {
    std::cout << "Update of PieChartView." << std::endl;
  }

private:
  SpreadsheetModel& model;
};
```

I think it is time again to show an overview in the form of a class diagram. Figure 9-11 depicts the structure (classes and dependencies) that has arisen.

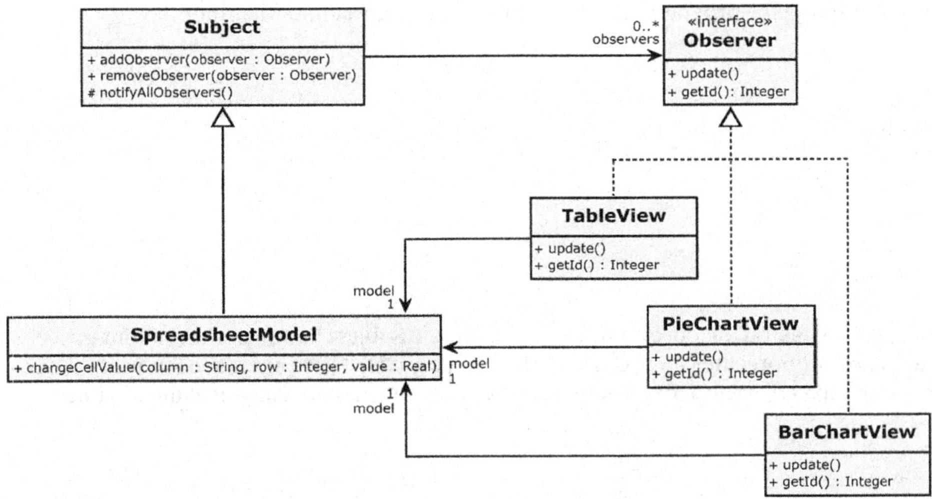

Figure 9-11. *When the SpreadsheetModel gets changed, it notifies all its observers*

In the `main()` function we now use the `SpreadsheetModel` and the three views as follows:

Listing 9-35. Our SpreadsheetModel and the three Views assembled together and in action

```cpp
#include "SpreadsheetModel.h"
#include "SpreadsheetViews.h"

int main() {
  SpreadsheetModel spreadsheetModel { };

  ObserverPtr observer1 = std::make_shared<TableView>(spreadsheetModel);
  spreadsheetModel.addObserver(observer1);

  ObserverPtr observer2 = std::make_shared<BarChartView>(spreadsheetModel);
  spreadsheetModel.addObserver(observer2);

  spreadsheetModel.changeCellValue("A", 1, 42);

  spreadsheetModel.removeObserver(observer1);

  spreadsheetModel.changeCellValue("B", 2, 23.1);

  ObserverPtr observer3 = std::make_shared<PieChartView>(spreadsheetModel);
  spreadsheetModel.addObserver(observer3);

  spreadsheetModel.changeCellValue("C", 3, 3.1415926);

  return 0;
}
```

After compiling and running the program, we see the following on the standard output:

```
Cell [A, 1] = 42
Update of TableView.
Update of BarChartView.
Cell [B, 2] = 23.1
Update of BarChartView.
Cell [C, 3] = 3.14153
Update of BarChartView.
Update of PieChartView.
```

In addition to the positive feature of loose coupling (the concrete Subject knows nothing about the Observers), this pattern also supports the Open-Closed Principle very well. New concrete observers (in our case, new views) can be added very easily since nothing needs to be adjusted or changed at the existing classes.

Factories

According to the Separation of Concerns (SoC) principle, object creation or procurement should be separated from the domain-specific tasks that an object has. The above discussed Dependency Injection pattern follows this principle in a straightforward way, because the whole object creation process is centralized in an infrastructure element, and the objects do not have to worry about it.

But what shall we do if it's required that an object must be dynamically created at some point at runtime? Well, this task can then be taken over by an object factory.

The *Factory* design pattern is basically relatively simple and appears in code bases in many different forms and varieties. In addition to the SoC principle, also Information Hiding (see Chapter 3) is greatly supported, because the creation process of an instance should be concealed from its users.

As already has been said, factories can be found in countless forms and variants. We discuss only a simple variant.

Simple Factory

The probably simplest implementation of a Factory looks like this (we take up the Logging example from the DI section above):

Listing 9-36. Probably the simplest imaginable object factory

```cpp
#include "LoggingFacility.h"
#include "StandardOutputLogger.h"

class LoggerFactory {
public:
  static Logger create() {
    return std::make_shared<StandardOutputLogger>();
  }
};
```

The usage of this very simple factory looks as follows:

Listing 9-37. Using the LoggerFactory to create a Logger instance

```cpp
#include "LoggerFactory.h"

int main() {
  Logger logger = LoggerFactory::create();
  // ...log something...
  return 0;
}
```

Maybe you'll ask now, whether it is at all worth it to spend an extra class for such a puny task. Well, maybe not. It's more sensible, if the factory were able to create various loggers, and decides which type it shall be. This can be done, for example, by reading and evaluating a configuration file, or a certain key is read out from the Windows Registry database. It is also imaginable that the type of the generated object is made dependent on the time of the day. The possibilities are endless. It is important that this should be completely transparent to the client class. So, here's a little bit more sophisticated LoggerFactory that reads a configuration file (e.g., from hard disk) and decides on the current configuration, which specific Logger is created:

Listing 9-38. A more sophisticated Factory that reads and evaluates a configuration file

```cpp
#include "LoggingFacility.h"
#include "StandardOutputLogger.h"
#include "FilesystemLogger.h"

#include <fstream>
#include <string>
#include <string_view>

class LoggerFactory {
private:
  enum class OutputTarget : int {
    STDOUT,
    FILE
  };

public:
  explicit LoggerFactory(std::string_view configurationFileName) :
    configurationFileName { configurationFileName } { }

  Logger create() const {
    const std::string configurationFileContent = readConfigurationFile();
    OutputTarget outputTarget = evaluateConfiguration(configurationFileContent);
    return createLogger(outputTarget);
  }

private:
  std::string readConfigurationFile() const {
    std::ifstream filestream(configurationFileName);
    return std::string(std::istreambuf_iterator<char>(filestream),
      std::istreambuf_iterator<char>());  }
```

```cpp
OutputTarget evaluateConfiguration(std::string_view configurationFileContent) const {
  // Evaluate the content of the configuration file...
  return OutputTarget::STDOUT;
}

Logger createLogger(OutputTarget outputTarget) const {
  switch (outputTarget) {
  case OutputTarget::FILE:
    return std::make_shared<FilesystemLogger>();
  case OutputTarget::STDOUT:
  default:
    return std::make_shared<StandardOutputLogger>();
  }
}

const std::string configurationFileName;
};
```

The UML class diagram in Figure 9-12 depicts the structure that we basically know from the section about Dependency Injection (Figure 9-5), but now with our simple `LoggerFactory` instead of an Assembler.

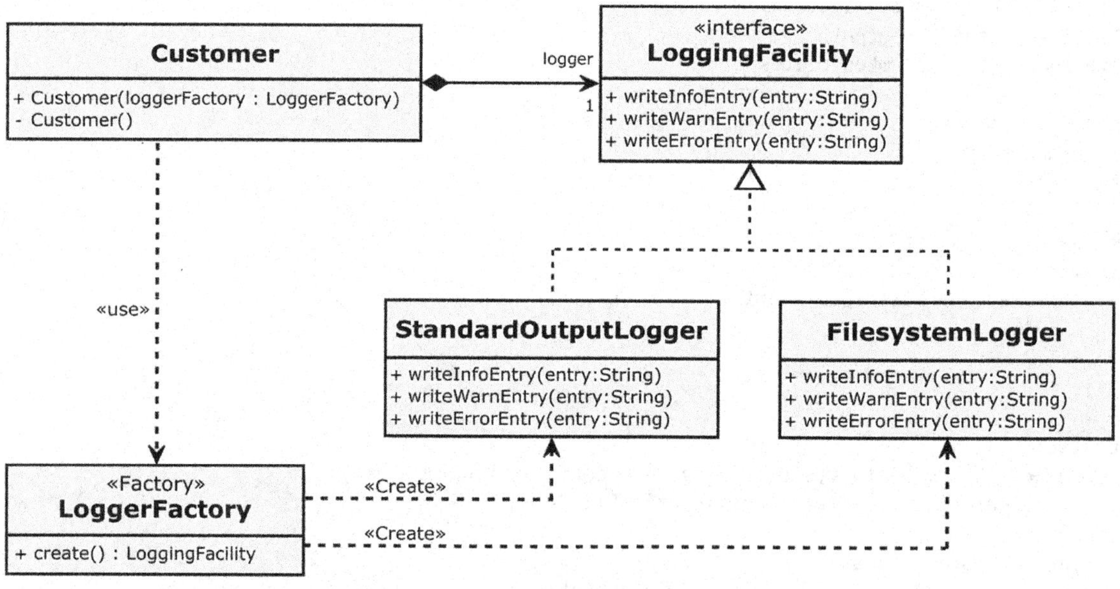

Figure 9-12. *The Customer uses a LoggerFactory to obtain concrete Loggers*

A comparison of this diagram with Figure 9-5 shows a significant difference: while the class `CustomerRepository` has no dependency on the Assembler, the Customer "knows" the factory class when using the Factory pattern. Presumably, this dependency is not a serious problem, but it makes clear once again that a loose coupling is brought to the maximum extent with Dependency Injection.

Facade

The *Facade* Pattern is a structural pattern that is often used on architectural level and has the following intent:

> *Provide a unified interface to a set of interfaces in a subsystem. Facade defines a higher-level interface that makes the subsystem easier to use.*
>
> —Erich Gamma et. al., *Design Patterns* [Gamma95]

Structuring a large software system according to the principles Separation of Concerns, Single Responsibility Principle (see Chapter 6), and Information Hiding (see Chapter 3) usually has the result that some kind of bigger components or modules are originated. Generally, these components or modules can sometimes be referred to as "subsystems." Even in a layered architecture, individual layers can be considered as subsystems.

In order to promote encapsulation, the internal structure of a component or subsystem should be hidden for its clients (see Information Hiding in Chapter 3). The communication between subsystems, and thus the amount of dependencies between them, should be minimized. It would be fatal, if clients of a subsystem must know details about its internal structure and the interaction of its parts.

A Facade regulates access to a complex subsystem by providing a well-defined and simple interface for clients. Any access to the subsystem must solely be done over the Facade.

The following UML diagram (Figure 9-13) shows a subsystem named `Billing` for preparing invoices. Its internal structure consists of several interconnected parts. Clients of the subsystem cannot access these parts directly. They have to use the Facade `BillingService`, which is represented by a UML Port (stereotype «facade») on the border of the subsystem.

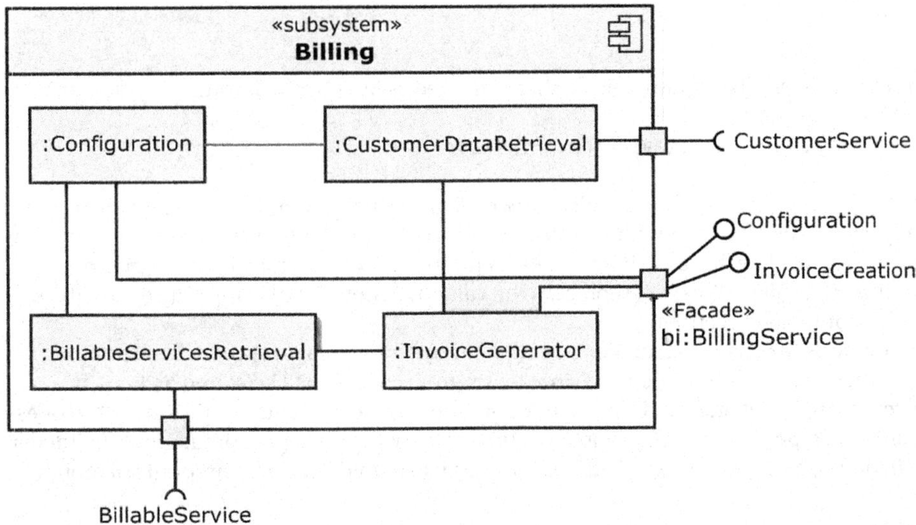

Figure 9-13. *The Billing subsystem provides a facade BillingService as an access point for clients*

In C++, and also in other languages, a Facade is nothing special. It is often just a simple class that is receiving calls at its public interface and forwards them to the internal structure of the subsystem. Sometimes it is only a simple forwarding of a call to one of the internal structural elements of the subsystem, but occasionally a Facade also carries out data conversions, then it is also an Adapter (see section about Adapter).

In our example, the Facade class `BillingService` implements two interfaces, represented by the UML ball-notation. According to the Interface Segregation Principle (ISP; see Chapter 6), the configuration of the `Billing` subsystem (interface `Configuration`) is separated from the generation of bills (interface `InvoiceCreation`). Thus, the Facade must override operations that are declared in both interfaces.

Money Class

If high accuracy is of any importance, you should avoid floating-point values. Floating-point variables of type `float`, `double`, or `long  double` fail already in simple additions, as this small example demonstrates:

Listing 9-39. When adding 10 floating point numbers this way, the result is possibly not accurate enough

```cpp
#include <assert.h>
#include <iostream>

int main() {

  double sum = 0.0;
  double addend = 0.3;

  for (int i = 0; i < 10; i++) {
    sum = sum + addend;
  };

  assert(sum == 3.0);
  return 0;
}
```

If you compile and run this small program, this is what you'll see as its console output:

```
Assertion failed: sum == 3.0, file ..\main.cpp, line 13
```

I think that the cause for this deviation is generally known. Floating-point numbers are stored in a binary format internally. Due to this it is impossible to store a value of 0.3 (and others) precisely in a variable of type `float`, `double`, or `long  double`, because it has no exact representation of finite length in binary. In decimal, we have a similar problem. We can't represent the value 1/3 (one-third) using only decimal notation. 0.33333333 isn't completely accurate.

There are several solutions for this problem. For currencies it can be a suitable approach to store the money value in an integer with the required precision, for example, $12.45 will be stored as 1245. If requirements are not very high, an integer can be a feasible solution. Please note that the C++ standard does not specify the size of integral types in bytes; thus you must be careful with very big amounts since an integer overflow can occur. If in doubt, a 64-bit integer should be used, as it can hold very large amounts of money.

DETERMINING THE RANGE OF AN ARITHMETIC TYPE

The actual implementation-specific ranges for arithmetic types (either integral or floating-point) can be found as class templates in header `<limits>`. For example, this is how you will find maximum range for `int`:

```cpp
#include <limits>
constexpr auto INT_LOWER_BOUND = std::numeric_limits<int>::min();
constexpr auto INT_UPPER_BOUND = std::numeric_limits<int>::max();
```

Another popular approach is to provide a special class for this purpose, the so-called *Money Class*:

Provide a class to represent exact amounts of money. A Money Class handles different currencies and exchanges between them.

— Martin Fowler, *Patterns of Enterprise Application Architecture* [Fowler02]

Money
- amount : Integer - currency : Currency
+ Money() + Money(other : Money) + Money(amount : Integer, currency : Currency) + operator=(other : Money) : Money + operator=(newAmount : Integer) : Money + operator==(other : Money) : Boolean + operator+(addend : Money) : Money + operator-(subtrahend : Money) : Money + operator*(multiplier : Integer) : Money + getAsFloatingPointValue() : double + getAsPrintableString() : String

Figure 9-14. A Money Class

The Money Class pattern is basically a class encapsulating a financial amount and its currency, but dealing with money is just one example for this category of classes. There are many other properties, or dimensions, that must be accurately represented, for example, precise measurements in physics (Time, Voltage, Current, Distance, Mass, Frequency, Amount of substances ...).

1991: PATRIOT MISSILE MISTIMING

MIM-104 Patriot is a surface-to-air missile (SAM) system that was designed and manufactured by the *Raytheon Company* of the United States. Its typical application is to counter high-altitude tactical ballistic missiles, cruise missiles and advanced aircraft. During the first Persian Gulf War (1990 – 1991), a.k.a. operation "Desert Storm," Patriot was used to shoot down incoming Iraqi SCUD or Al Hussein short-range ballistic missiles.

On February 25, 1991, a battery in Dhahran, a city located in the Eastern Province of Saudi Arabia, failed to intercept a SCUD. The missile struck an Army barracks and caused 28 deaths and 98 injuries.

An investigation report [GAOIMTEC92] revealed that the cause for this failure was an inaccurate calculation of the time since power-up of the system due to computer arithmetic errors. So that Patriot's missiles can detect and hit the target after launch, they must be spatially approximated to the target, a.k.a. the "range gate." To predict where the target will appear next (the so-called deflection angle), some calculations with the system's time and the target's flying speed has to be performed. The elapsed time since system's start was measured in tenths of a second and expressed as an integer. The target's speed was measured in miles per second and expressed as a decimal value. To calculate the "range gate," the value of the system's timer has to be multiplied by 1/10 to get the time in seconds. This calculation was done by using registers that are only 24 bits long.

The problem was that the value of 1/10 in decimal can not be accurately represented in a 24-bit register. The value was chopped at 24 bits after the radix point. The consequence was that the conversion of time from an integer to a real number results in a small loss of precision causing a less accurate time calculation. This accuracy error would probably not have been a problem if the system would only been in operation for a few hours, according to its Concept Of Operation as a mobile system. But in this case, the system has been running for more than 100 hours. The number representing the system's up-time was quite large. This meant that the small conversion error of 1/10 into its decimal 24-bit-representation resulted in a large deviation error of nearly half of a second! An Iraqi SCUD missile travels approx. 800 meters in this time span – far enough to be outside the "range gate" of an approaching Patriot missile.

Although the accurate dealing with amounts of money is a very common case in many business IT systems, you will struggle in vain to find a Money Class in most mainstream C++ base class libraries. But don't reinvent the wheel! There are multitudes of different C++ Money Class implementations out there, just ask the search engine of your trust and you will get thousands of hits. As so often, one implementation doesn't satisfy all requirements. The key is to understand your problem domain. While choosing (or designing) a Money Class, you may consider several constraints and requirements. Here are a few questions that you may have to clarify first:

- What is the full range of values to be handled (minimum, maximum)?

- Which rounding rules apply? There are national laws or practices for roundings in some countries.

- Are there legal requirements for accuracy?

- Which standards must be considered (e.g., ISO 4217 *International Standard for Currency Codes*)?

- How will the values be displayed to the user?

- How often will conversion take place?

From my perspective it is absolutely essential to have 100% unit test coverage (see Chapter 2 about Unit Tests) for a Money Class to check whether the class is working as expected under all circumstances. Of course, Money Class has a small drawback compared to the pure number representation with an integer: you lose a smidgen of performance. This might be an issue in some systems. But I'm convinced that in most cases the advantages will predominate (always keep in mind that premature optimization is bad).

Special Case Object (Null Object)

In section "Don't Pass or Return 0 (NULL, nullptr)" in Chapter 4 we learned that returning a `nullptr` from a function or method is bad and should be avoided. There we had also discussed various strategies to avoid regular (raw) pointers in a modern C++ program. In the section "An Exception Is an Exception – Literally!" in Chapter 5 we learned that exceptions should only be used for real exceptional cases and not for the purpose of controlling the normal program flow.

The open and interesting question is now this: How do we treat those special cases, which are not real exceptions (e.g., a failed memory allocation), without using a non-semantic `nullptr` or other weird values?

Let's pick up our code example again, which we have seen several times before: the query of a `Customer` by name.

Listing 9-40. A look up method for customers by name

```
Customer CustomerService::findCustomerByName(const std::string& name) {
  // Code that searches the customer by name...
  // ...but what shall we do, if a customer with the given name does not exist?!
}
```

Well, one possibility would be to return always lists instead of a single instance. If the returned list is empty, the queried business object does not exist:

Listing 9-41. An alternative to nullptr: Returning an empty list if the look-up for a customer fails

```
#include "Customer.h"
#include <vector>

using CustomerList = std::vector<Customer>;

CustomerList CustomerService::findCustomerByName(const std::string& name) {
  // Code that searches the customer by name...
  // ...and if a customer with the given name does not exist:
  return CustomerList();
}
```

The returned list can now be queried in the further program sequence whether it is empty. But what semantics has an empty list? Was an error responsible for the emptiness of the list? Well, the member function `std::vector<T>::empty()` is not able to answer this question. Being empty is a state of a list, but this state has no domain-specific semantics.

Folks, no doubt, this solution is much better than returning a `nullptr`, but maybe not good enough in some cases. What would be much more comfortable is a return value that can be queried about its origination cause, and about what can be done with it. The answer is the *Special Case* pattern!

A subclass that provides special behavior for particular cases.

—Martin Fowler, *Patterns of Enterprise Application Architecture* [Fowler02]

The idea behind the Special Case pattern is that we take advantage of polymorphism, and that we provide classes representing the special cases, instead of returning `nullptr`, or some other odd value. These special case classes have the same interface as the "normal" class that is expected by the callers. The class diagram in Figure 9-15 depicts such a specialization.

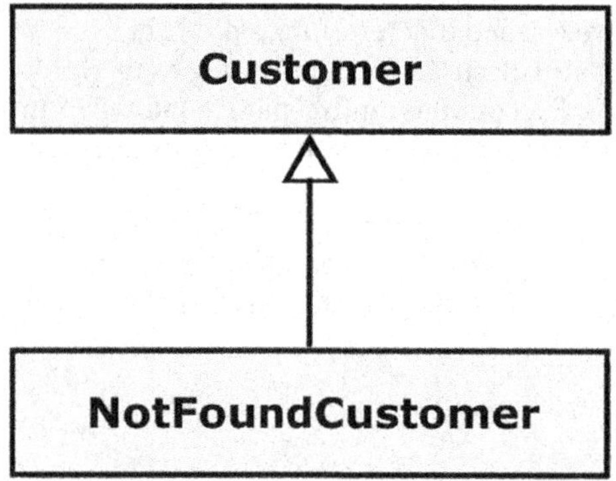

Figure 9-15. *The class(es) representing a special case are derived from class Customer*

In C++ source code, an implementation of the `Customer` class and the `NotFoundCustomer` class representing the special case looks something like this (only the relevant parts are shown):

Listing 9-42. An excerpt from file Customer.h with the classes Customer and NotFoundCustomer

```cpp
#ifndef CUSTOMER_H_
#define CUSTOMER_H_

#include "Address.h"
#include "CustomerId.h"
#include <memory>
#include <string>

class Customer {
public:
  // ...more member functions here...
  virtual ~Customer() = default;

  virtual bool isPersistable() const noexcept {
    return (customerId.isValid() && ! forename.empty() && ! surname.empty() &&
      billingAddress->isValid() && shippingAddress->isValid());
  }
```

```cpp
private:
  CustomerId customerId;
  std::string forename;
  std::string surname;
  std::shared_ptr<Address> billingAddress;
  std::shared_ptr<Address> shippingAddress;
};

class NotFoundCustomer final : public Customer {
public:
  virtual bool isPersistable() const noexcept override {
    return false;
  }
};

using CustomerPtr = std::unique_ptr<Customer>;

#endif /* CUSTOMER_H_ */
```

The objects that represent the special case can now be used largely as if they were valid (normal) instances of class Customer. Permanent null-checks, even when the object is passed around between different parts of the program, are superfluous, since there is always a valid object. Many things can be done with the NotFoundCustomer object, as if it were an instance of Customer, for example, presenting it in a user interface. The object can even reveal whether it is persistable. For the "real" Customer, this is done by analyzing its data fields. In the case of the NotFoundCustomer, however, this check has always a negative result.

And compared to the meaningless null-checks, a statement like the following one makes significantly more sense:

```cpp
if (customer.isPersistable()) {
  // ...write the customer to a database here...
}
```

std::optional<T> [C++17]

Since C++17, there is another interesting alternative that could be used for a possibly missing result or value: std::optional<T> (defined in header <optional>). Instances of this class template represent an "optional contained value," that is, a value that may or may not be present.

The class Customer can be used as an optional value using std::optional<T> by introducing a type alias as follows:

```cpp
#include "Customer.h"
#include <optional>
using OptionalCustomer = std::optional<Customer>;
```

Our search function CustomerService::findCustomerByName() can now be implemented as follows:

```cpp
class CustomerRepository {
public:
  OptionalCustomer findCustomerByName(const std::string& name) {
```

```cpp
    if ( /* the search was successful */ ) {
      return Customer();
    } else {
      return {};
    }
  }
};
```

At the call site of the function, you now have two ways to handle the return value, as illustrated in the following example:

```cpp
int main() {
  CustomerRepository repository { };
  auto optionalCustomer = repository.findCustomerByName("John Doe");

  // Option 1: Catch an exception, if 'optionalCustomer' is empty
  try {
    auto customer = optionalCustomer.value();
  } catch (std::bad_optional_access& ex) {
    std::cerr << ex.what() << std::endl;
  }

  // Option 2: Provide a substitute for a possibly missing object
  auto customer = optionalCustomer.value_or(NotFoundCustomer());

  return 0;
}
```

In the second option, for instance, it is possible to either provide a standard (default) customer, or – as in this case – an instance of a special case object, if `optionalCustomer` is empty. I recommend choosing the first option when the absence of an object is unexpected and is a clue that a serious error must have been occurred. For the other cases, where a missing object is nothing unusual, I recommend option 2.

What Is an Idiom?

A programming idiom is a special kind of pattern to solve a problem in a specific programming language or technology. That is, unlike the more general design patterns, idioms are limited in their applicability. Often, their applicability is limited to exactly one specific programming language or a certain technology, for example, a framework.

Idioms are typically used during detailed design and implementation, if programming problems must be solved at a low level of abstraction. A well-known idiom in the C and C++ domain is the so-called *Include Guard*, sometimes also called *Macro Guard* or *Header Guard*, which is used to avoid double inclusion of the same header file:

```cpp
#ifndef FILENAME_H_
#define FILENAME_H_

// ...content of header file...

#endif
```

One disadvantage of this idiom is that a consistent naming scheme for filenames, and thus also for Include-Guard macro names, must be ensured. Hence, most C and C++ compilers support a non-standard `#pragma` once directive nowadays. This directive, inserted at the top of a header file, will ensure that the header file is included only once.

By the way, we have already gotten to know a few idioms. In Chapter 4 we discussed the Resource Acquisition Is Initialization (RAII) idiom, and in Chapter 7 we have seen the Erase-Remove idiom.

Some Useful C++ Idioms

It is not a joke, but you can actually find an exhaustive collection of nearly 100(!) C++ idioms on the Internet (WikiBooks: *More C++ Idioms*; URL: `https://en.wikibooks.org/wiki/More_C++_Idioms`). The problem is that not all of these idioms are conducive to a modern and clean C++ program. They are sometimes very complex and barely comprehensible (e.g., *Algebraic Hierarchy*), even for fairly skilled C++ developers. Furthermore, some idioms have become largely obsolete by the publishing of C++11 and subsequent standards. Therefore, I present here only a small selection, which I consider interesting and still useful.

The Power of Immutability

Sometimes it is to be of great advantage to have classes for objects that cannot change its state once they have been created, a.k.a. immutable classes (what is really meant by this are in fact immutable objects, because properly speaking a class can only be altered by a developer). For instance, immutable objects can be used as key values in a hashed data structure, since the key value should never change after creation. Another known example for an immutable is the String class in several other languages like C# or Java.

The benefits of immutable classes, respectively, and objects are the following:

- Immutable objects are thread-safe by default, so you will not have any synchronization issues if several threads or processes access those objects in a non-deterministic way. Thus, immutability makes it easier to create a parallelizable software design as there are no conflicts among objects.

- Immutability makes it easier to write, use, and reason about the code, because a class invariant, that is, a set of constraints that must always be true, is established once at object creation, and is ensured to be unchanged during the object's lifetime.

To create an immutable class in C++, the following measures must be taken:

- The member variables of the class must all be made immutable, that is, they must all be made `const` (see section about Const correctness in Chapter 4). This means that they can only be initialized once in a constructor, using the constructor's member initializer list.

- Manipulating methods do not change the object on which they are called, but return a new instance of the class with an altered state. The original object is not changed. To emphasize this, there should be no setter, because a member function whos name starts with `set...()` is misleading. There is nothing to set on an immutable object.

- The class should be marked as `final`. This is not a hard rule, but if a new class can be inherited from an allegedly immutable class, it might be possible to circumvent its immutability.

Here is an example of an immutable class in C++:

Listing 9-43. Employee is designed as an immutable class

```cpp
#include "Identifier.h"
#include "Money.h"
#include <string>
#include <string_view>

class Employee final {
public:
  Employee(std::string_view forename,
    std::string_view surname,
    const Identifier& staffNumber,
    const Money& salary) noexcept :
    forename { forename },
    surname { surname },
    staffNumber { staffNumber },
    salary { salary } { }

  Identifier getStaffNumber() const noexcept {
    return staffNumber;
  }

  Money getSalary() const noexcept {
    return salary;
  }

  Employee changeSalary(const Money& newSalary) const noexcept {
    return Employee(forename, surname, staffNumber, newSalary);
  }

private:
  const std::string forename;
  const std::string surname;
  const Identifier  staffNumber;
  const Money       salary;
};
```

Substitution Failure Is Not an Error (SFINAE)

In fact, *Substitution failure is not an error* (short: SFINAE) is not a real idiom but a feature of the C++
compiler. It has already been a part of the C++98 standard, but with C++11 several new features have been
added. However, it is still referred to as an idiom, also because it is used in a very idiomatic style, especially
in template libraries, such as the C++ Standard Library, or Boost.

The defining text passage in the standard can be found in section 14.8.2 about Template argument deduction. There we can read in §8 the following statement:

If a substitution results in an invalid type or expression, type deduction fails. An invalid type or expression is one that would be ill-formed if written using the substituted arguments. Only invalid types and expressions in the immediate context of the function type and its template parameter types can result in a deduction failure.

—Standard for Programming Language C++ [ISO11]

Error messages in case of a faulty instantiation of C++ templates, for example, with wrong template arguments, can be very verbose and cryptic. SFINAE is a programming technique that ensures that a failed substitution of template arguments does not create an annoying compilation error. Simply put, it means that if the substitution of a template argument fails, the compiler continues with the search for a suitable template instead of aborting with an error.

Here is a very simple example with two overloaded function templates:

Listing 9-44. SFINAE by example of two overloaded function templates

```cpp
#include <iostream>

template <typename T>
void print(typename T::type) {
  std::cout << "Calling print(typename T::type)" << std::endl;
}

template <typename T>
void print(T) {
  std::cout << "Calling print(T)" << std::endl;
}

struct AStruct {
  using type = int;
};

int main() {
  print<AStruct>(42);
  print<int>(42);
  print(42);

  return 0;
}
```

The output of this small example on stdout will be:

```
Calling print(typename T::type)
Calling print(T)
Calling print(T)
```

As can be seen, the compiler uses the first version of print() for the first function call, and the second version for the two subsequent calls. And this code also works in C++98.

Well, but SFINAE prior C++11 had several drawbacks. The above very simple example is a bit deceptive regarding the real effort to use this technique in real projects. The application of SFINAE this way in template libraries has leaded to very verbose and tricky code that is difficult to understand. Furthermore, it is badly standardized and sometimes compiler specific.

With the advent of C++11, the so-called Type Traits library was introduced, which we have already got to know in Chapter 7. Especially the meta function `std::enable_if()` (defined in header `<type_traits>`), which is available since C++11, plays now a central role in SFINAE. With this function we get a conditionally "remove functions capability" from overload resolution based on type traits. In other words, we can, for example, pick a function its overloaded version depending on the argument's type like this:

Listing 9-45. SFINAE by using function template std::enable_if<>

```cpp
#include <iostream>
#include <type_traits>

template <typename T>
void print(T var, typename std::enable_if<std::is_enum<T>::value, T>::type* = 0) {
  std::cout << "Calling overloaded print() for enumerations." << std::endl;
}

template <typename T>
void print(T var, typename std::enable_if<std::is_integral<T>::value, T>::type = 0) {
  std::cout << "Calling overloaded print() for integral types." << std::endl;
}

template <typename T>
void print(T var, typename std::enable_if<std::is_floating_point<T>::value, T>::type = 0) {
  std::cout << "Calling overloaded print() for floating point types." << std::endl;
}

template <typename T>
void print(const T& var, typename std::enable_if<std::is_class<T>::value, T>::type* = 0) {
  std::cout << "Calling overloaded print() for classes." << std::endl;
}
```

The overloaded function templates can be used by simply calling them with arguments of different types, like this:

Listing 9-46. Thanks to SFINAE, there is a matching print() function for arguments of different type

```cpp
enum Enumeration1 {
  Literal1,
  Literal2
};

enum class Enumeration2 : int {
  Literal1,
  Literal2
};
```

```cpp
class Clazz { };

int main() {
  Enumeration1 enumVar1 { };
  print(enumVar1);

  Enumeration2 enumVar2 { };
  print(enumVar2);

  print(42);

  Clazz instance { };
  print(instance);

  print(42.0f);

  print(42.0);

  return 0;
}
```

After compiling and executing, we see the following result on standard output:

```
Calling overloaded print() for enumerations.
Calling overloaded print() for enumerations.
Calling overloaded print() for integral types.
Calling overloaded print() for classes.
Calling overloaded print() for floating point types.
Calling overloaded print() for floating point types.
```

Due to the fact that the C++11 version of `std::enable_if` is a little bit verbose, C++14 has added an alias named `std::enable_if_t`.

The Copy-and-Swap Idiom

In section "Prevention Is Better Than Aftercare" in Chapter 5, we have learned the four levels of exception-safety guarantee: no exception-safety, basic exception-safety, strong exception-safety, and the no-throw guarantee. What member functions of a class should always guarantee is the basic exception-safety, because this exception-safety level is usually easy to implement.

In section "The Rule of Zero" in Chapter 5 we've learned that we should design classes always in a way so that the automatically compiler-generated special member functions (copy constructor, copy assignment operator, etc.) automatically do the right things. Or in other words: when we are forced to provide a non-trivial destructor, we are dealing with an exceptional case that requires a special treatment during destruction of the object. As a consequence it follows that the special member functions generated by the compiler are not sufficient to deal with this situation, and we have to implement them by ourselves.

However, occasionally it is inevitable that the Rule of Zero cannot be fulfilled, that is, a developer has to implement the special member functions by herself. In this case, it may be a challenging task to create an exception safe implementation of an overloaded assignment operator. In such a case, the *Copy-and-Swap* Idiom is an elegant way to solve this problem.

Hence, the intent of this idiom is as follows:

Implement the copy assignment operator with strong exception safety.

The simplest way to explain the problem and its solution is a small example. Consider the following class:

Listing 9-47. A class that manages a resource that is allocated on the heap

```cpp
#include <cstddef>

class Clazz final {
public:
  Clazz(const std::size_t size) : resourceToManage { new char[size] }, size { size } { }
  ~Clazz() {
    delete [] resourceToManage;
  }

private:
  char* resourceToManage;
  std::size_t size;
};
```

This class is, of course, only for demonstration purposes and should not be part of a real program. Let's assume that we want to do the following with the class `Clazz`:

```cpp
int main() {
  Clazz instance1 { 1000 };
  Clazz instance2 { instance1 };
  return 0;
}
```

We already know from Chapter 5 that the compiler-generated version of a copy constructor does the wrong thing here: it only creates a flat copy of the character pointer `resourceToManage`!

Hence, we have to provide our own copy constructor, like this:

```cpp
#include <algorithm>

class Clazz final {
public:
  // ...
  Clazz(const Clazz& other) : Clazz { other.size } {
    std::copy(other.resourceToManage, other.resourceToManage + other.size, resourceToManage);
  }
  // ...
};
```

So far, so good. Now the copy construction will work fine. But now we'll also need a copy assignment operator. If you are not familiar with the copy-and-swap idiom, an implementation of an assignment operator might look like this:

```cpp
#include <algorithm>

class Clazz final {
public:
  // ...
  Clazz& operator=(const Clazz& other) {
    if (&other == this) {
      return *this;
    }
    delete [] resourceToManage;
    resourceToManage = new char[other.size];
    std::copy(other.resourceToManage, other.resourceToManage + other.size,
resourceToManage);
    size = other.size;
    return *this;
  }
  // ...
};
```

Basically, this assignment operator will work, but it has several drawbacks. For instance, the constructor and destructor code is duplicated in it, which is a violation of the DRY principle (see Chapter 3). Furthermore, there is a self-assignment check at the beginning. But the biggest disadvantage is that we cannot guarantee exception-safety. For example, if the new statement causes an exception, the object can be left behind in a weird state that violates elementary class invariants.

Now the copy-and-swap idiom comes into play, also known as "Create-Temporary-and-Swap"!

For a better understanding, I present the whole class Clazz now:

Listing 9-48. A much better implementation of an assignment operator using the copy-and-swap idiom

```cpp
#include <algorithm>
#include <cstddef>

class Clazz final {
public:
  Clazz(const std::size_t size) : resourceToManage { new char[size] }, size { size } { }

  ~Clazz() {
    delete [] resourceToManage;
  }

  Clazz(const Clazz& other) : Clazz { other.size } {
    std::copy(other.resourceToManage, other.resourceToManage + other.size,
resourceToManage);
  }

  Clazz& operator=(Clazz other) {
    swap(other);
    return *this;
  }
```

```cpp
private:
  void swap(Clazz& other) noexcept {
    using std::swap;
    swap(resourceToManage, other.resourceToManage);
    swap(size, other.size);
  }

  char* resourceToManage;
  std::size_t size;
};
```

What is the trick here? Let's look at the completely different assignment operator. This has no longer a const reference (`const Clazz& other`) as a parameter, but an ordinary value parameter (`Clazz other`). This means that when this assignment operator is called, first the copy constructor of `Clazz` is called. The copy constructor, in turn, calls the default constructor that allocates memory for the resource. And that is exactly what we want: we need a temporary copy of `other`!

Now we come to the heart of the idiom: the call of the private member function `Clazz::swap()`. Within this function, the contents of the temporary instance `other`, that is, its member variables, is exchanged ("swapped") with the contents of the same member variables of our own class context (`this`). This is done by using the non-throwing `std::swap()` function (defined in header `<utility>`). After the swap operations, the temporary object `other` now owns the resources that were previously owned by the `this` object, and vice versa.

Additionally, the `Clazz::swap()` member function now makes it very easy to implement a move constructor:

```cpp
class Clazz {
public:
  // ...
  Clazz(Clazz&& other) noexcept {
    swap(other);
  }
  // ...
};
```

Of course, the major goal in a good class design should be that it is not at all necessary to implement explicit copy constructors and assignment operators (Rule of Zero). But when you are forced to do it, you should remember the copy-and-swap idiom.

Pointer to Implementation (PIMPL)

The last section of this chapter is dedicated to an idiom with the funny acronym PIMPL. PIMPL stands for *Pointer to Implementation*; and the idiom is also known as *Handle Body*, the *Compilation Firewall*, or *Cheshire Cat technique* (The Cheshire Cat is a fictional character, a grinning cat, from Lewis Carroll's novel *Alice's Adventures in Wonderland*). And it has, by the way, some similarities with the *Bridge* pattern described in [Gamma95].

The intent of the PIMPL could be formulated as follows:

> *Remove compilation dependencies on internal class implementation details by relocating them into a hidden implementation class and thus improve compile times.*

Let's take a look at an excerpt from our Customer class, a class that we've seen in many examples before:

Listing 9-49. An excerpt from the content of header file Customer.h

```cpp
#ifndef CUSTOMER_H_
#define CUSTOMER_H_

#include "Address.h"
#include "Identifier.h"
#include <string>

class Customer {
public:
  Customer();
  virtual ~Customer() = default;
  std::string getFullName() const;
  void setShippingAddress(const Address& address);
  // ...

private:
  Identifier customerId;
  std::string forename;
  std::string surname;
  Address shippingAddress;
};

#endif /* CUSTOMER_H_ */
```

Let's assume that this is a central business entity in our commercial software system and that it is used (#include "Customer.h") by many other classes. When this header file changes, any files that uses that file will need to be recompiled, even if only one private member variable is added, renamed, etc.

In order to reduce these recompilations to the absolute minimum, the PIMPL idiom comes in to play.

First we rebuild the class interface of the class Customer as follows:

Listing 9-50. The altered header file Customer.h

```cpp
#ifndef CUSTOMER_H_
#define CUSTOMER_H_

#include <memory>
#include <string>

class Address;

class Customer {
public:
  Customer();
  virtual ~Customer();
  std::string getFullName() const;
  void setShippingAddress(const Address& address);
  // ...
```

```
private:
  class Impl;
  std::unique_ptr<Impl> impl;
};
```

```
#endif /* CUSTOMER_H_ */
```

It is conspicuous that all previous private member variables, as well as their associated include-directives, have now disappeared. Instead, a forward declaration for a class named Impl, as well as a `std::unique_ptr<T>` to this forward-declared class is present.

And now let's take a look into the coressponding implementation file:

Listing 9-51. The content of file Customer.cpp

```
#include "Customer.h"

#include "Address.h"
#include "Identifier.h"

class Customer::Impl final {
public:
  std::string getFullName() const;
  void setShippingAddress(const Address& address);

private:
  Identifier customerId;
  std::string forename;
  std::string surname;
  Address shippingAddress;
};

std::string Customer::Impl::getFullName() const {
  return forename + " " + surname;
}

void Customer::Impl::setShippingAddress(const Address& address) {
  shippingAddress = address;
}

// Implementation of class Customer starts here...

Customer::Customer() : impl { std::make_unique<Customer::Impl>() } { }

Customer::~Customer() = default;

std::string Customer::getFullName() const {
  return impl->getFullName();
}

void Customer::setShippingAddress(const Address& address) {
  impl->setShippingAddress(address);
}
```

In the upper part of the implementation file (until the source code comment), we can see the class `Customer::Impl`. Into this class, everything has now been relocated, which former has been done by the class `Customer` directly. Here we also find all member variables.

In the lower section (beginning with the comment), we now find the implementation of the class `Customer`. The constructor creates an instance of `Customer::Impl` and holds it in the smart pointer `impl`. As to the rest, any call of the API of class `Customer` is delegated to the internal implementation object.

If now something has to be changed in the internal implementation in `Customer::Impl`, the compiler must only compile `Customer.h`/`Customer.cpp`, and then the linker can start its work immediately. Such change does not have any effect to the outside, and a time-consuming compilation of the almost entire project is avoided.

Small UML Guide

The OMG Unified Modeling Language™ (OMG UML) is a standardized graphical language to create models of software and other systems. Its main purpose is to enable developers, software architects, and other stakeholders to design, specify, visualize, construct, and document artifacts of a software system. UML models support the discussion between different stakeholders, serve as an aid for a clarification of requirements and other issues related to the system of interest, and can capture design decisions.

This appendix provides a brief overview of that subset of UML notations that are used in this book. Each UML element is illustrated (syntax) and briefly explained (semantic). The short definition for an element is based on the current UML specification [OMG15] that can be downloaded for free from OMG's website. An in-depth introduction to the Unified Modeling Language should be made with the help of appropriate literature, or by taking a course at a training provider.

Class Diagrams

Among varied other applications, class diagrams are usually used to depict structures of an object-oriented software design.

Class

The central element in class diagrams is the **class**.

CLASS

A class describes a set of objects that share the same specifications of features, constraints, and semantics.

An instance of a class is commonly referred to as an **object**. Therefore, classes can be considered as blueprints for objects. The UML symbol for a class is a rectangle, as depicted in Figure A-1.

© Stephan Roth 2017
S. Roth, *Clean C++*, DOI 10.1007/978-1-4842-2793-0

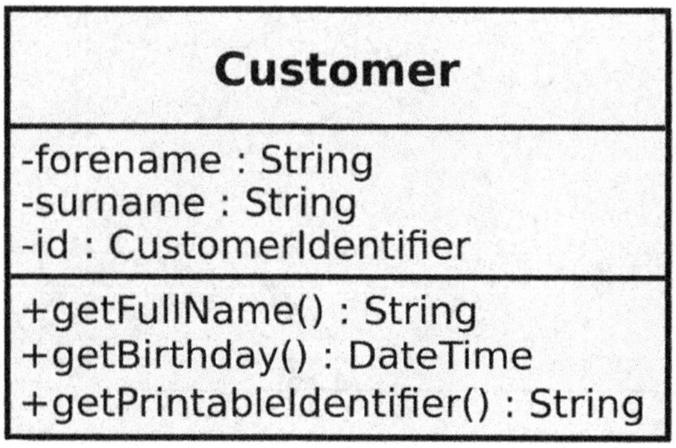

Customer

-forename : String
-surname : String
-id : CustomerIdentifier

+getFullName() : String
+getBirthday() : DateTime
+getPrintableIdentifier() : String

Figure A-1. *A class named Customer*

A class has a name (in this case "Customer"), which is shown centered in the first compartment of the rectangled symbol. If a class is abstract, that is, it cannot be instantiated, its name is typically shown in italicized letters. Classes can have **attributes** (data, structure) and **operations** (behavior), which are shown in the second, respective, and third compartments. The type of an attribute is noted separated by a colon after the attribute's name. The same applies to the type of the return value of an operation. Operations can have parameters that are specified within the parentheses (round brackets). Static attributes or operations are underlined.

Classes have a mechanism to regulate the access to attributes and operations. In UML they are called visibilities. The **visibility kind** is put in front of the attribute's or operation's name and may be one of the characters that are described in Table A-1.

Table A-1. *Visibilities*

Character	Visibility kind
+	**public:** This attribute or operation is visible to all elements that can access the class.
#	**protected:** This attribute or operation is not only visible inside the class itself, but also visible to elements that are derived from the class that owns it (see Generalization Relationship).
~	**package:** This attribute or operation is visible to elements that are in the same package as its owning class. This kind of visibility doesn't have an appropriate representation in C++ and is not used in this book.
-	**private:** This attribute or operation is only visible inside the class, nowhere else.

A C++ class definition corresponding to the UML class shown in the above Figure A-1 may look like this:

Listing A-1. The Customer class in C++

```cpp
#include <string>
#include "DateTime.h"
#include "CustomerIdentifier.h"

class Customer {
public:
  Customer();
  virtual ~Customer();
```

```
  std::string getFullName() const;
  DateTime getBirthday() const;
  std::string getPrintableIdentifier() const;

private:
  std::string forename;
  std::string surname;
  CustomerIdentifier id;
};
```

The graphical representation of instances is rarely necessary, so the so-called object diagrams of the UML play only a minor role. The UML symbol to depict a created instance (that is, an object) of a class, a so-called **Instance Specification**, is very similar to that of a class. The main difference is that the caption in the first compartment is underlined. It shows the name of the specified instance, separated by a colon from its type, for example, the class (see Figure A-2). The name may also be missing (anonymous instance).

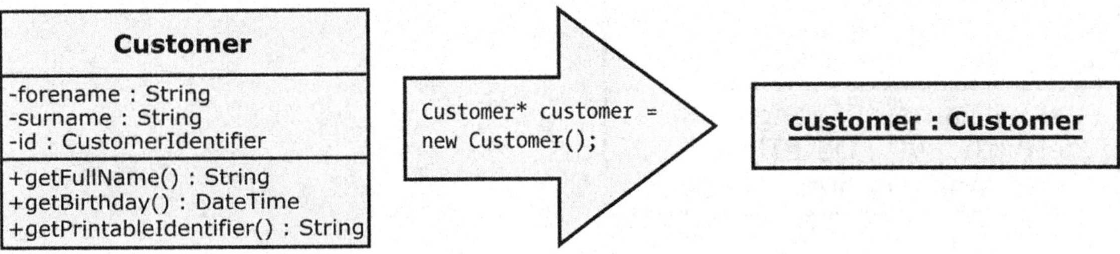

Figure A-2. *The Instance Specification on the right represents a possible or actual existence of an instance of class Customer*

Interface

An **interface** defines a kind of a contract: a class that realizes the interface must fulfill that contract.

> ## INTERFACE
>
> An interface is a declaration of a set of coherent public obligations.

Interfaces are always abstract, that is, they cannot be instantiated by default. The UML symbol for an interface is very similar to a class, with the keyword «interface» (surrounded by French quotation marks that are called "guillemets") preceding the name, as depicted in Figure A-3.

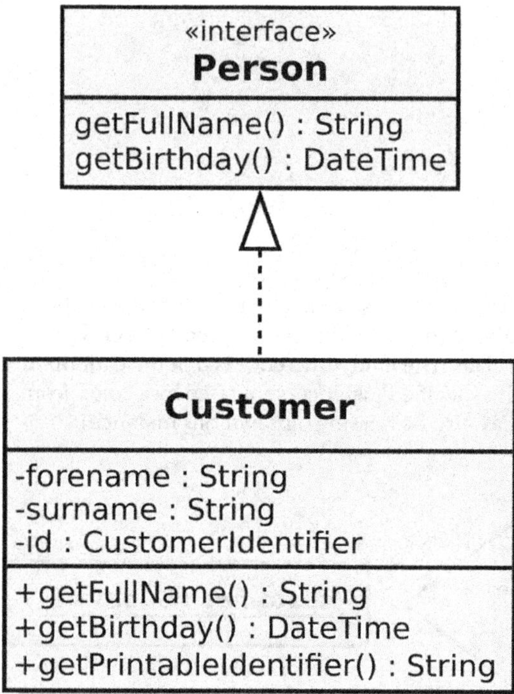

Figure A-3. *Class Customer implements operations that are declared in interface Person*

The dashed arrow with the closed but not filled arrowhead is the **interface realization** relationship. This relationship expresses that the class conforms to the contract specified by the interface, that is, the class implements those operations that are declared by the interface. It is, of course, allowed that a class implements multiple interfaces.

Unlike some other object-oriented languages, such as Java or C#, there is no `interface` keyword in C++. Interfaces are therefore usually emulated with the help of abstract classes that solely consist of pure virtual member functions as shown in the following code examples.

Listing A-2. The Person interface in C++

```cpp
#include <string>
#include "DateTime.h"

class Person {
public:
  virtual ~Person() { }
  virtual std::string getFullName() const = 0;
  virtual DateTime getBirthday() const = 0;
};
```

Listing A-3. The Customer class realizing the Person interface

```cpp
#include "Person.h"
#include "CustomerIdentifier.h"

class Customer : public Person {
public:
  Customer();
  virtual ~Customer();

  virtual std::string getFullName() const override;
  virtual DateTime getBirthday() const override;
  std::string getPrintableIdentifier() const;

private:
  std::string forename;
  std::string surname;
  CustomerIdentifier id;
};
```

To show that a class or component (see section Components below) provides or requires interfaces, you can use the so-called **ball-and-socket notation**. A provided interface is depicted using a ball (a.k.a. "lollipop"), a required interface is depicted with a socket. Strictly speaking, this is an alternative notation, as Figure A-4 clarifies.

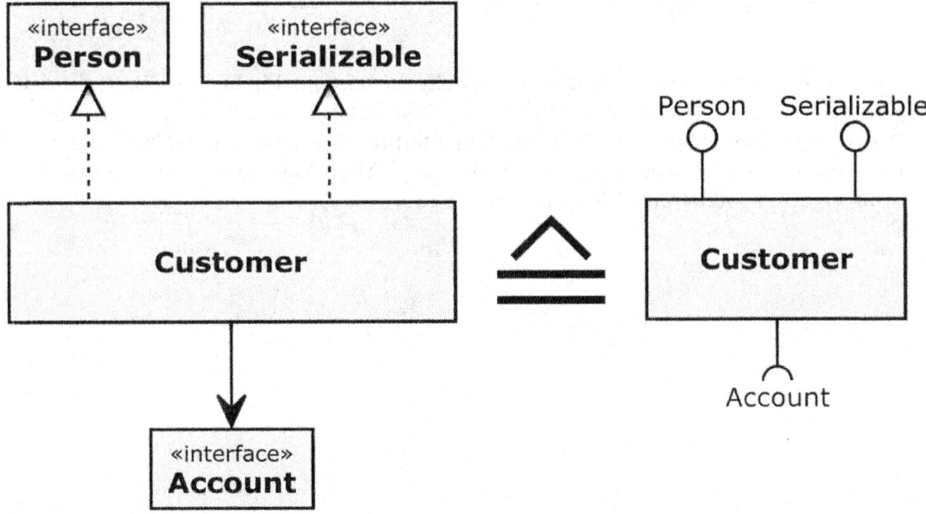

Figure A-4. *The ball-and-socket notation for provided and required interfaces*

The arrow between class Customer and interface Account is a navigable association, which is explained in the following section about UML associations.

Association

Classes usually have static relationships to other classes. The UML **association** specifies such a kind of relationship.

ASSOCIATION

An association relationship allows one instance of a classifier (e.g., a class or a component) to access another.

In its simplest form, the UML syntax for an association is a solid line between two classes as depicted in Figure A-5.

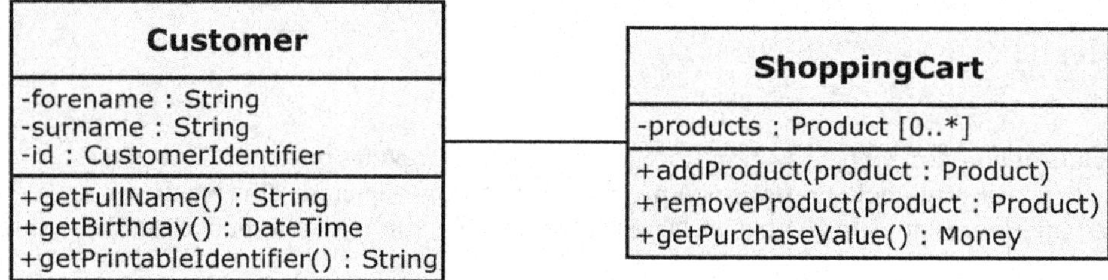

Figure A-5. *A simple association relationship between two classes*

This simple association is often not sufficient to properly specify the relationship between both classes. For instance, the navigation direction across such a simple association, that is, who is able to access whom, is undefined by default. However, navigability in this case is often interpreted as bidirectional by convention, that is, Customer has an attribute to access ShoppingCart and vice versa. Therefore, more information can be provided to an association. Figure A-6 illustrates a few of the possibilities.

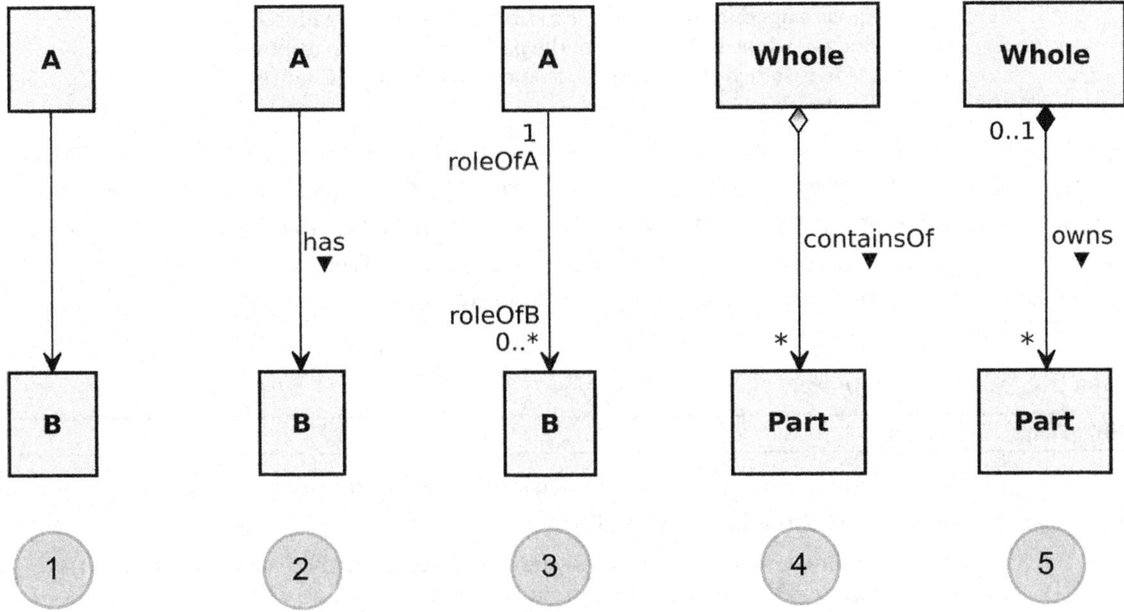

Figure A-6. *Some examples of associations between classes*

1. This example shows an association with one end **navigable** (depicted by an arrowhead) and the other having unspecified navigability. The semantic is: class A is able to navigate to class B. In the other direction it is unspecified, that is, class B might be able to navigate to class A.

■ **Note**   It is strongly recommended to define the interpretation of the navigability of such an unspecified association end in your project. **My recommendation is to consider them as non-navigable.** This interpretation is also used in this book.

---

2. This navigable association has a **name** ("has"). The solid triangle indicates the direction of reading. Apart from that, the semantics of this association is fully identical to example 1.

3. In this example, both association ends have **labels** (names) and **multiplicities**. The labels are typically used to specify the roles of the classes in an association.

   A multiplicity specifies the allowed quantity of instances of the classes that are involved in an association. It is an inclusive interval of non-negative integers beginning with a lower bound and ending with a (possibly infinite) upper bound. In this case, any A has zero to any number of B's, whereas any B has exactly one A. Table A-2 shows some examples of valid multiplicities.

4. This is a special association called **aggregation**. It represents a whole-part-relationship, that is, the one class (the part) is hierarchically subordinated to the other class (the whole). The shallow diamond is just a marker in this kind of association and identifies the whole. Otherwise everything that applies to associations applies to an aggregation too.

279

5. This is a **composite aggregation**, which is a strong form of aggregation. It expresses that the whole is the owner of the parts, and thus also responsible for the parts. If an instance of the whole is deleted, all of its part instances are normally deleted with it.

Note Please note that a part can (where allowed) be removed from a composite before the whole is deleted, and thus not be deleted as part of the whole. This can be made possible by a multiplicity of 0..1 at the association end that is connected to the whole, that is, the end with the filled diamond. The only allowed multiplicities at this end are 1 or 0..1; all other multiplicities are prohibited.

Table A-2. *Multiplicity examples*

Multiplicity	Meaning
1	Exactly one. If no multiplicity is shown on an association end, this is the default.
1..10	An inclusive interval between 1 and 10.
0..*	An inclusive interval between 0 and any number (zero-to-many). The star character (*) is used to represent the unlimited (or infinite) upper bound.
*	Abbreviated form of 0..*.
1..*	An inclusive interval between 1 and any number (one-to-many).

In programming languages, associations and the mechanism of navigation from one class to another can be implemented in various ways. In C++, associations are usually implemented by members having the other class as its type, for example, as a reference or a pointer, as shown in the following example.

Listing A-4. Sample implementation of a navigable association between classes A and B

```cpp
class B; // Forward declaration

class A {
private:
  B* b;
  // ...
};

class B {
  // No pointer or any other reference to class A here!
};
```

Generalization

A central concept in object-oriented software development is the so-called inheritance. What is meant by this is the generalization of the respective specialization of classes.

GENERALIZATION

A generalization is a taxonomic relationship between a general class and a more specific class.

The **generalization** relationship is used to represent the concept of inheritance: the specific class (subclass) inherits attributes and operations of the more general class (base class). The UML syntax of the generalization relationship is a solid arrow with a closed but not filled arrowhead as depicted in Figure A-7.

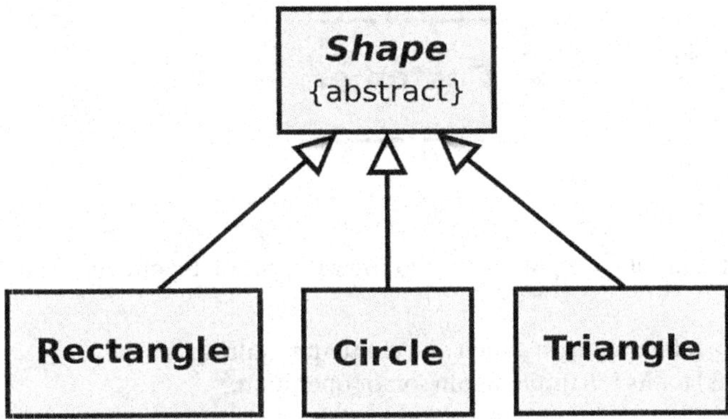

Figure A-7. *An abstract base class Shape and three concrete classes that are specializations of it*

In the direction of the arrow, this relationship is read as the following: "<Subclass> is a kind of <Baseclass>," for example, "Rectangle is a kind of Shape."

Dependency

In addition to the already mentioned associations, classes (and components) can have further relationships with other classes (and components). For instance, if a class is used as a type for a parameter of a member function, this is not an association, but it is quite a kind of dependency to that used class.

DEPENDENCY

A dependency is a relationship that signifies that a single or a set of elements requires other elements for their specification or implementation.

As depicted in Figure A-8, a dependency is shown as a dashed arrow between two elements, for example, between two classes or components. It implies that the element at the arrowhead is required by the element at the tail of the arrow, for example, for implementation purposes. In other words: the dependent element is incomplete without the independent element.

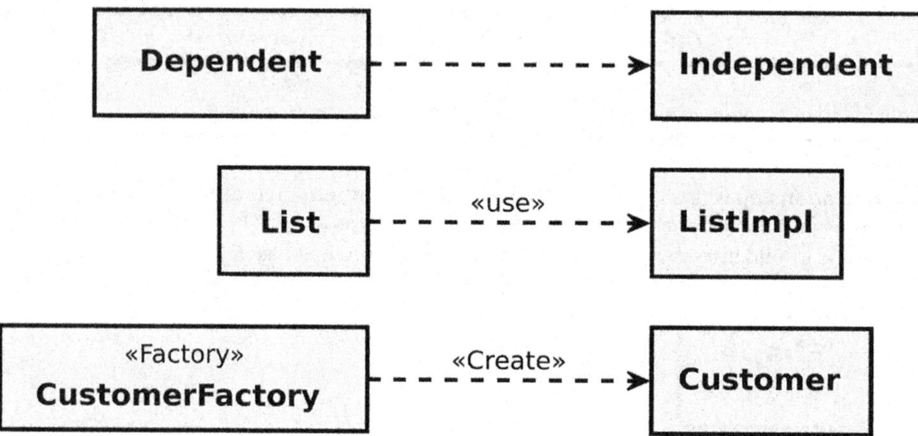

Figure A-8. *Miscellaneous dependencies*

In addition to its simple form (see the first example in Figure A-8), two special types of dependency can be distinguished:

1. The **usage dependency** («use») is a relationship in which one element requires another element (or set of elements) for its full implementation or operation.

2. The **creation dependency** («Create») is a special kind of usage dependency indicating that the element at the tail of the arrow creates instances of the type at the arrowhead.

Components

The UML element **component** represents a modular part of a system that is usually on a higher abstraction level than a single class. A component serves as a kind of "capsule" or "envelope" for a set of classes that together fulfill certain functionality. The UML syntax for a component is depicted in the Figure A-9.

Figure A-9. *The UML notation for a component*

Due to the fact that a component encapsulates its content, it defines its behavior in terms of so-called provided and required interfaces. Only these interfaces are available to the environment for the use of a component. This means that a component may be replaced by another if and only if their provided and required interfaces are identical. The concrete syntax for interfaces (ball-and-socket notation) is exactly the same as the one depicted in Figure A-4 and described in the section on Interfaces.

Stereotypes

Among other ways, the vocabulary of UML can be extended with the help of so-called stereotypes. This lightweight mechanism allows the introduction of platform- or domain-specific extensions of standard UML elements. For instance, by the application of the stereotype «Factory» on the standard UML element Class, designers can express that those specific classes are object factories.

The name of an applied stereotype is shown within a pair of guillemets (French quotation marks) above or before the name of the model element. Some stereotypes also introduce a new graphical symbol, an icon.

Table A-3 contains a list of the stereotypes used in this book.

Table A-3. *Stereotypes used in this book*

Stereotype	Meaning
«Factory»	A class that creates objects without exposing the instantiation logic to the client.
«Facade»	A class that provides a unified interface to a set of interfaces in a complex component or subsystem.
«SUT»	The System Under Test. Classes or components with this stereotype are the entities to be tested, for example, with the help of Unit Tests.
«TestContext»	A test context is a software entity, for example, a class that acts as a grouping mechanism for a set of test cases (see stereotype «TestCase»).
«TestCase»	A test case is an operation that interacts with the «SUT» to verify its correctness. Test cases are grouped in a «TestContext».

Bibliography

[Beck01] Kent Beck, Mike Beedle, Arie van Bennekum, et al. Manifesto for Agile Software Development. 2001. `http://agilemanifesto.org`, retrieved 9-24-2016.

[Beck02] Kent Beck. Test-Driven Development: By Example. Addison-Wesley Professional, 2002.

[Busch96] Frank Buschmann, Regine Meunier, Hans Rohnert, and Peter Sommerlad. Pattern-Oriented Software Architecture Volume 1: A System of Patterns. Wiley, 1996.

[Cohn09] Mike Cohn. Succeeding with Agile: Software Development Using Scrum (1st Edition). Addison-Wesley, 2009.

[Evans04] Eric J. Evans. Domain-Driven Design: Tackling Complexity in the Heart of Software (1st Edition). Addison-Wesley, 2004.

[Fernandes12] R. Martinho Fernandes: Rule of Zero. `https://rmf.io/cxx11/rule-of-zero`, retrieved 6-4-2017.

[Fowler02] Martin Fowler. Patterns of Enterprise Application Architecture. Addison-Wesley, 2002.

[Fowler03] Martin Fowler. Anemic Domain Model. November 2003. URL: `https://martinfowler.com/bliki/AnemicDomainModel.html`, retrieved 5-1-2017.

[Fowler04] Martin Fowler. Inversion of Control Containers and the Dependency Injection pattern. January 2004. URL: `https://martinfowler.com/articles/injection.html`, retrieved 7-19-2017.

[Gamma95] Erich Gamma, Richard Helm, Ralph Johnson, and John Vlissides. Design Patterns: Elements of Reusable, Object-Oriented Software. Addison-Wesley, 1995.

[GAOIMTEC92] United States General Accounting Office. GAO/IMTEC-92-26: Patriot Missile Defense: Software Problem Led to System Failure at Dhahran, Saudi Arabia, 1992. `http://www.fas.org/spp/starwars/gao/im92026.htm`, retrieved 12-26-2013.

[Hunt99] Andrew Hunt, David Thomas. The Pragmatic Programmer: From Journeyman to Master. Addison-Wesley, 1999.

[ISO11] International Standardization Organization (ISO), JTC1/SC22/WG21 (The C++ Standards Committee). ISO/IEC 14882:2011, Standard for Programming Language C++.

[Jeffries98] Ron Jeffries. You're NOT Gonna Need It! `http://ronjeffries.com/xprog/articles/practices/pracnotneed/`, retrieved 9-24-2016.

[JPL99] NASA Jet Propulsion Laboratory (JPL). Mars Climate Orbiter Team Finds Likely Cause of Loss. September 1999. URL: `http://mars.jpl.nasa.gov/msp98/news/mco990930.html`, retrieved 7-7-2013.

[Knuth74] Donald E. Knuth. Structured Programming with Go To Statements, ACM Journal Computing Surveys, Vol. 6, No. 4, December 1974. `http://cs.sjsu.edu/~mak/CS185C/KnuthStructuredProgrammingGoTo.pdf`, retrieved 5-3-2014.

[Koenig01] Andrew Koenig and Barbara E. Moo. C++ Made Easier: The Rule of Three. June 2001. `http://www.drdobbs.com/c-made-easier-the-rule-of-three/184401400`, retrieved 5-16-2017.

[Langr13] Jeff Langr. Modern C++ Programming with Test-Driven Development: Code Better, Sleep Better. Pragmatic Bookshelf, 2013.

[Liskov94] Barbara H. Liskov and Jeanette M. Wing: A Behavioral Notion of Subtyping. ACM Transactions on Programming Languages and Systems (TOPLAS) 16 (6): 1811–1841. November 1994. `http://dl.acm.org/citation.cfm?doid=197320.197383`, retrieved 12-30-2014.

© Stephan Roth 2017

S. Roth, *Clean C++*, DOI 10.1007/978-1-4842-2793-0

[Martin96] Robert C. Martin. The Liskov Substitution Principle. ObjectMentor, March 1996.
http://www.objectmentor.com/resources/articles/lsp.pdf, retrieved 12-30-2014.

[Martin03] Robert C. Martin. Agile Software Development: Principles, Patterns, and Practices. Prentice Hall, 2003.

[Martin09] Robert C. Martin. Clean Code: A Handbook Of Agile Software Craftsmanship. Prentice Hall, 2009.

[Martin11] Robert C. Martin. The Clean Coder: A Code of Conduct for Professional Programmers. Prentice Hall, 2011.

[Meyers05] Scott Meyers. Effective C++: 55 Specific Ways to Improve Your Programs and Designs (Third Edition). Addison-Wesley, 2005.

[OMG15] Object Management Group. OMG Unified Modeling Language™ (OMG UML), Version 2.5. OMG Document Number: formal/2015-03-01. http://www.omg.org/spec/UML/2.5, retrieved 11-5-2016.

[Parnas07] ACM Special Interest Group on Software Engineering: ACM Fellow Profile of David Lorge Parnas. http://www.sigsoft.org/SEN/parnas.html, retrieved 9-24-2016.

[Ram03] Stefan Ram. Homepage: Dr. Alan Kay on the Meaning of "Object-Oriented Programming." http://www.purl.org/stefan_ram/pub/doc_kay_oop_en), retrieved 11-3-2013.

[Sommerlad13] Peter Sommerlad. Meeting C++ 2013: Simpler C++ with C++11/14. November 2013. http://wiki.hsr.ch/PeterSommerlad/files/MeetingCPP2013_SimpleC++.pdf, retrieved 1-2-2014.

[Thought08] ThoughtWorks, Inc. (multiple authors). The ThoughtWorks® Anthology: Essays on Software Technology and Innovation. Pragmatic Bookshelf, 2008.

[Wipo1886] World Intellectual Property Organization (WIPO): Berne Convention for the Protection of Literary and Artistic Works. http://www.wipo.int/treaties/en/ip/berne/index.html, retrieved 3-9-2014.

Index

© Stephan Roth 2017

S. Roth, *Clean C++*, DOI 10.1007/978-1-4842-2793-0

■ U, V

■ W

■ X, Y, Z

Get the eBook for only $5!

Why limit yourself?

With most of our titles available in both PDF and ePUB format, you can access your content wherever and however you wish—on your PC, phone, tablet, or reader.

Since you've purchased this print book, we are happy to offer you the eBook for just $5.

To learn more, go to http://www.apress.com/companion or contact support@apress.com.

Apress®

All Apress eBooks are subject to copyright. All rights are reserved by the Publisher, whether the whole or part of the material is concerned, specifically the rights of translation, reprinting, reuse of illustrations, recitation, broadcasting, reproduction on microfilms or in any other physical way, and transmission or information storage and retrieval, electronic adaptation, computer software, or by similar or dissimilar methodology now known or hereafter developed. Exempted from this legal reservation are brief excerpts in connection with reviews or scholarly analysis or material supplied specifically for the purpose of being entered and executed on a computer system, for exclusive use by the purchaser of the work. Duplication of this publication or parts thereof is permitted only under the provisions of the Copyright Law of the Publisher's location, in its current version, and permission for use must always be obtained from Springer. Permissions for use may be obtained through RightsLink at the Copyright Clearance Center. Violations are liable to prosecution under the respective Copyright Law.

CPSIA information can be obtained
at www.ICGtesting.com
Printed in the USA
FSOW04n0027241217
42679FS

9 781484 227923